witches and pagans:
women in european folk religion

web of life portal, urnes stavkirk, norway

*Deer, snakes, and other creatures interlaced in heathen style
on the earliest surviving church in Norway, at Urnes circa 1000 CE*

witches and pagans:

women in European folk religion, 700-1100

max dashu

veleda press 2016

Witches and Pagans: Women in European Folk Religion
First edition

© 2016 Maxine Hammond Dashu

Dashu, Max, 1950-
Witches and Pagans: Women in European Folk Religion
Vol. VII of *Secret History of the Witches*
Includes bibliographic references
The index is online at:
www.veleda.net/witchesandpagans/bookindex.html

ISBN 978-0-692-74028-6   Paperback

1. Women - Europe - ethnohistory.   2. Witchcraft - History.
3. History - medieval - to 1100.   4. Folklore - Europe
5. Paganism - philosophy.   6. Art - Europe - medieval
7. Healers - women - medieval.   9. Divination - Europe
10. Penitential books - history and criticism
11. Persecution (witchcraft) - Europe
I. *Witches and Pagans: Women in European Folk Religion*

Illustration and book design by Max Dashu
Cover photo: "Panel from the Franks casket,"
Photo credit to Mike Peel (www.mikepeel.com) CC

Printed in USA by McNaughton-Gunn

CONTENTS

Cultural influence of the Sámi. *Útiseta*: "sitting out" on the land. Thorbjörg Litilvölva: traveling seeresses. Heiðr in *Völuspá* and in the sagas. The *gyðjur*. The sexual politics of *seiðr*. Medieval misogyny and modern interpretations. Oðinn's rapes, the "taming wand," and forced "marriages." Misogynist sexual insult and shaming: *ergi*, *argr*, and *org*. The emasculating distaff—and female spheres of power.

RUNES

Divination, fire and water, crystal balls. Heathens, *ethne*, *bruxas*; pagans and *gentili*. Rune magic. Mystery, symbols, and lots. Meanings of runic characters. Women rune-makers in the sagas. *Haliorunnae*, *heliruna*, and *hellerune*: ancestor-mysteries. *Leódrune* and *burgrune*. *Hægtesse* again, and *pythonissa*. Chants to the dead: *dotruna* and *dadsisas*. Elves, prophecy, and night-goers. "Secret crimes": repressing women's graveside ceremonies. Norse concepts of mind, soul, spirit.

CAILLEACHAN, DÍSIR, AND HAGS

The Cailleach Bhéara: ancestor, megalith builder, and shaper of land-scapes. Her staff of power. Buí, Bói, and Bóand. Cnogba: "Hill of the Cow" (Knowth). The great age of the Cailleach, and her wisdom as cultural teach-er. Megalithic traditions of Sliabh na Callighe: the cairns at Loughcrew, and the Hag's Chair. The Lament of Buí. *Cailleachan* of Scotland: wells, deer, and place-names. The Manx Caillagh. *Idisi*, *ides*, and *dísir*; halls and assemblies of the *dís*. Expansive view of valkyries: as nature spirits, spinners, and fates. Patriarchal myth and Odinist supercession. Giantesses and female power. Hags vs. Heroes: *glaisteagean*, the Morrigan, Louhi, witches and *wælcyrgean*.

THE WITCH HOLDA AND HER RETINUE

Women who go by night with "Diana, goddess of the pagans"—or other goddesses. The witches' ride, from *Corrector sive Medicus* to the Canon Episcopi, 850-1100. Spread of the Herodias legend, and its possible roots in Haera, Ero, Mother Earth. "The witch Holda," and Frau Holle, Perchta: the spinning Old Goddess of the Winternights. Wendish Pši-Polnitsa. Peniten-tial interrogatories: "Is there any woman who?" The timeless spinning of

Berthe, the Swanfooted; la Reine Pédauque; and St Néomaye. Women who lay tables for the Fates. From Mother Earth who nurtures all, to Luxuria, "Sensuality."

WITCH BURNINGS

Frankish and German persecutions. Female ordeals. Burning women by iron and fire in Spain. English witch hunting laws: of clerics and kings. Patterns of verbal abuse: "Witch and Whore." Invented, back-projected Scottish hunts. Witch persecutions of 1000-1100, in France, Germany, Russia, Denmark, Bohemia, and Hungary. Secular witch hunts, and modern myths about medieval church burnings.

VÖLUSPÁ

The Sibyl's Prophecy. Norse cosmogony: nine worlds in the Tree, nine wood-women, nine giantesses. Three Maidens: the Norns revisited, with variant tales in Hauksbók. Gullveig, Heiðr, and the "war first in the world." Scape-goating Gullveig, then and now. Theories about the Vanir, Álfar, ethnicity, and conquest. Gods/not-gods and the *h2ensus root in Proto-Indo-European. The Norse mead of poetry and Vedic *amrita*. Aesir oath-breaking and the giants. Freyja and Frigg. Oðinn and the *völva*. Doom of the Powers. Heathen and christian themes in the *Völuspá*. Female skálds, the *völva* and women's voice. Ceremonial space defined by women: a sphere of power.

acknowledgements

Thanks to Nava Mizrahhi who has walked this road with me.

Thanks to Sarah Hoagland for her editorial insights; to Mary Condren
for illuminating conversations and for generously sharing sources;
to Judy Grahn, Marna Hauk, and all those who have supported
my work, especially the subscribers to my online courses,
who made completion of this book possible.

PREFACE

Writing this book has been a forty-year process of excavation, gathering, sorting, comparison, verification, tossing, re-reading, and serial discovery. It meant assembling a mosaic of many bits of information, arranging and rearranging them to see what patterns emerged. It has taken decades to chase down and assemble the relevant documentation—a search that has proved to be virtually bottomless. The book I had originally envisioned burst its bounds as chapters grew into volumes. And yet more remains to be uncovered.

This is the first published volume of a multiple-volume sourcebook, but it is not volume I. *Witches and Pagans* falls at the mid-point, as Volume VII. The books overlap chronologically—especially this one and the preceding volume, *Women in a Time of Overlords*. For a variety of reasons, I decided to start at the tipping point of the early Middle Ages, when the war on heathen culture was in full cry. Evidence from those hostile witnesses, the clergy, testifies to beliefs and observances that would have otherwise been lost to us.

Researching this subject means confronting how the cultural history of Europe has been organized up until now. Christian and Roman bias has ruled in the general studies, most of which present a sterile aristocratic front. Specialized articles offer more depth of detail, but often fail to make broader connections between cultures. Historians are making progress in synthesizing archaeology, history, literature and orature, but it is still difficult to find the women—most of all the common women who were at the center.

My approach is ethnohistorical: looking for traces of folk religions and philosophies by going through archaeology, the written record, and orature. It has also meant searching for what language can tell us about the fabric of cultures that were ripped apart more than a millennium ago. Much of the book turns on language, the names and meanings that are an important part of the cultural record, but which remain mostly hidden in obscure texts, unknown to all but a narrow slice of specialists. Linguistics may seem arcane to most people, but it illuminates concepts held by the old ethnic spiritual philosophies.

A hundred different paths branch out from every subject, name, story and ceremony in this book. It is impossible to pursue them all in a single volume. My way of organizing the information has been to draft it out and see what constellates: delving into the origins of *witch, heathen, rune, fate, faery, weird* and *worship*; tracking how the words morph and migrate in meaning; and accounting for the filters through which the heritage passes, the distorting lenses that obscure old cultural foundations. By plunging down to the deep layers, we find names for spirit and soul, for the sacred mead of vision, the illuminating wisdom that the Irish called *imbas forosnai.*

In this search for what has survived, and how it has shifted under pressure and over time, several thematic strands emerge. Among them are distaff, spindle, weaving, fortune, and the Fates (in all their many ethnic titles). Ceremonial strands include incantation, prophecy and divination, rites of healing, herb-gathering and medicines. Other strands belong to consecrated tools: witch's wands and seiðstaffs, crystal balls, sieve pendulums, knots, runes, and pouches for *taufr* or *lyb* amulets. The strands of place take us into weirding at Nature sanctuaries—wells, stones, and trees ("peace-spots")—and to the rich megalithic lore. Those in turn connect to faeries, elves, and ancestors, who are interwoven with folk goddesses and the lore of place.

The seeresses and goddesses can be found in the corners of the andro-centric poems and sagas. Snake-suckling Mother Earth appears at the margins of 10th century Christian missals, and Romanesque church sculpture gradually transforms her into the sexualized figure of "Luxuria." Diviners and chanters over herbs are scolded in the bishops' polemics, as the canonists and penitential writers catalogue forbidden aspects of the ethnic cultures. They also show us, through a dark glass, an old mythology of witches who go by night with the goddess, whether she is called Diana, Herodias, or Holda. From this folk base the demonologists constructed their persecutory mythology, which has been so successful in redefining the meaning of witch, and in substituting a male anti-god for the heathen goddesses.

All this information is fragmented, but the aggregate sketches out a picture that falsifies the assumption of swift and complete christianization. The torn web of culture can't be completely reconstructed, but it is possible to glimpse parts and patterns. History does not go in straight lines or line up in neat rows; it grows and curves in a tangle of interrelating cultures. Orthodox history frowns on introducing modern comparisons, but we need the insights offered by Romanian women's way of gathering herbs, or Scottish cures with the "wresting thread." They illustrate the kind of folkways that early medieval canonists were trying to stamp out.

Mixing historical and spiritual themes is also disapproved as not fitting the proper historical grid; but that is itself a distorting lens that steers us away from the untold stories (and from the politicization of culture in the early feudal period). So this book moves from Norns and *fatas,* to the meaning of names for witches, to the archaeomythology of Irish megalithic lore, and then to the women who go by night with a goddess. Casting a wide net is the only way to get at the texture of culture, the weave of concepts that people lived in, and their social realities. The myths shift—they do—but that does not mean they contain no ancient memory. Some very old through-lines are visible in the megalithic traditions, the faith in *dísir,* and chanting over herbs.

This book does not posit a feminist wonderland for the early Middle Ages. These were patriarchal societies, rife with rape and abuse, captivity, slavery, and serfdom, and harsh enforcement of the sexual double standard. Some of them burned or drowned witches, or imposed female ordeals of red-hot iron. This sexual politics demands a critical eye. But it is past time to recognize that female spheres of power existed too, which repression and bias have rendered invisible. The complex of meanings around *weaving, distaff,* and *fates* is grounded in women's work, women's power and knowledge and ceremony. Even stereotypes of witch's wands and crystal balls have a material basis in history and archaeology, beyond the undervalued cultural testimony of folk orature, with its deep conservational substrate.

For forty years I presented slide talks under the title *Witches and Pagans.* While completing this book, I wondered whether *Witches and Heathens* might not be a more suitable title, as the percentage of Germanic material ballooned. But "heathens" has taken on a culturally specific meaning today, and in the end I decided to go with the broader title. In presenting witch names from masculine-default languages, I choose to use the female forms. They are the hardest to find, buried under the preferred masculine convention—and eclipsed by it in most linguistic discussions.

For Norse and Old English, I've kept the accent marks and the *eth* (ð), but decided not use the *thorn* character (Þ) because it looks too much like a P, and would be confusing or incomprehensible to most readers. I use ö for Norse o-with-cedilla. Names like *cailleach, calliagh, caillech* are given as spelled in the sources, as they vary according to dialect. Words preceded by an asterisk indicate linguistic reconstructions using the comparative method.

After decades of chasing down information, and fact-checking it multiple times, errors are inevitable. I kept finding them in many of the sources, as I got to know the terrain better. These were factual errors in scholarly sources, not just in books that indulge in inventions like "Celtic Wicca." Out of the hundreds of books and articles I read since 1970, it wasn't possible to retrieve every citation. As it is, I hope non-scholarly readers will not be daunted by the thicket of annotations. This book is intended as a sourcebook, and on a subject as controversial as this one, documentation is a necessity.

The table of contents gives a basic overview of where information is located in this book. The number of names and topics is quite large, so for reasons of space (and the digital advantage of searchability) the index is available online: www.veleda.net/witchesandpagans/index/

Most terms are explained in the text, but it covers such a large number of ethnic concepts that readers may find the glossary useful: www.veleda.net/witchesandpagans/glossary/ .

Further commentaries can be found at www.suppressedhistories.net/witchesandpagans/commentaries/

Volumes in the forthcoming series *Secret History of the Witches* are listed on the final page of this book.

1

THE WEBS OF WYRD

There stands an ash i know
called Yggdrasil,
a mighty tree moist with shining drops
from it come dews that fall adown.
it stands green over Urd's well.

...

Thence come the all-knowing maidens
three in the hall under the tree.
Urd is one called, another Verdandi—
they scored on the wood—and Skuld the third.
they lay down laws, they allot life
for humankind's children, speaking fates.
—*Völuspá*, Icelandic Edda, circa 1100 [1]

T he sacred Well of Life flows out of the Earth beneath a Mystery Tree, whose roots reach into the underworld, its branches into the heavens. From this great ash tree fall vitalizing dews that moisten the soil underneath and nurture swarms of bees. The Tree bears life-giving fruit. Four stags browse off its branches, and two swans draw sustenance from the Well. A wise eagle lives at the Tree's top, and a serpent lies beneath its root. Between them, the squirrel Ratatosk darts up and down, carrying messages.

Three primeval Maidens live under this holy Tree, says the *Völuspá*, the oldest poem in the Icelandic Edda. They lay down the laws of Nature and shape the destiny of all beings, carving runes into the Tree. These are the deepest Mysteries. The Maidens are named from the Norse verb *verða*, "to turn, to become."[2] They are Urð, which means "Became"; Verðandi, "becoming"; and Skuld, "Shall Be," "Must Be," or "Will-happen."[3] Skuld is related to English "shall," and carries the

völuspa

"Prophecy of the Seeress"

Old Icelandic poem circa 1000 CE

same sense of intention, propulsion or necessity.[4] Some translators highlight its connotation of of necessity or "Inevitability."[5] Rather than progressing in a straight line, the Norns spiral through revolutions of Time. What "was" must lead to what "shall be", which inexorably turns into "what was." In this philosophy, time as well as space curves, turns, spirals: "*Völuspá* seems to show traces of a cyclic arrangement of time..."[6]

Latin:	*Verto*	to turn, revolve
Old Norse:	*Verða*	to be
Saxon:	*Weorthan*	to be
German:	*Werden*	to be, become

In fact, the Norns' names have very deep Indo-European roots. They go back to a distant proto-Indo-European root *Wert (*Uert, *Uerth) meaning "to turn, revolve, spin, move in a circle." In some European daughter languages, this taproot concept evolved into a verb of being and becoming.[7]

This complex of meanings gave rise in turn to Germanic names for a Fate goddess who personified causation, change, and movement through time. The Norse knew her as Urðr, the Germans as Wurt, and the Old Saxons called her Wurð. In Old English her name was Wyrd or Werd, giving rise to the medieval word for destiny: *weird*.[8] All these fate-names derive from the ancient verb of turning, in its completed form. The shaper of destiny is herself the sum of fates fulfilled, and in turn brings new things into being.

The Norns "shape" destiny, or "lay" fate, lay down natural law. Poems and sagas speak of their fate-shaping (*sköpum norna*).[9] The three Norns "shape every human term of life," *skapa mönnum aldr*, or *skôp î ârdaga*, "shaped the yeardays."[10] This shaping (*skop*) is named from a root that means "to create."

Anglo-Saxons had the same concept: *wyrðigiscapu*, "shaped by Wyrd." She is the etymological equivalent of Norse Urðr. The "shaped" metaphor refers to destiny in Germanic tongues: Old Norse *scop*, Old Saxon *giscapu*, Anglo-Saxon *gesceapu*. In Old Saxon proverb, fate was literally "shaped by Wyrd," *wurðigiscapu*, or "shaped by the Powers," *reganogiscapu*.[11] So too the Edda speaks of the "shapings of the Norns": when the birds tell Sigurðr that he will meet an enchanted valkyrie, they warn: "you are not able to stop / Sigrdrífa's sleep / against the Norns' shapings."[12]

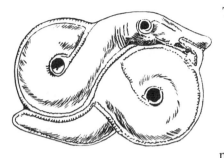

The giant Maidens create and maintain the order of things.[13] Icelandic sagas speak of the Norns as perceiving, decreeing, and pronouncing destiny.[14] *Nornir vîsa*, said the heathen Norse: "The Fates are wise."[15] Their speech carries determinative power: "Against Urðr's word | no one speaks," says *Fjölsvinnsmál* 47.

Where a single Norn is named, it is usually Urðr, but occasionally Skuld. Blessing her son from the Otherworld, Gróa chants: "Long is the journey, long are the ways, long are the wishes of humankind; if it may be, may you keep the goodwill of Skuld so that her shaping turns in your favor."[16]

The Norse word for destiny, *ørlög*, means "primeval law," literally "what was laid down at the origin."[17] The Eddic poem *Fáfnismál* says that the "Norn's judgment" ordains not only the fate of all humans, but of gods as well.[18] No one can overturn "the judgment of the Norns," a phrase that in the sagas usually connotes the finality of death.[19]

However, later works push the Three Maidens into the background. A more detailed account of them seems to have been excised from the *Völuspá*, and replaced with the Dwarf Intrusion. (See chapter 9.) The Icelandic skald Snorri remakes Urð's Well, still "exceedingly sacred," into the judgment seat of the Aesir.[20]

But the ancient Norns predate the patriarchal Norse gods called the Aesir. The *Völuspá* intimates that the Fates will outlast those gods and their wars, living on to lay down the foundation of another world cycle, as they did began the present round of human history.

The Norns are timeless Beings at the core of existence, "the Maidens that over the Sea of Ages travel in deep foreknowledge."[21] Although the *Völuspá* does not use the word "norns," Snorri made this connection, filling out the picture painted by that old poem:

> **A beautiful hall stands there under the ash tree by the well,**
> **and out of that hall come three maidens, those who are thus named:**
> **Urð, Verðandi, Skuld. These maidens shape lives for people;**
> **we call them Norns.**[22]

The Well is named Urðrbrunni, after the eldest Maiden Urð. Her Well is a reservoir of ancient Being, fed by a living spring. Its surface ripples and roils with power and consciousness. Within it resides "the unfathomable secret of the beginnings of life, deeply hidden..."[23] Two other wells lie under the Tree, that of Mímir, which is associated with the frost giants, and the well of Hel, whose underworld waters are filled with huge serpents.

It is further said that these Norns who dwell by the Well of Urðr take water of the well every day, and with it that clay which lies about the well, and sprinkle it over the Ash, to the end that its limbs shall not wither nor rot; for that water is so holy that all things which come there into the well become as white as the film which lies within the egg-shell.[24]

Anything that enters the Well of Urð is stripped of all previous qualities, passing into primeval essence, as within an egg, to be regenerated. The *aurr* that the Maidens pour onto the tree is often translated as "white clay," but there is another possibility for this regenerating substance. Snorri's next line says, "That dew which falls from it onto the earth is called by men honey-dew, and thereon are bees nourished." The dews that fall from the great life-tree correspond to the sweet exudations produced by many species of ash trees, which is known as "manna."[25]

"The white film of Urð's spring and the white clay of the ash tree have puzzled scholars," as Darl Dumont remarks. He quotes Hilda Ellis Davidson: "It is clear enough that *aurr* is ash tree manna." Dumont notes connections between the Greek name for ash manna, *melía*, the dryads associated with that tree, and the word for honey, *melí*. He quotes Victor Rydberg, who wrote: "Thus the world tree is among the Teutons, as it is among their kins-men the Iranians, a mead tree..." [26]

The *Völuspá* describes the great Tree as *miötvith*, which has been vari-ously translated as "measuring tree"[27] or "Fate tree."[28] (Some suggest that the word might have originally been *miöðvid*, "mead tree.") The Tree is called Læraðr in other sources, which also describe the vital essence it exudes as mead: "The goat Heiðrún ('bright mystery') eats its leaves, and she gives milk from it. Her flow is so abundant that it fills a barrel "with the bright mead; that drink can never run out."[29] The stag Eikthyrnir also eats from the tree, and from his antlers, vital essence flows down into the source of all waters, Hvergelmir.[30] This too is a cycle of return.

The "dews that fall adown" have parallels in northeastern Asia. In their *olonkho* long-poems, the Sakha reverently speak of a "foamy moisture" that drips from the branches of the Tree of Life and flows forever in an endless stream. This life-giving foam "oozed on the holy Earth" and collected in a lake of pure milk. "Nourished with the juices of this tree, bathing in its enlivening flow, the weak grew strong, they grow; the small filled out, the sickly were made whole. Such was the purpose, for the happiness of the living, of that created blessed regal tree."[31]

INVOKING THE NORNS

A recognition has grown that the many kinds of supernatural women—norns, *dísir* and *fylgjur*, valkyries, giantesses and troll-women—overlap rather than being distinct categories. The *Völuspá* itself implies that the Three Maidens are of the giant kindred. It does not name them as Norns, but another Eddic poem, *Vafthrúðnismál*, makes a cryptic allusion to Three Maidens who descend upon human dwellings, and who are "the only fortunes in the world, although nurtured amidst giants."[32] *Dísir* (female ancestors) and *nornir* also appear "to have been at least partially synonymous."[33]

Eddic poetry made a distinction between different kinds of norns: the majestic primordial powers of the Tree and Well come from the giant kindred, while others are guardian spirits of clans, individuals, or even groups of deities. The Eddic poem *Fáfnismál* explains, "Of many births / I say the Norns are / some descended from Aesir / some descended from Álfar / some are daughters of Dvalin [dwarves]."[34]

The *Fáfnismál* says that the Norns draw near when mothers prepare to give birth, a theme that recurs in other texts.[35] Two Eddic poems refer to the norns as spinners of destiny. In *Reginsmál*, Sigurðr's fate-threads (*ørlogsímo*) extend across all the lands.[36] In *Helgakviða Hundingsbana* I, the norns arrive at night to shape the life of the newborn prince: "They twisted very strongly the strand of fate... they prepared the golden thread and fastened it in the middle of the moon's hall."[37] They secured the strand's two ends to the east and west, fating the newborn prince to have all the land between. One of the norns threw a strand to the north, to hold forever. This norn looks like a *dís* (ancestral woman) since she is identified by clan ties, called "the kinswoman of Neri."[38]

A few sagas refer to chants invoking the Norns or the goddess Freyja. The heroine of *Oddrúnagrátr* uses charms to help Borgný through a dangerous labor: "mightily chanted Oddrún, magically chanted Oddrún | powerful charms for Borgný." The mother in turn thanks the midwife with a blessing, "So many the holy spirits help you | Frigg and Freyja and other gods | as you delivered me from near death."[39]

Rural Scandanavian women retained a birth custom of preparing an offering called "norn porridge."[40] Among the Sámi, it was Sarakka porridge which was eaten, to honor the goddess who shaped the child in the womb.[41]

The *Fjölsvinnsmál* speaks of a deathless Tree of Memory that spreads its branches over every land, "but few know from what roots it springs… neither fire not iron will harm it."[42] The poet names the Tree after the giant Mímir, whose well is one of three that lie beneath the roots of the great Tree. It belongs to the realm of the frost giants where the void of Ginnungagap exists in primeval time. In this account, it is the fruit of the Tree that confers creative vitality:

> its fruit must be laid on the fire
> for the weal of travailing women
> they shall then come out
> who had been within.
> to [humanity] 'tis the giver of life.[43]

FATAS AND FATES

The Fates cast a long reflection across millennia of European folk culture. They were older than the Indo-European migrations that divided the Celts and Italians from the Germanics and Balts and Slavs, and from more remote cousins in Central Asia. The Norse called the three fates Nornir, the Romans called them Parcae, and the Greeks knew them as the ancient, mighty Moirae. In borrowed Latin, they were called the Matres in Gaul and Britain, Matronae in Germania.[44] These fates are nearly always triune. A

Frisian archbishop alludes to *tha thriu wüfer*, and a medieval source names *die drei heilräthinnen*, "the three healing counselors" (feminine).[45] In Dutch they are the Three Sisters (Old Dutch *dry sustren*, Modern *dreie gezuster*). Later German proverb calls them the Wisewomen, the Advisors of Welfare, the Measurers, and the Quick Judges.[46] Or they are the *Drei Heilige Frauen*, "Three Holy Women."

The fates are also threefold in Slavic culture. (No early medieval sources on them seem to exist, what follows looks at more recent folk culture.) Serbs and Croats spoke of the *sudnice* or *sudjenice*, "judges," Slovenians of the *sojanice*, and Czechs of the *sudice*.[47] The Czech word *osud*, "fate," like Russian судьба, comes from the same root, meaning "judgment"—a divine dispensation. The *sudiče* were also seen as spinners; the *sudička* (eldest fate) determined the length of a life by cutting the thread. In the 19th century, it was still customary for Czechs to "set out spinning wheels and scissors so that the fates would decide a more pleasant fate for the child." Ukrainians pictured the *sudci* playing with a ball of yarn, unwinding the thread of life.[48]

Slovenian women would leave a loaf of bread as an offering to the three fates whenever a child was born.[49] Slovenians also used the name *rojenice*, from the old Slavic root род, "birth," and these birth fairies had a Russian cognate, the рожаницы. Russian women embroidered *rozhanitsy* spirits on ceremonial cloths. Bulgarians had several names for the Fates: *urisnici*, "establishers, determiners," related to Romanian *ursitoare*[50] and *narečnice* or *rečenica*, "deciders, judges."[51] And: "The spindle and distaff are understood to be their attributes, they are said to decide fate while spinning, and the length of the thread spun around the child's head embodies his or her destiny."[52]

The *rečenice* are plural goddesses, but a singular Slavic fate goddess was named from the same root, *ryech'*, which means "decision, judgement, decree, foretelling." She was called Srecha in Russian and Serbian, and Srashcha in the Ukraine. The Serbs pictured Srecha as a spinner of golden thread who assigns fortune to souls. Unwilling to relinquish her under Christianity, they assimilated her into the new religion over the centuries: "In national songs and traditions the Srecha frequently occurs as an independent being by the side of God."[53]

The Lithuanian fate goddess, Laima, also persisted in christianized folk culture. Her name is closely related to *laimé*, "good fortune, happiness."

Lithuanians would say, "So Laima fated" (*taip Laima lemė*), using a verb that means "to declare, to pronounce (on questions that concern the future)," but also "to divine, wish."[54] (This fascinating ambiguity recurs in other cultures.) Another Lithuanian tradition says Verpėja ("Spinner") fastens the thread of each newborn life to a star.[55] Sometimes the fate is called Laima-dalia, literally "fortune-part."[56]

Laima occasionally takes multiple form, as three or seven fates who "wander" through the world. They too are spinners and weavers. The seven sisters are called Deivės Valdytojos, "governing goddesses." Among them are Verpiančioji who spins the life-threads, Metančioji who lays the loom warp, Audėja the weaver, and Gadintoja who breaks the thread. (See below for connections between weaving, fate, and fortune in Germanic traditions.) Latvians revered three fates named Dekla, Laima and Karta.[57] One of three witch sisters who governed the tribal Czechs is also named Tekla or Tekta.[58]

An 8th century Irish manuscript refers to "the seven daughters of the sea who are forming the thread of life."[59] Old Irish sources often refer to lives being destined, though not usually with a personified Fate. A commonly used word for fating is *cinnid*, from "decide" (like the Slavic fates). Another, *tocaid*, "refers to divination."[60]

In Welsh, an outcome could be spoken into fulfilment. Arianrhod said, *Mi a dinghaf dynghet*, "I destine a destiny."[61] In Irish literature, too, women use the power of speech when they lay a *geis* (mandate or taboo) on men, either mandating an action, or refraining from specified acts. Though Irish lore doesn't speak of fates under the latinate name, the raven goddess Badb ordains who is to fall in battle. The banshee (*bansithe*, faery* "woman of the mound") acts as a fateful protector, appearing in omen of momentous events, to warn and counsel.

In many European traditions, three Fates shape destiny on their distaff and their spindle, with their fingers twisting the thread of wool. There are three periods of Time: the past which is already spun and wound onto the spindle, the present which passes between the fingers of the spinster; the future is the wool wound around the distaff which must pass through the spinner's fingers, as the present must become the past.[62]

---

*The archaic spelling is used to bypass Victorian and Disney stereotypes of "fairy."

*Fate goddess in the Utrecht Psalter, plate 64, 9th century. She holds strands
of fate; one leads to a Greco-Roman altar, the other reaches toward a cornucopia. In her lap are a globe and two snaky cornucopias filled with herbs.
Beside her is a tree and an angel reading from a scroll, a symbol connected
with the Parcae. In illustrating Psalm 68, the Dutch artist interpolated
pagan symbols of Terra Mater, Fortuna and the Fatae.*

Birth rituals in western Europe offered reverence to the Fates or fatas,
who eventually became *las fadas*, *fées*, faeries, or "good women." Many
medieval sources say that women prepared tables of offerings for these
spirits. It seems likely that elders and midwives conducted other rites,
perhaps spinning ceremonial threads at births, knotting them on infants as
protective amulets, or tucking them into cradles. Or they might have buried
them under a tree with the afterbirth.

References to these customs were preserved by churchmen in the very act
of fighting to stamp them out. Around 1015, the German bishop Burchard
of Worms was hunting for women who made offerings to the "Three Sisters":

**Have you done as some women do, at certain times in the year,
spread a table with meat and drink and three knives, so that if
those Three Sisters come, whom past generations and ancient
stupidity call the Fates, they can regale themselves?**[63]

Burchard believed that the women were attributing to the devil what belongs to the Divine, which according to his dogma can only be male: "as to believe that those whom thou callest 'the Sisters' can do or avail aught for thee either now or in the future." (He ordered a year's penance, in the *Corrector sive Medicus* penitential.)[64] This German canonist described the Three Sisters as Parcae, just like his Anglo-Saxon contemporaries.

The *Corrector sive Medicus*, also called the *Corrector Burchardi*, is Book 19 in the *Decretum* of Burchard of Worms, circa 1020. It holds a trove of heathen customs and beliefs that the priesthood was attempting to stamp out.

The Danish cleric Saxo Grammaticus covered similar ground a couple of centuries later; but he was talking about norns, and the father of a child comes *to their temple*.[65]

Some scholars insist that all the diverse ethnic traditions of the Fates were nothing more than borrowings from Greco-Roman literature. But they are assuming that spinning and weaving had no mythic dimensions in tribal European cultures before Roman influence; that they were like a tabula rasa with no traditions of their own. Those assumptions do not account for the luxuriant pervasiveness of spinner goddesses, whether it is swan-footed Berthe spinning at the beginning of time, the weaving of Wyrd or Laima, or the magical distaffs of female spirits, witches and saints.

They also ignore the fact that there are few written records of northern European culture before the Christian era. The lack of evidence about non-literate cultures is a historiographical problem. Just because a cultural theme is attested earlier in writing is no reason to assume that it must be the source of parallel themes in non-literate cultures—or even predate them. Roman influence was a reality, visible in the iconography; but the question is how it combined with pre-existing ethnic women's cultures, which left visible tracks of their own.

All early medieval written sources were produced by the male clergy, who insisted on filtering everything through a masculinizing *interpretatio romana*. But that should not fool us into believing that all their references to Fates or spinner goddesses were borrowed from Mediterranean texts. Northern sources indicate that tribal Europeans had concepts parallel to the Roman fate-spinners, but not the same. An English scribe used the Anglo-Saxon word *wicce* to name the Roman Fates who preside over birth:

Wiccena Parcarum.[66] Another Old English writer described the Parcae as *wyrdae*, Wyrds or weirds.[67]

Old linguistic connections predate the imperial Roman influence. The name of the Greek Moirae derives from *smer, "apportion," a root shared by the Gaulish goddesses Rosmerta and Cantismerta (who also takes a plural form).[68] Proto-Celtic *Rho- means "great," as in Rhône, *Rho-Danu, "great river," and Ro-smerta, whose name is usually translated as "great provider."

Other evidence suggests that the goddesses who spin out destiny have distant Indo-European roots. In the earliest written IE language, Hittite, the goddesses Papaya and Isdustaya spin the threads of fate.[69] In one ritual text, the king sends an eagle to report who is sitting in field and forest. The eagle returns, saying, "I have looked. It is Isdustaya and Papaya, the ancient, infernal deities, who are sitting huddled there... She holds a spindle, they hold mirrors filled [with images]; and they are spinning the king's years."[70] The Gulses are another group of fateful goddesses who are shown in company with Isdustaya and Papaya, or with Hannahannes, "Grandmothers." The Gulses (Gulzannikes in Palaic) are both individual fates present at births and the creators of humankind.[71]

"Infernal deities": the underworld

Hittite spinning fates who showed things in mirrors were connected to the ancestral dead

Thus the spinning Fates seem to predate the long-ago Indo-European migrations. Another of these old IE connections points to Central Asia. Eva Pócs compares the "striking number of similar features" between Romanian and Tadjik spinner goddesses, who both "appear on Tuesdays, have chthonic goddess characteristics and also control the spinning."[72] The Vedas do not show spinner goddesses, but uses the metaphors of thread and weaving for human lives. M.L. West emphasizes "the unity of the conception over such a large part of the Indo-European area, which makes it likely that it goes back to the deepest level of Indo-European."[73]

The theme extends deep into Eurasia, where it crosses language families. The Ugrians honored Vagneg-imi, "Old Woman," as goddess of birth and fate. She hangs threads for each newborn on her wooden staff, and makes a knot in the thread that determines how long the child will live.[74]

❖

fatas, sorores fatalis, anᴅ faeries

The Latin word *fata* comes from *fari*, "to speak," with overtones of prophecy. This was recognized even by such a hostile witness as Augustine of Hippo.[75] In ancient Rome, the Fatae "speak the divine word," foretelling and advising on human destiny.[76] The *fata* was an oracular goddess of destiny, and she was also a woman who speaks prophetically, revealing how power will move through time and space.[77]

Threeness was a trait of the original Roman *fatae*, as shown by the city's monument to Ta Tria Fata. Even earlier, three stelae were inscribed to Neuna Fata (Nine Fatas), "to the Nine," and to Parca Maurtia at Tor Tignosa (ancient Lavinium).[78] The Parcae were the primary Roman form of the Fates, presiding over births and deaths. Tombstones show them spinning or writing scrolls of destiny.[79] In funerary inscriptions, the Parcae chant at the time of a person's birth.[80]

The name *fata* spread with Latin to western Europe during the Roman empire. In the fifth century, Martianus Capella wrote that the wilderness is populated by fauns and nymphs (spirits of the woods and fountains) as well as Fatuae or Fanae "and from this name is drawn that of Fana which is given to their prophecies."[81] (*Fane*, "shrine," came from the same root.) Early medieval clerics recorded that people paid honor to *fatales deae*, "fate goddesses", or simply *fatae*, "fates." The common people understood them "as prophetesses, endowed with a divinatory power in fits of sacred delirium."[82]

The core concept was "fatedness," as Noel Williams describes. Over time, "*fata* became attached to the Celtic goddesses in vulgar Latin and, as that language became Old French, the /t/ was dropped to give *fa'a, thence *fae.*"[83] Williams points to "the frequency with which Celtic females appear in multiples of three, their gifts of prophecy, their association with spinning or their association with the world of the dead."[84] He also pulls in the poetic Old English word *faege*, "fated, doomed to die," suggesting "that the notion of female supernatural beings who mark or select the dead may have been an important one in Anglo-Saxon pagan belief."[85]

Old French romances of the 1100s use the word *fai, fae, fay*, for a spirit woman or a woman with powers, but its meaning was broad: "By far the most popular phrase is *c'est chose faee*," which meant a fated thing..."[86] and

*Maison des Fées
(Fairies' House)
Tressé, Bretagne*

*A pair of ancestral
women on a neolithic
dolmen came to be
called* fées, *a word
descended from
Latin* fata

which later came to mean an enchanted thing. (As with *weird*, the concepts
of fating and enchanting overlapped.) When used for a being, *faé* took on
the meaning of "enchantress," but as Williams notes, the name of Morgne
la Fay "may perhaps be better translated 'the magical,' 'the strange,' '(of)
unusual power,' or '(of) the strangeness,' than 'the fairy'..."[87] (Chapter 5 shows
ælfe / elf used in this same otherwordly sense.)

Isidore of Seville and Burchard of Worms refer to the Fates as Parcae,
the old Roman triad of birth goddesses. Isidore of Seville shows them in
the same light as the Moirae. One ordains lives, the second spins them into
being, the third cuts them off.[88] Parcae comes from a verb meaning "to spare,
save," but the 7th-century archbishop reversed its meaning: "They are called
Parcae because they spare nothing."[89] But the name would have originated in
women's propitiation of the birth fates: "Save the mother, spare the child!"[90]

Isidore was well aware that *fatum* meant prophetic speech, from the
verb *fari*: "They call fate whatever the gods speak." He added that *fatum* is
what is said "by speaking" (*a fando*).[91] (This had come to mean "destiny,
oracle, utterance, fortune.") While *fata* was originally a neuter plural, it
had acquired the sense of "female speaker," as well as a "fate" who ordains.
Isidore acknowledged that there were three fates represented with distaff and
spindle. But the *tria fata* were too powerful a goddess symbolism—and far
too pagan—for Isidore to leave alone. Through a sleight of words, he flipped
fata around to the pejorative *fatua*, "foolish, fatuous." He accomplished
this switch by invoking the story of Fenta Fauna, also known as Fatua
Fauna, the taboo name of the Roman women's goddess Bona Dea: "Some
say that this word comes from the admirers of Fatua, the prophetic wife of

Faunus, who predicted the future, and called *fatuous* those who, stupefied by her prophecies, lost their minds." Isidore tried to discredit the divine fate-speakers, by reducing them to nothing more than delusional "foolish women."[92] Such defamation was standard priestly output.

In spite of priestly machinations, the name *fata* gradually became assimilated to goddesses immanent in the natural sanctuaries of springs, caverns, groves and peaks. Their veneration persisted long after Christianity was decreed the state religion. Over a thousand years, the name *fata* branched off in multiple phonological directions, metamorphosizing into *fae, fada, hada, hague, fadette, fée, fay, fayule*, and dozens of other variants in Portuguese, Spanish, French, Occitan, Italian, German, and other languages. Thus, *fata* is the root for the most common words for faery in Western Europe, as well as for the English word "fate." These imported names blended with older cultural forms: the ancestral dead, particularly ancestral mothers, and the megalithic mounds of past ages.

However, *faée* was a complex term. At times it referred to supernatural beings, but it often meant "enchanted" or "gifted with marvelous powers." It interweaves with Latin *fatalitas*, as the meaning "fate" became displaced by "faery nature."[93] In French, the realm of *fées*, or their actions, came to be called *faérie*, which connoted enchantment. English speakers turned this word into a name for the beings themselves: *fairy*.[94] These concepts rested on ancient foundations, as the archaeology of triune Mothers shows.

Under the Roman empire, the Gallo-Romans and Britons began to create

altar stones to the Matres ("mothers"). Nearly always they depict a three-fold goddess. In the Rhineland, Germans dedicated carved stelae to the Matronae ("great mothers"). They often inscribed the names of particular clans, in a pattern of female ancestor veneration. Veneration of triune Mothers certainly did not originate with the staunchly patrilineal Romans, who did not dedicate maternal stelae. But their custom of dedicating stone altars, once adopted in

Matres at Burwell,
Cambridgeshire

the empire's northern provinces, had the effect of precipitating the maternal veneration of tribal Europe into historical visibility.[95]

Another trace of maternal veneration is visible in an 8th century description of a winter holiday called Modranecht, "Mothers' Night."[96] The Anglo-Saxon year began with this night, December 25—winter solstice by the old calendar—when people celebrated "heathen ceremonies" all through the night, as Bede related.[97] One of the Welsh names for the faeries, Bendith Y Mamau—"Blessing of the Mothers"—also strongly resonates with the Matres and Matronae.[98]

The symbolism of some Matronae stones ties in with the Latin fates. In eastern France and among the Treveri, the Matres often hold scrolls, distaffs, and spindles, which were symbols of the Roman Parcae. A British inscription even names them as Parcae.[99] One of the goddess trinity at Metz holds a distaff and spindle[100], as do two of three Matronae on a stone at Trier.[101] But other stones reflect native themes, like the baskets of apples in the Rhineland, the tree and snake.

Some scholars think that an oracular culture was centered around the Matronae, who "may have been able to predict the future, since they seem to have some control over fate as seen in the symbolism of the spinning material, the globe, and the rudder."[102] Their inscriptions lead to the same conclusion: "Isabella Horn has pointed out that the frequent formula *ex imperio ipsarum*, 'at their command,' indicates that the sanctuaries of the Matres served oracular purposes."[103] Horn connects inscriptions to the Audrinehae (and variant names) to the weaving/fate/fortune complex in Germanic and Baltic languages (*auðinn, ēaden, auðna*).[104]

Other faery names are derived from the goddess Diana, or rather her plural form *dianae*: *janas* in Sardinia, *xanas* in northern Spain, and *ianare* in the Neopolitan region. In eastern Europe a phonological shift of d > dz caused *dianae* to morph to *dzine* in Romania, where Diana became Dzina, and Dzewanna in Poland. This Polish form of the goddess retained the most ancient Indo-European meaning of "shining" (present in Di-ana), visible in her linkage with Midsummers. It is celebrated with torches made of mullein, which is also called *dziewanna*.

Under whatever names, *faery* eventually took on the meaning of a goddess immanent in natural places, who sometimes bestows gifts of power, especial-

ly healing or prophecy, but who can be offended by disrespectful or careless people. "The faeries" also encompassed the ancestral dead, who could
be encountered on the land, often in procession, or seen riding the skies in
storms. These ancestors included the elder kindreds as well as the waves of
immigrants, Celtic or Germanic or Italic, who intermarried with them over
millennia.

Over time, latinate faery names became entwined around much older traditions of the megalithic monuments. In France these were called House or
Hut or Cave of the *fées* or *fades,* or whatever local form *fata* had taken. "The
name Grotte-aux-fées ["faery cave"] is so frequently given that one could
consider it as one of the synonyms of dolmen in common parlance, whenever it does not refer to caverns."[105] In some places, the spirits in these places
were called "people of the mound": *siddhe* in Irish, *bergfolk* in Danish, or
liudkova gora in Lusatian. The Irish also called the megalithic spirits Tuatha
Dé Danann, the Tribe of Danand or Tribe of the "gods of Danand."[106]

One of the most striking survivals of ancestor veneration is the Dutch
tradition of *witte wieven,* female spirits who lived in old burial mounds. The
name originated with the meaning "wise women," which is still preserved in
some dialects; but in others it drifted over to a new meaning of "white wom-
en" (thus taking on a racialized context in the colonialist era). In 1660, Johan
Picardt wrote that people brought offerings to the *witte wieven* to ask for
healing, for aid in childbirth, for knowledge of the future and help in finding
lost valuables.[107] These very things were repeatedly listed as activities of the
witches throughout the Middle Ages.

An engraved illustration, entitled "With Witte Wieven in Gravemounds,"
shows one of the *witte wieven* prophesying from the doorway of her house
—a burial mound—to people praying in front. Human and animal skulls
lie on the ground, emphasizing that these precincts belong to the dead. Two
more skulls rest on roof-posts, near the *witte wieven*'s chimney which puffs
merrily away—with mushrooms in the foreground.[108]

Land spirits continued to play a central part in ethnic cultures. Medieval
faery traditions of place told of their spinning and dancing, their gift-giving,
healing, harvest- and herd-protecting. The *fatas* and *fées* and *hadas* were
revered as spirits of springs, caverns, groves, stones, and peaks. In spite of
churchly interdictions, the common people made ceremonial visits to sanc-

"Witte wieven in grave-mounds," by Gerrit van Goedesbergh, 1660

tuaries where they made offerings and vows, and sat vigils in meditation.

The reputation of pagan shrines as the gathering place of witches was engrained by the late Middle Ages. That is why inquisitors interrogated Jeanne d'Arc about her girlhood participation in garlanding and dancing around the village faery tree. In 1431 performing pagan acts was still understood as connected with witchcraft; and they were determined to burn her as a witch. In the most dramatic instance of this connection, a persistent memory of a 7th century pagan tree shrine at Benevento, Italy, became transformed into a mythology that governed Italian witch trials a thousand years later. It said that witches flew in from all over to dance around the Walnut Tree of Benevento, just as the pagan Lombards had done.[10]

wyꜳᴅ ::: weaver oꜰ beiɴɢ

Germanic traditions preserved a dynamic cosmology of the Three Fates. The Norse conceived of the Fates as Being in motion, spinning and turning. They called the eldest Norn Urð, while the Saxons called Fate Wurð, the Germans Wurt, and the Anglo-Saxons Wyrd.[110] These names are the completed aspect of the verb "to be, to become."[111] "Became": the shaper of destiny herself sums up fates already fulfilled, as she brings new things into being. In Old English sources, "The creation of the Fates changes the world under the heavens."[112] Wyrd or Werd gave rise to the medieval word for destiny: *weird*.

Wyrd byð swiðost: ƿyꞃð iſ miᵹhꞇieſꞇ.
—Cotton Maxims, England, ca. 900 CE[113]

These concepts of the divine go deep into Proto-Indo-European history, before Latin and German, or even Sanskrit, had branched off into distinct languages. The names of the Norns (most obviously that of Verðandi) are related to Sanskrit *vartana*, "turning," a word that appears frequently in Indic deity litanies—and which also means "spindle." From the same root *wert, the rotating movement of the spindle is named *wirtel* in German, *vreteno* in Slavonic, and *gwerthyd* in Welsh.[114] It also shows in the Latin verb "to turn"—*vertere* or *vortere*.

The fateful goddesses had deep roots in tribal Germanic cultures. They show up in Icelandic sagas, Frisian common law, and Anglo-Saxon epics and proverbs.[115] Wyrd appears often in Old English gnomic verse, which encoded folk wisdom in mnemonic rhymes. The gnomic proverbs encoded nuggets of heathen lore. *Bith*-gnomes described the essence of things, and *sceal*-gnomes called for action.[116] Anglo-Saxon *sceal* is the word "shall," related to Skuld, the third Norn. The Old English *sceal* carries a sense of imperative necessity, as that which must be, and connoted strong intention. "Wyrd goes as she shall," it says in Beowulf: *Gaeth a wyrd swa hio scel.*[117]

In gnomic verse, the Old Goddess brings into being, moves and changes. *Seo Wyrd geweard*: So Wyrd became, or happened. She arrives at moments of destiny: "The Wurth drew near,"[118] and "*Thiu Wurðh is at handun.*"[119] She also dissolves and transforms what already exists: "Wyrd swept all away."[120]

Wyrd is shown as a fateful presence at births in the Corpus Gloss (circa 725), which renders the Roman fate-name Parcae into Old English as *wyrdae*, "weirds."[121] Anglo-Saxon manuscripts refer to Wyrd as knotting, writing, ordaining, causing and arousing.[123] She grants good fortune, or she withholds it: "Wyrd did not allot him so." She escapes the notice of mortals, sometimes fooling them, leading them astray, or causing their fall. Ultimately, Wyrd deals death to all. In the words of one German source, "Wurth took him away."[124]

Some Old English gnomic sayings conceive of Wyrd as a weaver: "what Wyrd wove for me" (*me thæt Wyrd gewaf*).[125] Another phrase is "woven by the decrees of fate."[126] Anglo-Saxon *gewif*, "fortune," is closely related to *gewæf*, "wove." The connection of these concepts is spread out over several northern European languages. Old English *ēad*, "fortune," is related to the Lithuanian verb *audmi*, "I weave," and to Norse *authna* "fate, fortune, luck," and *authenn* "fated, destined."[127]

In Norse *auðna* meant "to be fated, ordained by fate." From the same root came *vaðmál*, "homespun cloth," which was a basic unit of exchange in Iceland, and thus a measure of wealth, or fortune. "The ancient Indo-European

Three Wyrds, Franks Casket, carved whalebone, England, ca 700 CE

At right, three women in long hooded robes work strands between them, ordaining a warrior's fate. To their left, a dís or valkyrie stands beside a warrior's grave-barrow, holding a staff and cup. His horse mourns beside the mound, with a raven beneath. At far left, the helmeted warrior stands before a spirit woman seated on a stone. She is winged and has the head and feet of a deer. She holds out a flowering tree or branch, proffering regeneration to the dead warrior. Translating the runes is difficult, since the characters run together, some are broken, and several are unknown. Consequently, interpretation of the images has been all over the map. Most readings fail to perceive the powerful female presence in this panel. The idea that it shows the Fates has been around for half a century, but has not been picked up on until recently.[122]

idea linking *auðun* and *vaðmal* is weaving," writes William Miller. He adds that the link of weaving, wealth, and fortune goes to the Fates, "whether as Norns, Moirae, or Parcae."[128]

"whaτ wypō wore for me..."

The Anglo-Saxon word *wyrdstæf* was a name for what Fate ordains. The term resonates with the Norse *rūnstæf*, which were divinatory wooden lots. The only surviving use of *wyrdstæf* combines it with the word "woven": "when comes that season woven by fate's decrees."[129] This same line is also translated as "the time woven on Wyrd's loom." (*thrāg ... wefen wyrdstafum*, taking *wyrdstæf* as "loom")[130]

These heathen concepts survived christianization. Literate clergy parsed them according to the *interpretatio romana*. An entire series of medieval Latin glosses equates Wyrd with Fata and the goddess Fortuna, and with fate and lots: *Fati wyrde oððe gegonges*; *Fata wyrde*; *Fatis wyrdum*; *Fors wyrd*; *Fortuna wyrd*; *Fortunae wyrde*; *Sortem wyrd*; *Fatu wyrde*."[131] These glosses show that the concept of Wyrd was active in Anglo-Saxon culture.

An engrained belief in the supreme power of Wyrd persisted among the people long after pagan religion was officially abolished. In England, the Cotton Maxims accommodated Christianity but still asserted the primacy of the Fate Goddess: "the glories of Christ are great; Wyrd is mightiest."[132] Or as another translation has it, "Wyrd is strongest of all."[133] The Anglo-Saxon *Dream of the Rood* makes several references to Wyrd while recounting Christian mythology.[134] The missionary king Alfred tried to redefine the terms: "What we call Wyrd is really the work of God...."[135]

Though the clergy repressed mention of the Fate Goddess over several centuries, popular culture kept her alive. Wyrd resurfaces, still vigorous, in secular literature after 1300. Weird or Werd remained a common English name for Fate to the end of the middle ages. "Werd drives the world's things to the end."[136] The name also referred to the destinies the Fates shaped at birth: *Whan thei at my nativite/ My weerdes setten as they wolde*. ("When they at my birth set my weirds as they would.")[137]

Attempts to assimilate Wyrd's powers to the Christian god begin as early as the 7th century. The fateful webs of war survive in *Beowulf* in a christianized form: "the Lord gave the people of the Weders webs to speed

them in their battles."[138] Around 1300, the Curson Manuscript replaces
the fate goddess with Jesus, who "weirded er unto the bliss (destined a
soul for heaven)."[139] Eventually the priests succeeded in recasting Wyrd as
Providence, an attribute of the Christian god; "...but for some time during
the transition period Wyrd is remembered in Old English writings as
all-powerful with the Christian God himself subject to her power."[140] A
manuscript of the early 1400s praises "the werdes of my gracious goddis,
the grettest in erde."[141]

The Three Weird Sisters

Wyrd becomes plural in the Middle English of 1385, when Chaucer
wrote of *the Werdis that we clepyn destene* ("the Weirds that we call Destiny").[142]
Elsewhere he called them the *fatal sustrin*, anglicizing the old Latin phrase
sorores fatales.[143] Then, around 1420, the Thre Werd Systeris appear in the
Wyntoun Chronicles.[144] *The Complaynt of Scotland* (1548) also mentions a
story of the *thre weirdsystirs*.[145]

In 1577, Hollinshed's *Chronicles* referred to "the prophesie of three wom-
en supposed to be the weird sisters or feiries."[146] (Notice that he linked the
faeries to Weirds.) He wrote an early version of the Macbeth story, describing how as Macbeth and Banquo journeyed through the woods and fields

there met them three women in strange and wild apparell,
resembling creatures of elder world...[147]

elder, eldritch, eld

"Elder world," or "eldritch world," is an archaic name of the Otherworld,
with eerie, even terrifying connotations. *Online Etymological Dictionary* is
uncertain about its derivation, but suggests that it may be related to *elf*
(compare Scottish variant *elphrish*). But Calvert Watkins views it as a
compound of Old English *el-* "else, otherwise" and *rice*, "realm," thus:
"otherworld."[151] *Weird* and *eld* (a supernatural realm) were associated
as late as 1863: "Stories of *eld* and *weirddom* are vanishing too."[152]

Fifty years after Hollinshed, Heylin repeated his connection of faeries and
wyrds, while adding witches to the mix: "These two ...were mette by three

Fairies, or Witches (Weirds the Scots calle them)."[148]

Shakespeare drew on these accounts of the Three Weird Sisters for one of his most popular plays. He set the opening scene in *MacBeth* this way: "A cavern. In the middle, a boiling cauldron. Thunder. Enter the three Witches."[149]

MacBeth: How now, you secret, black and midnight hags! What is't you do?

[The Witches]: A deed without a name.[150]

John Gilbert, "MacBeth Visits the Three Witches," 1868

Shakespeare still understood the Three Sisters as foreknowing Beings, and showed their prophecies coming to fruition. But he also called them "witches," like the women being hunted in his time. They meet on the open heath and gather in a cavern to chant around a steaming cauldron. These are no mortal women, however, but haggard goddesses:

> **What are these?**
> **So withered and so wild in their attire,**
> **That look not like the inhabitants of the earth,**
> **And yet are on't? Live you? Or are you aught**
> **That man may question? You seem to understand me**
> **By each at once her choppy finger laying**
> **Upon her skinny lips: You should be women**
> **And yet your beards forbid me to interpret**
> **That you are so.**[153]

The three crones are unimaginably old, self-possessed, and foreknowing beings. Unfortunately, Shakespeare's portrayal of the Weird Sisters (circa 1630) is heavily stained with witch-hunt doctrines. He shows them putting

ghastly ingredients into their witches' brew, including parts of human bodies. In the playwright's time, such accusations were killing real women,
especially old ones. Bearded women, like the old Sisters in MacBeth, were
among those at risk. A border English aphorism declared, "A hairy man's a
geary (wealthy) man, but a hairy wife's a witch."[154] Old women tend to develop facial hair, but so do some young women. The saying shows the danger to
a woman who diverged from norms of femininity in the witch hunt era.

The Fates survived in christianized disguise as a triad of saints, or as
three ladies, three nuns, or three Marys. They were widely venerated as saints
in Belgium under their old name the Three Sisters (*dry-susters*).[155] In modern
Flemish, especially in the Limburg region, they are called *De Drie Gezusters*.[156]
Other traditions refer to three women in white or black who sing at the birth of
a child, or who become visible at summer solstice.[157]

Similar folk imperatives created *las tres Marías* in Spain, who appear as the
three spinning Marys, *die drei Marien*, or *tras feyes* in Alsace-Lorraine. These
spirits are often spinners, as Italian used to say of the spring gossamer, "Look
how much *le tre Marie* have spun tonight!"[158]

weoròuncj anò weiròincj

One English name for the witch was "weirding woman." The Scots called
her "weird-woman" or "weird-wife," or sometimes, under Norse influence,
"spaeing woman" (after *spákona*, "prophetic woman"). She cast lots, scanned
the signs and advised of currents to come. Weirding encompassed foreknowledge and prophecy and all the shamanic arts. A Scottish reference to
"weirding peas" harks back to the divinatory way of casting lots.[159]

Divination with peas continued to be practiced even in colonial New
England. Cotton Mather wrote: "They say that in some towns it has been a

usual thing for people to cure hurts with spells, or to use detestable conjurations with sieves, keys, peas, and nails..."[160] The Spanish had a parallel system of casting lots with beans (as did Hungarians) and in their colonization of South America, found Peruvians practicing divination with beans.[161] The sieves, too, have a long history of divinatory use in Europe.[162]

Far from being considered evil or harmful, as its sinister modern connotations suggest, *weirding* was a sacred act in pagan Saxon culture. Its Old English form, *weorðung* or *weorþung* meant "honoring, showing reverence." A related form, *weorðscipe*, developed into the word "worship."[163] It took centuries of repression to change the cultural prestige of *weorðung*. A thousand years ago, an English canonist forbade devotions at sacred trees and wells: *treow-weorðung* and *wylle-weorðung*. Long afterward, people continued to seek out these natural sanctuaries. The clergy often took them over, replacing the well goddess with the image of a bishop or or some saint.

In well-weirding, a seeker made offerings to the waters. She may have invoked the Powers to illumine her spirit while gazing at the waters, at how light and power moved in them. Or she entered trance through immersion in the water. In the Icelandic Edda, a seeker after wisdom sits in silence at the Urðrbrunnr:

> tis time to chant in the sage's chair
> at the well of uror
> i saw and said naught
> i saw and took thought...[164]

Holy springs appear in Old German manuscripts and place-names, as *helicbrunno, heilacprunno, heiligbrunno, heilbronn*.[165] English had the same name: the Holy Bournes. These fountains often preserved a continuity of sacred observance from tribal Europe under romanization and christianization, through the middle ages, and even beyond.

Old sources describe how water drawn from such fountains was used to heal diseases and wounds. It was collected ceremonially, at certain times and in certain ways: "Water drawn at a holy season, at midnight, before sunrise, and in solemn silence, bore til a recent time the name of *heilawāc, heilwāc, heilwæge*."[166] A person might draw living water before sunrise on Sunday from three flowing springs, for example, and then light a candle before it.

Meditation by the waters was a very old custom. The 8th century penitential of Egbert of York not only forbade making libations and other offerings at wells, but also the custom of sitting out beside a spring: "If any has waked at a well..."[167] or "who keeps night watches by rapids..."[168] Burchard of Worms advised confessors to check up on people who went to natural sanctuaries, by asking them:

> **Hast thou come to any other place to pray other than a church or other religious place which thy bishop or thy priest showed thee, that is, either to springs or to stones or to trees or to crossroads, and there in reverence for the place lighted a candle or a torch, or carried there bread or any offering, or eaten there, or sought there any healing of body or mind?**[169]

The *Gesta Herwardus Saxonis* (1068) described how English women held nocturnal dialogues with the spirit guardian of a spring (*custos fontium*):

> **In the middle of the night, the women go out in silence to the springs of east-flowing waters; Hereward saw them go out of the house beside the garden; and he immediately followed them, and heard them from a distance, conversing with I know not what guardian of the spring, asking questions and waiting for answers.**[170]

The Anglo-Saxon well-weirding women recall the ancient Germanic seeresses Aurinia and Veleda who gained knowledge by gazing into river eddies.[171] The custom survived into early modern times, when a poem shows a woman sitting out overnight beside a holy spring: "I the welle woke."[172]

The forbidden *wurðungan* included healing ceremonies. King Edgar's law calls the ritual of passing children through openings in the earth "devil's craft."[173] Anglo-Saxon women treated babies who cried constantly, by making a hole in the ground and ceremonially pulling the child through it.[174] Abbot Aelfric of Eynsham inveighed against this custom: "Likewise some witless women go to cross-roads, and draw their children through the earth, and thus commit themselves and their children to the devil."[175] (This was priestly code for invoking non-christian spirits.) The Frankish *Corrector sive Medicus* also says that women performed the rite as a treatment for babies who cried all the time.[176] The Arundel penitential describes the same healing in the middle of the night, the women go out in silence to the springs of east-flowing waters ... conversing with i know not what guardian of the spring, asking questions and waiting for answers.

rite in contemporary France, along with other charms and divinations.[177]

Germans used hollow trees for this kind of blessing rite, or trees whose boughs had twisted and bored into each other, creating apertures in the wood. The Swedes called these magical openings "elf-bores." Birthing women passed through them.[178] In modern times, sick or disabled people used

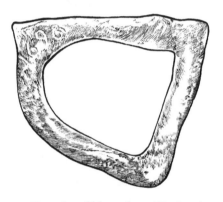

Curative elf-bore from Uppland, Sweden, inscribed 1690.[182]

to crawl through a gnarled old oak at Wittstock, Altmark. Children or cattle were made to walk or crawl through earth tunnels, stone hollows, or the cloven trunk of a young tree.[179] In Ireland, a wisewoman brought a child before sunrise and passed it through a split ash sapling. The Irish also passed sick children through holey stones.[180] These healing ceremonies of passing-through were also carried out in Spain, the Balkans, and other regions of Europe. Three penitential books refer to women who sought to heal sick children by suspending them in a net over a sacred well.[181] Theodore's penitential orders long penance for "any woman who puts her daughter upon a roof or into an oven for the cure of a fever."[183]

Many other priestly texts forbid paying tribute at trees described as *fanatici* (shrines) or *sacrivi* (sacred) or *sacrilegi* (because their sacredness was outside of the bounds declared by priestcraft). Other polemics call the sanctuaries of trees, stones, waters, "abominated places." Bishop Arno of Salzburg preached that it was wrong to look for spiritual help "whether at trees or springs or anywhere" except in church.[184] Condemnations of spiritual acts "anywhere except in church" are repeated over and over in the penitential manuals.

A WORD TREE OF WYRD

From the Proto-Indo-European root *Wert (*Uerth) arose verbs of turning, being, and becoming. From them came the names of the Norns, as well as words for Fate in Germanic languages, including Anglo-Saxon Wyrd and the Three Weird Sisters. Other descendants are weorðung (later weirding) "honoring, reverence," and weorð, "worth," from which came weorðscipe (later worship). Weird figured in names for women of power and divination. Scottish weirdfu' parallels the formation of English worthful. But in modern English weird ("destiny") shifted in meaning to "eerie."

Wyrd span names into the web of language. She tucked under their origins and hid their deepest meanings, before herself sinking out of sight. She concealed her signatures even in the language of religion. *Weorðung* ("honoring, reverence:) and *weordscipe* (the revering of deities) gave rise to the modern English "worship." These words are related to "worthy" and "worth," as well as to "Wyrd."[185]

Wyrd governs what is revered and honored, valued and striven toward, and, ultimately, in its deepest linguistic roots, the turning, spinning movement that is Being. Her proverbs survived longest on the lips of the common folk. In spite of Church hostility to Wyrd's divine kennings, they continue to surface in written literature to the end of the Middle Ages.

The negative modern connotations of "weird" are the result of the severing of witchen spirituality from the cultural mainstream, via a long histosry of persecution. Anything supernatural that did not take a christianized form, a protective veil, was banned and, eventually, feared. In modern English *weird* means "strange, eerie."

The anthropologist Bronislaw Malinowski used the word to describe how special or archaic words were used in ceremonial speech in Trobriand Island culture: "powerful magical language is distinguished by a very high coefficient of weirdness."[186] His comparison to Melanesian concepts is worth reflecting on in the European context: "A spell is believed to be a primeval text which somehow came into being side by side with animals and plants, with winds and waves, with human disease, human courage and human frailty. Why should such words be as the words of common speech? ... the magical theology of the Trobrianders declares that there are words of primeval origin which produce their specific mystical effect by being breathed into the substance, spiritual or physical, which has to be influenced."[187]

The old ethnic European religions shared an understanding of this numinous essence, and of the power of ancestral legacy. But the overwhelming tendency of moderns has been to deny them any philosophical basis. The old demonologists left their mark on modern academe, which has continued to issue anathemata against anyone who has the temerity to say the word "goddess." However, the costs of this "disenchantment of the world" are beginning to be understood.

Behind the dense wall of Christian literature, a few precious shreds of folk culture lay hidden. One is the Anglo-Saxon Æcer-Bot charm, a "field remedy" for land that has grown infertile.[188] Under its christianized surface a pagan ceremony is recognizable. Before dawn, the farmer takes chunks of turf from the four quarters of the land, and pours over them a mixture of milk and oil and honey, with bits from all the trees and plants that grow there, and then puts the turf back into the ground. Other substances are placed on the plow, as an invocation to Mother Earth is spoken.

It begins with the archaic formula, "Erce, Erce, Erce, Eorðan Modor." Who or what Erce might be has been much debated. It could be an old vocative word, similar to Latin *Ave* or Sanskrit *Om*,

earth

Eorth: Old English
Airtha ::: Gothic
Erda: Old High German
(later Erde)
Eerde ::: Old Dutch
(later Aarde)
Jörd ::: Old Norse

or the name of "an old goddess,"[189] or of Earth herself. But *Eorðan Moder* literally means "Mother of Earth," rather than Earth Mother. So Erce might be a name for that Grandmother.

Jacob Grimm nominated the Low Saxon folk goddess Herke or Harke as the German equivalent for a now-lost Anglo-Saxon goddess Erce. Herke flies over the land in the Winter Nights, "dispensing earthly goods in abundance," and belongs to the larger European pattern of spinner goddesses.[190]

The invocation continues *Hāl wes thū folde, fira mōder*: "Hale be thou, Folde, mother of [humans]..." *Folde* turns out to be an extremely old Indo-European name for Earth. It derives from a root meaning "Broad One," from which come Vedic Prthivī and the archaic Greek Plataia, both Earth goddesses.[191] Her title *fira moder*, "mother of humans," places her "not only as the personified land from which produce comes forth, but as the mother of all humankind."[192]

Snorri, in his attempt to explain heathen religion, wrote that ancient people saw that Earth was alive, "and they realized that she was extremely old in years and mighty in nature. She fed all living things, and took to herself everything that died."[193] This idea that Earth received the dead was shared by Latvians and Old Prussians as well as Greeks and Romans.[194] In fact, it was pan-European, and can be traced back as far as the megalithic womb-tombs of the elder kindreds in the 4th millennium BCE, when people lay the cremated remains of their loved ones in uterine chambers covered by earthen mounds—and held ceremony in them.

Heathen culture was the cultural ground floor for customs and beliefs of the commoners. It was overlaid by Christianity to a greater or lesser degree, depending on region and century, and the process of syncretization had begun. But the influence of the old beliefs—in festivals, proverbs, hearth observances, place names and legends— has been underestimated. Even the scribal monks picture Mother Earth as a living being. Underneath their romanizing symbolism (Romulus and Remus appear more than once, and the cornucopia had long since been adopted in imperial times) the old goddess of the common people makes her influence felt. Though she is literally marginalized, she is there.

Earth Swallows the Flood Waters

Frankish manuscript

Northern France, early 800s

As christianization proceeded, these images fade from view. After 1100 they were replaced by saints and Black Madonnas and sirenas, at least in the visible iconographic record, as well as by the allegorical figure of Luxuria. As later chapters will show, ethnic oral tradition carried along a rich pagan freight, so culturally pervasive that it shows up in ecclesiastical literature. There, it collides with misogynist theology, and is overwritten from that perspective. But in trying to stamp it out, the priesthood inadvertantly preserved bits of the culture for posterity. Songs would have been the motherlode, but they are lost. The common people conserved some of the stories, which survived as late as the industrial era in rural areas.

Educated men considered the old ethnic cultural streams to be low-class superstition. They learned it was preferable to think of the Fates, if at all,

Mother Earth exudes life, holding a distaff loaded with flax, with babies at her breast, and proliferating flowers and greenery, even between her toes.

in Greco-Roman terms. Some pictured them spinning in the company of Astrologia, or as the Roman goddess Fortuna—whose wheel also turns in a circle. The Wheel of Fate or Fortuna, or *Rad der Saelde*, became a common theme in the later middle ages.

The royally mandated conversions failed to uproot the people's deep-seated veneration of Eorthan Moder. Earth was for them a great Presence, the source of abundance, revered as a goddess. A thousand years ago, Christian artists were still depicting her in the corners of their ivory psalters, suckling a serpent under the Tree of Life, or a pair of babies, or holding her horn-shaped basket of herbs. In the corners of 12th-century manuscripts, scribes painted Earth among exuberant plant growth, with the spinner's distaff that represents her fateful power, her weirding that becomes, turns, and revolves. Earth herself revolves and turns through time. Spinning on her axis, the Old Goddess creates in the whirl of time.

2
WYCCECRÆFT

When missionaries arrived in pagan Europe, Wyrd's webs were venerated under many names. Spinners and weavers handed down to their daughters customs and beliefs of their craft. They taught them to invoke fateful goddesses while spinning their flax or wool, and to chant and observe omens while weaving. Spinning and weaving were sacraments of the Fates, whose wand of power was the distaff, from which spinners draw fiber to make thread.

Since ancient times, European goddesses have been depicted as spinners. In Greece, the Moirae spin the life-strands (Clotho), measure them (Lachesis) and irrevocably cut them (Atropos). Fate also appears as a singular goddess, Aisa. Greek poets often described goddesses as holding a "golden distaff."[1]

Athena Ergane, horned, with distaff, Sicily

Artemis is sometimes titled *chryselokatos*, "she of the golden distaff." An ivory statue of Artemis Ephesia holding a distaff was found in her Lydian temple from the 6th century bce.[2] In Rome, the distaff and spindle of the founding mother Gaia Caecilia was guarded in the Sabine temple of Semo Sancus. This figure was based on the Etruscan seeress Tanaquil, and her distaff had sacred and blessing qualities.[3]

The distaff figures as a magical tool—and spirit being—in ethnic orature. In Sardinia, it is the spirit-wand of the witch-goddess Lughia Rajosa, who lived in one of the *nuraghe* towers of the bronze age. Her enchanted distaff (*Rocca fatata*) guarded great wealth: herds of animals and thousands of jars of grain and oil. The distaff moved around in the day while Lughia slept, and whistled to warn her of intruders. People recounted how young men often tried to steal her animals or firewood. She defeated many of these intruders, but one managed to push her magical distaff into the oven. Not knowing how to cry, Lughia turned into many insects, which cried for her. Now she

flies as a cicada amidst the *nuraghe* towers.[4]
The distaff acts as a spirit wand in
French legends about St. Germaine
de Pibrac. When she stuck her
distaff in the ground, it looked
after her sheep—and never lost
a lamb to the wolves.[5]

Saint Berthe d'Aveney
(d. 690) was said to have been
spiritually inspired to discover
"a fountain of living water."
She used her distaff to increase
its flow and to lead the water to
her abbey. She left the mark of
her knees on a stone there "with
two little holes at the place where
she rested her distaff and spindle."[6]
(See chapter 4 on spirit wands.)

Roman-influenced Gaulish
sculpture shows goddesses as

*Horned goddess with distaff, wearing an
archaic cape. Chesters, Northumberland.*

spinners, such as Sequana, she for whom the Seine river was named.[7] A
horned goddess holds a loaded distaff in a lead icon from Chesters, Britain.[8]
She has an archaic, feral look, with an off-the-shoulder capelet of fringed
vegetal fiber string, or possibly of strips woven on a backstrap loom. She
reflects a very different cultural reality than Roman reliefs of the Parcae
spinning with a distaff. She is from the borders of Pictland, the tribal northern Britons that the legions could never defeat.

Spinner goddesses persisted in medieval European culture despite con-
tinual attempts to quash their veneration. Early bishops of Spain, France and
Germany campaigned against women's spiritual practices "in their webs."
In Galicia, Martin of Braga insisted it was forbidden "for women to invoke
Minerva in their weaving." He admonished women to invoke only "the
Lord," and not "to observe whatever vanities in their weaving." He revealed
that weavers had the custom of calling on a goddess (whose name was not
necessarily the Roman one he gave) with some ceremony or incantation. As
a hostile outsider, the bishop was unlikely to have witnessed them.[9]

Invocations of a goddess—possibly entire litanies—were practiced at the loom. Her indigenous name was not recorded. The *interpretatio romana* demanded Latin names, so the priesthood frequently used that of Minerva, a goddess of weaving. It may be that she had become syncretized with a local Celt-Iberian or Germanic goddess. Anne Ross has shown that native British and Gaulish goddesses were often conflated with Minerva, especially those associated with healing springs, like Sul of Bath. Stone reliefs of the goddess Brigantia are visually indistinguishable from Roman Minerva; but the name they bear is Brittonic (Celtic).[10]

Another reference to women's weaving invocations implies that women did call on their goddess by her native names. In north Gaul, bishop Eligius of Noyon refused to acknowledge those names even as he prohibited them:

No woman should hang succinos [amber amulets] from her neck, nor in weaving or dyeing or textile work name Minerva *or other unpropitious persons...*[11]

But this was where the weavers disagreed. The common women believed that their goddess was preëminently propitious, and brought good fortune to those who revered her, whatever she was called. Around 750, another prohibition of "women naming Minerva in their weaving" comes from Pirmin of Reichenau, who calls it the "culture of the devil." Pirmin probably borrowed the wording from Eligius, but the fact that he considered such a ban relevant signals the possibility that these German websters were invoking a goddess, possibly Holda / Holle.[12]

Around 700, a penitential at Silos listed "woolen work, or magical practices"—among them divination, enchantment, soothsaying, and dream interpretation. The priests prescribed a five-year penance for these observances, adding this enticing but frustratingly brief fragment: "It is not permitted *to observe wool at the kalends,* or the collections of herbs, or to give heed to incantations..."[13] (Emphasis added; the calends are the first day of the year or month.) So too the Frankish *Homilia*

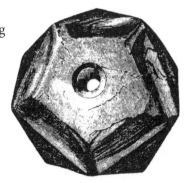

Crystal spindle whorl, Emscote Warwicks, Britain

Frankish women weaving outdoors, circa 800. Several sources refer to the incantations women sang "in their webs," invoking goddesses and observing omens as they wove. These workspaces were called gynecaea, *"women-places."*

de sacrilegiis condemns a divination by drawing out tufts of wool with needles.[14] Such prohibitions yield the barest glimpse of women's divinatory practices, but show that they were related to spinning and weaving *cræft*.

Pagan weaving customs were still thriving in Hispania five centuries after Martin's sermons first assailed them. This time, the clergy was upset over the weavers using amulets or sacred images. In 1065 the council of Santiago inveighed against women's custom of "hanging on looms little figures of women or filthy animals or other similar things, all of which is idolatrous."[15] In Provence, a sermon of Caesarius of Arles deplores the fact that "wretched women" refused to weave or spin on Thursdays, which were widely observed as a pagan day of rest in this period. Several centuries later, the Pseudo-Gregorii penitential ascribes this custom to sorcerers and sorceresses.[16] Thursday was still viewed as a witches' holiday in early modern witch trials.

Weaving was associated with wisdom, prophecy, poetry, and blessing in Indo-European culture. The *Rg Veda* speaks of poetry as weaving, and later Indic scriptures are called *sutra,* "threads." Avestan *vaf,* originally "weave," acquired the meaning of "hymn, praise-song." In Greece, Pindar spoke of having "woven a song." In Welsh the weaving metaphor was applied to poetic composition, just as the Old English writer Cynewulf "wove the art of words" (*wordcræft wœf*).[17]

The poet-goddess Brigit was called the first weaver in Ireland, and it was she who "put the white threads in the loom that have a healing power to this day."[18] Cloth, as in so many other world cultures, had sacred power. Not only did the mantle of Brigit figure in countless stories of blessing grace, but it was invoked every Imbolc (the eve before Feb. 2) when women laid a cloth (the Brat Bhríde) out overnight to gather Brigit's blessing power to be used through the year.

Christianizing the goddess made it possible for such customs to survive, but only some of them. An Irish hagiography of Ciarán shows that women wanted no males around while they were doing textile work. His *muimme* (foster-mother) sent him out of the house while she dyed wool, for which the juvenile saint cursed her heathen impiety.[19] The story implies that the women were performing some kind of ritual.

í am ꝼeðelm ꝛhe banꝼílí oꝼ connauꝼhꞇ...

A weaving prophetess appears at the beginning of the *Táin Bó Cuailnge*. Fedelm the *banfháidh* comes in a chariot drawn by black horses to prophesy to queen Medb. Her divine vision is underlined by the triple irises in her eyes. She is richly dressed in a speckled cloak with a gold pin, an embroi--dered hood, and her hair in three plaits, with two of them wound around her head and the other "brushing her calves."

Holding a bronze weaver's sword, she speaks to Medb: "I am Fedelm the *banfíli* of Connaught." The queen asks if she has *imbas forosna*, the power of prophecy, and she replies that she does. Addressing her as "Fedelm, prophetess," Medb asks her to forecast the battle, again and again. Each time the *banfíli* replies, "I see it bloody, I see it red," chanting a prediction of defeat for Connaught. And so it happens; many die, and nothing is gained by the conflict.[20]

The prophetess says solemnly, "I am Fedelm. I hide nothing." She calls herself a *banfíli*, a name often translated as "woman poet," but the Irish title carries the broader meaning of seership. In fact, she proclaims her mastery of *imbas forosna*, prophetic inspiration. She is also called *banfháith*, "prophetess."[21] Fedelm is not a personal name, but an ancient title, a strand from the same root as *filidh*. In the second recension of the *Táin*, Fedelm is again presented as chanting, and she not only carries a weaver's sword, but is actually weaving while prophesying.[22] Maire West views the weaving tool as "a symbol of her office as prophetess." She notes that scholars have emphasized the importance of the weaver's sword of Fedelm, "associated with her intrinsic magical and prophetic powers."[23] C. O'Rahilly compared it to modern Scots women who were described as "framing witchcrafts by crossing threads of varied colors in varied manners..."[24]

omens "that women call 'what comes upon' in their spinning and wearing work"

A ninth century bishop reported a Frankish women's custom of drawing omens during the spiritually charged act of weaving. Bishop Hincmar of Reims classified the auguries that women observed from things that happened while they were working fibers as "sorceries": "to these belong those which women call *superventas* [what "comes upon"] in their spinning and weaving work."[25] A similar concept survived in the German *Angang*, omens observed from encounters with people or animals, especially first thing in the morning.[26] It might be a bird's flight, animal cries or meeting up with a fox.

Hincmar also disparaged women's practice of "measuring with threads," abundantly documented in European folk healing into modern times. He condemned "the execrable remedy of *ligaturas*" (magical ties worn on the body).[27] He complained that some people wore "clothing that had been sung over," thus showing that Frankish women were using incantations to

Norman weavers laying warps, Eadwine Psalter, circa 1100. Copied from Carolingian weavers scene (see page 38), adding veils, tree, and animals.

bless the clothing they made.[28] Irish and Scottish weavers continued to sing protective blessings over newly-made clothing into the modern era. Norse sagas also show women enchanting tunics so that "iron would not bite" the wearer.[29] In Denmark, Saxo Grammaticus says that Ulfhild gave Frodi "a coat which no steel could pierce, so that when he wore it no missile's point could hurt him." He also shows the wood-maidens bestowing a coat or belt of invulnerability on Hother.[30]

Another important priestly allusion to women's weaving mysteries, circa 1015, indicates that German women chanted as they wove. The *Corrector sive Medicus* reproaches "the vanities which women practice in their wool work, in their weaving":

> **When they lay their warps, they hope with both their incantations and actions it will be possible, as the threads of warp and woof may become so tangled together that if they did not supplement these in turn with other counter-incantations of the devil, the whole will perish.**[31]

The Latin in this passage is muddled and difficult. Like Eligius, the writer obscures the real purpose of the women's chants, and associates women's weaving chants with "the devil," instead of heathen goddesses who were hallowed as weavers of fate. The same source condemns women's ritual observances on January 1: "who on that holy night wind magic skeins, spin, sew, all at the prompting of the devil beginning whatever task they can begin on account of the new year."[32]

The Fates governed birth and death, and the symbolism of spinning and weaving entered into funerary custom. The *Corrector sive Medicus* tells us that women performed a ritual act of clapping carding combs together over a dead person before they were carried out for burial. Bernadette Filotas notes that carding combs and other weaving tools are often found in Germanic ship burials, like Sutton Hoo in England. She connects these funerary offerings to Fate goddesses.[33]

Women's threadboxes, which they seem to have worn on belts, hold other clues. In Francia and Scandinavia their "aromatic and sometimes exotic contents," including stones, led archaeologists to consider them "amulet-capsules."[34] They often contain scraps of cloth. In her study of Anglo-Saxon amulets, Audrey Meaney comments, "...what is clear is that to the people of the early Middle Ages, 'weaving spells' was no mere empty phrase, and therefore these scraps of textile could have been preserved because of the magic power within them."[35]

Secular writers were less taciturn about the details of these beliefs. They connected weaving with the revelation of fate. Anglo-Saxon chroniclers described an oracular banner that Danish warriors carried before them in battle in 878. It was called Reafan ("Raven"). Women wove these cloth battle standards under special ritual conditions. One was that the banner needed to be started and completed in one sitting:

> **... for they say that three sisters, daughters of Loderocus, wove that banner and finished it in a single afternoon. And they said that in all wars, whenever that sign preceded them, if they were to get the victory it would appear as if a crow flying; but if in the future they were going to be defeated, it would hang there not moving.**[36]

Another account appears in the Annals of St Neots, circa 1105. It says that the flag was of plain white silk, in which a raven became visible only in wartime. Then it appeared rippling with victory, or drooped motionless in defeat.[37] Jarl Sigurd possessed such a magical banner, according to *Orkneyinga saga*. His mother, a skilled witch, wove it for him after he was challenged by a rival. She foretold that the banner would give victory to the leader before whom it was carried, but death to whoever bore it. Three men died carrying the banner. Another saga reports that Sigurd used it again at the battle of Clontarf, but his men refused to carry it. So he did, and was killed.[38] A Norman woman depicted one of these raven-banners on the Bayeux tapestry (below).

The valkyries are said to weave a web while singing; when the web is finished they have decided the outcome of battle.[39] A horrific "web of war" appears in the 13th century Norse poem *Darraðarljóð*. Twelve valkyries

*Raven-banner
embroidered on
the Bayeux Tapestry,
Normandy, northern France*

Irish proverb speaks of "the knowledge of the raven's head."[44]

Illustration by John D. Batten from Celtic Fairy Tales, *1902*

arrive on horseback early in the morning before a battle. They enter the *dyngja* (women's weaving quarters) and set up a loom. Its warp and woof are men's entrails, and their heads the loom weights. The supernatural women use an arrow as the shuttle and a sword as the beater. As they weave, they sing a poem: "Let us wind, let us wind the weaving of the pennant." They prophesy the outcome of the battle, and conclude with, "Now the fabric is wove and the field dyed red."[40] When the battle is over, they take the cloth down, rip it up, and each one takes a piece away on her horse, with six heading south and six to the north.[41]

Germanic peoples associated the valkyries with ravens. The Anglo-Saxons gave the valkyrie title *wæl-ceásega* ("chooser of the slain") to the raven.[42] Battle-fating ravens also existed in Celtic culture. The Morrigan often took this form. The Irish goddess Badb Catha ("battle raven") dealt out fate on the battlefield, over which she flies screaming, and is seen washing the clothing of those about to die in battle.[43] The Gaulish goddess Cathubodua had nearly the same name, though little is known about her. Nantosuelta also had a raven aspect.

The Badb was a prophetic goddess, as explained in the *Second Cath Maige Tuiread*: "Then after the battle was won and the slaughter had been cleaned away, the Morrígan... proceeded to announce the battle and the great victory which had occurred there to the royal heights of Ireland and to its *síd*-hosts, to its chief waters and to its river-mouths. And that is the reason Badb still relates great deeds. 'Have you any news?' everyone asked her then. [She replied:] 'Peace up to heaven. Heaven down to earth. | Earth beneath heaven, Strength in each | A cup very full, Full of honey | Mead in abundance…"[45]

. In those violent times, traces also remain of an old suasion against war. The 6th-century Alemans had diviners (*manteis* and *khismologoi*) who dissuaded from battle.[46] The Anglo-Saxons called certain women *freoðu-webbe*, "peace-weaver," and their male counterparts *freoðu-weard*, "peace-guardian." Scholars have described how *freoðu-webbe* meant a woman married into an adversarial family, but L.J. Sklute makes a case for such women playing an active part in improving relations between groups: "making peace by weaving to the best of her art a tapestry of friendship and amnesty."[47] Similarly, the abbess of Kildare is called "a woman who turns back the streams of war."[48]

Anglo-Saxon heathens called Nature sanctuaries *frith-freoðu*, "peace-places," as holy places were by definition sacrosanct from all acts of violence. *Frith* connoted peace, concordance,

ᚠᚱᛁᚦ-ᚠᚱᛖᛟᚦᚢ,
ᚠᚱᛁᚦ-ᛋᛈᛚᛟᛏ:
"peace-places"

treaties, and also asylum. The *frithsplot* was "a plot of land, encircling some stone, tree, or well, considered sacred, and therefore offering sanctuary…"[49] A 10th century English priest's denunciation of the *frithsplots* shows they were closely connected with the veneration of certain trees:

The elder was revered in England as Lady Ellhorn (later, as Old Gal) and by Danes as the Hyldemoer

"the vain practices which are carried on with various spells and with *frith-splots,* and with elders, and also with various other trees, and with many various delusions."[50] A related term, *frith-geard*, meant an enclosure that gave asylum to a fugitive, and "a place where peace prevails."[51] *Frith* was still understood as "an enclosed wood" into the late middle ages, in the poem *Piers Plowman*.[52] These shrines resemble the latticed enclosures that the Roman Penitential forbade Christians to approach.[53]

In southern Europe, web-working was associated with spiritual power. The Italian witch-name *magliaia* arose from the same root as words for "knitting" and "mesh-cloth." The Corsican *magliaia* performed the classical work of the witch: healing, sooth-saying, love-magic, the making of amulets, and turning away the evil eye.[54]

Placing a blessing cloth on the sick person or animal was a widespread pagan method of healing. In Ireland, people still place Brigit's Mantle (*brat Bhríde*) outside on her holy night to receive the dew, and attribute healing and blessing power to them. Christians adapted customs of consecrated weavings to altar coverings, often in precious purple and gold, or by draping cloths over saints' tombs for magical uses. The English called these magical cloths *Godwebbe*.[55]

The Godwebbe appears "especially often in stories about supernatural curative practices."[56] One recipe for women's discharge of blood involved wrapping a ritually gathered berry in a red Godwebbe to bind on her forehead or belly. The Lacnunga contains a charm for smudging sick cattle with herbs or incense and with the Godwebbe, which was not for waving smoke over the animals but actually was itself burned as a sacred substance.[57] All of these are adaptations of far older animistic rites with yarn or skeins or woven cloth.

Women often used belts in midwifery and healing. Their methods were sometimes adapted to Christian use, as with the Moylough Belt Shrine of 8th century Ireland. It is the only surviving example of sacred belts "imbued with mystical powers" to heal or to establish truth, as described in early Irish literature: "For example, the girdle/belt of St. Bridget was reputed to cure any illness or sickness."[58]

The church declared pre-christian sacraments, especially those associated with spinning and and other animist *cræfts,* to be devilish. Women carried on most of their fabric *cræft* outside church contexts. As late as 1870, a country person told a folklorist about animistic customs around the spinner's craft: "The old soul have a bit of belief like in witch-stones, and allus sets one aside her spinning jenny."[59]

Tbe ORIGINS OF WITCb

Linguists disagree on the deep etymology of the word "witch." Several possible Indo-European genealogies have been proposed, but so far none have been agreed upon. The recent line of descent in Germanic languages is better known; the root *wik- or *weik gave rise to Old English *wicce*, Dutch and East Frisian *wikke* and Low German *wikken*.[60] Anglo-Saxon also had the verb *wiccian*, "enchant, make magic." Though *wicca* was the name for male witches, popular usage leaned heavily toward the female form: *wycce, wicche, wychche, wyche, wiche, wich, wech, witche and wytch*.[61] The plural was *wiccan* or *wiccana*. An early Latin gloss for English "witch" translates it as *saga*, "wise woman."[63]

In northwestern Germany, *wihken* and *wicken* survived as words for soothsaying, predicting, divination, and conjuring. Their Dutch parallels were *wikken* and *wichelin*. "In [Lower] Saxony they still say for conjuring or soothsaying, *wihken, wicken* and *wigelen* (*wichelen*), for fortune-teller *wicker* or *wichler*, for witch *wikkerske*, for sorcery *witchelie*."[62] In the 1600s, *wickhersen* ("foretellers") appears in a list of witch-names recorded by Johannes Pott —along with Töchter des Donners, "Thunder Daughter."[64]

Names for magic wands also arose from the *wik-* root. From *wicken* came the northern German word *wickerode,* for hazelwood wishing-wands or divining rods. The *wickerode* was used to find ores, water and other "hidden treasures," like the dowsers of Anglo folk culture,[65] whose art is still called "water-witching." The Dutch call the divining rod *wichelroede,* and the action of moving it back and forth is *wichelen.*[66] A lexical linkage of "witch" and "wand" occurs in the modern German *wünschelwip* "wish-woman" and *wünschelrute,* "divining rod."[67] Memory of the witch's wand was kept alive in faery tales. Its deep history belongs to a global context of shamanic staffs.[68]

The oldest attestation of *wicca* occurs around 890, when the laws of king Alfred translated Exodus into Old English—with alterations. Instead of "Suffer not a witch to live," his law reads, "Women who are accustomed to receiving enchanters [*gealdorcraeftigan*] and sorceresses [*scinlaecan*] and witches [*wiccan*], do not let them live!"[69] (This expansion of the scope of persecution to those who consult witches is also found in the Lombard laws of north Italy in the 7 th century.)[70]

In spite of their antipathy toward heathen spiritual culture, the writings of Anglo-Saxon churchmen contain important testimony about witches. Some of it underlines how popular and sought-out they were. Archbishop Wulfstan denounced *wiccecræft* in a sermon that exhorted people: "do not pay heed either to spells [*galdra*, literally "incantations"], or idle divination, nor to sorceries or witchcraft".[71]

Abbot Aelfric of Eynsham provided abundant evidence that people saw *wiccan* (the plural of "witches") as prophetic and healing figures. He conceded that witches did know things, but condemned the source of their inspiration as demonic:

**Now some soothsayers [*wiglere*] say that witches often speak the truth
of how things go. Now we say in truth that the invisible devil that flies
yonder around this world sees many things and reveals to the witch
what she may say to men [sic], so that those who seek out this *drycræft*
may be destroyed.**[72]

Priestcraft's standard explanation for the *wicce's* prophetic insight is that
her powers come from the devil. Churchmen inverted the folk recognition
of spirits and substituted the christian anti-god for the rich spirit-names
of the old culture. They attempted to convince people that they would be
destroyed for seeking counsel from the *wicce*.

Aelfric acknowledged that people went to witches for healing, though in
the most disparaging terms: "Nor ought a Christian man to enquire from
the foul witch about his health..."[73] He insisted that whatever helpful things
she was able to tell people came from the devil. Aelfric belonged to a host of
priestly writers and preachers who urged people to suffer illness, even unto
death, rather than consult witches or perform any forbidden pagan rites:

**The christian man, who in any of this like is afflicted, and he then will
seek his health at unallowed practices, or at accursed enchantments,
or at any witchcraft, then will he be like to those heathen men, who
offered to an idol for their bodies' health, and so destroyed their
souls. Let him who is sick pray for his health to his Lord, and patiently
endure the stripes.... It is not allowed to any christian man to fetch his
health from any stone, nor from any tree, unless it be the holy sign
of the rood [cross], nor from any place, unless it be the holy house of
God: he who does otherwise, undoubtedly commits idolatry.**[74]

Here *stane-weordhunga* and *treow-weordhunga* appear in a healing
context; but priestcraft defines them as illict and intrisically evil. Elsewhere,
Aelfric described how witches went to crossroads or to *hæðanum byrgelsum*,
"heathen graves," a phrase connoting mounds or megalithic passage graves:

**Yet fare *wiccan* to where roads meet, and to heathen burials with their
phantom craft, and call to them the devil, and he comes to them in the
dead man's likeness, as if he from death arises, but she cannot cause that to
happen, the dead to rise through her *drycræft*.**[75]

Reading through the diabolism, an explicitly female *wicce* is perceptible,
a woman who communes with the ancestral dead. She goes to crossroads

or to ancient burial grounds for her ceremonies, which Aelfric derided as *gedwimore* ("phantom-craft" or "illusion, fantasm"). *Drycræft* is another name for witchcraft; Anglo-Saxon *dry* is a loan-word derived from Irish *draoi or drui*—the same root as *druid*.[76]

Aelfric's condemnation of witches' ceremonies at crossroads corresponds to the penitentials' denunciation of such rites as "pagan" acts. In the early middle ages, "witch" overlaps with "pagan." As the Council of Paris declared in 825, "witches, diviners, and enchanters" practiced "very certainly the remains of the pagan cult."[76a] But this connection has been heavily contested in academia, where it has become doctrinal to deny it, no matter how often the witches' priestly contemporaries denounced them as "pagan."

Priestly diabolism collided with the old ethnic cultures. Its biased interpretations of witchcraft are still prevalent in modern analysis. The old wisewomen are cut out of the historical picture, which continues to be framed by an engrained cultural bias formed over a long history of persecution. Most scholars, including many specialists in witchcraft studies, still define "witch" in very negative terms: "In the most general sense a witch is a person who possesses a supernatural, occult, or mysterious power to cause misfortune or injury to others."[77] Dictionary definitions run along the same lines. Anthropologists continue to use "witch" in a specific, negative sense: "According to the traditional anthropological definition, witchcraft is an inborn, involuntary, and often unconscious capacity to cause harm to other people."[78] Without realizing it, they agree with the diabolist clergy.

Compounding the problem is the anthropological convention of using sex-marked words to designate harm-doers (witch : female), which are counterposed to terms considered neutral or ambiguous (sorcerer or magician : male).[79] Thus Claude Lecouteux refuses to use "witch" in the belief that "it applies only to black and evil magic."[80] But this terminology is not sex-neutral, as a massive accumulation of culture shows. These word choices are loaded with assumptions engrained by priestcraft. They carry a heavy historical charge, loaded with the misogynist sexual politics and racialized stereotypes of the witch hunts. By insisting on a "bad" definition of witch, they perpetuate misogynist and anti-pagan church doctrines.

They also ignore the old ethnic context of "witch," which had a very different valence that sometimes leaks through even some priestly accounts. The oldest usage of witch meant a woman of spiritual knowledge, and this meaning continued for a long time. As late as 1584, Reginald Scot could write in *The Discoverie of Witchcraft*:

> At this day it is indifferent to say in the English tongue, "she is a witch," or "she is a wise woman."[81]

The etymologies of wicce

Attempts to trace *witch* to its Indo-European roots have so far been inconclusive. Among its proposed sources are two separate Proto-Indo-European roots reconstructed as *weik, each with different meanings. The first, which has been favored by many sources, including the Oxford English Dictionary, is *weik2, with the meaning "to bend, turn, move." From it came Anglo-Saxon *wik-*: "to bend, twine, twist, turn." This word is connected to spinning, twining, and plaiting. (The second *weik root, meaning "sacred," will be discussed below.)

The Anglo-Saxons used *wich* to mean a bundle of fiber, originally plant fibers like tow, flax, or rushes. Women twisted them into *wicks*, which they dipped in tallow and burned for light. Turning split willow wands into baskets and other forms made *wicker*. The word "weak" is related to this crafting of pliable stalks. Witch hazel is named from Old English *wice*, for its pliant branches rather than from any herbal use of the plant. The turning motion of a gate or door gave *wicket*; a turning of time gave rise to the word *week*.[82]

In spinning and weaving and knotting, weirding women partook of the Fates' power to shape and transform reality. They were literally witches, bending and twining and binding the fibers of Being. Spinning was one form of the *cræft* of *wicces*. The Old English word *cræft* expresses a broad range of meanings: "... it is power, force, strength; cunning, knowledge, ability and skill; prescription and remedy."[83] It was combined with other words to create compounds such as *gealdor-cræft* and *leoðucræft* (incantation), *læce-cræft* (medicine), *hyge-cræft* (knowledge), and *dry-cræft*. The Cotton Maxims condemn a woman who seeks a lover *thurh dyrne cræfte* ("by secret craft").[84]

Women's *cræft* of spinning, weaving, plaiting, wickerwork and knotting reflected a central sacrament of tribal European religion. It was the image of the Fates' transformative power, under whatever names they were known.

For the Estonians as for Saxons, they symbolized the creative power of Goddess.[85] The symbolism of spinning, especially the distaff, would persist in folk observances and through the entire course of the witch hunts, and in place-lore too. In Wales, a crag named Ystol Gwiddon, "Witch's Chair," was said to be the place "where a witch is said to have planted herself to weave the woof of human destiny."[86]

The twisting of fibers, the bending of osier twigs into baskets and wattle was literally "wicked," in its most archaic sense. But eventually, quite late in fact, *wicked* came to mean evil. The *Unabridged Oxford* shows that it was used in this sense no earlier than 1275. In modern English, the word survives primarily in the phrase "wicked witch." It is still linked to a woman of power, but a demonized one, far from the original meaning of *wik-.

Returning to the second Proto-Indo-European *weik root, another strand of meaning appears in the linguistic web. This *weik- meant "holy, sacred." In Common Germanic, it became *wihs. The word survived in Gothic as *weihs*, "holy." Other descendants of the root include several verbs meaning "to consecrate" (Old High German *wihen,* modern *weihen,* and Old Icelandic *vigja*).[87]

Old Icelandic *vé* (temple) descends from *wihs, as do Old English *wîg,* "idol," and *wêofod* "altar," along with its Northumbrian equivalent *wigbed.* The linguist Jacob Grimm saw English *wiccian* and Dutch *wichelin* as flowing out of this "sacredness" grouping, and linked them with Low German *wikken,* "foretell."[88] This directly parallels the relation of *diviner* and *divination* to *divine.*

Some sources also throw *wigle,* "divination," into the mix. *Wiccian* and *wiglian* both meant "to cast a spell," but are not etymologically related.[89] The latter term, from the root *wih-l, produced Old English *wigla* "divination, sorcery" and *wiglera* "sorcerer," and the closely related Old Frisian *wigila* "sorcery." It also extended into medieval Norse, English and French words for "craftiness": *wihl, wile, guile.*[90] *Wiglian* might also relate to Germanic *wiegan,* "rock, sway," which yields Middle High German and Middle Dutch *wigelen,* "sway, shake." That could suggest diviners entering ecstasy. English "wiggle" and OHG *wegan,* "weigh," are also part of this complex.

But like Grimm, Anatoly Lieberman sees medieval Dutch *wijchelen, wichelin, wîkelen* as growing out of the *wihs "holy" root, not the "shake and sway" root.[91] He lays out the confusion and contradictions between the many proposed etymologies for *witch*. His highly technical discussions about phonological shifts (such as how *wik-* went to *wig-* according to Verner's Law) explain how certain changes were likely and others, unlikely. "The quickest search will reveal the fact that the only reliable connection is between OE [Old English] *wicca* and OE *wiccian* and the almost identical verb in Low German..."[92]

The Neopagan use of Wicca as a name for pagan religion is a modern development. It denotes the masculine singular for witch, which governs the plural form *wiccan / wiccana*. But *wicca* was not even a preferred designation for male witches in Anglo-Saxon. The most common terms was *wiglera*, "diviner." W*itaga*, an unrelated word meaning "wise man," came from the same root as "wit." Royal counselors were called *witaga*, and an annual assembly was called the *Witenagemot*. (This crumbling, all-male survival of an elders' council was choked out by feudalism by the end of the 10th century.) But the primary usage, by all accounts, was the female *wicce*.

Neopagans often cite the *wit*-root as the source of "witch," a derivation that has been forcefully rejected by most modern etymologists. Some older Anglo-Saxonists like Walter Skeat did see *wicce* as descending from Old English *witka*, which he compared to Old Icelandic *vitki*, "conjurer, magician," and a verb of knowing, *witan*. Recently, Lieberman has resurrected this line of reasoning in a new form. He starts from *wîteg*, "seeing," and *witeg*, "knowing" (a very old pairing in Indo-European languages, including Slavic and Celtic) and lays out a progression of *wîtega* > *witga* in Anglo-Saxon, and to *wîzzago* and *wizzago* in Old High German.

Lieberman recognizes that *wicca* can't derive from *witega* since they were used concurrently. Instead he proposes a root **witja* that became *wicca* (and *wicce*).[93] He points to parallel formations in Old English; the word "craftsman" went from *cræft-ig-a* to *cræftga*, *cræftca*, and even *cræfca*. Similarly the "knowing" root *wîtan* might have shifted to wît-ig-a > *witga*. He points to a Slavic analogue: "A close parallel to witch derived from **wit-ja* is Russ *ved'ma* (morphologically ved'-m-a). Old Russ *vêd* meant both 'knowledge' and 'witchcraft.'"[94] (A similar conceptual pairing in Celtic is shown in the next chapter). Anglo-Saxon linguist Alaric Hall accepts the derivation of **witege / witega* > *wicce / wicca*.[95] This proposal of *wit*-as-"knowing" is a new twist in a still-unresolved discussion.

In any case, contra another popular etymology, *witan* is not connected to "wizard," which derives from "wise," and is not attested until the 15th century. Even then it does not yet designate a magician, a meaning that took another century to develop.[96] Another common word for male sorcerers, "warlock," comes from a word meaning "oathbreaker," and is completely unrelated to any of these terms.[98]

WICH AS VITALITY

There's one more proposed Proto-Indo-European root to consider: *weg-, "to be strong, lively, or *gweih3, "to live," from which flowed Latin *vivere*, Spanish *vivir*, French *vivre*, and English *revive* and *survive*. This root is related to the English "awaken," and "wake" as an expression for all-night vigils, "waking the well." (*Vigil, wait* and *watch* are derived from it too.) In Old English the verb form was *wacian*. An old German word *wikkiyaz*, "one who wakes the dead," bears enough similarity to be a candidate for relationship to "witch."[98]

The Indo-Europeanists Calvert Watkins and Jan Puhvel favor this root as the origin for "witch." Puhvel ties in "waking" with the *völur* being called up in the Icelandic Eddas. (or rather the single instance in Baldrsdraumr).[99] A later form of this root is *wik-*, which designates "living place" in many languages: Latin *vicus* ("town"), Norse *vik*, Gothic *weihs* ("village"), and Greek *oikos* ("house"). (From *oikos* sprang "economics" and the newer term "ecology"). The same root survived in English words like "bailiwick" and place-names like Warwick and Sandwich.[100] Middle High German also uses *wich* in this sense of habitation.[101]

From the *weg root came the now-archaic English usage of *quick*, meaning "alive." It survives in the expression "cut to the quick," and as a word for the sensitive tissue under fingernails. The King James Bible (1611) used the phrase "the quick and the dead" three times, in Acts 10:42, 2 Timothy 4:1, and the First Epistle of Peter. From there the expression made its way into the Book of Common Prayer. Later, the English meaning of *quick* changed to "fast, speedy." Conversely, *vegetable* comes from a Latin derivative of the same root "vital, lively," for a plant full of life force—but modern English has reversed it out to a symbol of passive inactivity!

The antique sense of *wick* as life-force was preserved in some rural English dialects. In *The Secret Garden*, the Yorkshire gardener's son shows a dried-out bush to his female friend and, cutting away the dead surface, says:

> "This part's wick. See the green?
>
> "Wick? What's wick?"
>
> "Alive. Full of life."[102]

*Wik- also referred to the movement of vitality in Nature: the coiling turns of tree branches and roots, the winding patterns of a river or sinuous coastline. Two trees of mythical importance derived their names from this root: the wych elm and the mountain ash (pyrus aucuparia). Anglo-Saxons called both of these trees *wych* or *wich* (later forms whicken tree, quicken tree, wittan tree, or witchwood).[103]

The mountain ash had a wide reputation of sacredness. The Finns planted it in their holy places.[104.] The Norse called the tree Rönn, "red," adapted by the Scots as "rowan."[105] Scottish folklore persisted in connecting witches with the rowan, though in a form corrupted by witch-hunting. The tree's magic uses, and its association with witches, morphed into using its

Swirling flow of growth in the wych elm

wood as a charm against witchcraft—and against the faeries. Blessing rites and chants around "rowan tree and red thread" lasted into modern times.[106]

Rowan wood also had an association with sorcery in Ireland. In the poem *Tochmarc Étaíne*, Fuamnach uses a rowan wand to enchant her rival Étaíne. Fuamnach is a woman of the Tuatha Dé Danann, well versed in the magical arts. The story turns on her rejection of her husband's prerogative of taking a second wife. In classic patriarchal wifely mode—typified by Olympian Hera—Fuamnach cannot stop her husband but attacks her rival. When Midir brings Étaine home, she welcomes them and seats her new co-wife in the center of the hall. Then she strikes her with a red rowan wand, changing her into a pool of water. Like Hera, Fuamnach transforms, pursues, and torments "the other woman," who in this story assumes diverse guises in various incarnations. Étaíne later marries Mac Oc. The story ends with him beheading Fuamnach, in a rare (if mythical) Irish reference to the execution of a witch.

Ancient Irish traditions affirmed the great virtues of the rowan tree, called *cáerthann*. People thought of it as a "healing physician to the people."[107] The Tuatha Dé Danann were said to owe their immortality to its brilliant crimson berries. It was said that "no disease attacks those who eat them, but they feel the exhilaration of wine and old mead; and were it at the age of a century, they would return again to be thirty years old."[108]

Another legend said that the Tuatha Dé Danann brought rowanberries from the Land of Promise, along with crimson nuts and catkin apples. A rowanberry fell to earth and took root; the quicken-tree that grew from it bore berries of life-prolonging virtue. Irish tales describe a *cáerthann* with a dragon coiled around its roots, or guarded by some other magical beast. "Every month it bore sweetest fruit, and one berry satisfied hunger for a long time, while its juice prolonged life for a year and healed sickness."[109]

Ligatura

Our first etymological trail of *wycce* led to the spinning of fibers, twining strands and casting knots. In pagan women's culture these crafts were used to create protective amulets, to charge with sacred power for healing, and to bless newborns. Their making would have been accompanied by chants and undertaken according to season, time of day or moon cycle, and sometimes carried out in special places. A host of ecclesiastical prohibitions denounced and forbade the binding and attaching of *ligaturas* for healing purposes.[110]

Ligatura literally means "tying," though it had become a synonym for "amulet," from a consecrated knot, or something tied on with one. People tied on herbs, animal teeth, horns, or stones—natural objects charged with vital esssence. But the cord itself could be ritually endowed with potency, by spinning incantations, knotting, measuring, anointing, smudging or immersing in spring water. The *Bedan Penitential* refers to "diabolical amulets whether of grass or amber," which suggests that people were wearing plaited straw[111], like the "Brigit's Crosses" that are made in Ireland and its diaspora.

Folklore and some ecclesiastical accounts indicate that witches used

*Women
smudging
a baby,
passing her
through
herbal smoke
over a brazier.
11th century*

strands and knots for healing and protection. For centuries the Scots used multi-colored strings in healing charms known as *Eolas* ("knowledge") or *Teachasg* ("teaching"). Often they worked them with stones of power: frog stones, snail stones, egg stones, or the *Clach Nathrach*, a serpent stone.[112]

The Irish kept healing stones wrapped around with "straining strings" on boulder altars. When someone was injured, they removed the string, wrapped it around the sprained limb, and replaced it with a fresh new string around the stone. These animist healings drew on vitality in the stones.[113]

Early priestly writers also used the Greek word *phylacteria* for "amulet." Caesarius of Arles admitted that "at times *phylacteria* themselves seem to have power and to be of benefit," but attributed any positive effects to "the devil."[114] Gregory of Tours referred to a sick boy who was treated by "murmuring incantations, casting lots, and wearing *ligaturas* around the neck." Bede related that St Cuthbert had scolded Northumbrians for using "incantations or *alligaturas*."[115] Boniface described women who in a pagan rite tied amulets and knots on their bodies. Hincmar of Reims condemned singing incantations over multicolored threads and various herbs.[116]

Scottish witches performed healings by passing the sick through hasps of yarn. A common treatment for sprain was called "casting the wresting thread." Those skilled in this art took a thread spun of black wool, cast nine

The witch Ilmatar revivifies her slain son, with the help of a bee who brings vital essence from the celestial realm. Painting by Gallen-Kallela, 1895.

knots on it, and tied it around the sprain, softly saying a charm all the while: "bone to bone, sinew to sinew..."[117] This archaic healing litany is found all over northern Europe: in Ireland, Britain, Germany, Denmark, Iceland, Latvia and Finland.[118] It seems to go back to Proto-Indo-European, since a form of it appears in the Atharva Veda.[119] The earliest versions are heathen, though the charm was christianized in most places by the end of the middle ages. So was the wresting thread charm; this was the price of its preservation.

A rare survival of old German heathen incantation was preserved in the Second Merseberg Charm. In it the goddesses Sinthgunt and Sunna her sister, and Frija and Volla her sister, along with Wodan, conjured a horse's sprained foot: "Be it sprain of the bone, be it sprain of the blood, be it sprain of the limb: Bone to bone, blood to blood, limb to limb, thus be they fitted together."[120] This knitting together of tissue invoked and affirmed the body's own natural healing process.

The charm also occurs in the Irish *Lebor Gabála Erenn*, when Miach heals Nuada "joint to joint, vein to vein."[121] A modern Scottish example invokes Brigit: "Bríde went out in the morning early, with a pair of horses. One broke his leg... She put bone to bone, she put flesh to flesh, she put sinew to sinew, she put vein to vein. As she healed that, may I heal this."[122]

In the Finnish *Kalevala,* the charm describes how the witch-mother of Lemminkainen puts his dismembered body back together:

> Then the flesh to flesh she fitted,
> And the bones together fitted,
> And the joints together fitted,
> And the veins she pressed together.
> Then she bound the veins together,
> All their ends she knit together,
> And with care the threads she counted...[123]

Knotting was commonly used in a rite of binding disease. Often the knots were in groups of nine, as with the Scottish charm *Eòlas Sguchadh*.[124] Many charms invoked Nine Sisters on a distant island, counting down from nine to clear away diseases. Modern Rumanian healers used ritual knotting charms to cure people of various ailments. A woman who was described treating lower back pain in 1910 took hemp cord in her hands and placed it over the man's back. She proceeded to tie nine knots, each while repeated a healing charm:

> I do not bind the knot, but the pain in the heart, I do not bind the
> knot, but the pain in the intestines, I do not bind the knot, but
> the pain in the liver...the ribs...the shoulders...the breast...
> the throat...the neck, ears and teeth...the pain in all the joints
> and all the other parts of the body.[125]

When the last knot was finished the healer placed the cord in water, speaking another charm, then crossed this cord over the man's chest. She had him wear it for three days, after which the healer removed the cord and cast it into running water. Binding pain or disease into the knots, and then exposing them to the power of the elements was a common way of neutralizing them. Scottish wisewomen also threw their knotted "wresting cords" into running waters. Old texts say that healers placed these cords in tree hollows or other places in Nature.

Belief in the shamanic uses of knots is widespread. Mesopotamian, Arab and Hebrew magicians wore knots, and sacramental *tzitzit* are still tied into Jewish prayer shawls with consecratory prayers. The Lapps traditionally wore cords tied with nine *turknutar* (luck-knots) around their necks to bring good fortune. In Russian, wizards are called *uzol'nik*, "knot-tier," and the words for amulet (*nauzu*) and knot (*uzelu*) come from the same root.[126]

The Latin *fascino* ("binding, fastening") gave rise to *fascinum*, "magical spell," which shifted again to the modern meaning of "fascination." Another old knot-word with very different connotations is "religion," from *religare*, to tie together. It is etymologically related to *ligatura*, the name for witch knots.

Knots possessed spiritual, social and even legal significance in European folk cultures. The complex knot patterns in Celtic crosses and illuminated manuscripts would have had names and meanings. Medieval people made love knots, friendship knots, and betrothal knots. Some knots signified a marriage contract. Court witnesses who were unable to sign would attach a knotted leather strap to the document as their corroboration. These were binding, legally and magically. A legal term for witness, the *nodater*, evolved from this old practice.[127]

Wheat-straw was used similarly in making engagement vows and other contracts. The straws were cut into equal lengths, and each person kept one, not so much as proof, since it would be easy for the other to destroy theirs, but as a magical bond of the agreement. Old Welsh poetry refers to engagements being ended in this way: "If she converse no more, break the straw with my fair one."[128]

Why would people use something as common and fragile as straw to make vows and agreements? Wheat-straw was sacred to goddesses—Cerridwen in Wales, Brígid in Ireland—so pledges made in this substance carried spiritual power.[129] Wheat-straw also represented the grain mothers who were revered in agricultural rituals all over Europe. Peasants plaited corn grannies out of the first or last sheaf harvested each year. The Irish plaited wheatstraw in the name of Brigit, hanging it in their homesteads to bless people, animals and grain. Among the Franks and Germans, too, amulets were made of plaited grass.[130]

The sacredness of wheat-straw may have figured in another old custom, the drawing of lots. A straw was cut into uneven lengths and then arranged so that the tips were even, and the lengths of the straws concealed. Whoever "drew the short straw" was the one chosen to carry out an act no one wanted to do, a custom that has survived into the present.

Straws were also used in conjuring. A Welsh proverb indicates that they could be used in magical combat: "The keen-eyed Gwrnerth killed the largest bear ever seen, with a wheat-straw."[132] Rushes could also be used for shamanic flight. In the 13th century, William of Auvergne wrote of sorcerers who made magical horses from a reed by "writing and painting on it unspeakable characters and scriptures."

Weaving tools had their own power. We saw that Brigit was associated with weaving threads in a healing context. An 8th century weaving sword of yew (another magical wood) had runes carved on it.[133] The Irish prophetess Fedelm held a weaver's sword as she foretold the future.

Brigida with wheat straw

In another Irish text, Eithne grasps a hazelwood weavers' sword during a difficult childbirth.[134] The author eclipsed women's use of a weaving tool in their birth rites, choosing to emphasize the miracles of a male saint instead. He showed Máedóc planting the hazelwood slay, which miraculously became a living tree, while the soil

Weaver's Sword

weaver's slay

weaver's slew

weaver's reed

shed stick

(often erroneously translated as "weaver's beam")[134]

it stood in received the power to dissolve the chains of prisoners. The magical significance of the weaver's tool was retained, but its power was stripped away from women and transferred to a priest.

To ensure that no pagan spirits lingered, Máedóc prescribed saying nine masses over the earth gathered beneath the hazelwood.[135] Thus the new religion appropriated the old ninefold blessing. Hazelwood had

German woman using a weaver's sword

an ancient significance, as the bush that bears the purple nuts of wisdom, which fall into the Well of Ségais to be eaten by the holy salmon, whose bellies show the same purple essence.

Yet the pagan traditions persisted in names and stories about the land, and the ancient great-stone chambers. Women kept them alive in spinning and weaving ceremonies, and in the symbols they wove. Spinning itself remained a metaphor for life, creation, and transformation. An Irish text speaks of "spinning the threads of wisdom."[136]

As late as 1851, Croatians from Križevci and Zagorje spoke about a *vila* (faery) who taught the healing art to women, within the symbolic context of spinning. The *vila* descended every Friday, the day of the spinner goddesses across Europe. Women went to a green grove with their hair unbound, and climbed a tree to listen to the *vila*: "and while they were listening to the fairy they had to eat yarn in order to better remember what the fairy was teaching them; when they had learned, they became *vilenicas*. The two women in the tree, and everyone else who was listening beneath the tree, are connected by a thread from the yarn which they hold in their hands, and as long as the fairy is speaking, they have to spin together, or as the people say, pound the thread... Anyone who doesn't do so can't hear the fairy, and doesn't learn a thing."[137]

Spinning and weaving were deeply intertwined with concepts of fate, creation, lifespan—and the *wyccecræft* of blessing, healing, and protection. Now we turn to look at how various peoples conceived of the power of witchcraft: as wisdom, prophecy, divination, healing, shapeshifting, flight, and the invocation of deities and spirits.

3
NAMES OF THE WITCH

Modern "Western" culture is saturated with demonized concepts of the witch, while lacking knowledge about authentic cultural practices in its own past. For this reason, many readers will be surprised to find that the oldest names for witch in European languages emphasize their spiritual gifts: powers of prophecy, divination, and incantation; of healing, herbal knowledge, shapeshifting and shamanic flight. Some cultures named witches after their magical staffs or masks or animal spirits. Others described them in language relating to Wisdom, Fate, and the Mysteries. With few exceptions, the old witch-titles honored these women as cultural authorities, in sharp contrast to later diabolist stereotypes that portrayed witches exclusively as demonic cursers and destroyers.

One of the Norse names used for such women was *fjölkynngi*, "of manifold knowledge."[1] The English cognate *cunning woman* is based on the same ancient root of "knowing," which also survives in the expression "beyond his ken." It is related to *know* and *gnostic* and Sanskrit *jñana*, "wisdom." The Norse *vísendakona*, literally "wise woman," and *vítka* ("sorceress") both derived from an archaic root of seeing and knowing. The Latin *saga* ("wisewoman") survived in French as *sage-femme*. The Russian healer-name знахарка (znakharka) means a "woman who knows."[2] Crossing into the Uralic language family, the Finnish word *tietäjä* is an ungendered term for "knower." The more common Finnish word for "witch" is *noita* (again, not gendered) which is closely related to *noaidi*, the Sámi title for a shaman, and to shaman-words in other Uralic languages.

PROPHETIC WITCHES

The Fates I fathom, yet farther I see | See far and wide the worlds around.[3]

Many names in Slavic and Celtic languages describe the witch as a foreknowing seeress. In Russian she is *vyed'ma*, in Polish *wiedzma*, and in southern Slavic tongues, *vyeshchitsa* or *vedavica*: all meaning "knower."

(Every Slavic language has some form of this word for "wisewoman"; see table at the end of this chapter.) The Slavic names come from the same Proto-Indo-European root *weid, "to see," as the Russian verb видеть or видать, "to see," and as the Indic Veda, "knowledge."

The Old Celtic root *wel-, "to see," shares the same deep root. It in turn yielded the Gaulish word for "witch," *uidlua*,[4] and its close relatives: Welsh *gwelet*, "seer," and Old Irish *velet*, later *fili, filed, banfilé*, "poet, seer."[5] The name of the Irish prophetess Fedelm descends from that root.[6] So does Veleda, the title of a revolutionary Bructerian seeress in ancient Germania.[7]

The English translation of *fíli* as "poet" fails to convey its spiritual context or its cultural prestige. The *fíli* was expected to be skilled in three powers. First and foremost was *imbas forosnai*, the "wisdom that illuminates," which was inspired prophetic vision. The seeress Fedelm and the woman warrior Scáthach were said to prophesy from *imbas forosnai*.[8]

The significance of the second concept, *teinm láida*, "breaking of pith or marrow," is no longer understood, except that it involved chanting. The third technique was *díchetal di chennaib*, "chanting from heads," a spontaneous incantation.[9]

Proto-Indo-European *weid also gave rise to the Old Irish word *wissuh, "knowledge," which produced *ban-fissid*, "seeresss."[10] More recent Irish titles—*ban feasa* "wisewoman" and *cailleach feasa* "wise old woman"—derive from that same root.[11] So does the pivotal concept *imbas*, "wisdom," from *imb-fiuss or *imb-fess, "great knowledge." This derivation is quite old, given in the prologue to the *Senchas Mór*, in the early 700s.[12]

The *fáith* or *ban-fáith* was a prophetic woman who was "expert in supernatural wisdom."[13] The modern Irish form *banfháidh* (also *fáidhbhean*) is based on *fáidh*, "seer, prophet, sage," a word with an interesting late usage as "the Fates."[14]

The related noun *fáth* meant "divination."[15] The title *ban-fílid / ban-fíle*, from the same root as Gaulish *uidliua*, "witch," signified a female bard or poet, which in Irish had strong spiritual connotations. The druid-names will be more familiar to most people: *ban-drui* or

France, circa 600-700

ban-draoi, "druid-woman."[16] Linguists think that Celtic *fáith* was borrowed into Latin as *vates,* "divinely inspired seer, soothsayer," and *vaticination,* "prediction, prophecy." Its Indo-European root meant "possessed, frenzied, inspired."[17]

Spiritual inspiration is also the basis of the Latin *divina,* "diviner, one who performs divination."[18] Isidore of Seville admitted that *divinus/divina* means a person filled with the divine, although he saw these soothsayers in a very negative light. But like other priests of his time, he was obliged to acknowledge the cultural consensus that the *divini* were usually right.

Isidore identified two kinds of seer-ship, "one which comes from art"— such as casting and reading lots—and "the other from prophetic frenzy," or in other words, an oracular ecstasy.[19] Latin *divina* flowed out into French

Merovingian France

devine or *devineresse,* Italian *indovina,* English *diviner,* and Welsh *dewines.*

The English word *soothsayer* literally means "truth-sayer." There was a verbal form, "to say sooth." The same meaning pops up in Church Latin as *veratrix.*[20] The *auguriatrix* ("woman who reads omens") is listed among people targeted in Charlemagne's repression of pagans, circa 800 CE. Arno of Salzburg also listed the *auguriatrix* among *incantatores* and other "sorcerers" that people turned to in times of trouble. They were reputed to heal sick people and animals.[21]

The clergy preferred to use Latin titles, and occasionally Greek ones like *sybil* and *pythonissa.* *Pythia* ("snake woman") was the ancient title of the Delphic oracle who, inspired by her serpent-spirit, prophesied in spiritual ecstasy. After the Christian empire suppressed the ancient lineage of Pythias, medieval clergymen adopted the latinized *pythonissa* from the Vulgate Bible as a term for entranced and prophetic witches. Thus, an 8th century Irish text quotes the condemnation in Leviticus of people who had "a python or divinatory spirit."[22] Around the same time, the *Homilia de sacrilegiis* says,

And those who are *divinus* or *divinas,* that is, *pitonissas,* through whom the demons give answers to those who come to question them, who believe what they say, and go to the hidden place,

**or listens to anything from the demons, is not a Christian,
but a pagan.**[23]

Romanized terms have obscured and eclipsed indigenous witch names
in many places. By late antiquity, the Gauls and Hispani were calling healer-
diviners *ariolae* (female) and *arioli* (male). Though the masculine plural
supposedly included females, French bishops went out of their way to
specify women in their attacks on the "*arioli* and *ariolae*."[24] People consulted
them in Nature sanctuaries, or invited them to their homes for divinations,
healings and purifications. The priesthood insisted that their ceremonies
and incantations were made to demons, but this barely dented their prestige
among the people.[25]

German bishops at the synod of Erfurt (932) went so far as to prohibit
fasting "because it is perceived as being done more for the sake of divination
[*ariolandi*] than as a supplement to Catholic law."[26] A 9th century penitential
reveals that people were undertaking fasts "in honor of the Moon for the
sake of a cure."[27]

δIVINERS

An influential group of witch-names derives from Latin *sortiaria*: "one
who reads or influences fate, fortune." It is based on *sors* (genitive *sortis)*,
meaning "destiny," "oracular response," and "lots."[28] From the same root
came *sortilega*: "reading or gathering of lots"—or of "fates." The root *legere*

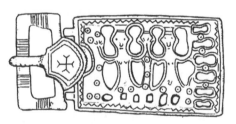

Invokers: Merovingian buckle, France

means "to gather, select, read."
Modern Italian still retains the
sense of "read," but the word's
oldest foundation is found in the
Greek *legein*, "to gather."

In the early middle ages,
sortilega still signified a diviner, a
lot-caster, as in Isidore of Sevilla.
(In modern Spanish, *sortiaria* means divination by lots or cards.) From
sortiaria came *sorcière*, which became the primary word for "witch" in
French. It was borrowed into English as *sorceress*, and strongly marked as
female. Its first known use (circa 1384) predated *sorcerer* (1526) by 150 years.[29]

Sortiaria soon lost its specific meaning of divination, and began to be used for many kinds of witchcraft, including healing and weather magic. Pirmin of Reichenau ordered his parishioners, "Do not believe weather-sorceresses, nor give them anything for that reason, nor *inpuriae* who, they say, men put on the roof so that they can tell them the future, whatever of good or evil is coming to them."[30] The *Corrector sive Medicus* also deplored the custom of sitting on the roof to see future events. An anonymous sermon uses the same epithet *inpurae* for "impure" women who set out offering tables on January 1.[31]

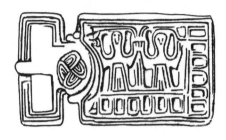

Invoking: buckle at Arbon, France

A denunciation of soothsayers and enchanters in the early 800s refers to people who interpret dreams.[32] So does the Capitularia written by an archbishop of Tours in the same period.[33] Ghärbald of Liège placed "those who observe dreams" among lot-casters, soothsayers, and amulet-wearers in his Belgian capitulary.[34] In fact, over twenty penitential books refer to dream interpreters (*somniarii*), though none give much detail.[35] An 11th century Spanish manual warns priests against those who "practiced or scrutinized dreams, woolwork or sorcery."[36] (Once again, textile arts are connected to divination and witchcraft.) Old High German sources also refer occasionally to old women who interpreted dreams.[37] Words for "dream-readers" are recorded for Norse and Old English.[38]

Sermons, penitentials, and other priestly sources conflate the *sortilegi, divini, arioli, incantatores and praecantatores*, often using them interchangeably.[39] The writers are deliberately cryptic, avoiding detailed description of the customs. Their language is confusing, with the meanings of the Latin words drifting on ethnic tongues. But however poor their mastery of Latin, the priests adhered to its masculine default, which obscures women from view except when the writer goes out of his way to name them. About two dozen texts do explicitly name female diviners and enchanters. But language conceals many others, as Bernadette Filotas points out: "Burchard of Worms himself, who time and again identified women as the principal practitioners of magic, never gave the feminine form of any word for magician."[40]

The Norse had an expression for consulting a diviner: *ganga til frétta* "go for news," or "institute an inquiry."[41] Old Norse *frétt* corresponded to Old High German *freht* and Old English *fyrht*, "divination, oracle."[42] *Fyrht* appears in King Cnut's catalog of forbidden heathenisms in the year 1020, along with "the worship of heathen gods, and the sun or the moon, fire or rivers, water-wells or stones, or forest-trees..."[43] Icelandic sagas refer to another kind of divination, *thriefa*, in which a woman touched a person's body in order to read and foresee events to come, especially fate in battle.[44]

The Latvian word for "witch," *burt* (male *burtneks*) derives from *burtas*, lots, and *burten*, "to divine or conjure." These words are related to Lithuanian *burtas*, "lot," and *burtininkas*, "lot-caster."[45]

The Basque *sorguiñ* or *xorguiña* derives from the same root as *sorceress*, adding the suffix *guiñ / eguiñ* "which means somebody who does or makes something."[46] So a *sorguiña* is a fate-maker, who sees and works with destiny. The British *weirding-woman* and *weirdwife* also act upon destiny, which is the meaning of Old English Wyrd.

Similarly, a complex of Latin-root words (*hechicera, faytillera, facturière, faiturière, fatucchiera,* etc.) describe the witch as a "doer, maker"—one who causes things to happen. The deep meaning of the Slavic root *charodeia* (as in Russian чародейка) also originated from an Indo-European root "to make." It has the same root as Sanskrit *krti*, "do, make"; Lithuanian *keraī*, "magic"; and Middle Irish *creth*, "poetry."[47]

The Basque diviner was called *azti*. Like healers and the *sorguiñes*, she acquired spirit helpers called Mamarro or Galtzagorri. The *azti* were said to keep as many as four of these spirits living in their needlecases. The Basque word for these containers, *kuthun*, can also mean "amulet, book, or letter"— all magically charged things.[48]

The witchen nature of the needlecase seems to grow out of its association with spinning. Early medieval archaeological finds suggest a spiritual charge for threadboxes buried with women, some of which contained herbs, including camomile (Gumbsheim, Germany), henbane (St Aubin, Switzerland), and umbelliferous seeds (Yverdon, Vaud). But only one kind of herb was found in any box, making it likely that they are amuletic rather than medicinal.[49]

Threadbox, Burwell, Cambridgeshire

The going assumption has too often been that no prophetic women really existed in the early "Christian" period. Priestly denunciations prove otherwise. The women are there, being reviled by men like Aldhelm of Malmesbury, who have nothing useful to say about them. Writing around the year 700, he inveighed against the "empty gibberish of falsity from talkative prophetesses and soothsayers."[50] This English abbot was obsessed with degrees of sexual purity—and with stamping out heathen culture, which as yet remain barely touched by the royal decrees of conversion.

The clergy showed contempt, but they also projected their fear. Before long, priestly opposition had pushed the meaning of "sorcery" toward illicit and harmful magic. Early medieval capitularies were already assigning negative meanings to *sorciarius / sorciaria* ("sorcerer").[51] This trend would only accelerate with time.

CHANT, INVOCATION AND CHARMS

Incantation was called *galdr* in Norse. The witch-name *galdrakona* referred specifically to a woman who chanted. From a related word in Saxon, *galdor*, came names for the *galstre* or *gealdricge / galdriggei*: (female) "enchanter." The cognate in Middle High German, *galster*, meant "spoken magic, spell."[52] The Anglo-Saxon *wyrtgælstre* was an "herb-chanter." Through their voice and breath and words, the chanting women brought spirit to bear on matter, and by infusing it with consciousness, caused transformation.

The Latin *incantation* means "singing into," invoking through chant, from *canto*, "song, chant." The clergy sometimes called witches by the Latin title of *incantatrix*, which gave rise to French *enchanteresse* and, in turn, to English *enchantress*. Church councils were constantly prohibiting the singing of charms. They usually included divinations alongside incantations, as the council of Clovesho did in 750.[53] Also in England, Theodore's Penitential prescribed penance for "a woman [who] performs diabolical [sic] incantations or divinations," as well as for any who observe "omens from birds, or dreams, or any divinations according to the custom of the heathen."[54] Authors of penitential books were doing their damnedest to stamp out the *incantatores* and *praecantatores* to which people flocked for healing, protection, and other blessings. These witches did more than chant; they gave counsel, and with it healing and protective remedies, in the

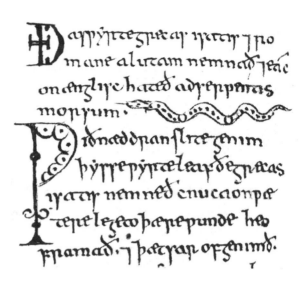

*Anglo-Saxon
birth charm
(with serpents!)
in the Lacnunga,
a compendium of
medical remedies,
circa 1000 CE.*

form of herbs, amulets, knotted ties, and other medicine objects.[55]

Back in the 5th century, Caesarius of Arles singled out female *incanta-trices*, warning Christians (men specifically) not to seek them out for healing or prophecy. He declared it was better for a man "if he does not send for a soothsayer, if he does not make bindings, he does not admit any enchant-resses. The woman enchants, the serpent enchants."[56] That misogynist trope is foundational priestcraft, in the stamp of the church patriarchs. But it is a commentary on a real female sphere of power. As Bernadette Filotas summarizes from English and Frankish sources, "enchantment was typically the practice of women." And they performed it for female purposes, which included weaving, conception and contraception, birth, and protection from men. For example, the Pseudo-Egbert penitential condemns Anglo-Saxon women for using incantations to conceive.[57]

The woman enchants, the serpent enchants

The *carminatrix* was named from *carmen*, another Latin word for "song." From it descends French *charme*, and in turn the English *charm* and *charm-er*. These medieval names referred to women who chanted healing verse and performed ritual cures. In Spanish such women were called *ensalmadoras*, a name that implies they used Christian prayers in their chants. Germans called them *segenœrinne*, "signers," for the gestures they made over people.[58] In modern Irish, *cailleach phiseogach* is a common name for an old sorceress who works spells or charms.[59]

The word "spell" itself originally meant "speak, tell" (Old English *spellian*, Anglo-French *espeller*, Old French *espelir*: "mean, signify, explain, interpret").[60] The meanings of these words stretched over time, so that a German source used *carmen* to mean amulet, as something that was sung over.[61] This kind of semantic drift is common. English "charming" referred to love spells, but now means "attractive."

In Ireland, incantation figured prominently in the druidic arts. It was a means of attaining *imbas forosnai*, the "wisdom that illumines," and also of revealing it. The *Táin* shows Fedelm chanting a long prophecy to Medb of Connaught. Nora Chadwick saw this state of inspiration as having originally been "the special métier of women." One of the old sources she mentions is the lost *Druim Snechta*, of which only fragments survive. One says that the British witch Scáthach practiced *imbas forosnai*. Other sources describe Imbas as "a process of revelation brought on by a mantic sleep."[62]

Imbas was classed with two other arts, both involving incantation. In the first, *teinm laida*, "illumination of song," inspiration comes through chanting, a signature of shamanic ecstasy. One source says that *teinm laida* belongs to the fourteen streams of poetry. *Teinm* is thought to derive from *tep-*, "heat," the same root as Sanskrit *tapas*, which is commonly used to describe intensive spiritual practices.

According to the Prologue to the *Senchas Mór*, different kinds of offerings were made for *imbas forosnai* and *teinm laida*. These "heathen rites" were the reason that Patrick abolished them, "for neither *tenm laida* nor *imbas forosnai* could be performed without the accompaniment of heathen offerings."[63] Laws of Patrick and his successors abolished these two forms of *filidecht* (seership). And they admonish Irish kings not to consult with druids or "pythonesses."[64]

Around 900, the *Sanas Cormaic* concurred that these arts were considered too pagan to be permitted. Only *dichetal*

*The Moylough Belt Shrine
8th century Ireland (detail)*

do chennaib was allowed to continue under Christianity. The phrase is variously translated as "to chant in prophetic strains," as "poetry from the head," or "chanting from the bones."[65] It was also described as "a declaration from the ends of his bones at once."

Early sources hint that *dichetal do chennaib* involved moving the fingertips in gestures.[66] One writer associates it with "chanting by means of the hazels of prophecy," apparently referring to divinatory wands.[67] This fragment calls to mind the hazelnuts of Wisdom that fall into the Well of Segais, at the source of the Boyne, where they turn the bellies of the salmon purple. This fountain was sought out in hopes of attaining illumination.

Anglo-Saxons called the chanting witch *leóð-rūne* or *leóth-rūne*, "song mysteries." *Leóð* means song, poetry, verse;[68] compare with Old High German *leod* (modern *Lied*) Irish *lóid*, Scots *laoidh*, "song, poem," French *lai* and English *lay*, medieval words for a longpoem.[69] There was also

leoducræft, the power or skill of chant.

leoꝼunan

Anglo-Saxon lexicographers marked the pagan underpinnings of *leóð-rūne*: "Cockayne translates the word 'heathen charm'," according to Toller-Bosworth, who also translates *fondien leódrunen* as "incantations".[70] Christine Fell reads *leod-rune* as a variant of the poetic Old English *leoðurun* ("sung mystery").[71] Alaric Hall concurs, "*Leoðurun* denotes holy mysteries and the Middle English *leodrune* prophecies..."[72] But this important word was choked out by persecutory stigma (see chapter 4).

Charmers cured by knotting hanks of colored thread, and by laying on hands, or touching with stones. Some invoked the Nine Maidens, common in healing spells across northern Europe. Audrey Meaney refers to an Old English charm invoking the Nothðæs (Needs), who are Nine Sisters, and compares it to a Danish runic inscription on a pine wand, in which the Nine Needs (*nouthær*) lying on a black stone out on the sea chase away a fever.[73] These Need-names might relate to invocation of the Norns, going by two lines in the *Sigrdrífumál*. The valkyrie Sigrdrífa recommends that runes should be cut "on the nail of the Norn" and "mark your nail with nauð" (the Need-rune).[74]

In an early modern Scottish witch trial, Bessie Smith said that she "charmed the heartfevers" by invoking "the nine maidens that died in the boortree in the Ladywell Bank," and giving her patients wayburn leaf to eat for nine mornings.[75] "Boortree" is another word for the elder, a tree rich in the goddess lore of Britain, Denmark and Holland.

The Gauls and Old Irish ascribed powers of incantation to women, using nearly identical phrases. A rare Gaulish inscription found in a tomb at Larzac, France, refers to a sisterhood of enchantresses (*uidlua*). It is a charm inscribed on a lead plaque, with the phrase *bnannom bricto*, "women's spell."

Historical linguist Yves Lambert derives the spell-name *bricto* from Indo-European **bhregh*, "to declare solemnly."[76]

Gaulish *Bnannom bricto* has an exact Irish correlate, *brichta ban*, in the *Liber Hymnorum*. This text, attributed to St Patrick but dating several centuries later, is itself a spell, a counter-charm of a Christian monk who chants "Against the spells of women, of smiths and druids."[77]

women's spells

Gaulish: *bnannom bricto*
(Plomb de Larzac)

Irish: *brichta ban*
(Liber Hymnorum)

Medieval bishops and canon lawyers attempted to wipe out the peasantry's use of incantations for vision, blessing, healing, and protection, because those chants had traditionally invoked pagan deities—and

against the spells of women, smiths and druids.

because the priesthood now arrogated the chanting of litanies to its own brotherhood: to men alone. The priest singing Mass is performing an incantation that is supposed to magically transform wine and wafer into the body of his god. But the Church claimed that power of enchanting only for a doctrinally restricted brotherhood, denying it to females or people of ecstatic spiritual traditions. Its hierarchy forbade the *incantatrix* to practice the universal human sacrament of invoking Spirit. It slandered the pagan European chants (and sometimes even christianized ones) as devilish. If the Night Chant of the Diné or the Maori Creation Chant had existed in Europe, they would have attempted to ban them just as they did the enchantment of European wisewomen. And eventually they did.

❖

healing witches

Many witch-titles have to do with medicine and healing. Some mean "herb-woman," like the Frankish *herbaria* and Spanish *herbolera*, both of which were demonized early on. The *Lex Alamanorum* gives "herbalist" as a synonym for "witch," in its most negative sense: *stria aut herbaria*. *Stria* (from Latin *strix*, "screech-owl") was a primary Roman name for "witch."

The priests often rendered *herbaria* as *venefica*, "poisoner," following old Roman patterns of vilification and demonization.[78] In eastern Europe, Orthodox missionaries engaged in the same vilification, using other epithets. The Greek priest St Cyril rebuked his Slavic parishoners for going in illness to healers he called "accursed women."[79]

But the witch-herbalist knew of plants for sickness and binding up wounds, for childbirth and purifying the blood. She brewed herbs and roots to make healing drinks, made salves, and combined these medicines with ceremonial acts, in what is now known as "wholistic healing." She used knotting on cords, healing belts, rubbing with stones, healing touch, and herbal smudges.[80] She gathered herbs to bless houses and barns, burned or scattered them, hung wreaths over doors and beams; and tied blessing plants around the necks of cows and other animals.

Penitential books are full of references to people using *ligaturas* (ties) for healing and protection, or wearing bundles of herbs, bones or pieces of iron, as pendants, tied on or sewn into clothing.[81] The *Homilia de Sacrilegis* gives a long list of illnesses and physical problems that were treated by "songs and incantations," and by various folk remedies, such as hanging amulets such as the "serpent's tongue around a person's neck.[82]

In Germanic languages, treatment through touch, stroking, and making passes over the body was sometimes called "bettering": Anglo-Saxon *bētan*, Middle Dutch *böten*, and Old German *puozan* all meant "to remedy, heal."[83] "Among our peasantry there are old women still who profess *böten*, stroking, pouring, and charming by spells."[84]

The Welsh had a constellation of words based on the same concept. *Swynaw* meant "to comfort or cure; to charm; to bless; to save harmless," and also "preserve"; *swynawg*, "possessed of a preserving virtue"; and *swynedigaeth*, "the act of preserving or remedying by some hidden virtue; a preserving by charm." A woman who did this was called a *darswynws*.[85]

The witches often treated people through animist ceremonies: laying healing stones on sick bodies, passing children through openings in the earth, or by immersions into south-running water. Modern Scottish healers tied black and white thread around the limbs of afflicted people or animals.[86] Silesian Germans consulted old women called *messerin*,

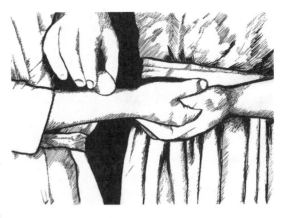

Healing with a serpent stone, Hungary, mid-20th century. (After Dömötör)

who took their measure with thread, from head to toe and across their outstretched fingertips, to cure consumption.[87]

These shamanic arts did not fade away of their own accord. They were much in demand, and in spite of centuries of repression, they persisted. In birth magic, for example, women used "herbal or animal remedies, amulets, girdle [belt], charms and invocations, physical manipulation and various rites relating to springs and stones."[88] The stones could be large boulders or rock "beds" in which women who desired to conceive a child would lie, or small stones that could be tied on the mother's body, or used in other ways.

Herbal mysteries were the province of the Old English *lybbestre* and Old German *lupparā*, "female healer."[89] These words for healing witches descend from *lyb* and *luppa*, which both mean "vitality," "medicine."[90] *Lyb* is related to the word "life" itself. The Anglo-Saxon verb *libban (lybban)* means "to live, be, exist."[91] It designates "medicine" both in the sense of curative herbs or powders, and as something animated by sacred power.

The Icelandic cognate *lyf* could mean either a healing plant, or some other spirit power.[92] Modern explanations define *lib / lyb* as "something medicinal and potent, a harmful or powerful drug, φάρμακον."[92] There is a special irony to translators' using the word "drug," and even "poison," rather than "medicine," to translate *lyb*,[93] which meant "life." The negative charge laid on these heathen terms dies very hard.

So *lybbestre* translates as "woman who works with life-force," or "medicine-woman." Many spiritual concepts of the Anglo-Saxons sprang from the etymological matrix of *lyb*. *Lyfja* meant "to heal." *Lybcræft* was the wisdom of witch-herbalists, who supplemented their pharmacological knowledge with transformative and protective magic.[95] Cognate words existed in Old German: *lupperie* "medicine, healing," *lüppærinne*, "sorceress" and, later, *lublerin*, "female healer."[96]

Amulets crafted from herbs, animal claws, crystal, amber and other essence-filled things, were called *lybesn*, *lyfesna*, or *lybesa*.[97] This word also

gloss

a translator's explanation, comparison

encompassed the meaning of "offering" and "favorable omen," as implied by the Latin gloss *strena*.[98] *Lybcorn* ("healing grain") referred to medicinal seeds, especially purgatives like euphoriba or spurge or hellebore.[99] Lybcorn leaves were also given in an herbal compound for people suffering from mental illness.[100]

Another word in this magical set was *lyblac*, which derives from *lyb-læca*, an Old English word for "doctoring" (later *leech*).[101] It had a Gothic cognate, *lubjaleisei*, which was glossed in Greek as φαρμακεία (*pharmakeia*).[102] (We only know of *lubjaleisei* because it was preserved in an early translation of Galatians 5:20, in which Paul denounces "the acts of the flesh," among them "idolatry and witchcraft.")[103] Both *lyblac* and φαρμακεία had an herbalist genealogy but were turned into general terms for witchcraft, acquiring an increasingly pejorative sense as time passed. *Lāchenærinne*, "female healer," the Middle German cognate of English *læca*, also took on the meaning of "enchantress."[104]

Because of its pagan dimensions, *lyblac* met with hostility from the Anglo-Saxon priesthood, who loaded it with negative connotations. So it came to be defined as "sorcery, witchcraft, the art of using drugs or potions for the purpose of poisoning, or for magical purposes."[105] In the same way, *lifesne* (consecrated things) are denounced in the same breath as "incantations or amulets or other hidden devil-crafts."[106]

The Anglo-Saxon preacher Aelfric chastised those who suffered an illness "and who then seeks health by forbidden practices, or in accursed incantations, or by any witchcraft."[107] Elsewhere he wrote, "Nor ought a Christian man to enquire from the foul witch about his health..." The priest acknowledged that she may be able to speak truths, but insisted that they come from the devil.[108] Priestly literature not only demonized folk religion, but disparaged its adherents, calling them "ignorant," "uncouth," "stupid," "the rabble," or "worthless women."[109]

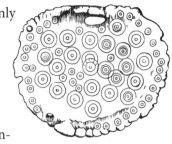

Antler pendant,
Friesland, Netherlands

Ultimately, the *lyb* witch-word survived in Anglo-Saxon only through a shadow-word that was its grammatical negation. In his denunciation of sorcerers and enchanters, archbishop Wulfstan of York names *unlybwyrhtan*, literally "unlife-workers."[110] No attestations survive for *lybwyrhtan*, the positive word on which this term was based—an absence that speaks volumes. A direct parallel is seen in the German transformation of *die holden*, "the beneficent" (female)" to *die unholden*, which demonologists introduced as a word for "witch" in the 1400s. But older names persisted, like the Anglo-Saxon *wortcunning*, "herb-knowledge," at least for a while.

From Norway comes a measure of how wide and deep the *lyb /lyfja* concept must have been in Common Germanic. *Lyf* is given as a Norse word for magical drugs as late as the early 1300s.[111] It survives in an anathema against "herbs, runes, and enchantment" (*lif runir oc galldra*) in witchcraft statutes issued by a Norwegian archbishop of Niðaróss.[112] In Norwegian, *lif* seems to have specialized into an herbal meaning, while in Anglo-Saxon it turned toward "amulet" or "charm."

In Icelandic, *lif* appears as the Lyfjaberg, the "Hill of Healing," a female sanctuary where the goddess Menglöd sits with her Nine Maidens:[113]

> *It is called lyfjaberg, and has long*
> *brought joy to sick and suffering.*
> *She will become whole, though gravely ill,*
> *every woman who climbs it.*[114]

Luppa also continued to be used in Central Europe, as shown by Swiss churchmen's prohibitions in a Zurich MS dated 1393: "You shall not believe in magic nor in magic ointment [*luppe*] nor in witchcraft [*hesse*] nor in magic cure [*lachene*], nor in fire gazing [*für sehen*], nor in measuring for healing, nor in the night women [*naht frowen*] nor in the cry of the magpie, nor in the twitching of the eyebrows and cheeks [as omens], nor even in the magic herb betony. All this is unbelief."[115] All this was *folk* belief, folk remedies, omens and divination.

In Old High German too, the meaning of *luppi* was turned inside out, directly reversed from "healing" to "poisonous." The same negative shift occurred with the Latin word *potio*, "a drink," which became specialized into "herbal brew," then torqued into the French word "poison," whence it was adopted into English.

In spite of her connection with life and healing, priestly writers often called the medicine witch *venefica*, Latin for "poisoner."[116] By early medieval times *venefica* had acquired the connotation of "sorceress." Thus Herard of Tours capped his 8th century listing of sorcerers, diviners, enchanters, and dream-readers with "the sorcery (*veneficis*) of women who invent various wonders."[117] Not all scribes agreed that herbalists were harmdoers; in two texts *veneficus* was emended to *beneficus*, "one who is beneficent."[118]

The use of *venefica* for herbalists and healers was stoked by the clergy's campaign to brand contraceptive users and providers as murderers and "poisoners." They used this staining epithet often.[119] Early European penitential books give abundant evidence of this distortion, which continued in the slander of midwives as babykillers in the 1400s, most famously in the *Malleus Maleficarum*.

From the 9th century on, the priesthood tried to scare people with the spectre of *maleficia*—harmful sorcery. But some of their writings reveal that the common people saw witch-herbalists as healers, and continued to consult them as their physicians and all-round life advisors, throughout the middle ages. In Scandinavia, "magical healers, especially women" were active from the Viking age up into the 20th century.[120]

One of Aelfric's sermons groups together three elements of women's witchcraft abhorred by the clergy: animistic child-blessings and healings; contraception and abortion; and female love potions. "Likewise some witless women go to cross-roads, and draw their children through the earth, and thus commit themselves and their children to the devil. Some of them kill their children before they are born, or after birth, that they may not be discovered, nor their wicked adultery be betrayed … Some of them devise drinks [philtres] for their wooers, or some mischief, that they may have them in marriage."[121] Assuming that married women never needed contraception, the abbot preferred to make the punitive claim that birth control was nothing but a way for women to hide evidence of their love affairs.

They bring their offering to earth-fast stone, and also to trees and to wellsprings, as the witches teach...

The Latin penitential of Halitgar of Cambrai also inveighed against animist ceremonies (using the usual masculine default): "Some men are so blind that they bring their offerings to earth-fast stone and also to trees and to wellsprings, and will not understand how stupidly they act or how this dead stone or that dumb tree might help them or give them health when these things themselves are never able to move from their place."

This condemnation of animist offerings at stones, trees, and springs was a standard priestly formula used in church councils and penitential texts. But an 11th century Anglo-Saxon translator contextualized the passage by adding to it this revealing phrase: *swa wiccan tæcað* ("as the witches teach").[122] His commentary emphasizes that the Anglo-Saxons still understood "witches" within the context of pagan ceremony, and it underlines the animist reverence of the witches for Earth, trees, and water.

The Austrian bishop Arno of Salzburg complained that people preferred folk healers and animist shrines to doctors and church. They dealt with plague and animal disease by going to "wicked men and women, seeresses, sorceresses and enchanters."[123] The English monk Cuthbert denounced "the false remedies of idolatry, as though they could ward off a blow inflicted by God the Creator by means of incantations or amulets or any other mysteries of devilish art."[124]

All this looks very different from the wisewoman's perspective. The herb woman chanted to the plants she found, invoking their powers and virtues. Old English had a specialized name, *wyrtgælstre*, for the "woman who chants over herbs."[125] But this sole attestation for the *wyrtgælstre*, dated around 1050 CE, appears in a menacing context: "a girl born on the fifth day of the moon will die worst, for she will be a witch and an enchantress with herbs (Lat. *herbaria*; OE *wyrtgælstre.*"[126]

Herb-chanting is referred to in an Anglo-Saxon remedy against "ælf-sickness." It explains "how one must sing over the plants before one picks them; and also how one must put those plants under an altar and sing over them…"[127] Early medieval priestly literature is full of prohibitions of pagan herb-chanting, from Martin of Braga (Portugal), Eligius of Noyon (Belgium), the

Healer infuses blessings into a herbal potion, her mortar and pestle in the foreground.

Theodore penitential (England), Regino of Prum and Burchard of Worms (Germany), and the *Medicina Antiqua.*[128] An 8th century sermon forbids incantation over herbs;[129] so does Burchard's German penitential, circa 1015: "Hast thou collected medicinal herbs with evil incantations, not with the creed and the Lord's Prayer…?"[130]

Healers also sang incantations over medicinal or blessing potions, as a condemnation in the *Homilia de Sacrilegiis* tells us.[131] The author intones that such people are "not Christian, but pagan." Meanwhile, priests everywhere threw up their hands and invented their own christianized charms to replace the pagan ones—and were often modeled on them.

In spite of their polemical tone, priestly sources demonstrate that gathering herbs was a religious act to pagan Europeans. Their use in blessing and protection was not restricted to witches. The common people gathered certain plants at the new or full or waning moon, or at dawn, midday, sunset, midnight, or on the ancient holidays such as Midsummers Eve. It was customary to approach the plant reverently, ceremonially asking its permission to cut or uproot it. Some placed offerings of grain or honey before it, or into the ground where they dug. Hungarians gathered the shamanic herb belladonna after offering bread, salt, and spices.[132]

Such herb-gathering rites survived in modern Romania. The *babele mestere* ("skilled old women") set out quietly at dawn to gather mandrake that they had previously "destined" for harvest by tying on a red ribbon. After digging up the earth around the plant, the wisewomen removed it, laid it on the ground and placed food and drink around it. They spoke a charm: "I give you bread and salt | It is for you to give me strength and health"; or they simply said, "So that you will cure me." The women shared a meal while embracing and caressing each other. Then they discussed the person the mandrake was for, and how it would help them.[133]

On Midsummers Eve young Rumanian women would go out to search for the *cusitza* creeper. They tied red yarn on their finds, and hid the plant under green leaves. Then they drew water from three fountains. Before dawn on Midsummer's Day, they dressed in their finest, gathered the vines, twined them around their heads, and went door to door singing and making merry. In the evening they carried out a divination using the jug of water collected from the three springs.[134]

Many herbal invocations took the form of praise-songs: "Good day, holy plant *pivoine*, you are queen of the plants." Medieval people honored the peony (*pivoine*) in what one writer called "a veritable cult."[135] Transylvanians used to greet the belladonna plant every morning, calling her *Nagyasszony*, "great lady," and paid similar honors to vervain.[136] The Gauls highly esteemed vervain for their rites, according to Pliny, and modern French herbalists continued to relate to it in a ceremonial manner.

As recently as a century ago, Jacques Esquirol accompanied a Lyonnaise witch on her search for vervain on March 21. (The herb was said to be most potent on the spring equinox.) After much wandering, the herbalist suddenly cried out and knelt before a clump of vervain. She began to move, sighing, speaking and praying, and only after that did she gather the plant.[137] This approach to plants aligns with Siberian shamanism and North American medicine ways.

The Anglo-Saxon *wyrtgaelstre* would have sung incantations something like those in the "Nine Herbs Charm," a series of plant-spirit invocations to mugwort, plantain, nettle, camomile, fennel and other herbs. A 10th-century priest recorded these pagan chants in a medical compendium called the Lacnunga. Though he mixed in names of the christian god, that of Wodan remains too, and the outlines of an older cosmology are still perceptible. The charm addresses plants as living powers, and foremost among them is Artemisia:

> Remember, mugwort, what you made known,
> what you arranged at the great proclamation.
> you were called una, oldest of herbs.
> you have power for three and against thirty,
> you have power against poison and infection,
> you have power against the loathsome foe
> roving through the land.[138]

Mugwort is a relative of North American desert sage, and closely related to the herb burned in Chinese medicinal moxibustion. On all three continents, the local form of Artemisia was revered for its power to bless and remove negative energy, disharmony and disease; and to purify and protect from danger. Pliny referred to the ancient belief that Artemis had revealed this herb, which even now retains the botanical name Artemisia.[139]

Invocation to Mugwort, "oldest of herbs," in the Nine Herbs Charm, Lacnunga, 10th century England

Around the year 870, German carvers of an ivory gospel cover showed Mother Earth holding a horn-shaped basket of herbs. Roman influence would suggest that acanthus is shown, but it is plausibly the local mugwort, whose leaves are shaped.[140] (See chapter 7, pp 258 and 261.)

Mugwort was said to reach its greatest power on the summer solstice. It was among the nine sacred herbs that peasant celebrants offered to the Midsummer bonfires, and which they brought home after the dancing to safeguard the household until next year's summer solstice.[141] It is likely to have been one of the herbs that Breton soothsayers used to lustrate houses in the mid-9th-century. Frankish authorities also list "fumigators" (*suffitores*) among pagan practitioners in the same period.[142]

Russians told a thoroughly shamanistic tale about mugwort, which carried the secret name *Chernobyl* ("black one"). They said that a girl went searching for mushrooms in the old oak forest of Starodubsk. She saw a group of serpents curled up, and tried to retreat, but fell into a pit where they lived.

*Pagan interlace: silverwork
from Ryazan, Russia*

It was dark there, and the snakes were hungry, but their golden-horned queen led them to a luminous stone. Licking it satisfied their hunger. The girl did as they did and remained with them until spring came. Then the snakes made a ladder for her by interlacing their bodies, and she ascended from the underworld. Before they parted, the serpent queen gave the girl the ability to understand the language of plants and to know their medicinal powers. But she warned her never to speak the name of Chernobyl or she would lose her knowledge.

The maiden had this gift until one day a man asked her the name of the plant that grows along the footpaths, and before she realized it she had answered, pronouncing the taboo name of Chernobyl. All her knowledge left her, as the serpent queen's prediction came true. People say that this is where mugwort acquired its other name: Zabytko, "herb of forgetfulness."[143]

Southern Slavs recounted similar stories of dragons or serpent queens who granted second sight to humans who lived in their underground world for seven or nine years. This initiation gave them the power to achieve wealth and to gain knowledge of the dead.[144] The tale of Chernobyl shows that mugwort was held to be very sacred—thus the secrecy around its ritual name—and that knowledge about it was transmitted after an initiation (communion with snakes in the underworld). The admonition to secrecy may also be seen as a reference to the danger of openly espousing the "Old Faith" (старая вера), the Russian name for pagan spirituality.

Just as the initiate must never reveal the name of Chernobyl, Russians gathered a "nameless herb" on the eve of *Kupala*—Midsummers' Eve. This so happens to be the time when people over many parts of Europe gathered mugwort for ceremony. Celebrants garlanded themselves, their children and animals; hung their homesteads with mugwort; cast it upon bonfires on the high places; and leaped over its smoke. The French made wreaths to wear at festival dances, then threw them into the bonfire along with their sorrows.[145] Russians called the sacred bundle of mugwort Kupala, "shower," from a blessing rite of sprinkling water with it. That byname may have come into use because the real name of mugwort was indeed taboo: sacred.

STAFF-WOMEN, AND OTHER GERMANIC TITLES

Scandanavia lay out of the church fathers' reach for a long time. The northern countries were not even nominally converted to Christianity until after 1000. As a result, pagan culture survived there in strength, and had many names for the wisewoman and seeress. Old Norse texts refer to the clairvoyant powers of the *spákona*, "prophet-woman."

She is also *seiðkona*, a word that has no English equivalent, but connotes "woman of ecstatic ceremony, enchantress." And she is the *völva*, which means "staff-woman" (from *völr*, "staff").[146] (The plural of *völva* is *völur*; later sources often use *vala* for the singular.) The ceremonial staff has been used by shamans and medicine women all over the world, from Zimbabwe to Japan to California.[147]

The *völva* was the Norse shaman par excellence. She went out on the land, gazing in silence and watching the signs of nature, a practice known as *utiseta*, "sitting out." She was adept in *seiðr*, a ceremony in which she entered trance at the center of a circle of women. Chanting of *seiðlati* (trance melodies) fueled her spirit-journey and her inspired prophecy. This induction of trance was called *efla seið*, "fixing magic."[148] Toward the end of the ceremony the *völva* gave oracular responses to people's questions. These seeresses roamed the countryside, often travelling with groups of singers.[149]

Another major group of sorcery-words come from more southerly Germanic languages: Dutch *toverij*, Old Frisian *tauwerie*, German *Zauber*, and the Old English *teafor*. From the same root came the Flemish *toveresse* and German *Zauberin*, "sorceress." The Old High German form *zoupar*, in its variant spellings, is glossed as "divination." Icelandic has various forms including *töfur* (amulet, talisman or other magical object, but also meaning "incantation" and magical "fascination").[150] A seeress was described as keeping *taufr*, "the instruments for making spells," in her skin bag, though the saga does not reveal what those might be.[151]

In Low German, *toverie* was sometimes paired with the *wykke* / *witch* words, as in *tovern und wykken*, or "go about with *toverye* and *wyckerie*"; and similar combinations.[152] Most intriguing is a single Icelandic attestation of *töfranorn*, which looks to be a fate, although the Latin gloss *saga* ("wise-woman") suggests a living woman.[153] The witch Búsla invokes the *töfranorn*, along with trolls, *álfar*, and giants, in her protective spell to prevent the saga's hero from being executed.[154]

shapeshifters and spirit flight

Some names of the witch highlight her shamanic nature, and the transformative powers she worked with. She is described as taking the form of an animal double to make journeys in the spirit. In northern Europe, she often rides upon the wolf, whale, or walrus, her animal spirit helpers. In Greece, the Pythia received power and knowledge from the serpent. The Italian *strix* assumed the form of an owl. If her flight was once revered as the dreamer's journey, by Roman times she was reviled as a devourer of life-force who stole children and caused people to waste away.[155] This idea was carried over into the Church's negative interpretation of shamanic ways.

Under Roman rule, the Latin *strix* was adopted into Gaulish culture, becoming the *striga* of Provence and *stria* of the Franks. The loanword imported the negative Roman connotations, which circulated ever more widely in Church Latin pronouncements against *strigae, stregonae, stregulae, or striones*. Only in her Italian homeland, among the peasantry, did the *strega* retain her positive associations with healing and second-sight. In other countries—notably France, early on, and Switzerland and Hungary centuries later—women were persecuted as witches under the imported name of *striga* / *striges*.

In seventh century Languedoc and in northern Italy, commoners called

the witch *masca*, She-of-the-Mask. The Lombard *Lex Rotharii* refers to
the burning of women as *mascae*. The law permitted lords to burn women
under their rule as witches, but forbade other men to lynch them: "No one
should presume to kill the serving-woman of another [man] as witch [*stria*],
which they call *masca*..."[156] The word comes from a late Latin term *masca* or
mascara that entered medieval languages as Italian *talamasca*, Old French
talmache and *tamasche*, Old Dutch *talmasge*.[157]

In the late 7th century, Cilian referred to *Talamascæ Litteræ*,
"Talamasca characters, or letters," explaining them thus: "for the hidden
things, and the things known only to sorcerers [soothsayers] and to the
Talamascas, and to those who are agreed upon the meaning of their characters."[158] This reference to characters comes very close to Germanic runes.

In Church Latin *talamasca* is given as a synonym for *larva*, which carries
the meanings of "mask, double, ghost, shadow, image," and especially,
"demon."[159] Here again there is an overlap between the witch and the dead,
with a suggestion that she channeled ancestral spirits, or enacted them in
ceremonies. Massimo Centini shows that *talamasca* was connected with
"masquerades organized on the day of the dead." He cites an 882 order
by the Frankish bishop Hincmar of Reims: "Do not permit them to do
shameful games with bears, nor consent to them going carrying in front of
them those masks of demons, which are commonly called *talamascae*."[160]

In medieval German, *talmasca* referred to a masked person. *Tal-* appears
to derive from *dalen*, "to whisper, speak in a droll manner, joke." Centini
concludes, "And so Talamasca would be a mask that mumbles or speaks in
a strange manner like a spirit or a madman."[161] In the modern folklore of
Piemonte, *masca* means "witch" and also "spirits, shadows of the dead."[162]
There it continued to be used as an insult toward women, as "witch," beyond
the middle ages.[163]

Medieval Latin sources used *larva* for spirits, including devouring hag-
spirits and night-maras, but also for the dead. Gervase of Tilbury equated
larvae with the old Greco-Roman *lamias*, "who the common people call
mascae or in Gallic language *strie*." He quoted physicians as saying that
they are "nocturnal visions that disturb the souls of sleepers, causing
oppression."[164] Countering this negative definition, interestingly, was the
Jesuit Gaspar Schott, who wrote in 1657, "*lamia* and *strix* mean the same
thing, namely, *saga* ('wisewoman')."[165] *Larva* was used in the first description

of the famous witch-mountain Horselberg, in the early 1500s.[166]

Masks were once used to invoke ancestors and land spirits. Innumerable canon laws forbade women's singing and dancing in churchyards, as well as masked ceremonial processions in the guise of stags and old women. Masked dancers and mummers were a common sight on medieval festival days, carried over from wholly pagan origins into a churchified calendar of saints' names. They survived into the 20th century in Switzerland, Bulgaria, and other remote regions.

A witch named Grima ("Mask") appears in an Icelandic saga. Her family were Norse from the Hebrides: "All of them were very skilled in magic and were great sorcerers.[167] The Norse called those who were able to assume another form *hamleipur*.[168] Alone among the gods, the witch Freyja possesses the shamanic *fyaðrhamr*, "feather-form," a magical cloak with the power to fly over the lands. Eddic poetry does not elaborate on this; the only mention of it is when she loans her witch-cloak to the trickster Loki.[169]

Many Celtic goddesses took the form of bears, wild pigs, deer and especially ravens, the allies of the prophetess. Flidais, the Irish goddess of wild animals, drove a chariot drawn by deer (as Artemis also had). The Scottish *glaisteag* oversaw, protected, and dealt out fates to the deer, and had deer feet herself. She punished hunters who were disrespectful to the deer. The Morrigan took many forms, but especially that of a crow or raven. Shape-shifting swan-cloaked women appear in Celtic lays and Germanic faery tales. Valkyries also sometimes took this form. Goddesses and *dísir* (female ancestors) take the form of *fylgjur*, apparitions that guide, warn, and protect. (See Chapter 6.) If analogies to other world traditions hold, these ancestral beings would also act as spirit helpers.

Folk tradition held that some people inherited or were divinely gifted with the shamanic power of shapeshifting. Around 1015 bishop Burchard of Worms asked in his penitential book if people believe "that those who are commonly called the Fates exist," or that when a person is being born, "they are able even then to determine his life to what they wish, so that... he can be transformed into a wolf, that which vulgar folly calls a werewolf, or into any other shape."[170]

The old Irish believed that people of certain clans possessed the power to take the form of wolves when they wished. One source reports that in the year 690 a wolf was heard speaking with a human voice.[171] Several centuries later, Giraldus Cambrensis recounted how "a monk wandering in a forest came upon two wolves, one of whom was dying. The other entreated him to give the dying wolf the last sacrament... [and] tore the skin from the breast of the dying wolf, laying bare the form of an old woman." Afterwards the monk worried that it was sinful to give the sacrament to such a being—was it human or animal?[172]

A more orthodox version of this story says that a priest traveling through the woods in Meath was accosted by a man who asked him to confess his sick wife. The priest saw nothing but a wolf lying on the ground, and turned to flee. The wolf and her husband calmed his fears, and he performed the rite. Thinking that the wolf-woman might possess prophetic insight because of her shamanic form, he asked her about the English who were then invading Ireland. The wolf answered that God was punishing the Irish for their sins.[173] In this way, pagan traditions of shapeshifting were turned to the service of Christian moralizing; but the story also bears witness to how shapeshifting was linked to spiritual vision.

A strong cultural expectation that wolf-witches were female seems to have prevailed in Ireland. One of three categories of women penalized with reduced compensation for wrongs in the *Bretha Crólige* was "the woman who likes to stray in wolf-shapes." A second category was the wandering woman "who goes off with *síd*-folk"—with the

Female wolf, Book of Kells, Ireland

faeries.[174] (This is a prime metaphor for Otherworld journeys in Ireland, and was faery doctors like Biddy Early and Máire Ni Murchú were still said to journey to faery realms in the 1800s.)[175]

The third kind of disapproved woman, "the sharp-tongued virago," was the female satirist.[176] She was seen as a kind of sorceress, whose words had the power to raise up blisters on a deserving target. Male satirists had this same power, but the legal codes did not socially penalize—or demonize—them for it. Tribal Irish society was not as sex-egalitarian as is often claimed. The suppression of sharp female social critique would have been a pivotal change in Irish culture.

Folk tradition knows of spells called *fith-fath* or *fath-fith*, which have the power to make a person invisible, to shift shapes, or to change things into different forms. Many Irish tales turn on transformations of this kind. Eithne went through many such changes after being cursed by her husband's first wife. But transformations that result from a curse are a very different matter than shapeshifting in ecstatic connection with spirit beings.

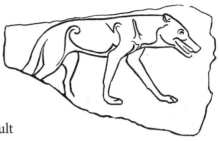

Female wolf on Pictish stone,
Ardross, Scotland

A hag riding on a giant white wolf was said to have stopped the Danish invasion of England under Harald Hardrada in 1066. A man named Gyth dreamed that a great witch stood on the island, opposing the king's fleet with a fork and a trough. Tord dreamed that "before the army of the people of the country was riding a huge witch-wife upon a wolf, and she tossed the invading soldiers into its mouth."[177]

Witches were famous for allying with animal guardians or helpers, especially ravens, wolves, snakes or dragons. During the early modern witch hunts, witches' doubles and spirit "familiars" were most often pictured as cats, toads, bats and hares, or occasionally foxes or birds. Savoyard tradition kept alive stories of witches who turned into wolves or bears.[178] Shapeshifting and consorting with animal spirits became stock accusations of the witch hunters, and in later persecutions up to the 20th century. Already around 1235 Etienne Bourbon was recording a French belief that wolf-riding old women (*striges*) killed babies.[179]

In the old lore, witches and goddesses ride on dream-animals: wolves, horses, goats, or geese. The Norse poetic kennings for wolf called it "the trollwoman's steed" and "the dusky stallion on which the Night-Farer goeth."[180] In their dream-journeys, witches attain foreknowledge of the unseen, of what is yet to come. The word used in the Helgakviða—*trollkona*—can mean a spirit, or a witch:

a witch woman on wolf did ride in the gloaming...
full well saw she that soon would fall
Sigrlinn's son on Sigarsvellir.[181]

Wolf-rider stone at Hunnestad, Sweden, in the 1600s. All but two of seven stones were later smashed.

A trollwoman mounted on a wolf is carved on a second-century runic stone at Hunnestad in Skåne, Sweden. She has often been compared to the supernatural Hyrrokin in Snorri's Edda. When the Aesir called her from Jötunheim to aid them, she came riding on a wolf with serpents for reins.[182] An old manuscript shows a witch riding on a wolf bridled with snakes.[183] In the Balkans, the *vila* (faery woman) rides a seven-year old stag bridled with snakes.[184]

Another term for shamanic flight was *gandreid*, "staff-ride." A spirit journey by Thordís of Löngueness in Greenland is described in *Fostbraethra saga*. She slept fitfully, tossing and turning; when she awoke, she told her son she had gone on a long ride on a *gand* through the heavens "and now I know the destiny of those of whom I knew nothing before."[185] Here again, as with the troll-woman riding a wolf in *Helgakviða*, a journey in the spirit reveals the future and hidden things. *Gandr* also signifies a helping spirit, enchantment or magic.

now i know the destiny of those of whom i knew nothing before.

The *gandreid* evokes the familiar image of witches riding on the broomstick, or on distaffs or oven-forks. The *völva* carried a ceremonial staff that was apparently understood as conveying her on journeys through the worlds, like the horse-staff of some Siberian shamans. Its equivalent is the witch's wand, whose potency is dramatized by its omnipresence in European faerie tales. The witch waves her wand, points it, or transforms a person or object by touching them with it. The Irish *luirgean* and Scottish *slachdán* were magical staves or wands that transformed what they struck. Even brooms figure as animated magical objects in Spanish tales of witchcraft, like the distaffs in French and Sardinian lore.

The Night-Farer's name is very old, predating the Germanic migrations: Old German *naht-fara*, *naht-frouwa*, *naht-rita*; Anglo-Saxon *niht-genge*; Old Norse *myrk-ritha* ("rider in the dark, the murk") or *qveld-ritha* or *trollritha*.[186] Because the witch hunts have so thoroughly ingrained the idea that darkness is evil, these names have a sinister ring to modern ears.

The Scandanavian *völva* was known both as "night-farer" and *spáfarar*, "prophetic traveller, a term that is known from 13th century Icelandic laws prohibiting witchcraft.[187] The repressive context for that single attestation of *spáfarar* parallels that of Anglo-Saxon *wyrtgælstre*. But the propitious evening star was also called *nahtfara*.[188] No one could ask for a clearer reference to the shaman's journey.

FROM HAGEDISSE TO HEXE

Another group of Germanic witch-names carried the double sense of a woman who traveled in the spirit, and also of an ancestor or supernatural crone. The name in Old High German was variously recorded as *hagedisse*, *hagazussa*, *hegizissa*, *hegitisse*, and *haghtessen*. In Anglo-Saxon the word was *hægtesse* or *hagtis*; in medieval Dutch *hagetisse* or *haghdisse*. Over long usage these words gradually contracted, in German to *hazus*, *hazusa*, *hazasa*. In Middle High German the word was already sliding into *hegxse* or *hexse*, in Swiss to *hagsch* or *hezze*, and in English to *hægesse* or *haetse*.[189] It's important to understand that these terms referred to female spirits, Otherworld beings, possibly ancestors, as well as to the witches who invoked them.

The etymologists say that the deep meaning of *haga* / *hæg* / *hœg* is "hedge, border, boundary." Old English *haga* meant "enclosed area," often a homestead or house.[190] (It is related to the *haw* in hawthorn—originally *hagathorn*—a tree with strong faery associations.) So *hagazussa* signified "hedge-woman" or "fence-woman," a liminal being who is a boundary-traveler.[191] She "courses between the worlds."[192]

The *hagazussa* is related to the *tunriða*, "hedge-riders" or "gate-riders" that Oðinn sees flying in the sky and tries to bring down.[193] The *tunriða* had a German counterpart in the *zunritha*, a term "used of witches and ghosts."[194] Late medieval Swedish laws refer to the fence-riding witch. In the Old Laws of Västergotland, a wild-haired woman is said to ride the gate "in a witch's shape, 'caught' between night and day."[195] These lines appear in the form of an accusation before an all-male Swedish court: "Woman, I saw you riding on a fence with loose hair and belt, in the troll skin, at the time when day and night are equal."[196]

The second component of the compound word *hægtesse (-disse, tesse, zussa)* is also significant. Its spirit-meaning is shared across a wide range of Indo-European languages. The Proto-Indo-European root is *dhewes- "to fly about, smoke, be scattered, vanish." It gave rise to "Norwegian *tysja* "fairy; crippled woman," Gaulish *dusius* 'demon,' [and] Lithuanian *dvasia* 'spirit.'"[197] It also relates to Westphalian German *dus*, Cornish *dus* or *diz*, and Breton *duz* (all christianized to mean "devil") and Old English *dust*.[198]

Romans equated the Gaulish god Dusios to Pan; this deity also took plural form as *dusioi* or, in Latin, *dusii*. In late antiquity, Augustine and Isidore both referred to *dusii* as "incubi," spirits who had sex with women.[199] But as late as the 8th century, *dusii* was still being used in France for spirits of the dead, *dusii manes*.[200]

The 10th century Anglo-Saxon cleric Aelfric used *hægtesse* in the sense of "woman of prophetic and oracular powers."[201] He connected the *hægtesse* with *pythonissa*, a Latin term for entranced seeress,[202] and linked both terms with another witch-word: *Helle-rúne vel hægtesse pythonissa*.[203] Both the *hægtesse* and *hellerune* were associated with female ancestors. (Chapter 5 looks at *hellerune* in more depth.)

The modern Anglo-Saxon dictionary of Boswoth-Toller defined *hægtesse* as "hag, witch, fury," while another source gives "witch, pythoness."[204] These names overlap and are compared in several sources: "In late glosses, *hellerune* is given as an alternative to *hægtesse*, and *hægtesse* glosses words for the furies."[205] One Anglo-Saxon source gives "Hægtesse Tissiphona," naming one of the Greek Erinnyes (Furies).[206] Another brings in a singular "Erinys," and compares the *hægtesse* with Anglo-Saxon forms of the valkyrie, the *wælcyrge/wælcyrre*.[207] The Furies were a wrathful form of maternal ancestors, which is worth recalling in light of Anglo-Saxon spells that interpreted disease as attacks by *haegtessen*.

The Old English charm *Wid færstice* attempted to expel *hægtessen gescot* ("hag-shot") along with *ésa gescot* [aesir-shot] and *ylfa gescot* (elf-shot).[208] The charm shows a fear of *hægtessen geworc*, which apparently means the "work" of a hag spirit, not a living witch.[209] Earlier in the charm, the *hægtessen* spirits are described as the "mighty women" who rode over the land and "sent screaming spears" (see chapter six).[210] *Hægtesse* also appears as *hætse*, a word that Aelfric used for Jezebel in translating the Vulgate's *maledictam illam*, "that accursed woman"[211] whose "sorceries" were "many."

Old English placenames meaning "witch's valley" gave modern Hascombe in Surrey and Hescombe in Somerset, "where the first element of the name is O.E. *hætse* or *hægtesse*, 'witch.'"[212] Similar phonological contractions occurred in Old High German *hesse* and *hezze*.[213] *Hægtesse* also relates to *hag*, symbolically if not etymologically. In folk tradition, "hag" designated a supernatural old woman at least as often a human witch or old woman.

Mary Daly drew attention to the evolution of *hag*, pointing to its archaic meaning given in *Webster's Dictionary* as "female demon: fury, harpy," and as *nightmare* (in the sense of a female spirit), but only later as "ugly old woman." She pulled up archaic meanings for the word *haggard*, which originally signified "untamed" (as of a hawk), "intractable," "willful," "wanton," and "unchaste." It also referred to a "wild-eyed" person. Daly's final touch was a discovery loaded with sexual politics: "As a noun, haggard has an 'obsolete' meaning: 'an intractable person, especially: a woman reluctant to yield to wooing.'"[214] She is untamable, indominable.

English is full of magical hag-words, such as the snake called *hagworm*, and the *hagstone*, "a naturally perforated stone used as an amulet against witchcraft."[215] These stones, also called holey stones or adder stones, were used in healing, especially for eye diseases. Another strand of meaning is found in Old Dutch *haghdisse*, with its variants *eghdisse*, *egdisse*, *haagdisse*, all meaning "lizard" (*hagedis* in modern Dutch). German *eidechse* has the same meaning,[216] as did the Old Saxon *egithassa*.[217]

In late medieval German, *hagazussa* was compressed into *hegxse*, *hecse* and finally *hexe*. In Swiss it became *hagsh*, *haagsch*, or *hezze*.[218] In Dutch it was *heks*. From German the word spread, with slightly different spellings, into the Scandinavian languages during the witch-hunt era, as continental demonologies migrated north. It was under the name of *Hexe* that multitudes of women would be burned.

Over many centuries, the priesthood gained a monopoly over the power of naming. Churchmen labored to remold folk culture to conform with their own worldview. They defined incantation, ecstatic dance, folk beliefs and ceremonies as devilish, and recast the old ethnic titles through a hostile lens.

The Anglo-Saxon *wycce*, French *sorcière*, Spanish *bruja*, Russian *vyed'ma* and Italian *strega* were diviners and healers who were, as the clergy often complained, respected among the people. Since the institutional priesthood felt rivalry with these old peasant women, it called their power dangerous. Later, they would define it as heretical, but in 700-1100 they still understood witchcraft as pagan, heathen, *bruixa*.

The witches were female in a male-dominated society, and animist peasants ruled by aristocrats who were enforcing Christianity as the state religion. Their position has similarities to that of Amazigh *kahinas* after the Islamic conquest of North Africa, to the legendary Nishan Shaman who faced repression from Confucian rulers in Manchuria, or the Maya and Diasporic Africans who were forced to catholicize their culture so that it could survive.

In the Spanish repression of Indigenous Peruvian culture, Irene Silverblatt observes, "Idolatry, curing, and witchcraft were blurred."[219] The priesthood invented penitential manuals to repress European paganism, internally colonizing the ethnic cultures there. A thousand years later, they used them to enforce Christianity on the Chumash in California.[220]

Patriarchal and imperial religions disapprove of women's shamanic powers and consider them a threat to the order of dominion. Men felt threatened by witches whose direct personal power could potentially overthrow their social privilege. Conquerors felt threatened by the peoples they colonized. The same was true for any people who resist hegemonic systems of sex, ethnicity, class, or gender. As the European witch hunts gained

Pictish Stone with snake, mirror and comb. Aberlemno, Scotland

momentum, all these groups ran a high risk of persecution for witchcraft.

The names for witches in the old ethnic cultures show that they were viewed as seers, prophetesses and diviners; as wisewomen, healers and herbalists; as chanters and invokers; as shapeshifters and women who journey in the spirit. The meanings of the English word "witch" were considered in chapter 2, and chapter 5 will go deeper into the *leóðrune* and women's ancestor ceremonies. The following pages offer a wider tabulation of witch-names, after which we will delve into the rich cultural testimony about the Norse *völur* and their ceremonies.

ethnic names for witches: attributes and powers

knower

Croatian: *vještica* (vyeshtitsa) "knower"
Serb: вештица (vyeshtitsa) "knower"
Bulgarian: вещица (vyeshitsa) "knower"
Macedonian: вештерка (vyeshterka) "knower"
     (also appears as *vjescirica, vedavica*)
Polish: *wieszczyce* (vyeshchitse) "knower"
Russian: ведьма (vyed'ma) "witch, hag, night-hag";
     znayushchie liudi, "people who know"
Ukrainan: відьма (veed'ma)
Belorus: ведзьма (vyedz'ma) also вядзьмарка (vyadzmarka)
Polish: *wiedźma* (pron. veejma) witch, hag, harridan
Russian: знахарка "woman who knows"
Lower Germania: *veleda,* "knower, seeress"
Gaulish: *uidlua, "witch"*
Welsh: *gweled, gwelea*
Old Irish *velet*
Irish: *filid, filed, file, banfilé* "poet, bard, prophet"

wisewoman

Latin: *saga,* "wisewoman, witch"
French: *sage-femme* "wise woman"
Spanish: *sabia* "wise woman"
English: *cunning-woman* (related to *ken:* "know")
Norse: *fjölkyningskona* "much-knowing woman"
Norse: *vísendakona* "wise woman"
Norse: *vitka* "wisewoman, sorceress"
Hungarian Roma: *cohalyi*
Irish: *ban feasa,* "wisewoman"
     cailleach feasa "wise old woman"
Finnish: *tietäjä,* "knower," "seer" (ungendered)
Slavonic: *hmana zena:* "common woman"

PROPHETESS

Norwegian, Icelandic: *spákona*, "prophetic woman,"
spámeyja, "-maiden," *spákerling* "-old woman
spáfara, "prophetic traveler"
Scottish: *spaeing woman, spaewife*, "prophetic woman" (from *spákona*)
Old Irish: *fá, fáth, fáidh*, "prophet, poet"
            banfáith, "woman-prophet, poet"
Latin: *vates*, prophet (loanword from Celtic)
Latin *sortiaria*, "fate-seeress," *sortilega*, "lot caster"
French: *sorcière*
English: *sorceress*

DIVINER

Latvian: *burt, apburt*, "lot-caster, diviner"
        burve "witch, sorceress, enchantress"
        burtininkė "witch, sorceress, sibyl, pythoness"
        zīlniece, "diviner"
Latin: *divina, divinatrix*
French: *devine, devineresse*
Welsh: *dewines*
Basque: *azti*, "diviner"
Russian: *vorozheia; otgadchitsa* "diviner"
Greek: *mantis*, "female diviner, seer," from PIE root *men- ("mind"),
        cognate with *maenad* and *maniac*; *mantic* still means "divinatory"
Sardinia: *visionaria*, "enspirited woman"
ispiridada: "seeress"

ENCHANTRESS

Norse: *galdrakona*, "chant-woman"
Anglo-Saxon: *galstre*, "female chanter"; *wyrtgælstre*, "herb-chanter"
        leodrune, "mystery-singer"
Finnish: *loitsija*: "chanter"
Latin: *incantatrix, praecantatrix, praecantrix*, "enchanter"
Italian: *ammaliatrice* "charmer, spell-caster, witch"

Sámi: *guaps* "woman who chants and divines"
Latvian: *vārdotāja*, "word-charmer"
Norse: *seiðkona* "trance-woman"

healer

Greek: *pharmakis*, herbalist," as in "pharmacy"; later, "witchcraft"
Anglo-Saxon: *lybbestre*, from the root *lyb*, "life."
German: *lupparara*, from *luppa*, "life," related to "medicine, amulet"
     lüppærinne, lāchenærinne, lublerin
Spanish: *saludadora*, "healer"
Italian: *guaratrice*, "healer"
Latvian: *dziedniece, dziedinātāja*,"healer"
English: *charmer*, "enchantress"
Italian: *erborista*, "herbalist"
Spanish: *herbaria* "herbalist" (became pejorative)
Romanian: *fermecătoare* "enchantress, charmer, mezmerizer"
Latin: *venefica* "poisoner" (pejorative word used of herbalists)
Spain: *ensalmadora*, "healer with chants or words"
German: *segenoerinne* "blesser, enchantress, signer," from *segen*, "blessing"
Croatian: *vilenica*, "faery-woman," one taught to cure by the *vile* / faeries
Ireland: *bean leighis*, "medical woman"
Hungarian: *vajakos*, "healer"
Romanian: *vrăjitoare*, "charmer, enchantress, spell-caster (from *vraji*,
     "spellbind, charm, enchant, entrance, fascinate")
Welsh: *swynwraig* or *darswnynws*, "woman who gives charms, remedies,
     amulets; who gives comfort, cures and blessings, who preserves."

olD woman

Polish: *kobieta stara*
French: *vieille-femme*
English, Scots: *old wife*
Polish: *baba* "crone, hag, old woman, witch"
Romanian: *hoanghină* "hag"
Lithuanian, Latvian: *ragana* "hag, crone, witch, harpy"
Irish: *cailleach*, "old woman"; *cailleach phiseogach* "sorceress, charmer"

ammait (archaic "witch, hag"; devolved into modern "fool, idiot")
Welsh: *gwrach*, "hag, witch"
Norse: *spákerling*, "prophetic crone"
    galdrakerling, "spell-chanting crone"
Sámi: *noajdiesaakka* "shaman old woman"

DOER, MAKER

Spanish: *hechicera, faytillera*, "doer, maker, causer"
French: *facturière* (medieval), "maker"
Portuguese, Galician: *feiticeira* (fayteesheyra), "maker"
Italian: *fattuchiera* (fatuukiera), "maker"
Polish: *czarownica* (accent on ni) *czarodziejka, czarujaça kobieta*
    "witch, enchantress" (from a root meaning "to do, make")
Russian: чародейка (charodyeika) s"orceress, enchantress, witch"
Slovenian: *čarovnica* (charovnitsa)
Slovak and Czech: *čarodejnice* (charodyeinitse)
Basque: *sorguiñ, xorguiña, "doer, maker" sorsain*, "birth guardian"

SHAPESHIFTER

Italian: *masca*, "mask, masked one, ancestral spirit, ghost"
Provençal: *masco*
French: *talmasque*
Dutch: *talmasche*
Norse: *hamleypur*, "shapeshifter"; **hamgengja*: "goer-in-a-form,"
Latin: *strix, strigis* "screech-owl (woman)"
Frankish (loan): *stria, striga*, "witch" (pejorative, supernatural vampire)
Italian: *strega, stregula, stregona* (from Latin *strix*, "screech owl")

FATEFUL WOMEN

Latvian: *laumė* related to word for "fairy"and to the fate goddess Laima;
    now often used as "hag, witch"
Icelandic: *norn* "fate"; *galdranorn*, "chanting fate," both used as "witch"
töfranorn, witch or fate spirit
English, Scots: *weird woman, weird-wife, weirding woman* "fateful"

SPIRITS OR ANCESTORS

Old German: *hagedisse* "hag, hedge-spirit, wild female being, witch"
Saxon: *hagetesse*
Old English: *hægtesse, haetse*
Middle Dutch: *haghetisse*
Old German: hagazussa, hagzissa,
Dutch: *hagazussa*
German: *Hexe,* "witch"
Swiss: *hegse, hecse, hezze*
Norwegian, Danish, Dutch: *heks*
Swedish: *häxa*
Gothic: *haliorunna, haliruna,* "holy mysteries"
Old German: *helrune, hellerune*: (related to *haliorunnae,* goddess Hel)
Anglo-Saxon: *burgrune*: "mound-mysteries"
Norwegian, Swedish: *trollkvinne*: "troll-woman"
Norwegian: *trollkjering,* "troll-crone"
Swedish: *trollkäring,* "troll-crone"
trollpacka, "troll-packer, carrier, stower"
trollgumma, "ogress"
trollhäxa "troll-witch"
fortjuserska, förtrollerska, "enchantress"
välvillig "kindly, beneficent"
trolldom, trolltyg, häxeri: "witchcraft"
Polish: *jędza,* "raging"; hag, witch
Welsh: *wrach, gwrach, gwrachod, gwrachïod, ngwrachïod, wrachïod,*
wrachod, ngwrach, "witch, hag, dwarf, bundles of thatch or grain"[221]
gwiddon, gwiddonod, widdon, widdonod, ngwiddon, ngwiddonod:
      "witch, hag, giantess"

VARIOUS

Spanish: *bruja,* "heathen" (*bruzha,* later *brukha*)
Portuguese, Galician: *bruxa* (pronounced bruusha) "heathen"
Catalán: *bruixa* (brueesha) "heathen"
Occitanian, Gascon: *broucho* (bruusho) "heathen"
English: *wycce, wicce, wich, wicche, witch*: "twiner, spinner, plaiter"

Dutch, German: *wykke, wikker*

Irish: *banthúathaid*, "woman of *túaith*," meaning "northern, on the left";
  in patriarchal terms, "perverse, wicked, evil" (Compare "sinister")

Sardinia: *magliaia*, "knitter, mesh-worker"

German: *zauberin*, "female sorcerer, magic-maker"

Dutch: *tzouverijen, toveres, toeverse* "sorceress"

Flemish: *toveresse* "sorceress"

Frisian: *töfranorn*: "witch, diviner, or fate"

Greek: μάγισσα (magissa) magic-maker

Latin: *maga* "adept, magic-maker"

Serbian: *macisnica*, "adept, magic-maker"

Finnish: *tenhotar* "adept, magic-make"r

Albanian: *magjistare*, "female magician"

Polish: *guślarka* "sorceress, witch, woman who plays the *guslar*
  (Slavic shamanic instrument)

Finnish: *noita, noita-akka*: "shaman, shaman-crone"

Estonian: *nõid* "shaman"

Finnish: *noita*, "witch," (ungendered)

    noita-akka, "shaman-grandmother"

  loitsija "spell-weaver"

  lumoojatar "enchantress, witch" (*lumota* "bewitch")

Sámi: *noida* "shaman"

kwepkas "woman versed in witchcraft"

rudok, "spokeswoman for the female supernatural"[222]

This list of witch names is provisional, not intended to be exhaustive.

4

The völur

The Norse *völur* are the best-documented tradition of female spiritual leadership in medieval Europe. Several factors account for this wealth of detail. Scandinavia was christianized relatively late, and was romanized to a far lesser degree than western Europe. Another factor was the strong prophetic tradition of women in Germanic cultures. There is also the Norse proximity to the indigenous Sámi, with their *noaidevuohtta* (shamanic spiritual culture). Above all, the rich orature of Eddic poetry and sagas preserved knowledge that would have otherwise been lost.

The title of *völva* (plural *völur*) comes from *völr*, "wand, staff."[1] The *völva* is a "staff-woman," named for the female shamanic wand that is attested both in Icelandic literature and Scandinavian archaeology. The word has an ancient Gothic correlate, *walus*, as well as a proposed Old High German form **wala*. These words are reflected in the title of an ancient Germanic seeress, Waluberg, written on a Greek ostracon from Elephantine—a very long way from her homeland.[2]

Romans recorded the names of other Germanic seeresses, Ganna and Gambara, whose names are related to the Norse *gandr*, a word for magical staffs and spirit helpers. Linguists reconstruct the latinized Ganna as Germanic Gand-no, and Gambara as Gand-bara, "staff-bearer."[3] Ganna was a prophetic priestess of the Semnones tribe who acted as a diplomat in the time of Domitian, with a say in treaties and political power to settle disputes.[4] Hers was not a personal name but a title, like that of the tribal Bructerian sibyl Veleda.[5]

The *völur* are especially associated with prophecy and the ecstatic ceremony known as *seiðr*. Snorri defined *seiðr* as "the skill from which follows the greatest power."[6] It included "the power to predict the future, control the weather and seasons, harm or heal humans, and expel public enemies..."[7] The *völur* accessed these powers through a trance state induced by incantation of special chants. They also may have "acted as mediators between the living and the dead."[8] (See below for more on *seiðr*.)

The *völur* are mentioned in numerous Norse texts. In fact, the *Völuspá*, the most venerable poem of the Icelandic Edda, is named the "Völva's Prophecy." Inspired oracular prophecy by female figures occurs in the plots of many sagas. Most of the descriptions have to do with a woman's "knowledge of someone's *ørlog*: the thread of a person's life that leads to their death." In the sagas, this precognitive power is strongly marked as female. Judy Quinn's analysis of Norse literature found that "knowledge of the future is closely, though not exclusively, associated with females."[9] She writes, "... when these saga-writers represented the ancient past there was a close association in their minds between verse prophecy — and the related enunciations of advice and curse (what to do and what not to do in the

future) — and certain kinds of women." These women include not only human *völur* but an array of supernaturals: goddesses, *dísir* (female ancestors), and troll-women who live in mountain rocks or sea.[10]

Prophecy looms large, but the sagas refer to more extensive powers of the *völur*. The *Landnamabok* described Norwegian *völva* Thurid the Sound-Filler thus: "She was called 'the Sound-Filler' because during a famine in Halogaland she filled every sound with fish by means of magic, *seið*. She also fixed the Kvíar fishing ground in the open sea in front of Isafjord Bay and took a hornless ewe in return from every farmer in Isafjord."[11] Ceremonies securing staple foods for families ensured survival of an entire region. The account of Thorbjörg *spákona* ("prophetess") in *Eiriks saga rauða* turns on the same theme.

Hilda Ellis Davidson cites several instances of a *völva* who acts on the weather or the land by waving an enchanted kerchief or hood. She writes, "The witch's equipment is simple: a platform, a staff, a hood or cloak, a skin, rug, kerchief, and possibly a sealskin bag..."[12] Shapeshifting and shamanic flight appear in the sagas, with women "taking the form of fish, whales, or seals."[13] In *Kormáks saga* 18, Thorveig the witch changes into a walrus, and dies after it was speared. In the *Hjalmthers ok Olvérs* saga, two *völur* leave their bodies behind on the *seiðhjallr* platform as they travel in the spirit, riding on the backs of whales.[14] The woman warrior Hervör shapeshifts into a porpoise for a sea battle with an enemy in the form of a walrus.[15] Thúriðr Drikinn, anticipating

Hopper -stad, Norway

an attack by enemies, sets up her bed by the door: "very little can come without her knowing about it." When rival witch Kerling arrives at the head of a pack of warriors, a great boar leaps out at her, "and at the same moment up sprang Thuríðr Drikinn..."[16] The name of Hamgláma, one of two *seiðkonur* in *Friðþjófs saga ins frœkna* 5, also alludes to her shapeshifting power.[17]

The völr or seiðstafr

Archaeological finds of women with staffs underline the etymology of *völva* as "staff-woman." Yet despite pervasive references to the *völur* in the sagas, until recently most archaeologists were still interpreting the many iron staffs found mainly in female graves as meat-roasting spits (women cook, you know) or as measuring sticks used in textile work. These interpretations became unsustainable as the shared patterns of these staffs emerged. They are too thick, for one thing, and usually have knobs or other protrusions which would have made spit-roasting impossible. Some of the adornments are gaping animal heads, like those on the iron staffs from Klinta, Gävle, and Birka (grave Bj.660).

In the 1990s, new scholarship by Anne Stine Ingstad and other female archaeologists led to wider recognition that the staffs relate to the *völr* or *seiðstafr* of the sagas.[18] The knobs on the iron staffs are even described in an account of the *völva* Thorbjörg: "A staff she had in her hand, with a knob thereon; it was ornamented with brass, and inlaid with gems round about the knob."[19]

Most of the surviving staffs are made of iron. Quite a few of them share a design feature in which the rod separates out into four or more bars that curve out around an enclosed space and then rejoin at a knob near the top of the staff. These formations have been compared to "baskets," or called an "expanded handle" or "basket-like handle" or "openwork device."[20] But those widened portions would make poor handles, awkward to hold because of their breadth, especially for women's hands. They're too airy for baskets, since they have no walls, only spokes

Mykle-bostad, Norway

sprouting out of the shaft, sometimes from the mouths of animal heads, which curve back to rejoin it. Occasionally a disc joins them at the center, as with the Swedish *völr* at Søreim.[21]

For years I puzzled over the peculiar spoked protrusions near the top of the *seið* staffs: what were they? What did they signify? The shape was distinctive, but had no obvious function or symbolism. Eldar Heide has unlocked the symbolic key: the staffs are modeled on distaffs.[22] Once this clue was supplied, it was easy to find pictures of European distaffs that track exactly with the shape of Norse *völr*. The French call this shape a "linen distaff," the English, a "birdcage distaff."

The distaff symbolism of the Norse *völr* or *seiðstafr* is not a theory, but an irrefutable reality. The staffs of the *völur* are modeled on wooden distaffs with curved supports for the skeins of flax or wool that women wound around them for spinning, a process known as "dressing the distaff." Distaff itself means "staff with flax" (Old English *distæf*). From the same root comes *bedizen*, the act of draping flax around the staff for spinning.[23] Spokes on the *völr* in archaeological finds occasionally are grooved with a yarn pattern, underlining the symbolism of spinning, as in the Swedish staffs from Gävle and Närke, and the Norwegian ones from Kaupang and Myklebostad.[24]

The symbolism of the *völva*'s staff emphasizes a connection between spinning, *seiðr*, and causation. It evokes a wider European pattern of distaff-bearing goddesses and threefold Fates or female ancestors.[25] It connects

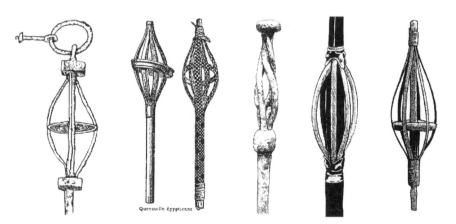

Iron staffs and wooden distaffs, from left: Swedish völr, Søreim; two Egyptian distaffs; Danish völr, Fuldby; Swedish völr, Klinta; French distaff

the shamanic ways of the *völur* with the early medieval women's sacraments detailed in Chapter 2, and ties in with a huge body of medieval and early modern stories and pictures of witches performing magic with distaffs or flying upon them, like a Norwegian *völva* who was buried astride her staff at Veka. So the *seiðstafr* of the *völva* belongs to a wide spectrum of female potency, while showing a culturally specific association with a Norse female spiritual office.

The distaff is presented as a staff of power in a northern Norwegian story brought forward by Eldar Heide. A Sámi woman takes her distaff up a mountaintop to call winds for her husband's ship to come home from faraway Bergen: "and she *yoiks* [chants in the Sámi way] on the mountain; she has her distaff on the mountain."[26] This hybrid story blends the Norse magical distaff with Sámi incantation.

Heide notes that magical acts of spinning have the power to render a person invisible, as described in *Eyrbyggja saga* and *Fóstbrœðra saga*. (In the former, the sorceress Katla uses the power of her distaff to conceal her son from his enemies.) A related theme is the sorceress who creates mind-sendings in the form of a ball of yarn or a rope.[27] The Norse witch-name *thraðriða*, "thread-rider," corresponds to these ideas.[28]

The seiðstafr in archaeology

Distaff-shaped *seiðstaffs* have been found in Sweden at Klinta, Birka (Bj.834), Gävle, Gnesta, and Närke; in Norway at Søreim and Kaupang, among others; and at Hardby, Denmark. On several of them, the corroded spokes have broken off, leaving only remnants. These include the staffs at Gnesta, and the lone example from Ireland. On the staffs from Närke and Fuldby, the spokes twist in a spiral. The bars of the Fuldby staff curve around sinuously as they ascend toward the staff head. Most of the staff finds catalogued by Price[29] are of the distaff type.

Norse seeresses are richly documented in archaeology, especially for the period 800-1000. Women have been found buried with ritual staffs of iron (or occasionally wood) in Norway, Sweden, and Denmark—often with regalia, herbs or other unusual items. One staff has turned up at Kilmainham near Dublin, another in the Manx islands, and another in Gnezdovo, Russia—all regions colonized by Vikings. The staffs were found in female graves, or on female sides of joint burials, except for three in Norwegian male graves; one in Denmark; and one in Finland. The sex ratio of known staffs is 34: 5, with six more found either in unsexed graves or in non-burial contexts.[30]

Kaupang, Norway

A distaff-shaped *völr* was placed next to a woman in an unusual ship burial at Kaupang-Skiringssal in Vestlandet. A woman and man were buried head to head on the ship's deck. The *völva* was seated at the stern, as if steering the ship, wearing an unusual leather over-garment with women's brooches. Metal rings hanging from the twisted rods of the distaff head would have rattled when she moved her staff. A large stone had been placed over the *völva's* iron staff.[31] Archaeologists usually interpret the placement of stones to weigh down the body of a dead person as attempts to keep their magical power in the Otherworld. This sometimes held true for their tools of power as well. Sagas describe this use of stones to weigh down the dead, which occurs in other ship burials.[32] A stone was placed over the Fuldby staff as well.[33] At Gerdrup, Zealand, a Danish woman lay under two large stones, with a man who had evidently been sacrificed, since he had been hanged with feet bound together. She has been interpreted as a *völva.*[34]

The Kaupang völr, the spokes of its distaff head corroded and broken

Klinta, Sweden

One of the most impressive staff burials was found at Klinta, in Köpingsvik, Öland Island. A woman was buried with a large iron wand (82 cm) with brass detailing of bear heads, their jaws gripping the distaff head above and below. The squared cap of the staff is topped by a little house with bears at its corners. This staff, now in the Swedish Museum of National Antiquities in Stockholm, may be the oldest dated *völr* of the distaff type (ca 900-950).[35]

Great care and effort was devoted to this ship burial. A woman and a man were laid out on bearskins with many rich offerings. (That makes a third bear connection in this burial.) The ship was set afire, after which their remains and goods were separated and buried in separate mounds. The woman's burial is the primary one, at the spot where the pyre was burned. After the cremation cooled, her bones were gathered together into a pit with the ashes and most of the offerings, including many animals. They were capped with a clay cover packed into a hexagonal twig frame. Her *seiðstafr* was placed under this cap, with its head protruding. Over all this was spread more debris from the pyre, then limestone chips, and finally a dome-shaped stone cairn.

The man's burial had no pit and fewer artifacts and ashes. It too was covered with a cairn, over which turf was laid. Both graves contained cross-gender artifacts. His included a needle, brooch and beads as well as a sword, balances, games, and whetstone. Hers held a battle-axe, tools for woodworking as well as female tools, most of the ship's rivets, and harnesses for draft horses, which would have pulled a cart (a marker of elite female burials).[36] Among the *völva's* imported goods were a costly copper ewer of Turkic workmanship and coins from western Asia.

The prominent placement of the Klinta *seiðstafr* is echoed in a Swedish woman's burial in a 10th century cemetery at Jägarbacken. Her staff was adorned with unusual bronze spirals that protruded above and below its distaff spokes. It was "thrust vertically into the ashes surrounding the woman's bones; around the staff two unburnt brooches had been placed," after which the whole burial was covered by a mound.[37] These burials gave central prominence to the *seiðstafr*.

Aska, Sweden

Another woman's cremation mound with an iron staff was found at Aska, Hagebyhöga, in southern Sweden. Among her rich grave goods, dated to 800-1000 CE, were a kettle, four horses with their harnesses and carriage, unusual jewelry, and an imported bronze jug. Two silver pendants depict spiritual themes: a man's head with a bird covering his forehead, and an unusual female figure adorned with many necklaces, which

The Klinta seiðstafr

have been compared to Freyja's shining Brisingamen. Most researchers think the figure represents this goddess. She takes a wide stance within an enclosing ring, with her hands joined over her bulging belly.[38] (See chapter 9.)

Tuna, Sweden

Women's ship graves were relatively rare, but Hilda Ellis Davidson highlights an earlier trove of Swedish women's ship burials at Tuna, Västmanland, "in what may have been an ancient cult centre associated with the goddess dating from long before the Viking Age."[39] One grave with fine gold jewelry is among the richest in Sweden; eight others were ship burials. One report suggests an oracular function for one of the women because "a seer's staff" was found in her grave goods. It adds that "the women in Tuna had a high status and that they had leading functions in a cult context. ... the women in the boat graves are placed in the middle of the grave-field while the men are buried at the edges." DNA tests show some of the women were related to each other, suggesting a matrilocal social pattern.[40]

Rich female burials were not uncommon in Norse society, as indicated by Swedish instances at Tuna, Valsgärde and Klinta; and others at Hedeby, Germany; Fyrkat, Denmark; Oseberg, Norway; and Peel, Manx Islands.[41] Spectacularly rich burials belonging to elite women go back into the Iron Age, such as those at Reinheim, Germany (ca 375 BCE), and Vix, France (circa 500 bce).

At Tuna, all the ship burials were of women, from the 4th to the 11th century. CE Kristen Ruffoni notes that "the dating suggests that approximately one woman per generation was given a boat or rich chamber burial." She adds, "The series of rich female boat burials and chamber graves, which date from the late Roman Iron Age into the Viking Age, indicate a very old burial tradition which was maintained throughout at least 7 centuries. We do not know who these women were. Some, such as the scholar Judith Jesch, have suggested that they represent a matriarchical society in which women were at the head of the family."[42] From what is known about Germanic societies (except for traces of matrilocality) it seems more

Distaff shaped völr with yarn pattern and spiral adornos. Närke, Sweden

likely that they represent a female sphere of power within a patrilineal society—as was true of their successors, the *völur* of the Viking era.

Birka, Sweden

Three female staff burials were uncovered in the cemetery at Birka, west of Stockholm. One was buried in the large chamber grave Bj.660. Only her teeth remain, her bones having dissolved into the soil. She was laid out on her back, in female dress, with standard female tools (scissors, awl, knife, whetstone) hanging from her belt. Among her jewelry was a silver crucifix, a trade item from the christian world to the south, and an apparent nose piercing. Her iron staff, which had knobs with animal heads rather than the distaff shape, was placed across her hips. Her rich grave goods included brooches that date to the early 900s.[43]

A smaller log-lined chamber grave at Bj.845 held a woman buried in a chair, richly dressed in a cloak lined with beaver skin and with a silk band embroidered with silver around her forehead. She held her staff on her knees, with one end resting on a wooden bucket. Hanging from her belt were a leather pouch, whetstone, and knife. At her feet was an iron box with "complex animal-head fasteners," probably holding clothing or other, now-disintegrated organic substances. Neil Price compares this chest to that of Oseberg with its "cultic" equipment. Her coin pendants put the burial no earlier than 925-943.[44]

The large timbered grave Bj.834 held a double burial of a woman seated on a man's lap. (Her placement raises a question since female sacrifice burials are mentioned in Norse sagas: did both people die at the same time, or does their burial together have more sinister implications?) The couple had rich grave goods; Arab coins in a leather pouch on the woman's belt date the burial to 913-932. Her *völr* was distaff-shaped, with multiple vertical "strands" tightly grouped between polyhedral knobs, with a central horizontal disc. On a platform were draft horses in harness to a cart, characteristic of elite female funeral regalia. Neil Price asks: "Does this imply that the woman in Bj. 834 was the most important occupant?" and suggests that she was a *völva*. Her staff was placed on the ground above the couple and the sword.[45]

Birka Bj.834: a tight distaff shape with knobs

Fyrkat, Denmark

A woman was buried with two staffs, one iron and one of wood, in this royal center of the late 900s. Her wagon burial was the richest in a cemetery of some thirty elite graves, and contained luxury goods imported from the eastern Baltic or Russia.[46] Her clothing was gold-embroidered, and her jewelry included two silver toe rings unique in northern Europe. Hanging from her belt were a knife and whetstone, a leather pouch, and several amulets. One of these was a miniature silver chair of a type found only in female burials, and is interpreted as a ritual "high seat." Another silver amulet, possibly of Finnish make, had pendants shaped like swans' feet.

Beside the Danish priestess rested a bronze bowl with organic residues and a tiny copper bowl that may have held ointment. Near her disintegrating leather pouch—and probably originally inside it—were hundreds of henbane seeds.[47] This psychotropic plant (Hyoscyamus Niger) belongs to the Datura family, which has shamanic associations in many parts of the world. It is connected to women's rainmaking ceremonies in a near-contemporary German penitenial, the *Corrector sive Medicus*. A engraving of a witch in the early 1500s depicts her with henbane, which is listed as a prime ingredient in witches' flying ointments in the same period.

The lady of Fyrkat had the usual female tools—shears, whetstone, spindle whorl—and even an actual meat spit with a spear-like end. Next to it was the shadow of a wooden staff that had fallen into dust. A box containing bones of birds and little animals was placed near her feet. At the foot of the wagon was an oaken chest containing the remains of clothing, in blue and red cloth and leather, embroidered with gold and silver. It also held more unusual items: the lower jawbone of a piglet, and an aged clump of owl pellets that long predated the burial. Finally, in or on the oak box were "the very corroded and fragmented remnants of a metal staff."[48] This is the third instance so far of a staff placed within a chest, or the fourth, if we count a mention in the sagas.

Silver amulet with swan feet pendants, Fyrkat

A magnificent *völr* was found in a Danish

woman's grave at Fuldby (shown at right). It is in the distaff shape, but with a twist, literally: the spokes curve around in a spiral form. Only a few, like the Swedish staff at Närke, have been found in this shape. The Fuldby staff bears traces of a reddish coating, perhaps ochre or cinnabar.

Several wooden staffs have been found. One belonged to the Fykat *völva*. Another had been thrown in a Danish bog in Hemdrup, Jutland. It was inscribed with runes and a cell-like pattern, and carved with humans, animals, and a triquetra knot. One end had been burned, possibly to "kill" the staff.[49] Another, much older *völr* was found in a woman's burial in Hordaland, western Norway. It had "a wooden staff hypothesized to be that of a seeress, dated to around 550 CE."[50] And another wooden staff was discovered in the famous female ship burial at Oseberg.

Oseberg, Norway

Although this site is celebrated as the richest of all Norse burials, the significance of the staff has only recently received due attention. In the early 1990s the woman was reinterpreted as a spiritual figure because of her hollowed birch staff, kept in a chest along with iron lamps, spindles, and distaffs, and many other ceremonial objects. While the Oseberg staff does not conform to the distaff form of the iron staffs, its placement in a chest with spinning equipment is suggestive. So is the thematic connection between the Oseberg staff, found in a chest with three iron locks, to a magical staff in *Fjölsvinnsmál*. It belonged to the giantess Sinmarra who kept it in a chest with nine iron locks (a comparison brought forward by Laszek Gardeła).[51]

Two women were buried in the ship: one in her seventies, the other her forties or fifties. This burial had long been interpreted as belonging to a queen and her sacrificed slave, with various historical figures being nominated as the queen. But archaeological research shows that the women were of the same rank, ate the same diet, and that both had died natural deaths. They lay in state on beds with posts carved with animal heads to which iron rattles were attached.[52] The ship burial held an elaborately carved

Völr *of* Fuldby

wagon, with one panel carved with nine intertwined cats and others with dragons, and three richly carved sledges.

Scholars have begun paying attention to the ceremonial context of the staff and other grave goods—and how they correspond to scenes in the grave's two tapestries. As Price observes, "the burial effectively provided the material requisites for the enaction of the scenes in the tapestries' ritual dramas."[53] The weavings depict processions of carts attended by people making ceremonial gestures, as ravens fly overhead. The carriages might have borne images of deities,[54] or priestesses. Women are shown raising swords, or carrying iron lamps like those found in the chest with the staff.

The Oseberg tapestries depict two women with animal heads, one with a boar mask-cloak and the other with the head of a vulture or falcon, wearing a wing-like cape. She evokes the *fjaðrhamr* ("feather-robe") of Freyja, as Anne Stine Ingstad Ingstad recognized.[55] She interpreted the burial as belonging to a priestess of Freyja, an intermediary between the human and divine. She noted that the name of the site itself means "Hill of the Aesir," and pointed to symbolism of Freyja and Oðinn in ritual scenes depicted on the two tapestries. They include sacrificed men hung from trees, a signature of Oðinn. Freyja's boar connection is attested in *Hyndluljóð* 5, where she rides on one. Other texts describe her as driving a cart drawn by cats[56]—a theme evoked by the cats carved on the wagon.

The Oseberg women were equipped with looms, spindles, and other textile tools. The staff was found among them, made of hollowed wood with five carved sections. It had been cut and the halves bound together.[57] Although the burial had no staff of the distaff-type, two iron chains made up of the same curved spoke distaff shapes were found in the chest that contained the wooden staff. Each link was made of four twisted strands of iron with terminal knobs at the top and bottom, just like the iron *völr* found in other burials.[58] Finally, cannabis seeds were discovered in a pile of feathers, possibly for a cushion stuffing. Their presence could be explained by the women working hemp into cloth, but another possible reason is the plant's psychoactive properties, like the henbane seeds in the Danish *völva's* pouch at Fyrkat and in the Swiss woman's threadbox at St-Aubin.

Isle of Man

Around 950, a bird-headed woman holding a staff was carved on a Manx stone cross
in Kirk Michael.[59] Her robes are shaped like
wings, similar to the falcon woman's dress in the
Oseberg tapestry. Both women are bird-headed. The staff in the Manx relief, with its dan-
gling pendants, compares with similar staffs in
Scandinavian women's burials. (Like Ireland
and Britain, the Isle of Man was colonized by
Vikings in this period.) The carving makes a
direct visual connection between the *völva's* staff
and a masked or shape-shifting woman.

A rich female burial was found in a slab-
lined grave at Peel Castle, on the Manx isle of
St Patrick. Dubbed the "Pagan Lady," she wore
a necklace of amber, jet and glass beads. Lying

*Manx bird-woman
in wing-like robes holding
staff with pendants*

next to her right side, probably placed in her hand, was an iron staff, with
a goose wing and various herbs. An ammonite fossil was among her grave
goods, along with shears, knives, needles, and comb. The woman did not
wear Norse female clothing, with its double brooches, though her burial
was surrounded by pagan Norse male graves.[60] But her staff is of Norse type,
linking her to the *völur*. Her goose wing, however, is reminiscent of 17th
century ritual deposits of swan skins, feathers, and eggs that were recently
found at Saveok in Cornwall.[61] A medieval English woman buried at Bidford-
on-Avon, Warwickshire, also had unusual amulets in her leather bag of
charms and jewelry, including an antler cone. Some scholars read the grave
as belonging to a "cunning woman."[62]

Ireland

A Viking *seiðstafr* turned up in an excavation at Kilmainham near Dublin. Damaged by time and weather, its spherical top has a distaff shape, with
its spokes contorted and broken. An old book on the Viking invasions provides written evidence that *völur* were active in Ireland. The *Cogadh Gaedhel*

re Gallaibh describes how a woman named Otta presided over ceremonies around 838-845. The chronicler says that her husband was a Viking chieftain who ruled over Clonmacnoise in Connaught. She took over the church there for oracular ceremonies: "It was on the altar of the great church she used to give her answers."[63] The *spákona* had need of a high seat, and she was no more reluctant than the Christians were to appropriate the sanctuary of another religion.

Many of the *völva* burials (the Norwegian ship grave at Oseberg, the Swedish one at Klinta, and the Danish wagon burial at Fuldby) belong to women at the highest levels of Norse society. But it seems likely that commoners would have used wooden staffs that have not survived the centuries. Price's summary of the archaeological finds shows eighteen burials with possible *seiðstafs* in Scandinavia; three from Russia, Ireland, and Man; fourteen other possible ceremonial staffs, and another four from from 8th century Norway and Finland.[64] The archeological record shows that the great majority of *seiðstafs* come from women's burials.

So do all of the silver chair amulets that are now interpreted as representing the "high seat" from which the *völur* conducted their ceremonies.[65] Chair amulets of bronze, amber, and silver are found in Swedish and Danish women's burials from the late 800s to about 1000 CE, and at slightly later dates in several buried hoards of looted wealth. None have been found in Christian graves. One silver chair amulet hung on a magnificent necklace of carnelian and rock crystal belonging to a woman at Birka (Bj.632); along with a coiled snake pendant. Price says, "The grave finds strongly suggest that such chairs were among the symbolic equipment of the *völur* and their kind."[66]

SEIÒR

What *seiðr* actually was has been the subject of much debate and speculation. The sagas describe it as a ceremony in which a woman entered an ecstatic state to prophesy or perform other acts of power, such as weathermaking or bringing fish to the shore. "There were *seiðr* rituals for divination and clairvoyance; for seeking out the hidden, both in the secrets of the mind and in physical locations; for healing the sick; for bringing good luck; for controlling the weather; for calling game animals and fish."[67] The magic could also be used to injure, restrain, and do battle.

Seiðr was a raising of power in a ceremony for the purpose of entering into profound states of awareness and connect with spirit realms, especially for the purpose of prophecy. A retinue of singers and other participants surrounded the *völva* in a circle, chanting the spirit-raising songs. *Seið* also appears as a verb of enchantment. Various expressions refer to "raising *seið*" (*efla seið*), or preparing, practicing, accomplishing, or working *seið*.[68] In *Egilssaga*, queen Gunnhildr gives the command for a ceremony to be held: *Lēt seið efla*.[69]

Animal-knobbed top of a völr, *Birka, Sweden (Grave Bj.660)*

For the ceremony, the *völva* mounted a high wooden platform, the *seiðhjallir*. Samplonius Kees compares the platform of the Norse *völur* with the "high tower" of the ancient Bructerian seeress Veleda in Lower Germania. The Latin text says *ipsa edita in turre* ("she sat in a tower") but Kees notes that Latin *turris* can refer to any kind of wood construction on posts.[70]

The origin of the word *seiðr* is still debated. Various proposed etymologies have linked it to "sitting," "sizzling," or "binding."[71] One suggested derivation is from Indo-European *sed, "to sit," related to French *séance*. (That would tie in with *útiseta*, the seeking of wisdom by "sitting-out" on the land.)

The *Encyclopedia of Indo-European Culture* gives the Proto-Indo-European root of *seiðr* as *soito, "sorcery," but also takes note of the root *seh-i (i), "bind," from which derives a different Old Norse meaning for *seiðr*, "band, belt," also found in Old English.[72] In the same vein, Eldar Heide points to a meaning of "cord or string" in Old High German and Old English, which accords with a Norse usage of *seiðr* in *Ragnarsdrápa* 15.[73]

Whatever the original root word was, the magical meaning of *seiðr* was foremost. This is true for its close relative *siden* / *sidsa* in Anglo-Saxon, but also for cognates in other Indo-European languages: Welsh *hud* ('magic'), *hudo* ('work magic, work by magic') and Lithuanian *saîsti* ('intepret a sign, prophesy')..."[74] All of these meanings roughly accord with the Norse sense.

The Old English forms *siden* and *sidsa* are connected with "elfen magic."[75] The Anglo-Saxon concept of *ælfsiden* is "well-paralleled by Snorri's association of the vanir with *seiðr*."[76] The Anglo-Saxon term *ælfsiden*, however, had come to refer primarily to illnesses or afflictions of supernatural origin.

One phrase is especially interesting: *uncuth sidsa*, "uncouth magic," with the original meaning of *uncouth* as "unknown, strange, unusual."[77] In the Norse world, however, the most salient context for *seiðr is* a formal ceremony, with a raised platform, ritual staff, and a repertoire of entrancing litanies sung to help the *völva* enter a profound spiritual state.

chanting galdr

Incantation is a key attribute of the *völva* in the sagas. The spirits had to be called through chants called *varðlokkur* ("binding protection") or *seiðlæti* ("ceremonial songs").[78] It is these songs that enabled the *völva* to enter a trance state. In *Eiriks saga rauða*, Thorbjörg Litilvölva "asked for women who knew the charms [*froeði*] necessary for carrying out *seiðr*."[79] Without them, the ceremony could not proceed.

The *völva* Heiðr traveled around with a chorus of 15 maidens and 15 lads, as recounted in the *Orvar-Odds saga*. "The spell was worked at night and was introduced by beautiful songs (*seiðlæti*) by which spirits were attracted, or else by recitation of formulas (*froeði*)..."[80] The loss of these entrancing litanies, outlawed under christianization, is incalculable.

The *völur* themselves are shown engaging in sacred chant during their ecstasies. As they entered into oracular trance on the *seiðhjallir*, they sang their prophecies to the people gathered around them. The incantatory quality of the *völva*'s revelations "in her [*seið*], in her long song" is underlined in the *Orms Tháttr Stórólfssonar.*[81]

Incantation, or *galdr*, is central to the witch-name *galdrakona*, "chant-woman." Her art is related to ceremonies of the *völur*: "the highest pitch to which the art of *galdr* could be carried was the *seiðr*, 'spell-craft,' a weird kind of chant performed seemingly under cover of nightly darkness."[82] It was indeed a weirding song. There was even a magical verse meter, the *galdralag*, in which the fourth line echoed and varied the preceding line.[83]

Strikingly, numerous sagas signal the onset of the *völva*'s prophetic song with a set refrain: *Ok verger henna ljód á munni*, "And a chant comes to her lips."[84] This refrain runs through many sagas, especially the *fornaldarsögur* ("ancient tellings"). Judy Quinn has shown that the phrase "a chant comes to her lips" almost always refers to a woman who sings oracular verse in an inspired state. Often it is used when a *völva* has been invited to a house for a *seið* ceremony.

and a chant came to her lips

"A chant came to her lips" also occurs in descriptions of women who spontaneously enter into a state of realization in highly charged settings and perform inspirited acts, as when a maiden recognizes a visiting king in disguise, and when an Irish princess fends off a rapist.[85] This chant-refrain also appears in tales about supernatural women, like the giantesses whose precognitive powers the sagas emphasize over and over.[86]

In *Orvar-Odds saga* the Christian hero battles a heathen king and queen, named Alfr ("elf") and Gyða ("priestess"). Queen Gyða is described as a *hofgyðja* (temple-priestess). She defends the city gates by shooting magical arrows from her fingers. When Oddr sets fire to the temples, "a chant comes to the priestess's lips" (*ok verðr henni ljóð á munni*).[87] Occasionally the same phrase is used for a man, but it takes a different form, as Quinn describes:

> When the speaker is male, however, the kind of utterance tends not to be the prophetic *ljóð* that casts such a long shadow over the narrative, but the more mundane *vísa* (verse) or *staka* (ditty), poetry arising from the speaker's own reflections. In both cases the phrase "verða henni / honum á munni" implies that the speakers are unable to suppress the words that come to their lips, but whereas the subject of a female speaker's revelation is characteristically the true nature of something she sees — either in the present or the future — the subject for a male speaker is most often his own deep feelings.[88]

In *Hrólfs saga kraka* 3, each time the *völva* was asked to prophesy, she let out a great yawn before she began speaking in verse. "She flung her jaws wide and yawned excessively, and a chant came to her lips.... Her mouth again gapes wide..."[89] Yawning is a sign of entering trance in many cultures, and it appears in other stories about *völur* in the sagas, as Judy Quinn demonstrates: "The verb *geispa* 'yawn' is found elsewhere in connection with women who have prophetic powers: *Sigrgarðs saga frœkna*, *Þáttr Halfdanar svarta*, and *Þáttr Þorsteins uxafóts*."[90] In *Njáls saga*, a man "wise in charms" yawns when he suddenly perceives imminent danger from hostile spirits:

"Now Svanr started to speak, his mouth yawning wide: 'Ósvífr's fetches are making an attack on us.'"[91] The story of Hauk Hábrók recounts how a sorceress (*heixr*) yawns while feeling men's bodies in order to divine where they will suffer wounds.[92]

Tbe völṛ oṛ seīðstaꝳ

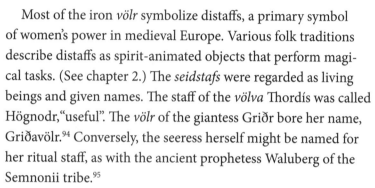

Most of the iron *völr* symbolize distaffs, a primary symbol of women's power in medieval Europe. Various folk traditions describe distaffs as spirit-animated objects that perform magical tasks. (See chapter 2.) The *seidstafs* were regarded as living beings and given names. The staff of the *völva* Thordís was called Högnodr, "useful". The *völr* of the giantess Gríðr bore her name, Gríðavölr.[94] Conversely, the seeress herself might be named for her ritual staff, as with the ancient prophetess Waluberg of the Semnonii tribe.[95]

The *völva* may have shaken her staff, as suggested by the spiraled pendants on the base of the Gävle *völr*. The rings hanging from the spokes on the Norwegian wand from Kaupang would have jangled as the *völva* swung or thumped her staff. Or she might have used her staff as a percussion instrument, pounding it on the ground, or striking it with a stick. Sámi drum paintings show female spirits with double staffs, one in each hand.[96] The *völva* may also have used her *seiðstafr* in ceremonial acts of spinning, like Katla in *Eyrbyggja saga*.

In *Orvar Oddr saga*, a *völva's* staff is shown as having the power to confuse an antagonist. Thordís spákona gives her staff and black cloak (also charged with potency) to a man who is being sued, and instructs him to touch his opponent's cheek with the staff three times. This act freezes the man's memory, causing him to forget what he wanted to say. When the staff-touch is repeated on the other side, it restores his memory.[97]

The *völur* apparently also rode on the *seiðstafr* in the manner of some Siberian shamans, or witches on their broomsticks and

*The flight-*völr *buried with a* völva *at Veka, Norway.*

distaffs. The Norwegian *völva* of Veka in Hordaland was buried astride her *seiðstafr*, as if flying on it.[98] The Norse had many words for a woman who rides by night, in the dark, on a fence or boundary line, or on a wolf or troll. This "riding," as Price comments, "would seem to refer to the soul journey in some way."[99] This is the witch in her shamanic aspect.

In *Hávamál*, Oðinn sees such riders up in the sky and tries to destroy them: "If I see witches riding through the air | I do something to make them lose their way | And they never find their own skin again | And they never find their own spirit again."[100] The word translated as "witches" is *túnriður*, "fence-rider"; and "skins" renders *hamr*, a person's psychic "form" with the capacity for spirit travel. Another word for this ride is *gandriða*, the "spirit-ride," "magical riding," or "staff-ride."[101]

A yew staff carved with a flying spirit or shaman was found in a Danish bog at Hemdrup. The entire surface had been divided into angular sections, in which images and two runic inscriptions had been placed. The runes include the name of a woman, to whom the staff seems to have belonged. Back Danielsson interprets it as a *seiðstafr*, inscribed with images of a shaman and helping spirits, meant to drive away spirits of illness. The staff did not come from a burial, but had been thrust down vertically into the marsh in a ritual act, sometime in the 900s.[102]

Five sets of miniature staffs attached to amulet rings have been found in women's burials. A ring from the Klinta burial has three staffs with several other miniature tools. One at Birka (Bj.60a) has four staffs, nothing else. Another from Kokemäki, Finland, has four staffs and a hook.[103] The magical significance of these amulets is underlined by a 12th century Norwegian law that forbids possession of a "staff or altar, device for sorcery or sacrificial offering, or whatever relates to heathen practice."[104] The staff is the first thing to be prohibited, a reflection of its importance in the old ceremonies, at a time when Christian repression was gaining momentum.

Seiðr was colored by cultural influence from the Sámi, the Aboriginal people of Scandinavia who had been the northern

Völr of distaff form, Gävle, Sweden

neighbors of the Norse for millennia. The sagas show that they were reputed to be powerful magicians. Most of the sorcerers in the *Heimskringla* are Sámi or have a Sámi connection.[105] They are presented as teachers to Norse *völur* or witches. Their ceremonial practice shows continuities with shamanic cultures in North Asia. The staffs of the *völur*, and their use of special chants to enter ecstasy, also have Siberian and Altaian parallels.

Later sagas often compare *völur* and (male) *seiðmaður* to Sámi people—displaying a negative and threatened attitude—or say that the Norse practitioners had learned *seið* from them. They often depict Sámi or Balto-Finnic men as practitioners of *seið*. At times this claim extends to other outsiders, from Britain or the Hebrides.[106] Awareness of the importance of Sámi influence has grown over the past century. However, a key difference is the predominantly male gendering of the *noaidi* among the Sámi, as compared with the predominantly female gendering of the Norse *völur*.

And here we circle back in time to the historic continuity of prophetic women in the Germanic cultures.[107] Over the expanse of Germanic history, remarks Jenny Jochens, "it appears that women did originally possess a monopoly on predicting the future which was an important aspect of magical activity."[108]

ÚTISETA

"Alone she sat out," says the *Völuspá*, when Oðinn came seeking wisdom from the *völva*.[109] She was absorbed in *útiseta*, or *sitja úti*: "sitting out" on the land as a heathen dreamer. Thus, the oldest Eddic poem shows a woman practicing the ancient way of "communing with spirits, out of doors at night."[110] A Latin text describes *sitja úti* as "paying attention with incantations by night in the open air."[111]

Later sagas refer to *útiseta*, and so do the Old Norwegian laws. They "strictly banned all 'sitting out at night for the sake of evoking spirits,' *útiseta at vekja troll upp,* or *útisetumenn er troll vekja,* 'people that sit out at night in order to evoke spirits.'" An 1178 law of an Icelandic bishop condemned those who "sit out at night for the sake of gaining knowledge,' *sitja úti til fródleiks.*"[112]

For the sake of gaining knowledge: that is the crux of it. These land-based vigils have parallels in North American vision quests, Siberian shamans

sitting out at night for the sake of evoking spirits ... [or] for the sake of gaining knowledge...

going alone into the forest for long periods, and Hindu, Buddhist, or Taoist sages meditating in the wilderness. But a nearer connection existed within Europe, in the early medieval German concept of *hliodarsaza*, "hearing-sitting." Kees Samplonius writes, "The compound gloss *hliodarsaza* shows that the practice of spirit-listening was known in Old High German. The last part of the word, *-saza*, derives from the same stem as Old Norse *(úti)seta*, and its first part corresponds to Old English *hleodor*, 'hearing.'"

The seeress of the Völuspá "sitting out" by a waterfall. Lorenz Frølich, 1895. Amazingly, he depicted her holding a distaff-shaped seiðstaf.

De Boor paraphrased the gloss as 'to sit down in order to listen attentively for something.'"[113] Old German *hliozan* was rendered in Latin as *augurari*, "diviner."[114] Its Anglo-Saxon cognate, *hleoðor*, was translated as "sound, divination," and the Old High German *hleodar-sāzo* as *ariolus*, "diviner."[115]

This "sitting-listening" can be compared to a more visual divinatory rite described in the *Corrector sive Medicus*. A circle would be drawn around the seer who would then sit out on the roof "so that you might see from there and understand what will happen to you in the coming year."[116] Another parallel exists in the Anglo-Saxon observance of "waking the well"—sitting up all night beside a fountain—and the brief but precious 11th century account of a woman who held dialogues in the night with the "guardian of the well."[117]

Outward silence would have been part of these practices. But the Norse sources also speak of *galdr* (incantation) in connection with *útiseta* / *at sitja úti*.[118] *Galdr* comes from the verb *gala*, "to sing, to crow, to chant," from which it turned to "enchant."[119] *Galan* was "used of birds' singing," leading one scholar to suggest that the chant might have been done in a twittering or screeching voice.[120] But it probably designated a full-throated song—perhaps like the Sámi *joik*.

Many modern writers create the impression, through selective citations, that *útiseta* was a masculine pursuit. They often emphasize sitting on grave mounds, which is a primarily male theme running through Norse and Celtic tradition.[121] For example, the Welsh prince Pwyll has his vision of Rhiannon while seated on a mound. But of *útiseta* in Nature, William Craigie wrote, "It was originally only done by women; the first mention of a man doing it belongs to the 12th century."[122] Jenny Jochens comments, "In the older literature the practice seems to have been performed mainly by women, although *Orkneyinga saga* mentions a man who '*sat úti um nottina*' [by night]." She contrasts this with later legal texts using *–maðr* and *–menn*, technically gender-neutral: "but the context would imply male performers."[123]

A *sitja úti* was undertaken when a divination was required about some important matter. The *Heimskringla* describes how it was done before a looming battle between two kings. "People say that Gunhild, who was married to Simon, king Hakon's foster-brother, had a witch employed to sit out all night and procure the victory for Hakon; and that the answer was obtained, that they should fight king Inge by night, and never by day, and then the result would be favorable. The witch who, as people say, *sat out* was called Thordís Skeggia…"[124]

An even more dramatic description of *útiseta* appears in the *Sólarljóð*, composed in Iceland around 1200. A sorceress sings: "On the chair of the norns | I sat nine days | then I was raised up on a horse | the giantesses' sun | shone grimly | from the cloud-dripper's clouds."[125] After sitting out for nine days, probably on a stone known as a portal for such journeys, a horse spirit carries her up into the heavens.

Norse literature contains numerous mentions of men sitting out on mounds, or, like Oðinn, under the hanged bodies of sacrificed men. Another wisdom-seeking practice was "going under the cloak." When Iceland was riven by conflict over whether the country should convert to Christianity, it was agreed that Thorgeirr the Lawspeaker should decide. "And when the people came to the booths, then Thorgeirr lay down, and spread his cloak over him, and he lay all day, and the night after, saying no word. And the next morning he sat up and called people to the law-rock."[126] (Keep in mind that these Icelandic legal assemblies were all-male affairs.). But the sagas also refer to women using magical cloaks or sealskins, which they may have drawn over themselves in an act of going-within.[127]

Another medieval source describes a folk practice of *utiseta*, which required a person to bring a gray cat, a gray sheepskin, a walrus or ox-hide, and an axe out to the land; then cover up with the hide and stare at the blade of the axe, looking neither right nor left no matter what happens. This somehow drives off the cat and gains its purpose. Commenting on this old source, Snorri mentions a popular saying about the *völva* Thórdís Skeggja "sitting out," "but a proof thereof I know not."[128] Magnusson and Morris comment, "We draw the conclusion that the modern folklore attribute of a Sitter-Out, the axe, a translation of *skeggja*, is the last that still remains of the old tale of Thórdís as current in the 13th century in Iceland."[129] She made her mark, but the tradition was fading under the Christian regime.

❖

THORBJÖRG LITILVÖLVA : STORIES ABOUT VÖLUR

In *Eiriks saga rauða*, a late medieval saga from Greenland, the *völva* Thorbjörg traveled from place to place, holding ceremonies and prophesying for the people. She wore a black lambskin hood lined with white catskin, and catskin gloves. In a large leather pouch hung on her belt, "she kept the charms (*taufr*) that she used for her sorcery (*fródleikr*)."[130] As discussed earlier, *taufr* is the Norse equivalent of German *zauber*, Dutch *toverie*, and other Germanic words for sorcery and amulets.

> There was in the settlement the woman whose name was Thorbjorg. She was a prophetess (spae-queen) [*spákona*], and was called Litilvolva (little sybil). She had had nine sisters, and they were all spae-queens, and she was the only one now living. It was a custom of Thorbjorg, in the wintertime, to make a circuit, and people invited her to their houses, especially those who had any curiosity about the season, or desired to know their fate...[131]

Each household received Thorbjörg with honors, "as was the custom when a woman of this kind was received."[132] The saga calls her a *vísendakona*, a "woman of knowledge," and *spákona* ("prophetic woman," anglicized in the translation above as "spae-queen").[133]

Eiriks saga rauða mythologizes the *völur* who were then in the process of being disappeared. It connects Thorbjörg with the Nine Sisters who figure prominently in European legends and incantations, ranging from the Nine Maidens of Welsh legend to the nine *korriganed* in Breton or the nine *sinziene* in Romanian faery lore. Norse tradition has its own female Nine: the nine daughters of the sea, the nine giantesses who live in the roots of the cosmic Tree, and the nine valkyries or nine *fylgjur* (protective female ancestral spirits) that figure in many sagas.

The saga presents Thorbjörg as a prestigious person who did not need to defer to anyone. "When she came in, everyone was supposed to offer her respectful greetings, which she received according to her opinion of each person."[134] After greetings, her hosts conducted her to a high seat with a feather cushion. Her host asked her "to cast an eye over his flock, his household and his homestead," but as he showed her around the settlement, she made little comment on what she saw. She was offered a meal that included "the hearts of all the animals available there," so that she tasted the essence of that land. When pressed for her assessment, under the urgent conditions of hardship, she replied she first needed to spend the night there. Having to sleep on it indicates that dreaming figured in her assessment: "An important part of the prophetic process was the nightly episode when the sleeping body traveled to other worlds."[135]

The next day, in preparation for the ceremony, Thorbjörg "asked for women who knew the charms [*froedi*] necessary for carrying out *seiðr* and which are called *varðlokkur*." Now the poem reflects its late medieval date of composition, in a time when christianization had decimated the old ways. It was difficult to find someone who knew the chants. It transpired that only one woman, who was a Christian, had learned them from her grandmother. Under pressure, she agreed to sing them. "Then the women formed a circle around the *seiðhjallr* on top of which was Thorbjörg."[136]

she asked for women who knew the charms necessary for carrying out seiðr and which are called varðlokkur.

A gap in the narrative appears at this crucial point, as the ceremony begins. The ceremony itself is not described, nor the transformation of the *völva*. We learn only that at some point after the chants, Thorbjörg made her prognostications in a ceremonial setting: "The people went up to the *vísendakona*, and each asked after that which they were most concerned to know; she gave them good answers, and little that she had said was not fulfilled." The Norse had a word for that, *sannspár*, which meant "prophesying what proves to be true." The *Orvar-Odds saga* also shows the *völva* greeting each querent who comes up to her with the words "It's good to see you here," addressing each by name.[137]

Even a poet of the Christian era, when the oracular culture was being destroyed, assessed Thorbjörg's abilities positively. Some scholars, starting with Dag Strömbäck, say that the poet aimed to glorify Guðriðr Thorbiarnardóttir, a bishop's mother who had several other ecclestical descendants, and to illustrate her superiority over the heathens.[138] That is likely; but there is more. Thorbjörg Litilvölva makes a point of blessing the Christian singer, sets her at ease, and shows appreciation for her contribution. The poet does not demonize her, even at that late date, and portrays her prophecy as accurate.

Other sagas repeat the theme of traveling seeresses. The *Nornagests tháttir* says that "*völur*, which were called *spákonur*, fared about the land then and prophesied the *ørlögs* of men, wherefore many men invited them home and prepared feasts for them and gave them good treasures when they parted."[139] (The story is borrowed from foreign traditions about the third fate who is offended and curses the child to live only until a designated log, or in this case a candle, burns out.)[140] The three legendary *völur* in *Nornagests tháttir* are conflated with the norns; but like living *spákonur* they are accompanied by *sveit manna*, "a following of people." In *Orms þáttr Stórólfssonnar* "a völva travels with her *sveit*, 'retinue,' again moving from farm to farm to give prophecies."[141]

völur, which were called spakonur, fared about the land then and prophesied orlög

The travels of the *völva* Oddbjörg are described in *Víga-Glums saga*. One hostess plies her with gifts and tries to extract a good prediction for her son, but "Oddbjörg replies that the quality of her welcome will not make any difference to her prediction." She gets a rude response to this, and the prophecy for the sons comes out badly.[142] The integrity of the seeresses was being maligned, as clergy had been doing for some time in more southerly regions.

The picture of traveling *seiðkonur* is fleshed out in *Orvar-Odds saga*, a *fornaldarsaga* from late 13th century Iceland. "There was a woman named Heiðr, and she was a *völva* and *seiðkona*, and by her art she knew beforehand matters which had not happened. She went to events widely throughout the land, when farmers invited her; she told people their fortunes and the seasons and other matters." So far, this is very much like the story of Thorbjörg in Greenland, and this account too refers to the necessity of chants for the *seiðr*. What comes next adds a new piece of information: "She had thirty people with her, fifteen lads and fifteen girls. It was a large company, since there had to be a great incantation wherever she was."[143] Again the chant is underlined as an essential foundation of the ceremony.

The *völur* clearly exerted considerable authority in Norse society. Lotte Hedeager writes: "The *völva* (staff-bearer) was the real power, and the most feared, in society and their power far exceeded even the most powerful kings and warriors."[144] At times it did, and the prestige and influence of the *völur* is undeniable, especially before 1100, but those were violent times riven by blood feuds. The sagas themselves show *völur* under pressure from powerful men, who sometimes attack them and try to coerce them.

Heiðr in Völuspá and the Sagas

Many Norse texts speak of a seeress named Heiðr. Some scholars translate her name as "bright, shining," referring, as Ursula Dronke remarks, to the radiance that the *spákona* brings into people's homes as she makes her circuit of oracular residencies. Dronke also calls attention to *heið* as a constant term of reference for the sacred mead that nourishes divinity, wisdom, and life. The goat from whose udders this mead flows at the Tree of Life is named Heiðrún. The theme of golden mead is underlined by a second name, Gullveig, closely connected to Heiðr, and interpreted many scholars as a form of Freyja.[145] (See chapter 9 for more on Gullveig).

A growing number of scholars relate the name Heið to English *heathen*, Old Norse *heiðinn*, modern Swedish *hed*, German *heide*, and Dutch *heiden*.[146] The word may be a loan from Old English *hæð* 'untilled, uncultivated land.'"[147] As in Britain and Germany, *heiðinn* had become a term for people who followed pre-christian ways. It is this strong heathen valence that propels the emergence of Heiðr as a name for the archtypical seeress in the Poetic Edda, and in later sagas.

There was a woman named Heiðr, and she was a völva and seiðkona, and by her art she knew beforehand matters which had not happened.

The earliest and most important Heiðr is the mythic *völva* described in *Völuspá* 22:

> **Heiðr they called her wherever she came to houses**
> **Völva who prophesies well, enchanter of spirits [or wands]**
> **She worked *seiðr* wherever she could, the *seið* of mind play**
> **She was ever the joy of an evil woman.**[148]

This stanza, succinct but loaded with possible meanings, has been translated and interpreted every which way. The multiple meanings and ambiguities in the Old Icelandic text have stimulated conflicting interpretations. They require considerable analysis, so we will take it line by line. The beginning is straightforward, since we have already looked at the possible meanings of Heið and the custom of *völur* traveling from house to house to hold *seiðr*. The second line is less clear—and not only because English equivalents for the concepts are lacking. It reads: *völu velspáa, vitti hún ganda.*

völva who prophesies well, enchanter of spirits / she worked seiðr wherever she could...

"*Völva* who prophesies well" is the favored reading of *völu velspáa*.[149] But because the 13th century manuscript contains no diacritics, *velspáa* has occasionally been read as *vélspáa*,[150] with a nearly opposite meaning. Is it *vel-*, "well," or *vél-*, "deceitful"? In a thoroughly heathen context, it is unlikely that the poet would disparage a *völva's* prophecy; but the stanza does just that a few lines down, and the poem was recorded by Christian scribes. However, *velspáa* has the savor of a timeworn phrase in praise of a *spákona*. Ursula Dronke translates *völu velspáa* as "a prophetess of good fortune."[151]

The next phrase, *vitti hún ganda*, is disputed, with many possible readings. Various translations render the line as "she charmed them with spells,"[152] or "she charmed spirits,"[153] or "conjured spirits to tell her."[154] Bray translates as "wands she enchanted."[155] "Staffs" works too: "she consecrated the staves."[156]

Gandr is related to the English "wand," but in Norse it has other meanings that refer to helping spirits and to a broader sense of "magic"—especially incantation. We even find *spáganda*, "a rod of divination," which points back toward the *seiðstafr*.[157] *Gandir* is sometimes used to describe wolves or other animals.[158] The "helping-spirit" sense of *ganda* is underlined by a reference to prophetic spirits of the Sámi "which are called *ganda*," and can predict many things to come, according to the (Christian) *Historia Norvegiae*.[159]

Seið hún hvar er hún kunni, seið hún hugleikin. (*Völuspá* 22:3) Translations of this line vary tremendously, because English has no equivalent for the verb *seið* or the noun *hugr*. So we get: "She made *seiðr* wherever she could, with *seiðr* she played with minds."[160] Or: "Cast spells where she could, cast spells on the mind."[161] A less literal rendition gives: "Spells many wove she, light-hearted wove them," interpreting *hugleikin* as playful magic.[162] Another translator conveys a sense of *seiðr* as magic: "Minds she bewitched, that were moved by her magic."[163]

But Ursula Dronke emphasized the ecstatic shamanic dimension: "Sorcery she practiced, possessed."[164] Her translation emphasized the use of the passive form of *leikin*, which implies that the spirit that Heiðr summoned was moving within her. Neil Price fleshes this out: "the verb can also mean 'to move' in the sense of drifting or swaying. The lines could equally well be rendered '*Seiðr* she had skill in / through *seiðr* she [was?] moved.'"[165] Price brings in an important connection; the same word *leikin* is used for the female *tunriður* flying in the sky in *Hávamál* 155. This is another usage of "motion"—and movement in the spirit at that. *Hugleikin* is a compound word, from *hugr*, "mind / spirit," and *leikin*, "play."[166] (See chapter 5.)

The final line of the stanza reads: *æ var hún angan illrar brúðar*. This phrase is usually translated, "She was ever the joy (or delight) of evil women." But the translation of *illrar brúðar* as "evil women" bears closer examination. *Brúðar* means "bride," or more broadly, "married woman"—and it is singular: "woman," not "women."[167] Jenny Blain notes that *illrar* also carries

The story of Gullveig and Heiðr follows verses about the Norns in the Codex Regius (stanzas 20-22)

meanings of "wretched, unhappy."[168] So a counter-reading of the passage sees a visiting *völva* bringing hope and help to women who are abused or alienated in patrilocal marriages.

Even if the definition of "evil" is accepted as the intended meaning, the poet's negative attitude toward the *völva* could be an artifact of Christian redactors. But there is something more: instead of *illrar brúðar*, the Codex Regius has instead *illrar thióðar*, "evil nations," or "peoples." Someone later emended *thióðar* to *brúðar* by adding three characters above it—but without erasing the original text.[169]

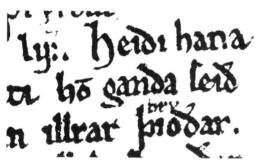

Superscript of brú *over* þioðar *Codex Regius*

Using "people," instead of "woman," casts a different light on things. If it was a slip, it was a revealing one, since the passages that follow are about a culture-war between peoples, and Norse sagas are full of allusions to the indigenous Sámi as "sorcerers." The witch in question, of course, remains a woman.

Either way, as a woman or as a people, the power of *seiðr* in the hands of an outsider or subaltern group was regarded as a threat and therefore judged negatively, to the point of being called "evil."

MANY VÖLUR NAMED HEIÐR

Heiðr is "a name often applied to wisewomen and prophetesses."[170] She of the *Völuspá* is the prototype for other Heiðs who appear later in the sagas. The *Örvar Odds saga* presented Heið as a woman endowed with second sight, who traveled with a 30-child chorus. The older version of the saga explains that their contribution was "great chanting" for the night ceremonies, which were done outdoors.[171] Incantation could not be more strongly underlined as an important element of the *völva's* ceremony.

As the refrain is repeated: "A chant came to her lips," the inspired *spákona* begins to foretell Oddr's fate in verse. He does not want to hear it, but Heiðr is "unwilling to be bullied or beaten"[172] (The later sagas often show warriors threatening violence against *völur*, and this one is no exception.) The seeress defies her antagonist: "I won't be put off by your threats, because your lot is to be made known. I may proclaim it, and you must listen." She prophesies a long and prosperous life for him, but predicts he will die from his horse Faxi. Oddr becomes furious and strikes her face, drawing blood. Declaring that such an attack is unprecedented, the *völva* leaves the hall, taking the host's gifts for her prophecies with her.[173]

The warrior goes off to kill his horse and buries it, muttering that he will ward off "that curse." Years later, he acts on a longing to visit his home farm. Walking around the land, he boasts that he has beaten the prophecy. At that moment, he trips over the horse's skull and is bitten by a snake inside it. In later versions of this story, a line is added emphasizing that a *völva* always speaks the truth.[174] Reverence for the old ways is palpable, and so is people's reluctance to forswear them. The expression *forspár* ("foreseeing the future") has a corollary, *sannspár*, "prophesying what proves to be true."[175]

Ukrainians told a similar story about the Kievan prince Oleg, again counterposing a pagan seer against a warlord. A *volkhv* (wolf-shaman) told the prince that his horse would cause his death. Oleg had the horse taken far away. Hearing it had died four years later, he went to see it, and put his foot on its head. A snake emerged from the head and gave him a fatal bite.[176] Both legends illustrate the persistence of popular belief in the prophetic power of the *volkhvy* and the *völur*—as well as Rus Viking influence on the eastern Slavs.

Another *völva* called Heiðr is described as traveling a circuit of settlements in *Hrólfs saga kraka*. She is invited to prophesy at a feast hosted by the wicked king Fróði. This account is important for its depiction of yawning as a sign of entering deep trance, as with Siberian shamans[177]: "She flung her jaws wide and yawned excessively, and a chant [*seiðrinn*] came to her lips."[178] Later, after the king threatens violence, she yawns again: "Her mouth again gapes wide, and the sorcery becomes difficult." That is because the *völva* is resisting, while in prophetic trance, Fróði's attempt to force her to reveal the whereabouts of two boys that he wants to kill to consolidate his power.

Yet another Heiðr is described in a classic shamanic flight on an animal. In *Friðþjófs saga*, Heiðr and Hamglama, two "women skilled in magic," went to the *seiðhjallr* "with charms and sorcery."[179] They sank into a trance, leaving their bodies behind. They flew in the spirit to prevent a ship full of warriors from landing, and approached them riding on the back of a whale.

These late heroic epics demonize the *seiðkonur* and show men overcoming them by hurling weapons at their animal doubles. Spearing the whale causes the witches to fall off the *seiðhjallr* and break their backs.

The same literal downfall of a seeress occurs in the English *Gesta Herwardi*. A sorceress on a high seat casts spells for the armies of William the Conqueror, but when they fail, she falls and breaks her neck.[180] The *Anglo-Saxon Chronicle* tells the story differently. During the seige at Ely in 1071, which was the last stand of the Saxons, a Norman witch made battle magic in a wooden tower (probably a *seið* platform) but Hereward brought down the tower by setting it on fire.[181]

Heið, a "foster mother" of Harald Fairhair, is described as a seeress, a tall woman in a skin dress, and a large gaping mouth. Harald sent two men to her with a ring—just as the *völur* were given jewelry in return for prophecy—and offerings of bacon and butter. "She made the two men he sent to her take off their clothes and kiss her, and then she stroked them all over, a familiar method of discovering whether they were to receive wounds, found in stories of witchcraft. She foretold what might happen on their journey, and gave them two magic stones, which they could use if attacked by their enemies."[182] This divinatory stroking was called *thriefa*.[183]

Finally, Heiðr is listed among the names of giants in the *Hyndluljóð*, in a section known as *Völuspá hin skamma*, "the Shorter Prophecy of the *Völva*." This poem within a poem includes a line (*Hyndluljóð* 33) about the mystic ancestry of seeresses: "All the *völur* sprang from Viðólfr ("wood-wolf"). Hyndla herself is a wolf-riding giantess who recites hidden wisdom at the request of Freyja. Another wolf-riding giantess, Hyrrokin, appears in *Gylfaginning* 49 (more about her in chapter 6).

So, many *völur* in the sagas are named Heiðr. But *heiðr* also appears as a *word* for "sorceress" in the prose sources, 66 times by Neil Price's count.[184] In her numerous appearances as a *völva*, "Heiðr's prophecies always come true."[185] Other mythologized seeresses appear as characters in the sagas. A *völva* called Skuld—named after the third Norn—goes into a black tent and mounts a *seiðhjallir* to make battle magic for Hrólf's army.[186] There is also a Huldr in Snorri's *Heimskringla*, whose name may relate to the German goddess Holda / Holle / Hulda, or the *huldre*, "hidden" forest faeries of Norway. In the story, Huldr s a Sámi *seiðkona* who is hired by queen Drifr to bring her faithless husband, Vanlandi, back to northern Norway, or failing

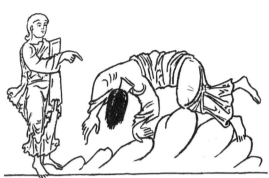

The overthrow and downfall of a powerful woman was a favored theme in the 11ᵗʰ century. In the Psychomachia *of Prudentius she is the allegorical Luxuria, Latin for "sensuality." Church sculptures depicted Luxuria with serpents at her breasts, like the Frankish Mother Earth*

that, to kill him. Huldr performs the *seiðr*, and Vanlandi is overcome by longing to go to "Finnland," but his men prevent him. Then he falls asleep and a *mara* created by Huldr presses him to death.[187] Although the story identifies her as Sámi, propagating the stereotype of Sámi sorcery, Huldr is a Norse name, and the Norse story is no more accurate than Greek legends about Libyan or Lemnian women—that is, not at all.

Another woman of magical power is Hildr, daughter of Hogni. She elopes with Hedinn and in the ensuing battles with her father, goes out every night to revive the dead warriors.[188] Other versions of the story of Hildr's reviving spells are repeated by Saxo Grammaticus and in the *Sörla Tháttr*.[189]

GYÐJUR

Another important category of Norse priestesses are the *gyðjur*. *Ynglingasaga* names Freyja as a *blotgydja*, "priestess of sacrifice." *Blót* refers to blood sacrifice, and comes from the same root as English *blessing*. "Blessing" descends from *bledsian / bloedsian*, "to consecrate, make holy (with blood)".[190] The *gydjur* are difficult to separate from the *seiðkonur*, and in fact Snorri juxtaposes these two forms of ritual (*seið* and *blót*) in describing Freyja—who is preeminent in both of them.[191] The "wise Vanir" are collectively expert in spiritual arts. After joining the Aesir, Njordr and Freyr are appointed as *blótgoð*.[192]

Icelandic linguists say that "goddess" was the original meaning of *gyðja*, and that "priestess" developed as a secondary meaning.[193] (There is the core of ceremony: divinity embodied.) So *gyðja* seems to be related to *goð*, a word that was gender-neutral in Norse—although "*goð* in the older poetry is

A painted stone at Kivik, circa 1500 bce, two millennia before the Viking era:
gyðjur *approaching an altar, snake-headed ancestral women, or both?*

used about female divinities such as the sun and the goddess Skaði."[194] *Goð*
appears in the singular "very seldom, and only if applied to a single goddess
or the like," as when Skaði is called *öndurgoðs* in *Haustlong* 7, or Freyja is
called Vanagoð ("deity of the Vanir").[195]

Gyðja is closely related to *gudja*, the Old Gothic word for "priest" in
Ulfila's Bible translation.[196] The Old Norse feminine *gyðja* perfectly corresponds to the Gothic form; the corresponding masculine form would have
been **gyði*, which is unattested in Norse. The male priestly title *goði* appears
relatively late in Icelandic, where it denotes an office that had become more
political than religious.[197]

The *gyðjur* poured out offerings on rock altars (*hörgr*). In *Herverar saga*,
the royal woman Álfhildr reddened the altar (*horgr*) with sacrificial blood
every night.[198] Fire offerings were used too. Freyja describes how a man
burned so many offerings on her stones that they became vitrified: "Always
Óttar put faith in goddesses."[199]

Antecedents of the *gyðjur* may be depicted on the painted stones at Kivik,
Sweden, where processions of women approach altars, nearly 2000 years
before the Viking era.[200] "Several indications point to an original preference
for women to perform the offices of sacrifice, and such *gyðjur* are still heard

of in the Viking period; to them belonged especially the sacrifice to the *dísir*, the sacrifice to the elves, and the cult of the spirits of the land."[201] In other words, these women led ceremonies for the ancestral mothers and Nature spirits. In the 11th century, the Christian skáld Sigvat described how in his travels in a remote region of Sweden, he came to a farm where the *álfablót* was going on. A woman stood in the doorway and drove him off, "For we are heathen people." She "declared that she held elf-sacrifice within."[202]

The sexual politics of seiðr

The sagas are overwhelmingly masculine narratives told from the standpoint of the social elite. The acts of men (and male gods) far outweigh those of women (and goddesses).[203] Still, Eddic poetry and the sagas indicate that *seiðr* constituted a female sphere of power that preceded what some are now calling "Oðinnic magic." *Seiðr*—and prophecy—are presented as female acts and powers. In the *Völuspá* itself, the seniority of the seeress is underlined in the *völva*'s sardonic questioning of why Oðinn, who is supposed to be "all-wise," must come to her for prophecy.[204]

Snorri's *Ynglingasaga* makes a key statement about the origins of *seiðr*, in which Freyja is the expert, not Oðinn: "The daughter of Njorðr was Freyja; she was a *blótgyðja* [sacrificial priestess]; she was the first to teach *seiðr* to the Aesir, as it was practiced among the Vanir."[205] This passage links Freyja to *seiðr*—as a priestess. It makes her its foundational (and therefore senior) practioner among the Aesir. And it describes *seiðr* as a ceremony of the Vanir, whose great spiritual wisdom is repeatedly emphasized in the lore.

The *Lokasenna* makes it clear that the Norse considered *seiðr* a female activity, to the point of unmanning a male who engaged in it. In a verbal duel, Oðinn taunts Loki for being womanish, and for living eight years underground, milking cows and bearing children fathered by giants. His line, "And I call that craven," actually uses the word *argr*, a word that conveyed gender-nonconformity with contemptuous overtones, "unmanly."[206] Loki retorts that Oðinn also ventured into women's realm, equating his practice of *seiðr* with femininity:

> **But you once practised *seiðr* on Samsey**
> **and you beat on a *vétt* as *völur* do**
> **like a *vitka* [wisewoman] you journeyed among**

the people, and I thought that showed an *argr* nature.[207]

By performing *seiðr,* Oðinn becomes "like a *vítka,*" which means a "wise one"—in the feminine—or "sorceress." Other translations say, "beat on a *vétt,* or "struck a *vétt,*" or "tapped on a *vétt* like the *völur.*"[208] Strömbäck, one of the most eminent scholars of Norse religion, interpreted this line as referring to shamanic drumming. *Vétt* can mean "lid" or shield," which brings to mind Roman references to Celts beating on shields before battle.[209] *Vétt* was used in kennings for shields, like that of a valkyrie—*Hildar véttin*—in the *Haustlong* poem.[210]

The passage shows that male wizardry had homosexual or transgender connotations, in accord with the statement in *Ynglingasaga* that it was considered shameful for men to practice *seiðr.* The declaration that doing *seiðr* was a female act of power, and thus *ergi* ("unmanly") is repeated in *Helgakviða Hundingsbana I,* when Sinfjötli accuses Guthmund of being a *völvi* and practicing sorcery: "A witch wast thou on Varins Isle | didst fashion falsehoods and fawn on me, hag | to no wight wouldst thou be wife but to me..."[211] This exemplifies Norse men's habit of claiming to have sexually dominated another man as a form of oneupmanship. Comparing other men to women in any way was in fact the classic mode of male insult, a way of declaring them to be social inferiors.

Besides expertise in *seiðr,* prophetic foreknowledge is female terrain in the Norse texts. In the *Lokasenna,* Freyja declares, "Frigga knows all fates (*ørlög*), though she herself says nothing." The statement is repeated in *Gylfaginning* 20: "She knows the fates of men even though she does not speak prophecies."[212] Also in the *Lokasenna,* Oðinn attributes the same foreknowledge of *ørlög* to Gefjon (while tacking on his own claim to it).[213] As the sagas attest, Oðinn craved this knowledge, is shown as competing in and appropriating this female sphere.

Since Freyja herself was a priestess (*blótgydja*), it seems likely that she would have taught her arts to women—not because the men wanted nothing to do with it, but because it was a recognized female sphere of power. In *Lokasenna* 32, Loki calls Freyja a *fordæða* ("sorceress"). The *Thrymksviða* refers to her feather-robe, the *fjaðrhamr,* which gives her the power of flight. Loki is described borrowing her shamanic garment for a mission[214]—but the skálds never show Freyja herself flying in this feather-robe.

A stray mention in the Prologue to *Snorra Edda* names one other goddess as a prophetess. It says that Thor found a *spákona* in the northern part of the world "who is named Sibyl, which we call Sif."[215] The name Sibyl shows a romanizing influence on the christian skálds, whether or not Snorri's identification of Sif as a *spákona* is authentic.

medieval misogyny and modern bias

The subject of *seiðr* in modern scholarship remains fraught with sexual politics and assumptions. There is a perceptible reluctance to acknowledge that *völva* and *seiðr* are strongly gendered female, in spite of the written and material evidence. Price writes, "The emphasis on women practitioners would seem to be reflected in the archaeological record, with the overwhelming predominance of objects from female graves."[216] But not so fast, he cautions, since the sagas do describe men performing *seiðr*. Well, yes; but the issue is not whether men ever did it; it is that female *seiðr* is the prevailing pattern, particularly in public ceremonies. And the Norse view that performing *seiðr* feminized males should be taken into account.

The skálds' salute to Oðinn as the most eminent figure of *seiðr* directly contests this female predominance. As Judy Quinn observes, "The euhemerising account of Óðinn's acquisition of knowledge in *Ynglinga saga* does not mention the existence of *völur*."[217] Nevertheless it is women who the sagas depict as leading *seiðr* in public ceremonies, as even Mircea Eliade had to admit.[218] Jenny Jochens presents ample reason for seeing prophecy and *seidr* as having originally been "a female monopoly."[219]

Eliade went to some lengths to discount the female preëminence in *seiðr*, arguing that what women did wasn't that important anyway. In his eyes it was only "sorcery" and "minor magic."[220] Here he flatly contradicted Snorri's definition of *seiðr* as "the art which has the greatest power."[221] Eliade also assigned "necromancy" to the "lesser" sphere of female magic; but in Norse tradition it is Oðinn and other male characters, not the *völur*, who practice necromancy and coercive sorcery.

While Eliade regarded the *völva* as engaged in mere "divination," he allowed wider shamanic latitude for the Celtic *fili* who sought answers to questions through incubation.[222] Eliade viewed shamanism as a male sphere that began to admit women only in its decadence. Even earlier, Dag

Strömbäck had claimed that *seiðr* was originally a male practice, which became despised as women took it up.[223] Stephen Glosecki responded to this male-dominance bias by dryly wondering whether "rather than being beneath men, the *seiðr* may not have been above them, originally."[224]

Ynglingasaga sings the praises of Oðinn as the great magical adept. It describes him as a shapeshifter who could travel in the spirit in animal form while his body lay motionless, among many other powers. It says, "Oðinn knew the skill from which follows the greatest power, and which he performed himself, that which is called *seiðr*." Snorri adds that this is what allowed him foreknowledge of the future and the power to cause harm. "But this sorcery [*fjolkyngi*], as is known, brings with it so much *ergi* that manly men thought it a shame to perform, and so this skill was taught to the priestesses."[225]

Before analyzing *ergi*, let's re-examine what is being claimed here. The poem states that the reason for teaching the priestesses *seiðr* was that men disdained it. But the *gyðjur* are known to have been were powerful, socially important women, with traditions of their own, even though male skálds barely allude to them. *Ynglingasaga* presents Oðinn as the great master of *seiðr*, even while acknowledging that Freyja was the one who taught the art to the Aesir, who did not know it before. Snorri does not actually say that Freyja taught Oðinn, as modern writers often assume, though that could be extrapolated from him being the foremost male practitioner of *seið* among the Aesir. The important thing is that prophecy remained entrenched as a female power, to the point that Oðinn himself is described going to a *völva* looking for prophecy on two occasions.

In *Völuspá*, the *völva* is "sitting out" alone on the land, when Oðinn comes to her offering rings and necklaces in return for her oracular wisdom. He cannot dominate her; on the contrary she speaks to him scornfully, and "implicitly warns Odin not to threaten her."[226] That exchange is discussed in more detail in the final chapter; but it is instructive to note that many commentators see Oðinn as *commanding* this *völva* to rise from the grave— in spite of the fact that she is clearly stated to be engaged in *útiseta*.

In *Baldrs Draumr*, the god seeks out a dead *völva* who is buried outside the eastern gates of Hel, in order to find out what the bad dreams of his son Baldr signify. Displeased at being roused from her sleep, she answers him, unwillingly, that in Hel they are preparing couches and mead for Baldr. But when he asks about the maidens who are not weeping for Baldr, the *völva* recognizes that the "Wanderer" is actually Oðinn. (Her discovery recalls that of the Witch of Endor who recognizes Saul once she has entered trance.) Exposed, Oðinn insults her: "No *vala* [*völva*] art thou, nor wise woman; rather art thou mother of three giants."[227] The non-weeping Maidens might be the Norns themselves.

Claims that women practiced "low magic" are common coin,[228] but in fact males, Oðinn in particular, are shown performing harmful sorcery much more than beneficial:

> **The strongest form of magic was the seiðr. This included two things: the art of enchantment and the art of prophecy, the latter with some suggestion that it actually exercised an influence on destiny. The first kind was regarded as an ignoble art, because it was usually aimed at causing harm to fellow men, as in producing disease, death, or madness. It was practiced in great part by men.... Prophecy on the other hand was practiced by women and the prophetess was given the name** *völva* **from her magic staff, the** *völr*.[229]

Prophecy was understood as influencing events, and this social reality is of great significance. This concept is sometimes called "operative divination."[230] Back in 1928, I. Reichborn-Kjennerud proposed that the seeress did more than predict: she shaped outcomes.[231] The Scottish name "weirding woman" implies the same kind of magnetic pull on the course of events.

sexual politics in norse myth

Numerous examples exist of individual men using *seiðr* in coercive sorcery, even on supernatural women. In *Skirnismál*, the hero comes to the giantess Gerðr in her underworld realm, as the messenger of Freyr, who wants to marry her. Skírnir breaches the boundaries of her realm—her very name Gerdr, "enclosure," symbolizes a protected boundary—and must pass through a fiery wall to reach her. The wall of flames is "traditionally the enclosure around the Otherworld."[232]

Skírnir accepts Gerðr's hospitality, and then proceeds to coerce her into an unwanted marriage. She forthrightly refuses Freyr's proposal, at which point Skírnir resorts to cursing and threatening her with his sword. At one point he says, *Ek síða thér*, "I *síða* to you," using the verb form of *seiðr* to indicate that he is magically forcing her.[233] He menaces Gerðr with a "taming wand": "I strike thee, maid, | with my magic staff | To tame thee to work my will..."[234] He goes on pronouncing dire curses against the giantess over the next twelve stanzas, until she is forced to yield.

Bizarrely, some scholars have interpreted this story as a "sacred marriage," highlighting Freyr's connection to fruitfulness of the land. But those who propose a hierogamy for this story disregard the obvious use of force on the woman. Such "marriages" are rape, and not to be confused with anything "sacred."

The *Lokasenna* presents a diametrically opposed view of Freyr, where Týr says that "he causes no girl to weep, nor any man's wife."[235] The other notable Vanr male, Njörd, is also distinguished by his mildness. So there is an incongruity; except in *Skírnirsmál*, Freyr presents as a peaceable figure. (The real contradiction is between love and male-dominant marriage systems.) Adam of Bremen, whose Latin account calls the Swedish god Fricco, wrote that he "bestows peace and pleasure on mortals."[236] He relates that libations were made to this god at weddings, and describes his phallic statue at the Swedish temple in Uppsala (1080 CE). Some scholars see Freyr in the many small *guldgubbar* foil plaques that were interred in building foundations, which often depict couples and have been interpreted as betrothals.

Ursula Dronke offers evidence that the ritual violence against women in *Skírnirsmál* has ancient Indo-European roots. The *Brhadaranyaka Upanishad* shows a parallel ceremony in which a man coerces a desired woman. The man is to approach a woman as Srī, goddess of abundance—but he treats her as an object, and even commits violence against her: "if she does not yield, he should buy her with presents [as Skírnir offers magical jewels and golden apples to Gerdr]. If she still does not grant him his desire, he should strike her with a rod [as Skírnir hits Gerðr with the *gambantein*] or with his hand, uttering the curse, 'I by my power and my glory take thy glory to myself,' and she becomes inglorious."[237] Another curse on a woman to force her to yield sexually is found in the *Atharva Veda* (I, 14).[238]

A Indo-European history of men using rods to punish resistant women goes deep. Roman law prescribed it, with the paterfamilias chastising women within the family and the *pontifex maximus* authorized to cane disobedient Vestals at the state level. Roman men saw no problem with whipping women. Norse men used the *gambantein*, in a sorcery of male dominance.[239]

A real-life example of such a curse is a 14th century charm carved on a rune-staff found in Bergen, Norway. The man calls on *álfar*, trolls, giants, and valkyries to deprive the woman he desires of all power of action and to afflict her until she yields to him: "I send to you, I *síða* to you a she-wolf's lust and restlessness... Never sit, never sleep... love me as you love yourself."[240] This unknown man uses very similar language to Skírnir—"I *síða* to you"—with the same imprecations that drive her to distraction and uncontrollable lust.

In Eddic poetry, Oðinn displays an oppositional and domineering attitude toward women. He rejoices in his sexual conquests and deceptions of women.[241] He claims that his power was greater than that of female magical adepts, boasting of overcoming them with magic: "Mighty love-spells I used on the witches | those who I seduced from their men."[242] Meanwhile Thórr brags that he fought berserk women, "she-wolves," on Hlésey Isle.[243]

In *Hávamál*, Oðinn boasts of using magic to trick seven witch sisters into sex, a "prolonged sexual conquest of sorceresses ... described over four strophes."[244] But in the same poem he condemns "the false love of women"[245] and warns men against sleeping in a witch's arms, lest she cast a spell over them.[246] (The word translated as "witch" is *fjölkunningi konu*, "a woman skilled in magic."[247]) This is the sexual double standard writ large, unabashed in its hypocrisy.

Only Billingr's daughter succeeds in fending off Oðinn's advances, in *Hárbarðzljóð*. He had hoped "to work his will with her," but she got the better of him, promising him love if he returned later on. But he got nothing, finding the hall locked and guarded, and a dog tied next to her empty bed.[248] Of course, women were not the only targets of Oðinn's deceit and trickery; he was well known for deliberately sowing strife and war.[249]

But like Zeus, Oðinn is a calculating rapist[250], most dramatically in the story of Rinðr the princess of Ruthenia.[251] Oðinn wants to impregnate her with a son who will become the instrument of his vengeance for Baldr's death, as foretold. But Rinðr refuses him.[252] In *Sigurðardrápa*, he uses magic to overcome her resistance: *seið Yggr til Rindar* (Yggr [Oðinn] did *seið* on Rindr").[253] In the version of the Dane Saxo Grammaticus, Othinus makes sexual advances on Rinda three times, and each time she physically repels him. After his fourth try fails, he drives her mad by striking her with a rune-carved stick (again the *gambantein*).

Then Oðinn comes in female disguise, calling himself the healer Wecha.[254] He tells Rinda's father that her only cure is a potion so hideous that the patient must be bound. So it is done, and then he rapes the maiden. The gods banish Oðinn—but for the scandalous cross-dressing, not for the rape.[255] In later centuries, friars and lay exorcists used the same tactics to get young women alone so they could rape them.[256] Modern commentators are still excusing Oðinn's rape of Rinðr: "whom he seduces [!] in her bed only on the fourth attempt"—"seduces," by having her tied up.[257]

In other poems, the giantess Gunnloð is guardian of the elixir of knowledge and poetry, within a deep mountain cavern. In *Hávamal* Oðinn makes sexual advances to Gunnloð in order to steal the mead-elixir of divine knowledge from her. *Skáldskaparmál* shows him penetrating the cave in the form of a serpent. He tricks the giantess into giving him three draughts of the mead, but gulps down all of it, then flies away as an eagle.

The giantess Gunnloð gives a cup of the mead of poetry to Oðinn, who steals all of it and escapes in the form of an eagle. Behind her is her father. They live in a cave deep within a mountain.

Oðinn's treatment of Gunnlöð leaves her ravaged, as he admits in *Hávamál*: "Gunnlöð gave me, from her golden throne | the precious drink of pure mead; a poor payment | I let her have in return | for her whole soul | for her burdened spirit."[258] A later stanza pours scorn on him for breaking his ring-oath to Gunnlöð, and stealing the mead "by treason," causing her "to weep."[259] But this does not seem to damage Oðinn's reputation.

As Maria Kvilhaug has noted, Gunnloð appears in a ceremonial setting, presenting the mead elixir of poetry from a golden throne.[260] This aspect represents an ancient goddess theme. But the storyteller makes her father the possessor of the mead, while she as its guardian is presented as a weak female (giantess or no) who can be sexually suborned, and then cheated, robbed of her treasure. The two surviving versions present her differently.

In one she agrees to give the mead in return for three nights of sex; in the other Oðinn cheats her. His prestige remains intact, while the all sexual shaming falls on Gunnloð.

It pleased the skálds to vaunt the upstart Oðinn as the greatest magician, but they failed to excise all the instances of female primacy from collective memory. According to the sagas, public ceremonies with *varðlokkur* and *seidstafr* were female-led affairs, while men's *seið* refers to individual magical acts outside a group context, except perhaps for battle.[261]

The feminizinç power of seiðr

The stretch Oðinn had to make to reach *seiðr* is visible in the accusation that doing so was *ergi*, "unmanly." His byname Jalkr – "Gelding"[262] may relate to this state of being. The most dramatic illustration of his assimilation to the female sphere may be a recently discovered figurine from Lejre, Denmark, circa 900 CE—if it indeed represents Oðinn and not Freyja or Frigg, as many believe.[263]

The little silver casting shows a person in women's clothing, wearing a long dress with an embroidered apron, a female headdress, and a heavy four-stranded necklace. Her mouth and lower face are covered by a wimple (mouth-veil). Her arms are tucked out of sight under a cape, and her feet under her long robe. The figure is seated on a throne with two birds perched on its arms, and two wolves on its back. These creatures look like Oðinn's familiars: the ravens Huginn and Munin, and the wolves Geri and Freki. It has been pointed out that both Freyja and Frigg have been described as sitting on Oðinn's throne.[264] Danish archaeologist Else Roesdahl leans toward identifying the figure as "the goddess

The Lejre figure from Denmark: Freyja, or Oðinn?

Freya, whose role in the pagan religion is probably understated in today's perceptions."[265]

In favor of a female interpretation are the dress and necklace, so like that of the silver Freyja from Aska, who is indubitably female and may even be pregnant. Against it is the glaring gaze of the Lejre figure, whose left eye bulges strangely, suggesting a one-eyed Oðinn. The wimple might have been meant to cover a beard, since no female figures of the Viking era are depicted wearing wimples or with mouths covered.

In fact, the figurine was found at the early center of royal power in Denmark, whose Skjolding dynasty Oðinn was said to have founded. But this is not a warrior figure, and if it does depict Oðinn, he is feminized in shamanic aspect. This strengthens the suspicion that the "unmanning" aspect of *seiðr* came in part from an expectation that male hierophants would dress as women—and possibly hold a distaff-shaped wand. In fact, several men were buried with the *völr*.

Several scholars have theorized that the reason *seiðr* was considered *ergi*, and unsuitable for men, must have been because the shamanic act itself involved a state of receptivity, seen as a "female" vulnerability arising from the nature of trance, in which spirits entered into the *seiðkona*. Thus they see *ergi* as "a sexually defined metaphor for the practice of sorcery itself."[266] But this comes uncomfortably close to Eliade's claim that male shamans command spirits, while women are mediums who merely submit to them.

Other theories go much further by asserting, on remarkably thin grounds, that sex was somehow a component of *seidr* itself. Central to this line of argument are repeated claims that the staff was a "phallic" symbol—of which there is not a single hint in descriptions of *seiðr* ceremonies. These theorists extrude an entire confection of sexual rites from a single mention of *göndull*, a less-common term for "staff," for "penis" in one lone saga.[267] *Bósa saga ok Herrauðs* uses the word *göndull* when the hero has sex with a farmer's daughter, with no ceremonial context whatsoever.[268] A "staff" metaphor for penis is nothing unique to the Norse. Many cultures use it in slang expressions.[269] But there is no reason to think this singular usage has any relation to the *seiðstaffs* or ceremonies led by the *völur*. It never occurs in any description of *seiðr* or *völur* or *gandr*.

A late medieval description of a rite by a seeress gives a far more believable illustration of how a *völva* might have used her staff. Ostacia "goes out and moves her *gandr,*" wielding her staff as a power object, a consecrated spiritual tool. The text goes on to say, "This performance we identify as the practice of *seiðr*, as it would have been done in ancient times, by women knowledgeable in sorcery [*fjölkynngar konur*] that were known as *völur*..."[270]

For the wild speculations that *seiðr* must have involved some sexual activity too shameful for men to engage in, there is absolutely no evidence—not the slightest allusion—in any accounts of ceremonies, or of *völur* (or for that matter, of *seiðmenn*). These Freudian projections are a backdoor way of identifying women—priestesses with recognized spiritual and social power—with "sex" in a way that the male gods and heroes never are. (The same impulse can be seen in the idea that ancient priestesses must have engaged in "sacred prostitution.")

Neil Price even refers to "the obscene mysteries of *seiðr*" in connection with the legendary *völva* Heiðr. Yet he rejects Clunies-Ross' suggestion that *seiðr* involved spirit frenzy on the grounds that "there is no real evidence" for such possession taking place in *seiðr*."[271] There is no *real* evidence for any sexual rites in *seiðr*—only conjecture, without any basis in the written descriptions.

The emasculating distaff

Instead of jumping to the conclusion that *seiðr* was marked female because it involved some rite of phallic penetration, more attention needs to go to the distaff symbolism of the *seiðstafr* in archaeology. A vast body of European folklore, custom, art, and legal nomenclature attests to the distaff's powerful female valence. It was the prototypical symbol of women, of female authority and power, to the point that Anglo-Saxon law speaks of "the spear side" and the "distaff side."

According to the Oxford English Dictionary, this nomenclature goes back at least to 885 when King Alfred's will bequeathed land to the *sperehealfe* or *spinhealfe* side of the family.[272] There would be no point to using a penis symbol as the sign of womanhood or, in this case, matrilineage. The same concept of "spindle kinship" existed in medieval German.[273] Although its economic and cultural basis has dissolved, "the distaff side" is still occasionally used in modern English.

As discussed earlier, distaffs figure prominently as power symbols of women, goddesses, faeries, saints and witches in Indo-European cultures. The connection of witches with distaffs as magical objects persisted in images and texts throughout the witch hunt era, and afterwards. According to Eldar Heide, even the word *seið* itself might have a linguistic connection to spinning.[274]

The femaleness of the distaff, and its symbolism in the *seiðstafr,* is crucial to understanding why the Norse considered *seiðr* to be *ergi* (unmanning and degrading) for men. Scandinavians were not the only European culture that saw the distaff as a symbol of feminization.[275] The theme of the emasculating distaff goes back a very long way in Indo-European culture. A Hittite charm to change a man's gender or sexual orientation or sexual impotence (it's not clear which) involved twining together red and white wool, and placing a mirror and distaff in his hand. He was made to pass under a gate; then the distaff and mirror were taken away from him and replaced by a bow and arrows, as this spell was pronounced: "See! I have taken womanliness away from thee and given thee back manliness. Thou hast cast off the ways of a woman, now [show] the ways of a man!"[276]

In classical Greece, the story of queen Omphale taming Hercules and

making him spin was the most popular expression of this theme. It was depicted in countless Greco-Roman statues, reliefs, mosaics and frescos, and was enthusiastically revived by Renaissance artists. Lucas Cranach the Elder did a series of paintings in which Omphale and her women wrap Hercules in female veils, put a distaff in his hand, and set him to spinning. This art belongs to a larger theme of the battle of the sexes, often called the "battle over the breeches," in which women try to take away men's pants, symbolizing male authority.[277]

A woman dominating her husband with a distaff was a popular misogynist theme in the middle ages and into the 1700s.

Medieval and early modern European art shows women wielding the distaff as a weapon against men. A vellum miniature depicts a woman jousting with a distaff

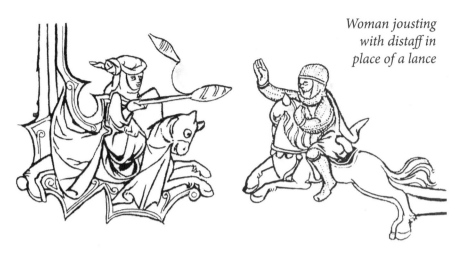

*Woman jousting
with distaff in
place of a lance*

against an (unarmed) man, and several other examples exist. In a French
manuscript from the Lancelot Cycle, circa 1300, a woman grabs a fleeing
man by one ankle and prepares to wallop him with her distaff, spindle
flying.[278] The artist emphasizes his emasculation; the man is thrusting a
sword into his anus and out through his genitals. The implication is that the
witch—note her snakey lower body—is making him castrate himself. (See
image on following page.)

An English manuscript of 1455 shows Thracian women attacking
Orpheus with their distaffs raised.[279] Later in the same century, Israhel van
Meckenem created his series on the "Evil Woman" who threatens or beats
a man with her distaff; one picture shows a feminized husband winding
thread from a spindle.[280]

A Dutch artist from the School of Leiden painted "Young Man from the
Rear, Holding a Distaff and Spindle," c. 1510–1550. His breeches are split,
and the spindle is suggestively positioned by his exposed buttocks.[281] Many
other examples of this gendered disdain exist in early modern art.

Another piece of this cross-cultural pattern were European punishments
that humiliated men by parading them through town carrying a distaff.
"So strong were the female associations of this implement that they were
exploited as the basis for one of the characteristic medieval punishments by
humiliation..."[282] In early modern English custom, men shamed "feeble" husbands in noisy processions "in which one man rode backwards on a horse or
donkey, holding a distaff, while another, enacting the role of the 'wife,' beat
him with a ladle.[283] It is no accident that men publicly satirized women for

baler chele part: 7 quant il idt
fi troeue vne biere bien atourt

The emasculating distaff in a French MS of the Lancelot cycle, circa 1300.
Her serpentine lower body shows the woman as a shapeshifting witch.

non-submission, or that male performance of female parts predominated in
European masquerades. Such commentary was a danger zone for women.

Norse culture didn't produce imagery of viragos wielding distaffs, or for
that matter, *any* images of spinners. But it did record ferocious social
disapproval of males who took on female attributes. As in the examples
above, the Norse consistently equated male feminization, on any symbolic
level, with being sexually penetrated and dominated. They would have seen
the distaff as intensely feminizing, and that would go for its symbolism in
the *seiðstafr* as well. Men did not use distaffs! Add to that the possibility
suggested by the Lejre figurine, that men put on female dress to perform
seiðr. All this more than explains why *seiðr* was considered *ergi*.

Several male burials with distaff-shaped *völr* have been found.[284] The dis-
integration of cloth over the course of a thousand years may not allow deter-
mination of whether they assumed female gender, as suggested by the Lejre
figurine. Maybe archaeology will uncover more evidence. But any further
consideration of the perception that *seiðr* was emasculating must take into
account the distaff symbolism of archaeological *seiðstafr* finds. Those are far
more concrete than any speculations that sex was part of *seiðr* ceremonies.

❖

ꟼENDERED SHAME ::: THE SEXUAL DOUBLE STANDARD

A copious literature has grown up around the concept of *ergi*, most of it in reference to gay or transgender people. That study is beyond the scope of this book, but the term definitely implied gender variance—though with different meanings for females than for males. Nearly all the scholarly discussion centers on male-bodied people, so we will start there. *Ergi* carried a variety of meanings, most of them considered insulting: "unmanly or effeminate," "perverted," "sexually impotent," "cowardly," or a man who is "acted upon sexually."[285] It also applied to the gender ambiguities that accumulate in old age, as *Hrafnkels saga* explained: "everyone becomes *argr* who gets older."[286]

Neil Price speaks of "highly complex concepts of dishonour and a special state of being called *ergi*, and there is a suggestion of other genders..." specifically males who in some way present as feminine. He emphasizes "the complex network of social and sexual taboos" encoded into *seiðr*, but elides the importance of its identification with women even while recognizing "the apparent contradiction of Oðinn's role as both a male god and a master of women." In his view, this contradiction is what gives Oðinn such great power; [287] but the oppositional nature of the god's relations with women— and with supernatural females is not to be passed over lightly. Speaking of "sexual taboos" can mean many things, but the key factor is that *seiðr* was considered female, and feminized men associated with it.[288]

Somehow, many writers think that feminization of males who participated in a female-marked profession equates to that profession being based on sexual activity. But in fact *argr* applied in the absence of outright sexual acts; it was enough for a man assume any female attributes whatsoever. *Thrymskviða* shows even hyper-masculine Thórr fearing that he'll be called "effeminate" (*argan*) when he has to dress as a bride in order to get his hammer back from the giants.[289] On the other hand, Loki—the character who actually is *ergi*—does not fear being slandered but aggressively throws accusations at others.[290] (Loki does not easily fit modern categories of gay or trans, and might even be described as intersex, since he bears children.) Another wrong track is the suggestion that *ergi* was dishonored because of women's magic was deceitful, "as its manipulative aspects ran counter to [the] masculine ideal of forthright, open behavior."[291]

Such views are ideology, not history, and simply reproduce misogyny; but that's Wikipedia.

The ultimate basis of the dishonor was male disdain for women, which made for a volatile mix when combined with the strong female associations of *seiðr* and the distaff wands of the *völur*. There men's fear of women's power came to the fore—but contempt for femaleness was a social norm. Masculine characterizations are used to describe strength in women as well as in men, "while *blauðr*, 'female,' is used of weak men and women alike."[292] To spell it out, femaleness itself was a stigmatized category, and abject by definition.

Norse men regularly insulted other men by comparing them to women. In poetic duels known as *flyting*, they derided each other with female epithets: mares, bitches, harlots—and *völur*. They flung accusations that their opponent did women's work (such as spinning!) or the work of slaves, and that they had been sexually used by other men. Such charges were so pervasive, and accompanied by violence, that penalties for them were codified in medieval laws.[293]

As in most patriarchal cultures, the Norse stigma on homosexuality did not apply to men who assumed the dominant role in sex with males. It was reserved for males who took (or were simply accused of taking) the female role, which was assumed to be submissive, subordinated and despised. In the blunt language of the Norse, such a man was called *sann-sorðinn*, "demonstrably fucked."[294] What counted was not whether a male had sex with another male, as Lotte Hedeager observes, but whether he was penetrated by that male: "Those who penetrated… were the powerful ('males'); those who became penetrated were the powerless ('females'). … The most severe accusations in the Old Norse society evolved around 'effeminacy' and penetration, implying that sexuality and hostility were two sides of the same coin."[295] Thus femininization was seen as degrading to males.

Ergi was a primary term of verbal abuse, and "deeply defamatory."[296] The Grágás laws of Iceland (2, 392) lay out penalties for anyone who calls a man *argr*, *ergi*, or *ragr*—but only if they cannot prove the accusation.[297] Males who did not fit the rigid gender norms had no legal defense against being publicly reviled and attacked. The law entitled a man to kill another man who called him by these names, to prevent being dishonored into social abjection, the defamed state known as *nið*.

But the law made open targets of gender variant males, whether they were what would now be called gays or trans women. (No mention is made of lesbians, who as usual are relegated to the realm of unthinkability.) Such non-comforming people were cast into the social shame of *níð*. (Old English had the same concept, from the same root as *beneath* and German *nieder*, "below."[298]) A disabled person, especially one who visibly limped, was also considered to be a *níthing* whose weakness was despised—and suspected of causing them to resort to sorcery.[299]

For women, however, *níð* meant a specifically female form of sexual shaming. Freyja, for example, refuses to go to giantland because their repute for sexual voracity would redound against her. She fears being seen as *vergiarnasta*, "most keen for men."[300] Promiscuity was expected from men, but counted heavily against women. Even involuntary sexual contact devalued a woman. The Grágás law compares rape with murder, since it destroyed a woman's honor, "and it was enough to ruin her reputation for the rest of her life."[301]

Although some women defied the sexual double standard, they were deeply stigmatized for it, as the sagas show. The most famous example was the Norwegian queen Gunnhild, whose rank and personal power allowed her to get away with a sexual affair. But several sagas reviled her for taking a young lover and spread nasty stories that she used sorcery to get him.

While males who did not conform to gender expectations were called *ergi*, the female correlate is hardly ever mentioned. When it is, it means something else. Under Norse patriarchy, women who defied female gender roles were derided for different reasons than men, and faced different constraints. *Org*, the female form of the term, implied rebellion against female gender norms, but does not seem to imply same-sex love or trans-genderism.[302] It meant a woman who was "sexually promiscuous" or "taking the sexual initiative," both of which were accepted, even admired, in men.[303] Among the curses used to force Gerðr to marry Freyr are threats that any other sexual relationships she may have will be afflicted with *ergi*, and madness, and the torment of raging sexual desire that cannot be assuaged.[304]

Another meaning of *org* was "a woman who desired a man far below her own social standing."[305] Patriarchal rules of hypergamy required that class rank not be allowed to confuse the code of female subordination, and they enacted reprisals against women who consorted with men of lower class.

Conversely, it was a given that men would have sex with (and rape) lower class women—especially enslaved women—without incurring the least dishonor. But female *org* enforced patriarchal constraints.

Female subordination also required self-restraint before men, since for women *ergi* connoted aggression or anger, as in the use of *argri konu* ("maleficent woman") in a curse on the Saleby Runestone.[306] "Angry" remains the primary meaning of the arg- root in modern Scandinavian languages (Swedish *arg*, or Norwegian and Danish *arrig*; Icelandic *ergilegur*, "irritable", Faroese *argur* "angry, annoyed," all of which compare to German *Ärgerlich*, "quick to anger, volatile," and probably English *irk* as well).[307]

A few sagas and historical legends mention women warriors and other women who defied gender rules by cross-dressing. Examples are the legendary woman warrior Hervör, and the historical Danish warrior Hlaðgerðr ("Lagertha" in English). For a woman to wear men's pants was grounds for divorce, as happened to "Breeches Aud" in *Laxdœla saga*. The same applied to men who wore low-cut shirts.[308]

By the later middle ages, gender resistance faced stronger legal penalties. The Norwegian Gulathing and the Icelandic Grágás forbade crossdressing, placing female crossdressing in the front line of fire: "If a woman dresses in men's clothing or cuts her hair like a man or uses weapons in a dangerous way, that should be punished by the lesser outlawry (*fjörbaugr*=life money). It is the same punishment if a man dresses like a woman."[309]

The idea that *seiðr* embroiled men in *ergi* is underlined by a common name for such witch-men: *seiðberendr*. The Norwegian *Gulathing* lists *berendr* among the proscribed words not to be used against men (except for gender-nonconformists, who could be lawfully targeted for insult). *Berendr* derives from *bera*, "to give birth," and was used for female brood animals, notably cows, especially for their sexual parts.[310] It was also "a very coarse word for female genitalia in Old Norse."[311] Contempt for females is the basis of these epithets used for gender-variant males.

The völr from Gnezdovo, Russia

But that doesn't explain anything about *seiðr* itself—except that it was recognized as a female sphere of power. Even some female scholars have gotten so caught up in the implications of *ergi* for male-bodied people that they end up losing sight of the significance of female power through *seiðr*.[312]

Völva dances on a seiðhjallir.
Olaus Magnus, Description of the Northern Peoples, *1553*

There is no doubt that these were patriarchal societies. But, underlying the intense ambivalence of Norse texts and modern interpretations alike, a female sphere of power is clearly perceptible. In fact, it becomes obvious once the testimony of the sagas and archaeology is brought together.

Then the broad scope of the history of *völur* and *spákonur* comes into view: their oracular ceremonies and shamanic staffs, their incantation, shapeshifting, and vision-seeking in Nature. This spiritual tradition of the Norse seeresses is a remarkable women's heritage that few people outside Scandinavia know about. It is a significant omission in the way most people are educated about European history.

Names and Meanings of the Runes

ᚠ	FEOH cattle, goods, wealth	ᚻ	HAEGL Hail, Sleet	ᛏ	TIR Victory, Warrior
ᚢ	UR Aurochs, wild cow, strength	ᚾ	NYD Need, hardship, constraint	ᛒ	BEORC Birch, rebirth.
ᚦ	THORN Thorn, enemy	ᛁ	IS Ice	ᛖ	EOH Horse, sun's course
ᚩ	OS River mouth	ᛄ	GER: Year, harvest	ᛗ	MAN People
ᚱ	RAD Riding, journey	ᛇ	EOH Yew tree, bow	ᛚ	LAGU Water, sea
ᚲ	CEN Torch, skiff	ᛈ	PEORTH Mystery	ᛝ	ING Fertility
ᚷ	GYFU Gift	ᛉ	EOLH- SECG Elk-sedge, protection	ᛟ	DAEG Homeland, heritage
ᚹ	WYN Joy	ᛋ	SIGEL Sun	ᛞ	ETHEL Daylight, Prosperity

5
RUNES AND ḣALIORUNNAS

Witches divined the path of Wyrd from movement, direction, synchronicity, pattern; from signs like the appearance and cries of animals, from happenings in human life and in the natural world. They watched the flow of water, wind and fire, as ancient Germanic priestesses gazed into rushing waters and as the Senae of Gaul looked into their sacred cauldron. The custom of gazing into water continued in early medieval France and Spain.[1]

Crystal balls, early medieval France

Another way of seeing was by contemplating glowing embers. A Swiss document circa 1300 names "fire-gazing" among various prohibited divinatory and healing practices.[2] As late as 1455, a German demonologist wrote, "There be women and men, which dare to make fires, and in the fire to see things past and to come." They carried out fire-gazing on particular days considered auspicious for clairvoyance.[3]

Other ways of divination include listening in grainfields by night, or sitting out on the house roof, or scapulimancy (examining patterns on an animal's shoulderbone). People also forecasted weather by reading goose bones (still done in some places).[4]

Crystal balls from early medieval France

Witches also looked into crystal balls, which have a historical reality beyond the stereotype. They are mostly found in female graves in early medieval England (especially Kent), France, Netherlands, Germany, Switzerland, Hungary, and Italy.[5]

"In England they have always been found in women's graves," observed Audrey Meaney in *Anglo-Saxon Amulets and Curing-Stones.* Usually the crystals are found between the woman's knees, indicating that they must have been suspended from her belt.

They often rest inside a sieve-spoon—another object with a long divinatory pedigree, which was used as a pendulum.[6] This divination, called sieve-driving, sieve-turning, -chasing, or -dancing, was practiced in many coun-

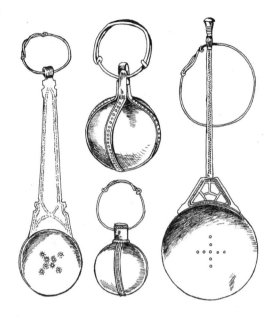

Sieves and crystal balls, Merovingian France

tries. It was compared to spell-speaking, especially in France and Germany.[7]

The historian Edouard Salin remarked on "the magical powers attributed to crystal balls and amulets hanging from belts" in these women's burials.[8] They continue into the Christian era; a 6th century princess was buried in the cathedral of Cologne with a crystal ball, knife, and small silver amulet case hanging from her belt.[9]

Meaney describes women's amulet bags found in Switzerland, Austria, and Germany, containing things like spindle whorls, bronze rings and discs, a bear tooth, chunks of iron, a boar tusk, or beads of amber and glass. A woman buried in Sussex in the late 6th century had an eagle's talon and a cowrie shell.[10] Other graves contained teeth of dogs, wolves, foxes, bears, and beavers; boar teeth in particular are usually found in graves of women and girls.[11] Cowries have been found all over medieval Europe, again mostly in female burials.[12] Meaney observed that "men are so rarely found with amulets."[13]

❖

heathens

All these customs were considered to be *heathen*. The word comes from "heath," wild shrubby land or moors, as in "heather." It became a designation—in all the Germanic languages—for people who followed old ethnic traditions: pagans, in Roman parlance. Its earliest form recorded is *haithno*, a feminine form in Gothic, followed by Anglo-Saxon *hēðin*, Old Frisian *hēthen*, Old Norse *heiðinn*, Old High German *heidan*, and modern German and Dutch, *heiden*.[14]

The 8th century monk Paulus Diaconus referred to rural people as *demo heidenin commane*; others called them "the wild heathen."[15] A custom survived of calling unbaptized children *heiden* or *heiden-wolf*,[16] just as Sardinians and Calabrians called them *paganeddu*, "little pagans."

There has been some speculation that these words were derived from Greek ἔθνη. The idea is that *ethne* would have entered Germanic languages via Ulfilas' Gothic translation of Mark 7:26, which calls a Syrian gentile woman *haithno*.[17] But linguists seem to reject this theory on phonological grounds,[18] nor does it explain the pervasive presence of "heath" and "heathen" in Germanic languages.

Nevertheless, as Catherine Coquery-Vidrovitch has pointed out, "in French, still in the 19th century, the first meaning of 'ethnique' was precisely pagan, by opposition to christian."[19] And in fact *ethnicus* does mean "pagan" in several early medieval Latin sources.[20] Priestly writers more commonly referred to pagans with the Latin *gentilis*—a usage that persisted in Romance languages. It came from the Greek word *gens* ("clan, tribe") which was used to translate Biblical references to *goyim*, non-Hebrew "nations."[21] *Gentile* took on connotations of a despised, othered culture, and entered Christian discourse with the meaning of "pagan."[21]

The priesthood also described pagans with words for "sorcerer," "witch," or "diviner." They redefined pagan ceremonies as devil-worship, idolatry, and sacrilege, considering any other religion than that of the Church to be *illicita*: "illegitimate" and "illegal." One 9th-century sermon states that "all the sacrifices and soothsayings of the pagans are sacrileges, as are the sacrifices of the dead around corpses or over tombs, or omens, or amulets, or the offerings made on stones, or to springs, trees..."[22]

The priesthood often used the formula, Whoever does or believes [X], " is not a Christian, but a pagan." Thus the *Homilia de Sacrilegiis* denounces

"Culture of the Old Gods" (Veterum Cultura Deorum) Fights Faith, assumed to be synonymous with Christianity, in the Psychomachia *of Prudentius.*

10th century English manuscript

anyone who "believes in bad or good fates," or who divines, or goes to hidden places to consult diviners, or who prognosticates by means of wool and needles.[23]

In an interesting new twist, recent scholarship has identified a word for "heath" as the root of the primary witch-name in Iberian and Occitanian languages: Spanish *bruja,* Portuguese and Galician *bruxa,* Catalán *bruixa,* Gascon *broucho.* (The o-ending is feminine in some southern French dialects; for example, Occitan has *fado,* instead of *fada,* for "female fairy.")

As with English "witch," the etymology of *bruja* has been murky. Julio Caro Baroja attempted to derive it from the Moorish root mBRSH, meaning "datura," a family of psychotropic herbs used ceremonially in many parts of the world. Others have suggested Latin *brusca,* "tree frog," or a relationship to Celtic *brixta* ("incantation, spell, magic") which occurs in Gaulish and Old Irish.[24] None of these proposed derivations are compelling.

But a theory by etymologist Joan Coromines has significant implications.

bꞅuxa, bꞅuixa
bꞅoucho, bꞅuia

He links *bruja* with a Gallo-Latin root *broiksa or *bru:ska. This word had three primary meanings: "heath," or more broadly wildlands; "woman of the heaths"; and by extension, people of the heaths as "pagan," in much the same way as English "heathen."[25] (The word is marked-female, as *bruja* continued to be in the middle ages.) Ton Sales remarks that these usages are "exactly paralleling the three senses of German Heide," as well as the oldest meaning of "pagan," as people of a rural locale. The English word "heather" is to *heathen* as German Heiderkraut ("heath-plant") is to *heiden*. Similarly, in Catalán the word for heath or heather is *bruc* or *bruguera*; in French *bruyère*; in Spanish *brezo*, in Gascon (Basque-French) *bròc*. Old Irish also has a form of this word, *froech*, for "heath."[26]

It is striking that in both Germanic and western Romance languages, a word meaning "people of the heath" came to mean "pagan" and, eventually, "witch." This usage parallels the rural connotations of Latin *paganus*. These words are reminders that for a long time Christianity mostly spread in urban areas, while people in the countryside adhered to much older forms of culture. This remained true throughout the middle ages, right up to the brink of industrialization. These usages recur in later European colonial designations of "the bush" in Africa and Australia, as "heathen" places lacking in "civilization."

RUNA

Most of what we know of witchen traditions comes in the form of laws and sermons intended to obliterate them.[27] Our primary historical sources are priests hostile to the old shamanic heritage. In their accounts, the witch's reflection is distorted and muddied by a competing worldview. Her sacraments are reviled, and veiled behind the devil-mask that priestcraft forced over heathen spiritual culture. Through this lens, prayer by the witch diviners seems unthinkable. Consider, too, the christianizing shift of that word's meaning; it originally meant "ask," as in "pray tell" and "prithee".

Yet when the goddesses invoked are the Fates, divination is inseparable from religion. People naturally expressed their aspirations in prayers to the threefold goddess of destiny—or to the ancestors, which as we'll see amounts to much the same thing. Weirding women sought to perceive how Wyrd was spinning out lives and interweaving them in her webs. People came to seers looking for illumination of their problems, for solutions and counsel to choose the right course. The impulse to divine the powers at work rested on a petition to the Fates.

The Fates first made the runes, scoring them onto the wood of the Tree of Life, as described in *Völuspá* 20:4. The nine daughters of Njörðr, giantesses living at the ends of the earth, are also described as carving runes.[28] Runes were not simply letters but essences, symbols of natural forces, lots cast as spells. *Spell* itself originally meant "story, saying, speech, command."[29]

Runes were an alphabet of powers and meanings, forming consellations in shifting relationships to each other. Divination with runes spelled out fate, and offered a chance to shape it. Working runes was an animist way of acting upon the world. The Lay of Sigrdrífa shows that runes were graven or painted on things imbued with vital power: wolf-claws, sun-horses' hooves, bear paws, eagles' beaks, bridgeheads, ceremonial seats, rings of gold, glass, amulets, and herbs. The valkyrie instructs her hearer to carve them "on the nails of Norns, and the night-owl's beak."[30] Women's rune magic appears in the sagas:

> **In Grettis saga there is an account of a tree-root which became magnat [charged with power] because a witch cut runes on it, rubbed blood into them, and recited charms over them, after which she cast the wood into the sea and gave it directions as to where it should float.**[31]

This rune-worker was a very old woman named Thuríður, who "had been very skilled in witchcraft and magic when she was young and the people were still heathen."[32] In the original Icelandic she is *fjölkunnig mjög og margkunnig mjög*, literally "full-knowing" and "great-knowing."[33] Her second attribute is near-synonymous with the Norns' attribute *margs vitandi*, "all things knowing," in *Völuspá* 20.

Thuríður was performing the rune ceremony to do away with Grettir, a violent outlaw who had killed many, burned down a family's hall, raped a serving-woman (though this was no factor in his outlawry), and stolen food from many farmers. He had eluded capture for nearly twenty years. Once a group of farmers caught him and were about to put him to death, but a woman of lordly clan intervened to save him. The trump card that won Grettir this reprieve was his social class.

Although people no longer believed in Thuríður's powers, her foster son asked for her help. First Thuríður insisted on attempting a last parley with Grettir, who ended it by breaking her leg with a thrown rock. That delayed her for some months. Once her wound had healed, the old woman walked along the seashore. She headed straight to a huge driftwood stump, and had the men turn it over. She pulled out her knife and began cutting runes into the wood, then cut herself and let her blood drip onto them while murmuring charms. She walked around the trunk counter-sunwise, still reciting spells. Finally she told the men to push it into the sea, saying that it would travel to the island of Drangey where Grettir was holed up. The stump arrived at his shore, and twice he succeeded in preventing his men from bringing it in for firewood, but the third time, a slave carried it in during a storm. Grettir went into a rage at its presence and struck it with an axe, which glanced off, dealing him a deep and fatal wound in the thigh.[34] This was "a 'thigh for a thigh' justice,"[35] as Arlea Hunt-Anschutz wittily called it.

CHARACTERS, MEANINGS, AND MAGIC

Runa means Mystery. The concept was sacred in the old Germanic languages. An Eddic poem describes the runes as *reginkunnom*, "of divine origin,"[36] literally "kin to the powers." The word *runa* was first written down in bishop Wufila's Gothic translation of the Christian scriptures, sixteen centuries ago.[37] It was the closest Germanic approximation to the Greek *mystérion* in Mark 4:11: "the mystery of the kingdom of God."[38] (The early Gothic Bible used a different word, *mēl*, to translate Greek words for writing.) The Anglo-Saxon cleric Caedmon defined *rūn* as both sacred Mystery and as magical symbol.[39] In the Old Saxon *Heliand*, the biblical passage "Lord, teach us to pray" is translated as "reveal to us the runes" (*gerihti us that geruni*).[40]

The Anglo-Saxon word *rūn* meant "mystery, secret, counsel, consultation, runic character."[41] Sometimes the characters are described as *rūnstæf*, showing their roots in divinatory wooden lots. The verb form *rūnian* meant "to whisper, murmur, talk secrets, conspire."[42] Other concepts include *rūnlic* ("mystical"), *rūncofa* ("chamber of secrets, breast, bosom"), and *rūncræftig* ("skilled in mysteries").[43] In Old High German *rūnēn* meant "to whisper," *rūnazan* "to murmur." Middle High German retained the word as *raunen*.

The range of meanings also encompasses Old Norse *rúnar* "secret consultation" and *rýna*, "carry on an intimate conversation." Both words had analogues in Old English and Old High German.[44] Celtic languages yield Old Irish *rún*, "mysterium, secret"; Scots Gaelic *rùn*, "secret, secret intention"; and Welsh *rhin*, "secret, virtue." *Rùn* also can mean "sweetheart, beloved person" in Gaelic and "intimate friend" (*rúna*) in Old Norse. The Finns borrowed *runo* to mean "magic song, charm"[45] and gave

RUNE WORDS

Anglo Saxon

rūnian "to whisper, murmur"

rūnlic: "mystical"

rūncofa "chamber of secrets, breast"

rūncræftig: "skilled in mysteries"

Old High German

rūnēn "to whisper,"

rūnazan "to murmur"

(*raunen* in Middle High German)

Old Norse

rúnar "secret consultation"

rýna, "converse intimately"

rúna "intimate friend"

Old Irish

rún "mystery, secret"

Scots Gaelic

rùn "secret, secret intention; also beloved person"

Welsh

rhin "secret, virtue."

their wandering bards the name of *runolainen*.[46]

All Germanic cultures had words for lots (OHG *hlōz*, Goth. *hláuts*, AS *hleát*, ON *hlutr*), each with their own divinatory customs. The Norse cast sticks or "let fall the blood-marked chip," reading the signs that fell facing up. They spoke of outcomes as how "the chips fell out."[47] This sheds light on the English expression, "Let the chips fall where they may." Another Norse name for lots was *spænir*: "a divining chip of wood, doubtless marked with runes… referring to fate in store for the consulter of the chip."[48]

The Icelandic Edda mentions rune-sticks with things wrapped and woven around them. In the north-ernmost Netherlands, the Frisians used wool-wrapped wicker lots called *tēnar*.[49] Their close relatives, the Anglo-Saxons, cast lots with twigs called *tān*. The historian Bede described the use of *tān* to select leaders of battle.[50]

Runes were engraved, painted, carved into amulets, on spindle whorls and weaver's swords, on weapons, or woven into cloth. As lots they were cut into slices of wood, usually beech or mountain ash. As letters they could be read from left to right or right to left, or alternately up and down. Germanic divination by casting bundles of sticks are mentioned in Tacitus and, later, the Frankish codes of Carloman and Charlemagne.[51] The Irish also used wooden lots, *fidlann*, for divination. The root *fid* means "tree, wood," from which also comes *fidba*, "sorcery."[52]

The Germanic runes may be based on Etruscan letters used in north Italy up to the first century.[53] These in turn go back to west Anatolian scripts such as Lydian, and ultimately to the Semitic alphabets. Some scholars think that the Goths may have been the first Germanic people to use runes, in the 3rd century CE. The three oldest runic inscriptions occur outside Scandinavia: in Rumania, Poland and eastern Germany, all lands where the Goths roamed in late antiquity.[54] The early Franks also had runic alphabets.[55] Anglo-Saxons cast lots with runes marked on sheep anklebones. In Burgundy, the synod of Auxerre prohibited people from "lotteries made of wood."[56]

Danes, Jutes, Norwegians, Swedes, Icelanders, Franks, Angles and Saxons: all knew the runes. In time the Norse runes settled into an alphabet arranged in three groups of eight, called *aettir*, "families." This rune order dates from the sixth century.[57] Related Germanic cultures varied in the name and number and form of basic runes. Only the Old English and Old Frisian runes include *ac*, "oak."[58] From the original 24, English runes expanded to 29 characters. The Scandinavian alphabet shrank to 16 characters, as the tradition declined.[59]

Several fragmentary Rune Poems have survived, transmitted orally for centuries before being written down. The *English Rune Poem* (recorded circa 1000) shows Christian revisions, as does the Norwegian one (1200s). The *Icelandic Rune Poem* is fully pagan, even though it was recorded last, in the 1400s.

Runecraft existed on a continuum with animist religion, cosmological meanings, and transformative power. Oðinn says in the *Hávamál*:

> **Know you how to carve them**
> **Know you how to read them?**
> **Know you how to paint them?**
> **Know you how to to prove them?**
> **Know you how to pray with them?**
> **Know you how to blood-sacrifice with them?**
> **Know you how to offer with them?**[60]

About blood-sacrifice of animals, the same poem warned: "A gift always looks for recompense."[61] Nor was working with runes carelessly undertaken. Instruction in the tradition and insight were needed.

Some writers create the impression that men controlled runic wisdom. However, F. B. Gummere highlighted female *runecræft*: "in Scandinavia, women seem to know most about the making and reading of runes." Early on, in his view, "knowledge of writing was largely in the hands of women."[62]

Grimm also saw German women as "the keepers of the sacred runes."[63] They appear on spinning and weaving tools, for example on an Anglo-Saxon spindle whorl. A Frisian weaver's sword made of yew and inscribed with runes was found at Westeremden, Groningen. It has been interpreted as a love spell, reading: "Aduyislu (man's name) with Jisuhildu (female name)."[64] The woman would have woven with the charmed wood, in a kind of weirding. The songs, words, intention of weavers: these are culturally charged acts, as many sources tell us, in the weft of countless lives.

Medieval poems show Óðinn in competition with a female runic wisdom. He brags of his rune-knowledge in the *Havamal*. His 18th boast declares that he will never teach "maid or man's wife" what he knows.[65] This chest-pounding rings hollow in light of the *Voluspá* and *Baldrsdraumr*, which show him seeking out female *völur* for oracular knowledge. As Óðinn went to the *völur* for prophecy, so the Niflung hero Sigurth asked the valkyrie Sigrdrífa to teach him wisdom, "if it so be that she had knowledge from all the worlds."[66]

Sigrdrífa instructs her lover in runecraft, filling 15 stanzas.[67] The poem gives glimpses of what mortal wisewomen might have known and done. Sigrdrífa knows runes for even-tempered speech and wisdom at council. She tells of beech runes, birth runes, victory runes, sea runes, and "mighty, magic runes." She explains runes for healing wounds, and help runes for childbirth. The midwife should put the help runes on her palms, grasp the mother's wrists, "and ask the *dísir*'s aid."[68] In other words, she invokes the ancestral mothers.

Icelandic epics depict women like Guðrún and Kostbera as having mastered runecraft. The prologue to *Guðrúnarkviða* shows Guðrún as having more than a touch of the witch in her; she had eaten of Fafnir's heart and understood the speech of birds.[69] In the *Atlakvitha*, Guðrún sent a runic warning to her sister-in-law: "Kostbera knew runes, deciphered the message by the bright fire..." She interpreted the runes' meaning to the men.[70]

Some rune messages were symbolic rather than lettered. In the *Atlamál*, Guðrún communicates a warning to her brothers without using any writing. She sends a ring wrapped with wolf hair, which Guðrún's sister-in-law correctly interprets as a signal of peril. That night, Kostbera receives a further premonition of danger through dreaming. She attempts to restrain her husband and brother-in-law from their fatal journey. So does the other sister-in-law, Glaumvor. But the brothers shake off the women's warnings with an arrogance alien to the ancient Germanic men that Tacitus had described as taking women's prophetic counsel seriously. Medieval sagas show a growing contempt of warriors for women's seeing.

HALIORUNNAS, HELRUNAN, AND LEÓDRUNAN

As the oldest Gothic history recounts, an Ostrogothic king persecuted seeresses called *aliorunae*: "He discovered among his people several wise-women [*magas mulieres*] who were called *haliorunnas* in the native language."[71] The spellings vary, but *haliorunnas* is conjectured to have been the original Gothic form. The word seems to derive from a proto-Germanic *haljo-rūnas*, in which *halja-* was equivalent to Old English *hell*, Old High German *hella*, Dutch and Icelandic *hel*, and to German *Hölle*: "underworld, realm of the dead." All these descend from a Proto-Indo-European root *kel*, "to cover, conceal, save."[72] Thus the *aliorunae* were priestesses of "underworld mysteries"—of the ancestors.[73]

he discovered among his people several wisewomen who were called haliorunnas in the native language.

The name persisted in cultural memory. In the 12th century, Michael Scot called these women by the latinized form Alarinas, and he interposed another name: Yriagas.[74] Where did this word come from? It is intriguingly reminiscent of Yrias in the *Indiculus superstitionum et Paganiarum*, 24: "The pagan course, which they call Yrias, with torn clothing or shoes."[75] Tearing garments is a classic custom of mourners, which accords well with the western Germanic sense of *hellerunes* as women who communed with the dead.

Even later, Trithemius inscribed this provocative fragment: "Keen perception (or far-sightedness) through divination they called Alyrunam."[76] That source dates to about 1500; yet his assessment aligns with the old meanings; Jacob Grimm emphasized the heathen concepts of Runa, with their long historical trajectory: "I believe it meant in the first place what is spoken softly and solemnly, then secondly a mystery: *symbólion* is secret counsel." Grimm traced the rūna-name back to one of its oldest attestations, the ancient witches of the Ostrogoths: "The wise woman of the ancient Germans is called Aliruna... and speaking words not understood of the common folk, has skill at once in writing and in magic; hers is the Gothic *runa*, hers the Anglo-Saxon *runecraft*."[77]

Centuries afterwards, linguistic counterparts of the *haliorunnas* are attested in fragments of west Germanic lore recorded by early medieval scribes. Old German and Old English give variants—*helliruna, helrun, helrune, helrynegu,* and *hellraun*.[78] The *helruna* is related to Hel, Norse goddess of the underworld, and the German underworld (Hölle).

The standard definition of *helrūn* / hellerūne / *helrynegu* is "sorceress, witch."[79] But its etymology gives strong indications that the name was rooted in ecstatic ceremonies of ancestor veneration. One suggested definition is "one having knowledge of the secrets of the dead."[80] Another translation is "one who knows the secrets of hell."[81] A third renders it as "those skilled in the mysteries of hell."[82] Another suggestion has been "hell-whisperer," because of the murmuring and secret connotations of *rūna*.[83] In all these cases, "hel" means the underworld of the dead, who have returned into the Earth—not the Christian place of fire and punishment.[84]

Medieval Latin sources equated *halioruna* with the calling up of the dead for soothsaying (which they called *necromantia*). They compared the *hellrune* with *hægtesse* (which meant both "witch" and "supernatural hag") and with *pythonissa*, the main Latin term for "trance oracle."[85] So the original *helrune* (when she was not a supernatural being) looks like a priestess with oracular powers, in touch with the earth and spirits of the dead. Linguistic analysis seems to bear this out, suggesting a Germanic "agent noun" *helliruna* meaning "female necromancer, sorceress."[86]

Kees Samplonius comments, "Word form and context show that the performers in the Old English and Gothic cases must have been women, but the OHG gloss shows that it was not an exclusively female practice." No, it was not; but the female preponderance is significant. The *Toller-Bosworth Dictionary* notes that names ending in *-rūn, -rūna* were feminine.[87] The early medieval sources predominantly name women—even though their use of the Latin term "necromancy" projects a distorted view of these ceremonies. The practices of Greco-Roman ceremonial magicians (typically men) were something quite distinct from the ancestral rites of Germanic women, or even from Roman-style ancestor veneration. As Ramsey MacMullan comments, "For the Romans and the subjects of their empire, ancestor worship constituted the most important manifestation of religion into the fifth century and beyond."[88] This was not called *necromancia*, but piety.

More about these ceremonies can be gleaned from archaic words out of the ethnic cultures. In Old German, funeral rites were called *dotruna*, "mystery of the dead." Frankish funeral songs, the *dadsisas*, were laments akin to the Irish *caoine* and the Greek *moiralogia*. They would likely have been sung over the ground where the dead were interred, "the lays sung after the heathen fashion on graves and barrows, to make the dead speak or send something out."[89] But priestcraft reviled these ceremonies. Around the year 800, the *Indiculus superstitionem* calls *dadsisas* "sacrilege over the dead."[90] The collision of values could not be starker.

In spite of the religious repression, positive interpretations of these pagan themes survived. The shamanic herb mandrake was called *Alrūna* in Old High German, and *Alraun* in modern German. The root was harvested and dried, and its human-like form was ceremonially dressed.[91] Alruna may have been the original name of Albruna, the oracular woman of the Germaniae that Tacitus names in some versions of *Germania* 8:2. Medieval Germans spoke of a mysterious cave of the *Alraun*, which Grimm thought might be linked to the mythical cave of the ancient spinster.[92]

LEÓD-RUNAN, ELVES, AND ANCESTOR VENERATION

Anglo-Saxons once named women who communed with the dead, with ancestors, as *leód-rūne* ("song-mysteries.") In Toller-Bosworth's classic *Anglo-Saxon Dictionary*, this word means "A witch, wise woman." It is also compared to "*burh-rūne* 'furia'; helle-rūne '*pythonissa*."[93] *Burh-rūne* or *burg-rūne* seems to mean "mysteries of the burial mound"; compare with *byrgen-leóth*, "tomb elegy, epitaph, burial song," and *byrgen-song*, "burial song."[94]

Burh-rūnan means fates or female ancestors, according to an old gloss in the Cotton manuscripts: "The fates, furies, fairies; *parcae, furiae, oreades*: *Burhrūnan furiae*, Cot. 92."[95] (The Parcae were the threefold fates of Rome; *furiae* is a Latin name for the Greek Erinyes, who were avengers of wrongs, especially against the mothers; and Oreades were female spirits of mountains and wild rugged country.) L.M.C. Weston, speaking of the "awe" towards women's connecion to spirit, comments, "*Burgunas* may be wisewomen of the community, but they may also be supernatural guardian spirits."[96] Over and over it is made clear that no sharp lines can be drawn.

The alternation between witches and fates, seeresses and supernatural hags (or "furies") recurs throughout early medieval culture. Here reference is made to shamanic women, there to ancestral grandmothers or supernatural hags. Some texts treat *leod-rūne* as a female spirit similar to *hægtesse*, but both words were also translated as "witch" (*pythonissa* or *striga*). Similarly, the Norse tradition conflates giantesses with witches or *völur*, and the other way around (as when Oðinn calls up a dead *völva* to prophesy for him, and ends up cursing her as "the mother of three *thursar* [ogres]).["97] *Trollkona* can mean a spirit or a human witch. It is sometimes hard to tell which is meant.

In France and Britain, the faeries or elves tie in with witchcraft, as well as with ceremonies honoring the dead, the "good women," or other fateful spirits. In the folk belief of later centuries, the faeries are often indistinguishable from the dead, or from land spirits. They could confer marvelous gifts, but were also the cause of afflictions, even death. Anglo-Saxons regarded the *ælfe* (elves) as causing fevers, boils, and other diseases, including mental illness.[98] The Old English leechbooks, circa 850-950 CE, prescribed salves and christianized charms to ward off misfortunes caused by the *ælfe*—which they linked with *hægtessen* or nightgoers. Demonization of witches was already well underway. Another change was the shift to literacy; the new christianizing charms were not sung in the old manner, but written.[99]

The Old English Leechbook III, 61, names *nihtgengan* ("nightgoers") together with the elves as the spirits to be warded off.[100] It is called "a salve against *ælfcynn* (elf-kin') and against a *nihtgenga* ('night-goer,' a common Anglo-Saxon name for a witch or hag-spirit).[101] The next charm, against "elf-sickness," stresses the need to sing over plants before gathering them, and after the gathering.[102] A similar passage in Bald's Leechbook associates the *leod-rūne* with "elfish magic," prescribing remedies "against every *leodrune* and *ælf-siden*, being a charm, powder, drinks and a salve, for fevers…"[103] Audrey Meaney views these charms as "examples of mumbo jumbo … which priests concocted to replace pagan incantations."[104] This spell demonizes the *leód-rūne*, who is no longer a "mystery singer" but

Urn with breasts, sun signs, and greenery, England, 6th century

Ƿiþ ælcyr-yfelne leoðrunan 7 ƿið ælf-
siðne- biɾ ʒeppc pprtchim biɾ ʒpecisai
fcapum 7 Λ + Ω + ỹ+l P B ɥ ᛗ ++++ :· B ᴇ-pp ɴ
ɴ I k ɴ ᴇ ᴛ ᴛ ᴀ ɴ I ·

*"Against each evil leodrunan
and against elf-magic..."*

a fearsome harmdoer: "Against each evil *leodrune* and against *ælfsiden,* this
writing."[105] Another translation runs: "Against each evil witch and against
elvish fascination, write this writing for him, these Greek letters."[106]

These spells show a significant link between "witch" and "elvish magic."
The remedy is a "dust or drink against *leódrunan*"—magical powders or
potions.[107] The magic of the Christian spell relied on Greek characters
"somewhat distorted by the Anglo-Saxon scribe," interspersed with crosses
and other magical markings.[108] A man is instructed to write the formula in
silence and wear it on his left breast as an amulet.

There was more to the elves than the supernatural causation of ailments
shown in these christianized charms. For one thing, *ælf*-names were common: Alfred, Alfhild, Alfrieda, and even Aelfric, the anti-heathen preacher
himself. No society names children after demons, so clearly the *ælfe* had
another, sacred valence. Alaric Hall points out that the term *ylfig* ("elvish")
was sometimes translated as 'mysterious' or 'strange.'[110] (This resembles early
meanings of French *fae* or *fai,* as discussed in chapter 1.) From the way texts
use this word Hall concludes that "*Ylfig* must, then, denote some altered
state of mind—possibly one which was '*maior et divinus*' ["great and divine"]
... [giving a basis for] understanding *ylfig* to mean 'one speaking propheticall-
ly through divine/demonic possession'..."[111] Similarly, "the term *ælfisc* (elfish)
in some contexts appears as causing hallucination."[112]

Hall proposes that "*ælf* was once sufficiently intimately associated with
people predicting the future, and possibly with possession, that a derived
adjective [*ylfig*] meant something like 'predicting the future.'"[113] He also
suggests that *ælfe*-inspired prophetic speech may have been why woody
nightshade (a member of the datura family) was named *ælfthone,* "elf-vine."
It may have been "deliberately eaten for its mind-altering effects." An 8th

century riddle describes the effects on a person who eats it: "mad with dizziness, he whirls his limbs in a circle." (This looks like an outsider view of ecstatic dance.) *Aelfthone* was also used as a treatment for fever or madness.[114]

The parallels between Anglo-Saxon *ælfe* and later British and Irish *faerie* need to be kept in mind, since the latter are paid reverence and are involved in curing, as well as causing illness ("fairy-struck") and death ("carried off by the faeries"). Their archaic connection with the ancestral dead, especially, must be taken into consideration when weighing the meanig of *ælfe*. One expert on the returning dead writes, "Elves collectively denoted living beings of the otherworld and, most specifically, good ancestors."[115]

The same was true for the Norse *álfar*. Hilda Ellis Davidson noted "some link between the elves and the dead within the earth." She pointed to the posthumous deification of king Olaf as the "Elf [Álfr] of Geirstad," with sacrifices made to him "and also to elves dwelling in mounds."[116] Experts in Norse studies suggest that the *álfablót* (offering to the elves) should "be regarded as worship of human souls," that is, as ancestor veneration.[117] In

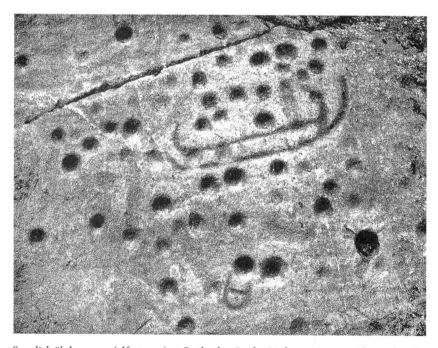

Swedish älvkvarnar *(elf-stones) at Botkyrka. In the Malar region, people made offerings at the* älvkvarnar *for healing, especially for "elf-blast" (skin eruptions). They made little dolls with the sufferer's hair and bits of clothing, and left them in one of the stone hollows for three Thursdays in a row. Or they poured fat or butter into the cupules.*

rural parts of Sweden, people made offerings in cup-shaped rock hollows called *älvkvarnar* ('elf-stones'), an observance that continued into the 20th century.[118]

People also appealed to the *álfar* for healing. In *Kormáks saga*, the witch Thórdís instructs a seriously wounded man to go to a mound of the elves, redden it with bull's blood, and make a feast for them, promising that this will heal him.[119]

Another important piece appears in the 8th century *Homilia de sacrilegiis*. It describes a Frankish custom of healing mentally ill people [*demoniacos*] by smudging them at old monuments, "that is, *sarandas antiquas*, which they call the Greater Ones (*maiores*)."[120] No one seems to know what "sarandas" means, but the conclusion seems inescapable that ancestors were being invoked for healing. *Maiores* could also be translated as "the elders." The ancient *sarandas* where these rites were carried out were very likely the ancient megalithic sanctuaries. The passage goes on to refer to other healing and protective measures: "those who by incantations and roots and herbal potions and wearing rings and iron bars on their bodies, or keep iron in their houses out of fear of the demons..." Using iron as a charm against faeries is a well-known and widespread custom in western Europe.

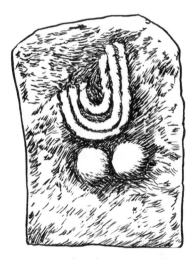

Grandmother stone at a megalithic tomb at Bellehaye, Oise, northern France

REPRESSING WOMEN'S CEREMONIES FOR THE DEAD

Returning to the ancestor-priestess, a Burgundian law punishing "women who violate graves" appears to refer to ceremonies of the *helliruna*,[121] or whatever their local counterparts were called. The law groups this vague category of women together with "adulteress" and "witch." These were the three categories of women that husbands could legally repudiate without consequences. An examination of the history and language of similar prohibitions shows that the law was really a ban on women's ceremonies of communicating with the dead, usually at gravesides.

As the Church spread its power in Spain, France and Germany, vigilant prelates forbade women's customary observances for the dead. As early as the 4th century, Spanish bishops had explicitly prohibited women's night vigils over graves, and burning candles on them, on pain of excommunication.[122] Prelates soon prevailed on kings to pass laws against such customs, using the same code phrase, "violation of graves"—which appears in some twenty-five penitential manuals and law codes.[123]

Ceremonies for the dead ("sacrilege at the graves of the dead") were the first entry in an 8th century list of pagan observances, the *Indiculus superstitionem et paganiarum*.[124] Priestly literature is full of other examples of this suppression. A 742 German edict against "pagan acts" also put ancestor veneration at the top of the list, asking bishops to "forbid sacrifice of the dead or sorcerers or soothsayers or amulets or omens or enchantments." Its target was "all those who love pagan observances."[125] (And they did; people loved their old customs, which is why they kept observing them in spite of priestly reproaches.) Prohibitions of "laying food and wine on the tumuli of the dead," and of eating it as part of a ceremony, are found in "almost every capitulary and church council in Germany."[126] Around the year 1000 an English cleric scolded, "The pagans learned the funerary incantations from their ancestors' vain songs and senseless stories."[127]

As late as 1015, the *Decretum* of Burchard of Worms repeated the prohibitions of the Elvira synod, saying that women "often commit secret crimes under the pretext of prayer and religion."[128] He alluded to divinatory consultations of the dead carried out during the winter holidays in his region of Germany.[129] Then he condemns wakes "surrounded by pagan rituals," advising priests to question people: "have you there sung devilish songs, and danced such dances as the heathen can devise at the devil's prompting, and have you there drunk and laughed..."[130]

Burchard also condemned the custom of burning grain for the "health of the living and of the house" when someone died. A dozen penitential books spanning the early middle ages refer to this offering for the dead, to protect the household. In Spain around the year 1060, the Penitential of Silo names women as the ones who make this offering.[131] Burchard forbids other ritual acts such as communal feasts from the offerings "placed by the graves, or by springs or trees or by certain stones or by forks in the roads," or raising burial mounds, and even bringing amulets to crosses at the crossroads.[132] The Arundel Penitential also described healing and divination taking place in graveyards, accusing people of devil-worship who "look into the future at tombs, funeral pyres, or elsewhere."[133]

Observances of ancestor veneration were pervasive, deep-rooted, and not easily stamped out. Over most of Europe, whether in Bulgaria, Scandanavia, or Czechoslovakia, people openly practiced them up through the 900s, and much later in some regions, bucking priestly repression over many centuries. In rural districts, families continued sacrifices to the "women of the tombs" long after the middle ages, supplicating the ancestors for wellbeing and life.[134]

Sardinian diviners known as *visionaria* or *ispiridada* ("inspirited women") communicated with spirits of the dead. They remained active into the twentieth century on this rural island that had escaped the witch hunts of the European mainland.[135]

Like *hægtesse*, the runa-titles are loaded with ambivalent meanings: "*Helrunas* may be human sybils or evil spirits. *Burgrunas* may be wisewomen of the community, but they may also be supernatural guardian spirits."[136] These words had acquired an undercurrent of negativity. It could be chalked up to Christian anti-heathenism—or to heathen misogyny, as a comparison with demonized giantesses in Norse lore suggests. In those transitional times, both could be factors.

The Old English epic *Beowulf* demonizes the *helrunan*, painting them as roaming devils.[137] Its villain, the male swamp-dwelling monster Grendel, is also described as *helruna*, even though the term was strongly gendered as female; but the real danger was Grendel's mother.[138] Animus against the heathens is even more explicit three stanzas below, where the poet treats their ceremonies as devil-worship:

> **Sometimes they vowed at their temples of idols**
> **To their gods' worship, with words they prayed**
> **The destroyer of spirits would render them help**
> **Against their folk-sorrows. Such was their custom,**
> **Hope of the heathen...**[139]

❖

CONCEpTS OF ϹΙΝΟ, SOUL, ANÒ SpΙRIT

The heathen language of Scandinavia was rich in shamanic concepts. The most common word for spiritual wisdom was *fjolkynngi*, "full knowing," "understanding many things." Power or mana was called *megin*; the verb of endowing with power, *magna*; and anything charged with this power was called *magnat* or *aukinn*, "increased." *Fjölkynngi* people were able to concentrate *megin* into stones, wands, belts, rings, and statues of deities. The Eddas speak of the *megin* of the earth and moon.[140]

Megin had equivalents in Anglo-Saxon (*mægin*) and Old High German (*magan*). Old English sources use *mægin* to mean strength, vigor, faculty, or ability—and also for the efficacy of herbs.[141] The Irish word *nért* carried much the same meaning.[142] Some scholars think that this Celtic word was borrowed into Germanic in ancient times: "The name Nerthus means 'power'; compare ON *njarðgjörð* = *meginjörð*, Thor's belt of strength. Norse *njarð* corresponds to Celtic *nerto-*, 'power (Irish *nert*, Welsh *nerth*)…'"[143] Through the same root, the name of the ancient Germanic goddess Nerthus is related to that of Njörðr, the medieval Norse god of prosperity and peace.

In Norse philosophy, every human has a consciousness called *hugr*, "mind, disposition, thought, way of thinking, desire, aspiration, perception or courage." [Shetelig and Falk, 407] The *hugr* is described as advising and warning, with overtones of precognition. Proverbial expressions say things like *mer segir hugr um*, "my heart tells me concerning this."[144] A weakened *hugr* resulted in illness or even death. The Goths had the same concept, *hugs*, which Ulfilas used to translate Greek *nous* (mind, thought, intelligence).[145]

Everyone also has *munr*, "desire, intention, will." And they possess a spirit-body, the *hamr*, which literally means "shape, skin, caul." This part of the being could travel and transform itself, especially for people of spiritual attainment. The word describes Freyja's *fjaðrhamr*, a "feather-robe

Panel from carved chest, circa 1000 CE, at Cammin cathedral, Denmark

or -skin" that enables her to fly; and the "troll-skin" that witches were said to possess. Those capable of shapeshifting were called *hamrammr* "having a powerful double," or *eigi einhamr*, "not possessing only one double."[146] An equivalent concept, *hama*, was known in Old English.[147]

A more common Norse word for "shapeshifter" was *hamleypur*.[148] Other terms for this, *vixla hömum* and *skipta hömum*, are also rooted in the concept of *hamr*.[149] A related concept was *sendingar*, spirit "sendings" that adepts could project to perform acts in far away places.

The wolf was often the tutelary spirit of such shamans. Night-riding witches and

Ancestor stone at Fornsalen, Visby, Gotland Island

troll-women traveled on the backs of wolves, the "dogs of the Norns" and "steeds of *jötun* women." The *Völuspá hin Skamma* explains, "All the valas [*völur*] sprang from Forest-wolf."[150]

Related to *hugr*, "spirit-mind," is "thought," *huginn*. The Norse sometimes conceived of it as a magic wind. Snorri comments that the *huginn* should be understood as the "wind of the *trollkvenna* (troll-woman)."[151] Eldar Heide suggests that it was common to conceptualize this magic wind as a spun thread, another spiritual connection to spinning.

Every person has a *fylgja*, guardian spirit or double, comparable to the archaic English *fetch*.[152] The *fylgja* took the form of a woman or an animal, and could be seen in dreams or by those possessing second-sight. The animal form might have expressed a person's individual nature, but the woman *fylgja* was more connected to family, and collective.[153]

Fylgjur are often compared to the protective ancestral *dísir*, who appear to warn of important happenings, especially death. (In this they resemble the Irish banshee.) To see your own *fylgja* is an omen of imminent death. But she is associated with birth too; *fylgja* is also used for the caul (amniotic sac) and sometimes the placenta.[154] The word *fylgja* literally means "one who follows." Icelandic midwives took care to bury the caul under the threshold, or sewed it into a band for the baby to wear. Destroying it would destroy the

Serpent woman under a dragon triquetra. The woman brandishing two serpents is also found in British and Gaulish art. Smiss Stone, Gotland Island, Baltic Sea

child's life, severing its link to the guardian *fylgja*.[155]

Also related to the *hamr* was *hamingja*, "fortune" or "personal luck." Like the *fyljgja*, it accompanied a person throughout life, but it could be transferred to someone else at death. The word *hamingja* seems to derive from *ham-gengja, "one who goes about in a form."[156] The *hamingja* was personified by a woman, who appeared to a person at crucial times.[157] At times the norns are conflated with *hamingjur*.[158]

Hamingja is also presented as "a power which can prevail against magic, and if it does not, then magic, and if it does not, then it was "veiled" or otherwise obstructed.[159] Régis Boyer breaks down these concepts in a useful way: "Visited (*hugr*), inhabited (*hamr*), or accompanied (*fylgja*)..."[160]

Because Scandinavian orature was so rich, and survived long enough to be written down before christianization wiped it out, its heathen philosophy survived more than in other western European countries. The only comparably extensive preservation of pagan orature is found in Ireland, where folk memory reaches back into the neolithic.

6

cailleachan, dísir, and hags

A rich lode of myths about a divine Old Woman were preserved at the northwest rim of Europe. She is called the Cailleach in Irish and Scots Gaelic, from *caille*, "mantle." This word came to mean "old woman," though for medieval sources it is sometimes translated as "nun." Hers is not a veil of modesty—the *cailleachan* are indominable and wild—but a mantle of mystery.

This Old Goddess inspired a vast complex of traditions, and no short description can hope to encompass her range, or depth. The Cailleach has universal qualities. She is not a goddess of "fertility," or "death," or of any single thing. She is a primordial being who is both transcendent and immanent. She is connected with rocks, mountains, boulders, rivers, lakes, wells, the sea and storms; with megalithic sanctuaries and standing stones; with deer, cows, goats, sheep, wolves, birds, fish, trees, and plants.[2]

Cailleach is an adjectival form of *caille*, "veil." It is a loanword from the Latin *pallium*, which originally meant "mantle," later "priestly stole," and then a woman's head covering.[1] The word's entry into Irish is dated by the p > q sound shift characteristic of early medieval Irish.

Ireland and Scotland are covered with natural shrines associated with the Cailleach. She cast her name across the landscape in hundreds of place-names, all with stories of an Old Woman of great cultural antiquity, who is more ancient than the present form of the Earth. J. G. Mackay called her "the most tremendous figure in Gaelic myth today."[3]

The cailleach Bhéara

The Cailleach Bhéara was an ancient being who "existed from the long eternity of the world."[4] Her oldest title is Sentainne, "Old Woman"—a native name that predates the use of "cailleach"—or Sentainne Bérri.[5] Cailleach Bhéara means the "Old Woman of Beara," a peninsula in Munster. She is often named Buí or Boí, "Cow," a title she shared with the ancient Irish goddess Bóand ("White Cow").

Tradition recognizes the Cailleach Bhéara as an extremely old—though not necessarily aged—woman. Her great age was a sign of power, venerable and proverbial: "as old as the Cailleach Bhéara." She is an ancestral mother to many peoples. The Prologue to the *Lament of the Old Woman of Beare* relates that "she passed into seven periods of youth, so that every husband used to pass to death from her of old age, so that her grandchildren and great-grandchildren were tribes and races."[6]

Thus the Cailleach Bhéara is the "epitome of longevity."[7] A proverb of Connaught places her in a triad of ancient beings: "Three great ages: the age of the yew tree, the age of the eagle, the age of the Cailleach Bhéarra."[8] Folk stories from Munster add the even longer-lived Otter of the Rock and the One-Eyed Salmon of Eas Rua.[9] The Welsh also told stories about the longest-lived animals who remember the history of the world.[10]

A woman of Tiree once asked the Cailleach how old she was. She replied that she remembered when the Skerryvore rocks were fields where barley was farmed and when the lakes were little wells.[11] The same is said of the Loughcrew monuments atop Sliabh-na-Caillíghe:

> **I am poor Cailleach Bhéara,**
> **Many a wonder have I ever seen;**
> **I have seen Carn-Bane a lake,**
> **Though it is now a mountain.**[12]

In Scotland, too, the age of Cailleach Bheurr is so great that great changes have come over the earth during her lifetime. In the headlands of Mull, people recounted her saying, "When the ocean was a forest with its firewood, I was then a young lass."[13] (This parallels Chinese traditions of the goddess Magu, who says that she had seen the Eastern Sea turn to mulberry fields three times, so many eons of time had she lived through.) In another Scottish verse, the Cailleach speaks of geophysical changes: "Dark, deep Crùlachan / The deepest loch in the world / The straits of Mull used to reach as far as my knees / but Crùlachan used to reach to my thighs."[14]

Numerous Irish stories demonstrate the great age of the Cailleach. In one story, St Patrick met her, and asked how old she was. "I buried nine times nine people on nine occasions in nine graves in Tralee." Then he asked how she managed to live so long: "I didn't ever carry the muddy dirt of one place beyond that of another place without washing my feet." She told him that every seven years she tossed the bones of a slaughtered bullock up into her loft. Patrick sent his servant up to count them, but after counting a great many of them, they had to give up, overwhelmed by the quantity that remained.[15] The theme of the Cailleach tossing innumerable bones up into the loft, and their witness to her great age, recurs in numerous folk accounts of the early 20th century.

The Beare peninsula in west Cork belonged to the Cailleach, and the island at its tip, off Dursey, was named Oileán Baoí after her. A sea rock was pointed out as the cailleach's great bull, Tarbh Conraidh. His bellow impregnated any cows who heard it. But one day the Cailleach became angry when he went off swimming after a cow, and she struck him with her staff, turning him to stone.[16] He became the Bull Rock, which is also known as Tech nDuinn, the "House of Donn," god of the underworld.[17] Irish tradition knows it as the realm of the dead.

A tradition of Kerry places the Cailleach Bhéara in a sisterhood of three old women. The other two were the hags of Dingle and Iveragh, two neighboring peninsulas. Once, during a time of hardship for Boí, the Cailleach of Dingle tried to render her aid by dragging another island over to her peninsula. The straw rope she was using broke, leaving the islands Scariff and Deenish off Iverach.[18] Another pairing of old women is preserved in the name of Meendacalliagh in Donegal, "mountain flat of the two hags."[19]

Other accounts relate the Cailleach, under the name Biróg, to the abundant-milking Glas Glaibhnann cow.[20] One story tells how "the celebrated witch Vera" possessed a fortune-bringing cow. (This anglicized spelling of Bhéara is one of many references to the Cailleach as "witch," which is an English word.) A neighbor and his son stole the cow and began driving her toward their farm. Giving chase, the Old Woman caught up with them, and struck all three with her staff, turning them to stone. The largest of these stones is called Clochtogla, the "lifted stone."[21]

The Cailleach's staff relates to other Irish shamanic wands. The Fé was made of aspen, sometimes with Ogham characters cut on it, and had power both in healing and cursing. The *Sanas Cormaic*, an early source on Irish paganism, calls the Fé a magic wand. It was used to strike what was detested and to banish ills; "and the wand was of such a purely pagan character that, in Christian times, it could be kept only in 'the cemeteries of the heathen.'"

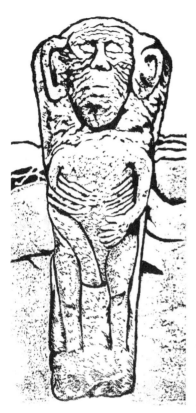

The classic sheela-na-gig is an old woman, bony, wrinkled, often hairless, and powerful. Fethard Abbey, Co. Tipperary

A 1509 remedy for a man who was made impotent through magic recommended cutting his name in Ogham characters on a wand, and then striking him with it.[22]

While the cailleach's staff evokes Irish and Norse magic wands, for Scots it also holds cosmological significance as the power of cold, darkness and winter. Her *slachdán* symbolizes the active force of the season of darkness. As the light half of the year begins, she hurls the *slachdán* to the base of the holly or gorse (both evergreen shrubs), storing her power of the cold and dark there until the advent of winter.[23] The Cailleach also creates rocks in Ireland and rearranges the coast of Scotland by hurling her *slachdán*.

Although slighted by medieval literature and epics, the Cailleach left her mark in innumerable folk stories and place names, including Slieve na Calliagh in Meath, Slieve Gullion in Armagh and Slieve Gallion in Derry, Sloc na Calliagh on Rathlin, Carnacally in Armagh, and Caislean na Caillighe island on Lough Carra in Mayo.[24] Just in Clare, there are Slievecallan and Ceann Caillí ("Hag's Head") at the southernmost tip of the Cliffs of Moher, Glennagalliagh Mountain, and Sliabh Ghleann na gCailleach. A cairn sits atop Bencullagh (Cailleach Mountain) in Galway.[25]

BUÍ, BÓI, AND BÓAND

The name Boí or Buí is ancient, and ties in with other Irish and Gaulish goddess names. Foremost among them is Bóand, "white cow," who gave her name to the Boyne River (An Bhóinn) and to two of the three colossal megalthic chambers that lie along it. The ancient geographer Ptolemy recorded the river's more archaic name Bouvinda Βουουίνδα.[26] The compound word is made up of *bou*, "cow," and *find*, meaning "white" but with the added sense of "brilliance." It derives from an Indo-European root meaning "wisdom, illumination."[27]

The cow goddess herself dates back to the Proto-Indo-European period. Bovinda, the earliest recorded form of her name, corresponds to the Sanskrit Gōvinda. (In India the name became masculinized as a title of Krishna, though it remains in the litanies of Devī). Sanskrit Gō is cognate to Irish Bó. Thus Bóand is a distant relative of Gō Mātā, the beloved Cow Mother of Vedic religion.[28] (Compare English "cow" and "bovine," divergent forms of the same root.) The Gauls also knew Bovinda, and had other cow-named goddesses like S(t)irona, "Heifer," and Damona, "Cow."[29] So the veneration of Boí has great time depth.

The colossal megalithic temple Brúgh na Bóinne is named for the White Cow Woman: "House of Bóand." The neighboring monument Knowth is named Hill of the Cow, Cnogba, anglicized as Knowth. Medieval sources connect it to Buí. The Dinnshenchas of Cnogba says that the name comes from Cnoc Buí, the hill of Buí or Bua. The Dinnshenchas of Nas calls Cnogba the hill of Buí "of the battles," and says she is also Called Bui in Broga (of the Brugh na Boinne). These are imaginative etymologies; linguists say that Cnogba cannot derive from "hill of Buí."[30] It means simply Hill of the Cow, using the genitive form (Bá) of "cow." Yet the mythical associations of Cnogba are another story. A poem in the *Book of Leinster* says that Buí is buried at Cnogba / Knowth.[31]

All these names are Indo-European, as Celtic tongues had long since replaced the languages of the elder kindreds, now lost. What they called the great stone sanctuaries that they built in the 4th millennium, no one knows. But much of the strong female symbolism of Irish cultural themes originates

Spiral kerbstone at entrance of Brú na Boinne, the "House of Bóand"

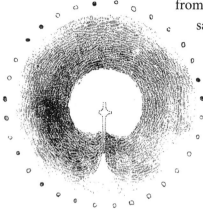

*Aerial view of Brú na Boinne shows
the sanctuary's womb shape*

from that very ancient people. Tradition says as much, naming Brú na Bóinne as the burial ground of the Tuatha Dé Danann, (Tribe of Danand). This goddess name of very ancient Indo-European vintage was applied to an older ethnic group of Ireland who were, apparently, perceived by the newcomers as a matriarchal people.[32]

The name Danand was already mostly submerged well before the time that these traditions began to be recorded in writing. She correlates to Don or Donwy, the Welsh mother of the gods (another faded goddess, mentioned in the *Mabinogion*), to Sanskrit Danu, and a myriad of river names across Europe, notably the Danube / Donau, Rhône, and Don. There are layers upon layers here; in many Irish accounts Buí's name is superseded by that of her "young son," Aengus Óg / Mac Ind Óg. Later come stories of kings of Tara who were buried there, in dynastic traditions that make much more of the men.

Bóand of the celebrated Brú na Bóinne sanctuary, Bó of Cnogba, and Boí or Buí, the Cailleach Bhéara: all carry the ancient name of Cow Woman. Other forms of the sacred cow persisted in Irish tradition, most famously as the Glas Ghaibhleann who gave rich and abundant milk as she roamed across Ireland. (This name is often given as Gavlen or an array of variant spellings that attempt to square Irish pronunciation with English spelling.) The cow was able to feed multitudes, filling any vessel no matter how large. Many place-names commemorate her passage. But the stories say that she disappeared after some greedy and selfish person tried to confine and exploit her, or wasted her milk, or otherwise failed to respect her generosity.[33]

Another Cow origin story explains the naming of ancient roads in Munster after a triad of spirit cows:

One May-eve, long ages ago, three enchanted cows suddenly emerged from the sea at Imokelly. The first was white; the second red; and the third black. They kept in company for about a mile; then the white cow

went northwest toward the county Limerick; the red cow went to the westward and passed around the coast of Ireland; the black cow going north-east towards the county Waterford.[34]

The same source adds that there is "hardly a county which does not possess a lake or well in which lives an enchanted cow which at certain times appears above the waters."[35]

The Corca Loighdhe ("Clan of the Calf") claimed the cow-woman Boí as their ancestor. They were a tribe of the Érainn living in the Beara peninsula of West Munster. Their king lived at Dun Buíthe (Dunboy), also named after Boí.[36] Another tribe of the Érainn, the Corca Dhuibhne, claimed Buí as their foster mother. Their own ancestor was the goddess Duibhne, whose name appears as Dovinia in several ogham inscriptions of west Munster.[37] Of the Corco Dhuibhne, the *Book of Lecan* says "... it was bequeathed to them that they shall never be without some wonderful Cailleach among them."[38] Thus oral tradition kept alive matrilineal origin stories.

But it also tells of violence that was tearing at those old kin bonds. The origins of the Corcu Dhuibhne are recounted in an 8th century text, *The Expulsion of the Déisi*. Duihind is raped by her brother Coirpre Músc, and conceives Corc and his twin brother Cormac. The violation reverberated upon her sons, who were in conflict even in her womb, one "reddening" the other. The crops failed, and people said it was because of the incest. "'Let them be burned,' the men of Munster said, 'so that the disgrace may not be in the land.' 'Let be given to me,' said the druid who was in the encampment, 'that Corc there so that I may bring him out of Ireland in order that the disgrace may not be there.'" So they gave him the infant Corc, "and he and his hag [*cailleach*] bore him into an island," as he recited a poem predicting great things for the boy's descendants.[39]

Departing from the norm of recounting the deeds of men, the story does not name the druid, only his wife Boí. This underlines her prominence, which is further emphasized by places named after her. The couple takes the boy to her eponymous island of Inis Boí off the tip of the Béare peninsula. The druid rescues him, but it is the Cailleach who restores him. Every morning for the next year, Boí performs a purification ritual in which she pours an ablution over Corc who sits on the back of an otherworldly white cow with red ears. One morning, Corc's curse finally leaves him and enters the cow, who jumps into the ocean and turns to stone, becoming the rock of Bó Boí ("cow of Boí"). Boí then takes Corc to his grandmother, Sárait, and convinces her to accept him back.[40] The Cailleach's restoration of Corc from exile, through ceremonial acts performed in the land's end realm of Donn, god of the dead, is a symbolic death and rebirth.[41] Other traditions say that Corc was only one of fifty foster children that the Cailleach had raised.[42] But those stories are lost.

τbe ოeçaᒐιτbιc caιᒐᒐeacb

Irish oral tradition associates the Cailleach with numerous megalithic hilltop monuments dating to the 4th millennium. Some passage graves bear her name, often as her "house." Other megaliths she is said to have built; or created by tossing boulders from hilltop to hilltop; or by carrying stones in her skirt or apron, which she drops, or else the apron-strings break and scatter the stones across the landscape. Similar acts of megalith building are told of the Martes or Margot-la-Fée in France, and of giantesses in Scandinavia.

Countless Irish stories tell how the Cailleach constructed huge cairns, mounds and megalithic monuments in a single night. Some, like megalithic "cairns" near Dundalk, Armagh and Heapstown, Sligo, are known by names like "one-night's-work."[43] (Later she is even said to have erected round towers of the Christian era.) The Cailleach Bhéara is commemorated in sacred sites all over Ireland. Some of the best-known Cailleach monuments are Slieve Gullion in Armagh, Loughcrew in Meath, and Carrownamadoo in Sligo. They are among the oldest megalithic sanctuaries in Ireland.[44]

In Armagh, people said the Cailleach lived in a deep megalithic chamber near the top of Slieve Gullion. (Sliabh gCullinn means "steep-sloped mountain"). It was called Calliagh Birra's House.[45] The highest-placed of all Irish megaliths, it sits on the southern summit, where it aligns with solar motion. It was surrounded by kerbstones and had three flat stone basins within its chamber. People visited this place on Blaeberry Sunday, a survival of of the pagan holiday Lughnasadh.[46] A lake near the summit is also named after the Cailleach, and on the western side of Slieve Gullion, the Ballykeel dolmen is known as Cathaoir na Caillí, the "Hag's Chair."[47]

In other accounts, a rock formation on Spellick hill in Aghadavoyle is

called the Cailleach Beara's Chair, and people
would come there on Blaeberry Sunday to sit
by turns on the rock.[48] Its Cailleach is sometimes called a "witch." She was
a guardian of the elixir of wisdom: "On the mountain somewhere, there is
a well of wisdom and magic meather [mead], from which if we only knew
the recipe, we could go to that marvelous ale, that once tasted — 'age could
not touch us, nor sickness, nor death.'"[49] Some versions of the Cailleach's
encounter with Finn at Slieve Gullion says that she gave him this restorative
elixir to drink (though not willingly).

By modern times, the ancestral Old Woman was often turned into a
"witch"—even in the absence of Irish witch hunts. (The word of course
comes from English). Over a century ago, Wood-Martin noticed "the transformation of the ancient goddesses, Aynia and Vera [Áine and Bhéara] into
witches of ordinary type… it is remarkable how stories of these mythical
beings have been so widely diffused, and have descended to the present day
from remote antiquity."[50]

Even the sun-maiden Grían ended up being presented as a witch. Five
warriors destroyed her father's "fairy mansion" (probably a megalith), and
she retaliated by turning them into badgers. Next their father came after her,
and since he rebuffed her conciliatory words, "she vanquished him by means
of a withering spell."[51]

In Sligo, the megalithic site Carrownamaddoo 2 (Castledargan) was
called Calliagh A Vera's House.[52] In the mountains above Kilross, in western
Tipperary, stands another stone formation the peasants call the House
of the Cailleach. A megalithic cavern near Collon in Louth is known as
Cailliagh Dirra's House.[53] The Labbacallee Wedge Tomb in Cork is said to be
her burial place; the Irish name means "the Old Woman's Bed" (Leabhadh

*Entrance to Calliagh Birra's
House, atop Slieve Gullion,
a mountain in Armagh,
northern Ireland*

Chailligh or Leaba Caillighe).[54]

loughcrew The Cailleach's most renowned namesake is the megalithic complex of Loughcrew. Its ancient stone chambers stand atop a low range in Westmeath, named Sliabh na Caillíghe, "the Old Woman's Mountains." The Cailleach was said to have dropped the megalithic monuments on its hilltops from her apron.[55] When Jonathan Swift visited Loughcrew in 1720, local people told him of her prodigious deeds, and of her stone chair:

> **Determined now her tomb to build,**
> **Her ample skirt with stones she filled,**
> **And dropped a heap on Carnmore;**
> **Then stepped one thousand yards, to Loar,**
> **And dropped another goodly heap;**
> **And then with one prodigious leap**
> **Gained Carnbeg; and on its height**
> **Displayed the wonders of her might.**
> **And when approached death's awful doom,**
> **Her chair was placed within the womb**
> **Of hills whose tops with heather bloom.**[56]

The three hilltops of Sliabh na Caillíghe are covered with cairns (an Irish term for what archaeologists call "passage graves," which many today call "womb tombs"). The best-preserved are Carnbane East and West in Loughcrew. The monuments on a third hill near Patrickstown were destroyed in recent centuries. There, the only surivals are a few kerbstones and a single interior slab engraved with signs. These megalithic chambers date to 3600-3400 bce, predating by several centuries the renowned monuments along the Boyne: Brugh na Boinne (New Grange), Knowth, and Dowth.

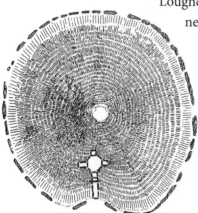

Aerial view of Cairn T, showing the quadrant shape formed by recesses

Of the Carnbane passage graves that have been excavated, all were collective burial sites, with remains of many cremations placed on the flat stone basins in their inner recesses. (They are unique to the megalithic chambers of Ireland.) But the monuments were more than graves; they were also sanctuaries of ceremonial renewal and of astronomical wisdom, as their solar alignments show. Covered in quartz pebbles, the cairns would have gleamed in the sun from a distance, like their more famous successor, Brú na Bóinne.

From the Hag's Chair on the summit of Carnbane East, half the counties of Ireland could once be seen. This massive stone seat rests on the north side of Cairn T, which is surrounded by six megalithic sanctuaries, now in ruins, but once all covered by earthen mounds. Their womb-shaped chambers received the dead, whose cremated remains gradually sank into the soil, returning to Earth to be reborn. The passageways to the uterine central chambers were lined with tall stones, many of them covered with engraved signs. The interior chambers are flanked by recessed areas, usually in threes that, in combination with the entrance halls, form a quadrant shape. The backstones of the recesses are engraved with patterns. That of Cairn L is elaborately engraved with spirals, vulvas, and concentric circles clustered in patterns that suggest cell division. On the backstone deep in the chamber of

Large stone basin and engraved backstone in one of three recessees off the main chamber in Cairn T, Loughcrew

Cairn T, solar symbols are aligned to catch the rays of the rising sun on the equinoxes.[56a]

Photos of the passageway stones at Cairn T are rarely published, which is amazing considering their age and importance. They are primeval, pulsing with concentric circles, curving lines, solar patterns, portals—and deeply engraved vulvas, portals of life, of rebirth, carved into the bones of Earth herself.[57] These symbols repeat in the recesses and on other engraved stones.

Also grooved into the rock are numerous round cupules, as deep as four inches, some of them clustered in honeycomb patterns. Stone cupules figure in conception magic in many cultures, as do the vulvas and concentric circles.

Women desiring to conceive children might have come to these ancestral sanctuaries, seeking to regen erate ancestral spirits in their wombs. Like women in other parts of the world, they would have touched, rubbed, painted, made ablutions, or ground out rock dust from the cupules, making them deeper over millennia. These old symbols of progeneration predate even the megalithic era, as they originate in older petroglyphs across the landscape of Ireland, Europe, and around the world.

Hag's Chair at Cairn T, Loughcrew, Westmeath.
From Wood-Martin, Traces of the Elder Faiths of Ireland *1902: 253*

Folklore says that the Cailleach looked out over her domain from the Hag's Chair, where she watched the stars.[58] The stone block of ten by six feet is engraved with concentric circles, vulvic portals, cupules, and other markings. Most of these have greatly eroded since Eugene Conwell published a drawing of the Hag's Chair in the mid-1800s, and a later sketch published in 1895.[59] Few of the markings remain visible, except for a supercessionist cross engraved on the seat. "Local lore states that a modern visitor, seated on the chair, will be granted a single wish."[60]

The Cailleach is named Garavogue in the Loughcrew stories recorded by Jonathan Swift. In faraway Sligo, megalithic tradition also names her as Gharbhóg (Garavogue). A river in the northwest of Ireland bears the same name.[61] So in addition to Boí, a second name for the Cailleach was fairly widespread, and others, if we count Dígdi and Bírog. But these seem to have yielded, ultimately, to the name of the Old Woman of Béare, as the stories became consolidated.

In another story, the Cailleach Bhéara came to Loughcrew from the north to perform a magical act that would give her great power. She filled her apron with stones, dropping a cairn on Carnbane; then jumped a mile to Slieve-na-cally (Hag's Mountain) to drop another, and on to the next hill, where she let another stone fall. On her fourth and final leap she slipped and fell to her death.[62] (This is one of many attempts to mythically kill off the Cailleach.) A different story says that if she had managed to keep all the stones in her apron during these prodigious leaps, "she would have gained rule over all of Ireland..."[63] But her power was of a different kind.

The many engraved stones at Cairn H on Carnbane West repeat the concentric circles and solar signs of the eastern cairns. This large passage grave is rimmed with 41 kerbstones. In its back recess lay the largest of all the stone basins found in the Irish megalithic chambers.

Backstone at Cairn L Loughcrew, Westmeath

It rested on six small stone balls and the remains of multiple cremations, which may have first been laid on the stone slab.

Bone pieces carved with swirling patterns in the La Tène style were found in Cairn H, along with bronze rings, bone pins, and beads. They show that people continued to frequent these shrines into the late Iron Age, thousands of years after their construction. It has been suggested that a diviner or oracle at Cairn used them in ceremony.[64]

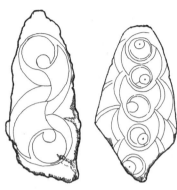

Boulders and stone formations are also named after the Cailleach. In Altagore, county Antrim, stood a stone called the Shanven, "Old Woman." Local people considered her sacred, and left offerings of oatcakes and butter there. It was said that a mason ignorant of the stone's power moved it for use as a gatepost. The next morning it had returned to its old place.[65] This story resembles French tales of the Black Madonnas being removed from and miraculously returning to their mountain sanctuaries.

It also recalls the medieval practice of taking sheela-na-gigs away from wells and fields to incorporate them into doorways and walls of churches, monasteries, and castles. Old Woman predominates in the iconography of sheelas. (That subject is a book in itself,[66] but for now it must be noted that one name for the sheela is "the witch on the wall").[67] Incorporating her icons into the churches was apparently a non-negotiable condition of christianization. People carried out rites of rubbing the sheela, or touching stones kept in hollows in the church walls, or enacted other ritual "patterns" that still continue today.

Stones of the Cailleach

The Cailleach is often said to have left her mark in stone. Near Antrim is a *bullaun* (rock basin) known as the Witch's Stone. When the Cailleach finished building the Round Tower, she leaped off the top and landed on this stone, leaving marks from her elbow and her knee. This stone used to lie near a stream, but later a wall was built that separated it from the water.[68] Another Witch's Stone is on the hill of Carrick, above the Boyne river. Legend says that a witch threw the boulder from the hill of Croghan at an early priest, but missed.[69] Originally it is the Cailleach who performs these feats, as a woman of extraordinary powers, who is imbued with a strong pagan valence. Later, as the culture changed under English rule, she began to be interpreted as a witch, remaining outside Christian orthodoxy and counterposed to the priest.

In many places standing stones are said to be people and animals that the Cailleach had transformed.[70] Her megalith-building aspect carried over into the Christian era, when traditions arose making her the builder of the Round Towers. It was she who built the unfinished tower at Meelick, carrying up stones in her pockets. She planned to raise up a tower to the sky, but when a boy passing by insulted her, she went into a rage and jumped down. Two dents in the rock below are said to have been left by her knees.[71]

Analogous stones are found in Britain. Any number of Scottish cairns and rock formations are named after mythic old women: Carlin's Cairn, Carlin Skerry, Carlin Tooth, and two Carlin's Stones, one by Dunlop, another near Waterside, Ayrshire. In Uist, Scotland are two Stones of the Black Hags (Leac nan Cailleacha Dubba). In Yorkshire several stones are called the Old Woman, and another on Bamford moor in Derbyshire.[72]

The Cailleach as Cultural Teacher

Marvelous long life is one of the many superlative qualities of the Cailleach. She possesses super-human strength and is able to walk long distances in very short times. She is often of colossal size, so huge that she easily wades rivers and lakes, or strides from hilltop to hilltop.[73] The Cailleach Bhéara was credited with extremely sharp sight, so that she was able to discern from a distance of twenty miles that her sister-hag's cow had wandered into her grainfield.[74]

Folk memory attributes the long life and other powers of the Old Woman to her way of living. In one story the Cailleach tells some women how she lived so long, "The morning breeze never blew on my empty stomach; the dew never wet my foot before sunrise; I consumed hot and I consumed cold, and that's the reason why I'm so lasting."[75] She never ate except when she was hungry, never stayed abed once awake, never carried mud on her feet from one place to another, and never threw out dirty water before bringing in clean.[76] (This last was a faery taboo widely observed across Ireland.) Many stories emphasize that in her constant walking across the country, the Cailleach would always wash the mud of one place off her legs before going on to the next place.

Traditions are very definite—but conflicting—about what foods the Cailleach ate to enhance her longevity. Here she took only cow's milk, there it was only seafood, or only grain.[77] A story of the Cailleach's encounter with saint Caithiarn depicts her as a forager who liked to gather food at the seashore. Or, roaming the glens, "she used to gather up all before her in her domination of the whole territory." Told about a salmon no one could catch, she caught it and brought it home to Béarra.[78]

These stories recall an ancient era of foraging peoples. That idea is supported by claims that the Cailleach dated back to the time of the Fir Bolg (according to the Book of Invasions, the first people in Ireland, an ancient non-agricultural society). It could be implied, too, by the theme of the Cailleach always traveling from place to place, from one end of Ireland to the other, and never staying anywhere for very long. But the same could be said for other stories that paint the Cailleach as a nomadic herdswoman: "She always had a large herd of cows … She used to travel from place to place, with the animals, from county to county. She didn't stay settled in any one place but always moved on."[79] Other accounts add goats and sheep to her herds. In Scotland, she ranges over the hills with herds of deer, rather than cattle. The Irish goddess Flidais also had herds of deer. These

The Scottish song "Little Cailleach of the Wild" (*Cailleach bheag an f hasaich*) joins her great age with the theme of her foraging for seaweed, garlic, fish and nuts:

What time the great sea
Was a grey mossy wood
I was a joyous little maiden
My wholesome morning meal
The dulse of the Rock of Agir
And the wild garlic of Sgoth
The water of Loch-a-Cheann-
dubhainn
And the fish of Ionnaire-more
Those would be my choice
sustenance
As long as I would live.
I would sow my nine lovely
rigs of lint
In the little trim glen of Corradale
And I would lift my skirtful of nuts
Between the two Torarnises.[84]

The "nine rigs of lint" are rows of flax. Thus this wild Old Woman is also a spinner and weaver, like Holle, Perchta, the Psi-Pol'nitsa, Laima, and other witch goddesses.

wild kine belong to the deepest cultural layer, overlaid as the economy changed to herding and farming.[80]

People in Connaught connected the Cailleach with the sowing and harvesting of grain. They say she taught the Irish how to thresh: using a holly-stick flail and a hazel-wood striker, she threshed sheaves on a clean floor, one at a time. Farmers there followed her custom of sowing in late winter—"the oats of February"—and of harvesting green corn before the autumn storms came. In many Gaelic-speaking areas of Scotland, the first or last sheaf harvested was called the Old Woman, and treated with ceremony.[81] Scots called this last sheaf A' Cailleach or Carlin, Carline, Carley ("old woman"). In Ireland, she was the Granny; the Old Witch in Yorkshire; and Wrach (meaning both "hag" and "witch") for the Welsh in Pembrokeshire.[82]

The key to these stories is not the obvious contradictions between the foraging, herding, and agricultural Cailleach—with their different historical layers—but their idea that the Cailleach was a model of wisdom and survival; that she was the ultimate elder who knew best how to manage things. This theme contrasts with a later group of tales that make the Cailleach wrong, foolish, or bad, and which show her on the losing end to males who rebuke, insult, and defeat her.

Some Scottish stories link the Cailleach with a flood, like Bóand in Ireland. But while Bóand acts in defiance of men's taboos—that a woman should never approach the sacred well, or that she should not walk counter-sunwise around the well, Scottish tales show the Cailleach dozing off or forgetting to replace the lid on a well she had opened to water her herd of cattle. This well would flood over if it was left uncovered by sunset. The Cailleach woke up to the sound of rushing water, just in time to push the stone lid back over the fountain, but not before it had formed loch Obha.[83] This story, and that of her pool of renewal, turn on the change of Time, at the edge of day and night.

LAMENT OF THE CAILLEACH BHÉARA

As she first enters written record around the year 900, this dynamic female figure has been rendered nearly unrecognizable. In a stunning example of patriarchal revisionism, the untamed cailleach who tossed boulders and leaped hilltops, roaming through the mountains with forest animals or, witch-like, taking their shape, was now pictured as an unhappy, tragic, powerless nun.

> **I am Buí, the Old Woman of Beare**
> **I used to wear a smock that was ever-renewed**
> **Today it has befallen me, by my low estate,**
> **That I could not have even a cast-off smock to wear.**[85]

This poem is the oldest written reference to the Cailleach Bhéara, dating to the 9th century, but surviving only in later copies in the *Otia Merseiana*.[86] The manuscript betrays priestly influences, recasting the Cailleach as the mother of St Fintan or as the wife of an 8th century poet. This pattern of stripping down ancient myths and reinterpreting them according to patriarchal norms is by now a familiar theme. Under the new order, female might of the magnitude expressed in folklore is unthinkable. The loss being lamented has more dimensions than the poet would have recognized.

In the poem, the Cailleach laments a cultural shift toward greed: "It is riches you love, and not people; when we were alive, it was people we loved. Beloved were the people whose lands we happily traverse; well did we fare among them, and it was little they boasted afterwards."[87] The final line seems to refer to hospitality offered for its own sake, not for prestige or status—but it has always struck me as a reference to an older, subjugated populace.

> **Lone is Femen: vacant, bare**
> **Stands in Bregon Ronan's chair.**
> **And the slow tooth of the sky**
> **Frets the stones where my dead lie.**[88]

The poem is about death, winter, decay. It is brimming over with female bitterness and intense loss. Age is no longer venerable and powerful—especially female age, which is seen as contemptible and weak. Her beauty gone, the Cailleach sits at the fringes of society, disregarded, in want. She is singing her death song: "My life ebbs from me like the sea | Old age has made me yellow."[89]

> **Ebb, flood, and ebb: I know**
> **Well the ebb, and well the flow.**
> **And the second ebb, all three,**
> **Have they not come home to me?**[90]

Buí of Béare laments that she used to wear a gown that was ever-renewed, but now her garment is threadbare. She laments her poverty and low status, the loss of her looks and therefore, of the company of chiefs and warriors. She remembers the men she loved, and how she raced with them on the fields. King Diarmaid no longer comes to her; he is rowing across the river of the dead. Buí drank mead with kings, but now sits with "shrivelled hags" swilling the whey-water of poverty. She has to follow the routines of a nun, against her will: "And as upon God I call | Turn my blood to angry gall."[91]

While the *Lament* reflects the bitter lot of old women in patriarchal society, it takes Buí far from her origins as the Cailleach of the peasantry: a being of immense antiquity who outlasts generations of offspring, whose age is not shameful but revered, who has tremendous strength, vitality and endurance, and who joyously heaves boulders and shapes the earth. The nun Buí has also been stripped of the power of the sovereignty goddess about whom so much ink has been spilled.

Some scholars say that Buí is not the name of the Cailleach, only that of the island off the tip of the Beare peninsula.[92] But one old book shows the island itself being named after her. The early story about Boí "the druid's wife" in *The Expulsion of the Déisi* explicitly links her name, and her cow, to that very island. However, the prose introduction to the *Lament* gives her yet another name: "Old Woman of Berri, named Digdi, of the Corcu Dubne."[93] Later, the *Book of Lecan* also names her as Digi or Duineach.[94]

For all her pervasiveness in folk orature, written Irish literature barely mentions the Cailleach Bhéara. None of the major medieval texts name her, only some minor 12th century texts and the *Metrical Dindsenchas*. Not much is said of her there, other than naming her (along with Naas) as one of Lugh's two wives.[95] Expressing a sentiment, echoed by other scholars, Mackay commented, "The implied indifference of the Irish aristocracy, contrasted with the universality of her legends among Gaelic-speaking Irish folk to this day, mark her as an aboriginal."[96] Not just indifference: it was outright antipathy.

Many stories tried to do away with this divinity. A thousand attempts were made to mythically kill off the deathless Cailleach, and the pagan past along with her. It is recounted how she drowned in a lake, fell off a mountain, or was overcome by the bark of a dog; how some saint caused her to be turned to stone or banished in a puff of smoke; or that some man killed her, or defeated her through trickery, and stole her enchanted objects. A Scottish tale even makes her into a witch whose powers a man is able to neutralize by dragging her through the fire by her heels.[97]

One tale says that the Cailleach was so tall that she was able to wade in all Ireland's lakes and rivers, but that she drowned while crossing the deepest loch in Sligo, the Lake of Two Geese. This lake is rumored to have an underground outlet and a monster that guarded treasure in its depths. Folk legends speak of how an attempt to dig out the treasure was foiled by the "good people."[98]

Modern stories show the Cailleach being disrespected and put down by men, even boys. When she scolded a servant boy for shaking out the hay when rain was on its way, he challenged her: "How do you know that it's going to rain?" Her reply invokes traditional omens drawn from observing Nature: "because the scald-crow screamed it and the deer spoke it." Then the boy repeats an Irish proverb, slightly altered for the story: "Heed not the scald-crow nor the deer | And heed not a woman's words | Whether it's early or late the sun rises | the day will be as God wills it."[99]

Another version of this saying is more pointedly anti-pagan: "Do not believe the scald-crow or the raven | Nor any false deity of the women."[100] But the faery woman Sín makes a retort to these misogynist tropes in the "Death of Muircertach Mac Erca":

Never believe the clerics | For they chant nothing save unreason | Follow not their unmelodious stave | for they do not reverence righteousness.[101]

The continually performed subordinations, defeats, and minimizations of the Cailleach failed to erase her memory, just as the monkish redactors of Irish orature were unable to get rid of the goddesses they kept trying to kill off. The Cailleach's near-omission from elite and learned accounts, and even the denunciations of pagan ways, failed to arrest transmission of her traditions among the people:

Regularly pronounced as overcome and appropriated, displaced and demonized since the early medieval period, the divine otherworld female is, nevertheless, retained and reinterpreted in Irish cultural consciousness and Irish expressive tradition...[102]

In spite of efforts of the priests and learned men, the lowly and powerful current of folklore carried the outlawed mythosophy of the Cailleach into modern times. She survived in Scotland, where the landscape was pollinated with tales of "great supernatural hags haunting mountain passes or driving their deer over the hills and conferring benefits and evils on humanity as they saw fit."[103]

The Cailleach in Scotland

The name of the Cailleach Bhéara changed after she was brought into Scotland, where she became known as Cailleach Bheur. In Gàidhlig *bheur* means "sharp, cutting," and refers to her winter-making power. Scots called the Cailleach the Old Wife of Thunder, and watched for the meteorological changes that signaled her coming. She brought snowfall over the heather-tinted hills and fields. As "daughter of the little sun," the Cailleach is an elemental power of winter cold, of wind and tempests. She comes into power as the days shorten and the sun courses low in the skies. She carries a *slachdán* (staff of power) with which she shapes the land and controls the weather. In the Skye folk-tale "Finlay the Changeling" she strikes the ground with it, making the earth harden with frost. By some accounts, wherever the Cailleach throws her *slachdán,* nothing grows.[104]

The last spurt of harsh winter weather is called *A' Chailleach.* Then comes *Latha na Caillich,* her day, which in the old calendar fell on March 25, the equinox, and this is when the hag was "overthrown"—until the next equinox. In the old calendar it was once New Years day, but is now called Lady Day.[105] In early spring the Cailleach hurls her *slachdán* into the root of the holly and gorse, plants symbolic of winter that were sacred to her. During the "big sun" —the light half of the year—she metamorphoses into a gray boulder that exudes moisture.[106]

Scots used to say that the Cailleach ushers in winter by washing her big plaid in the ocean whirlpool of Corryvreckan. Folklore holds that her action gave the turbulent gulf its name *Coire Bhreacain*: Cauldron of the Plaid. As the knowledgeable Mrs. Grant explained to a folklorist:

Before the washing the roar of a coming tempest is heard by people on the coast for a distance of 20 miles, and for a period of three days

before the cauldron boils. When the washing is over the plaid of old Scotland is virgin white.[107]

The 16th century poet Dunbar depicted the Cailleach descending from Lochlawn in a stormcloud, hurling thunder and lightning bolts: "She spittit Lochlomond with her lips | Thunner and fireflaucht flew from her hips."[108] The stormiest headlands in Mull used to be called Cailleach Point, where she sits on the rocks, looking out to sea.[109] A nearby cave was called the milking-place of the Cailleach's goats and sheep. The rocks at Lora Falls were steppingstones of the Cailleach and her goats.[110] The Irish Cailleach was also connected with the sea, both in the 9th century *Lament* and in the folk traditions of Béare.

A weather-making Old Woman was also known on the continent. In Lorraine, la Vieille de la Seille (Old Woman of the Seille River) travels through the seasons (or weather, or time: *qui court par le temps*). The "Days of the Old Woman" are usually said to be the last three days of March and the first three of April, when she sends spring frosts dangerous to the fruit orchards. And this is not her only resemblance to the Irish Cailleach: "Her great strength, which manifests when she throws boulders or carries masses of stones and earth to throw them in the sea, is a rather common trait."[111] That mightiness is shared by the Norse giantesses as well.

Like the Cailleach, la Vieille is an Old Woman associated with cows and cold weather. In various regions of France, the Days of the Old Woman run from the end of March into April, but the dates vary, sometimes beginning as early as February. They often bear a cow-name, like Les Jours de la Vachère (female cowherd), Vacairols, or Vaccharials. The story turns on the Old Woman celebrating getting her heifers through the winter, while March borrows days from April in order to bring cold that makes her beat her hands together.[112]

The Scottish Cailleach shaped the mountains and lakes, moving islands and striking rocks; she built the archaic cairns and megaliths.[113] She carried earth and stones on her back to make the hills of Ross-shire. Sometimes her basket or its strap broke, spilling the contents out to form the mounts of Ben Vaichaird and Ben Wyvis, and rock piles like Carn na Caillich. Deer faeries called *glaistigean* are credited with similar land-building feats.[114] They are often called Cailleach, as in stories of the *glaisteag* of Beinne Bhric.[115]

"Cailleach Beara" after John Duncan

The Cailleach nan Cruachan lives in Ben Cruachan, the highest point in Argyll. Countless other Scottish placenames commemorate her: Craig Cailleach, Glen Caillich, Loch na Cailleach, and various rocks, headlands, and meadows.[116]

The Cailleach's plowing created a crevice in the earth called the Hag's Furrow. She upturned huge piles of stones while ploughing on the Caledonian faery hill, mount Schiehallion. (In Gaelic Sídh Chaillean means "Mound of the Crone.") Many places are named Beinne na Cailleach (her mountain) or Sgríob na Cailleach (her "writing," which she inscribed in the earth). Scottish folklore says that the Crone turned into a boulder atop Beinn na Callich (Crone's Mount) in Skye's Red Hills, where a prehistoric cairn stands.[117]

In Perthshire there is a Glen Cailleach, with a stream named after the Crone, and a shrine to her. It is small shelterhouse called Tigh nan Cailleach ("House of the Old Woman") or Tigh nam Bodach (her husband's name). Inside are a group of stones, which are said to be the Cailleach, her husband the Bodach, and their children. Local people say that their ancestors gave shelter to the Cailleach and her family in the glen, which became fertile and prosperous during their stay. They gave the stones to the locals saying that the glen would continue to thrive as long as the stones were put out to look over the glen at Bealltainn and returned to the sheiling at Samhainn. People still observe this ritual today.[118]

Mountain springs were sanctuaries of the Scottish Cailleach. She was said to visit them to renew her strength, or to perform rites that bring on the seasons. Scottish stories of Loch Bá ("lake of the cow") in Mull said that the Cailleach came in the dead of night to the Well of Youth, to drink "before bird tasted water or dog was heard to bark." Her incredible longevity came from the water of life, which renewed her every hundred years. People said that the Cailleach had borne over five hundred children during her long life. (Once again, she is remembered as an ancestor.)

In many versions of this story, a dog barked before the Cailleach had bent to the water, and she crumbled into dust.[119] Other versions have her visiting before dawn on Bealtaine, but she had to come to the water before any dog barked. At last she was caught out while still making her way to the water. In a loud voice she cried out her death poem, which began, "It was early that the dog spoke..." Then she crashed to the ground, dead.[120]

A much-revered fountain in Banffshire was named Taber Cailleach, Well of the Old Woman. People made pilgrimages and offerings there. Religious trips to springs were as common in Scotland as in Spain, France, or Germany. Scots walked nine times around the Well of Virtues after drinking from its waters, then circumambulated the menhirs standing beside the well.[121]

The Scots knewCailleach Bhéurr was known as a wilderness spirit and protector of wild animals. The highest peak in Scotland, Ben Nevis, was sacred to her, and from it she is named Nícnevin. (The prefix Ní- or Nic means "daughter of" in Gàidhlig; Ben Nevis means "mountain of heaven.")[122] The Cailleach took her herds of deer to Glen Nevis and sang croons as she milked them. Hunters unable to find deer blamed her for protecting them.[123]

The Cailleach of Ben Bric herself took the form of a gray deer.[124] The great Cailleach of Clibhrich used witchcraft to keep the hunters away from her deer. Early one morning a man named William watched her milking her does at the door of her hut. When one of them ate some blue yarn she had hanging on a nail in her house, she took off her protection, predicting that the doe would be shot. And so it happened.[125]

The Scots had many songs known as faery croons, sung by *cailleachan* or other supernatural women associated with animist sanctuaries, such as the *glaisteagan* (deer-faeries). The old *glaistig* of Ben Breck in Lochaber sang a croon to her does as she drove them up the mountainside. The song has an incantatory quality, invoking the Crone of Ben Breck with a hailing cry:

> **Cailleach Beinne Bric, horó!**
> **Bric horó! Bric horó!**
> **Cailleach Beinne Bric, horó!**
> **Great hag of the fountain high!**

I ne'er would let my troop of deer,
Troop of deer, troop of deer;
I ne'er would let my troop of deer,
A'gathering shellfish to the tide.

Better liked they cooling cress,
Cooling cress, cooling cress;
Better liked they cooling cress,
That grows beside the fountain high.[126]

In another version of this croon, the Cailleach proclaims that she is an old woman who ranges the mountains and glens: "I am a carlin ranging bens, ranging bens, ranging glens..." She epitomizes freedom for all beings, saying, "I never set fetter on black or red cow in the herd.... I am the carlin who is light | Alone on the spur of the cairns."[127]

The Scottish cailleach's free-ranging cow was said to give great amounts of milk. In Benderloch, people called round green hollows "Cailleach Bheur's cheese-vats," because their rich grazing gave good milk. A rock shelter in Ardnamurchan was known as the Caillich's Byre, and she was said to keep her cattle there.[128] Like all faery cattle they were inviolate. An Irish legend tells how the Cailleach's neighbors once stole her magical cow and began driving her toward their farm. The crone gave chase, caught them and struck all three with her *slachdán*, turning them to stone. The largest of the rocks is called Clochtogla, the "lifted stone."[129]

The Scots often spoke of *beur cailleachan* in the plural. A Gaelic song mentions three *cailleachan* of the Scottish Hebrides. Other stories describe the *cailleachan* as powerful beings living in lochs and among the rushes. A certain tall lakeside reed was called "the distaff of the Bera wives," while a water plant similar to flag was their "staff."[130]

Another Scottish crone spirit is the Doonie, who appears to help people in trouble and to guide lost travelers.[131] A strange old woman called the Doonie once saved a boy who fell off a cliff and was hanging from a hazel-bush. She appeared below him, telling him to jump into her apron. He fell through it into the river, but she grabbed his neck and pulled him out. She warned him never again to hunt the rock-doves, "Or maybe the Doonie'll no be here tae keep ye."[132] She too was a protector of wildlife.

The Muilearteach was an ocean Cailleach armed with "two slender spears of battle." Upon her head the Muilearteach had "gnarled brushwood, like the clawed old wood of aspen root."[133]

> **Her face was blue-black of the lustre of coal**
> **And her bone-tufted tooth was like red rust.**
> **In her head was one pool-like eye,**
> **Swifter than a star in a winter sky.**[134]

Another blue-faced crone was Black Annis, who lived in a cave in Leicestershire. Even the Puritan poet Milton remembered a "blew, meager hag," but in his time she had become heavily demonized.[135] These dark British hag traditions have led to a modern folk etymology which tries to derive Cailleach from the Indian goddess Kālī. But Irish and Sanskrit are both descended from a common ancestor, not one from the other. And these two words are unrelated, with different etymologies: "black" in the case of Kālī; "mantle" for the Irish goddess. However, they have this much in common: both are primordial, untamed female spirits.

The Cailleach sometimes assumes the shape of gulls, eagles, herons, and cormorants. She rambles the hills followed by troops of deer and wild pigs, and leaps from hilltop to hilltop. Various accounts show Cailleach Bheura and her helpers riding on wolves and wild pigs (much like Norse and Russian witches) especially during the storms of February.[136] Similar stories are told of the Gyre Carline, a crone goddess of the Lowlands, who carried an iron club. When a pack of dogs attacked her, she turned into a pig and ran away. Some stories about the Gyre Carline reproduce the demonized stereotype of the witch hunts. But Sir Walter Scott called her the "mother witch of the Scottish peasantry," equating her with the Fairie Queen and Nicnevin.[137]

The Manx CailLagh

The Manx tell of Caillagh ny Groamagh ("the Gloomy") or Caillagh ny Gueshag ("Old Woman of the Spells").[138] Again, she is a witch, and a shapeshifter. She is seen on St. Bride's day as a gigantic bird who is carrying sticks in her beak.[139] As in Ireland, fine weather on this day portends a late spring, while a rainy one means good weather. An old Manx source explains:

> **Caillagh-ny-groamagh, the gloomy or sulky witch, was said to have**
> **been an Irish witch who had been thrown into the sea by the people in**

Ireland with the intention of drowning her. However, being a witch, she declined to be drowned, and floated easily until she came to the Isle of Man, where she landed on the morning of February 12th. It was a fine, bright day, and she set to work to gather 'brasnags'—sticks to light a fire, by which she was able to dry herself.[140]

Following her first arrival, the Caillagh goes out in the morning every February 12 to gather twigs for a fire. If she can dry herself before noon, then the spring will be wet, but if not, the weather will be dry.

The name of the Manx Caillagh-ny-Groamagh is related to Welsh *gwrach*, which means "hag" but was commonly understood as "witch." "Usually translated as 'Old Woman of the Gloom,' the linguistically astute might recognise that the Manx word 'groamagh' (pronounced with a m>w lenition as 'gro-ach') is the same as the name of legendary seaside female spirit in the Breton legends, the Gro'ach. This is also a metathesis of the Welsh word for 'hag', which is *gwrach* (as in 'Gwrach y Rhybin')."[141] Gwrach also means "witch" in Welsh.

Manx songs about the hag Berrey Dhone may relate to the Irish Cailleach Bhéara, and even offer "possible evidence that Bérri was there the hag's original name and not merely a toponym."[142] Berry Dhone appears as a witch or "an amazon who can stride over mountains," a feat very much in keeping with the Cailleach Bhéara.[143] Her bird aspect is also mirrored by the Irish name for the owl, *cailleach-oidhche* ("old woman of the night").

A headland in Maughold, the Gob ny Callee, was named after the Manx Caillagh. Like her Irish counterpart, she was reputed to leap from hilltop to hilltop (or in some Manx versions, was pushed). People said that a hollow at the top of Ballagilbert Glen in the southern part of the island was caused by the fall of Caillagh ny Groamagh when she was going from the hilltop of Barrule to that of Cronk yn Irree Lhaa.[144]

The Dísir

It was the belief in olden times that men were born again, but that is now called old women's superstition.[145]

Ancestral mothers lay along the strand of becoming that reached back to the Fates, the Norns, the Wyrd Sisters. They possessed prophetic knowledge and their appearance among the living was taken as an omen of birth, death, or momentous events. Heathen communities called upon ancestral grand-mothers to bless, counsel, protect, and provide

íðíѕí   Old German

íðeѕ   Old English

íṫíѕ   Old Saxon

ðíѕ   Old Norse

assistance to their living kindred. The Norse called these Old Ones *dísir*. The word had cognates in other Germanic languages, though their meaning is not as strongly connected to female ancestors as in Scandinavia: *idisi* in Old German, *itis* in Old Saxon and *ides* in Old English.[146] The Anglo-Saxon Dictionary defines *ides* as "a woman," but adds that it is often used for supernaturals.[147]

The Old Saxon and German *itis* was honorific and poetic, even sacred. Bible translators used it of Mary and the patriarch's wives.[148] But we also find it in a demonized context in the Old English epic of Beowulf. The hero's primary antagonist is the mother of the dragon Grendel. She is twice called *ides*, once as *ides aglæcwif*, "lady monster-woman."[149] But she is also given the title *gryndehyrde*, ruler or guardian of the Deep.[150]

The poet of *Beowulf* also uses *Ides* to describe two queens. Of Hildeburh, who was carried off to Denmark as booty after her male kin were slain in battle, he remarks, "that was a sad lady."[151] (And that was an understate-ment.) The second queen is called *ides Scildinga* ("lady of the Skildings"), a naming that corresponds to the Norse *dís Skiöldünga* in the Poetic Edda.[152]

In the First Merseberg Charm, the *idisi* knot and loosen strands of destiny, like the Fates:

> **Once the Idisi sat down, sat down here and there.**
> **Some fastened bonds, some held back the host**
> **Some tugged at the fetters:**
> **Leap forth from the bonds, escape from the enemy.**[153]

This curative charm of the Idisi was found among long forgotten manu-scripts at Merseburg cathedral. The charm and its companion represent the only surviving pagan texts in Old High German. They had been inscribed on a fly-leaf of a Christian liturgy during the 900s, and show that pagan charms were still in use, even by the clergy. In a century racked by feudal violence and invasions, the First Merseburg Charm depicts the Idisi as guardians who protect and release captives, using the witchcraft of knots to bind up the enemy—in this case, charming away a disease. The spell opens a window on people's desire to hold back armies, to escape from the enemy who chains captives. In Anglo-Saxon charms, too, warlords are metaphors for the attack of disease: "the loathsome foe roving through the land."[154]

Traces of the *itis / idisi* persisted in late medieval Germany: the faery world of Itislant, and a place called Itisburg, Mountain or Mound of the Itis. In the Middle High German romance *Wigamur*, a magical *eydes* (*idis*) sits under a linden tree near the fountain of youth. Other texts refer to an Itisland ("country of women").[155] In Brabant and Flanders, too, the names Ida, Itta, Iduberg were "all cognate with the word *itis*, an ancient term applied to the woman who exercised sacred functions."[156]

Norse *dís* leans even more toward the supernatural, to fates and ancestral women. *Vildu sva dísir*: so willed the *dísir*, said Snorri, and the *Haustlöng* too.[157] They are *spádísir*, "prophetic women," in *Völsunga saga* 19 and in *Ásmundr Saga Kappabana*, where they appear to the hero

vildu sva dísir

before battle and promise to help him. In the *Atlamál* a woman named Glaumvor has a warning dream from her husband's *dísir*, and tells him, "Dead women came here in the night."[158] In another saga, Ásmundr dreams that his *spádísir* come to promise him their protection on the eve of battle.[159]

Norse texts are replete with overlaps between female ancestors, valkyries, *dísir*, norns and land spirits. Hilda Ellis Davidson recognized fifty years ago that the "huge supernatural women" are not as distinct as old-school scholars imagined them to be, "whether they bear the name of *fylgjukona*, *valkyrja*, *hamingja* or *dís*."[160] Snorri called the giantess Skaði *öndurdís*, "snowshoe woman."[161] A valkyrie was referred to as *Herjans dís*, using a kenning for Oðinn.[162] Tribal goddesses such as Thorgerðr Hölgabruðr and Irpa look like ancestral *dísir*; by some accounts they were deified daughters of a king in Hálogaland.[163]

When the *dísir* "go away," the person's fortunes fall.[164] Many sagas complain that these female spirits are harsh toward warriors—"rough are the *dísir*"—or associate them with impending death—"I know your life is over, the *dísir* are against you."[165] The *Reginsmál* calls a maiden a "wolf-spirited *dís*" (*dís ulfhuguð*), and later calls the *dísir* "treacherous."[166] Many accounts show a *dís*, or a *fylgjakona*, appearing to a man who is about to die. They are huge and often armed.

It is key to remember that the main subject of the sagas is the doings (and views) of men. They are concerned with war and have far less to say about birth and women's concerns, which means that entire areas of testimony about the *dísir* (or norns) are missing from the surviving cultural record. Only a few brief mentions survive, like the valkyrie Sigrdrífa's counsel to midwives: to mark birth runes on their palms "and ask the dísirs' aid."[167]

The *dísir* often appear under other names, especially *fylgja* or *hamingja* (see chapter 5), but both of these always appear singly. In *Völsung saga*, Signy's *kynfylgja*—family *dís*—warns her against a planned marriage.[168] In another saga, Glúmr dreamed he saw a woman walking across the country, so colossal that her shoulders brushed the mountains. He went out to meet her and invited her to his house, then woke up. He understood the spirit's visitation as a sign of the death of his grandfather, whose *hamingja* (protective fortune) had now come to be with him.[169] The *dísir* not only protect their kindred, but at times also act as guardians to family friends.[170]

Scandinavians reared temples in honor of the *dísir*. Numerous prehistoric places of public worship are named after them: meadow, mount, cairn or spring of the *dísir* (*Dísavin, Dísaberg, Dísahrøys*).[171] Even in the 19th century, people in northwestern Iceland honored the *landdísasteinar*, "stones of the land *dísir*," which it was forbidden to mow around or play upon.[172] The ancient Swedes held an annual national assembly at Uppsala, called *Dísathing*, the Ancestress Council. A festival by that name was still being celebrated "as late as 1322."[173] Its vestiges survived in the yearly Distingen fair of modern times.

Blood sacrifices called *dísablot* or *bletuth dísir* were consecrated to the ancestral women. These ceremonies were local family affairs.[174] Norse priestesses called *gyðjur* sacrificed to the *dísir* at the spring festival to ensure the prosperity of their households. The hall where the *dísablot* were celebrated is called the Dísarsalinn. As Maria Kvilhaug explains, because *dísar* is a genitive singular, "we are dealing with the hall of the one (great) Dís rather than the hall of the many *dísir* who received sacrifice at this important celebration."[175]

Several sagas mention Halls of the Dís.[176] In *Ynglinga saga*, Snorri recounts that a Swedish king came to a sacrifice in the *dísir*-hall. As he rode his horse around the hall, his horse stumbled and threw him onto a stone, kill-

Dísarblót, by August Malmstrom, late 1800s

ing him. This fall has been interpreted as the *dís* calling the king to join her, with overtones of a sacrificial king.[177] However, the skáld Thjódólfr attributed his death to "a magic-making wight" (some sources translate as "witch") showing that by the 10th century, the sorcery charge had already begun to displace the concept of the *dísir*'s power, even in their own temple.[178]

In *Friðthjófs saga*, two kings come to make sacrifices at a *disarsalr* inside an meadow enclosure. They sit drinking and pouring libations, "and their wives meanwhile are said to sit by the fire and warm the figures of the gods."[179] Ellis Davidson thought the "wives" were actually wooden idols, like the famous statue of Thorgerðr Hölgabrúðr. This complex and murky figure is sometimes named as a deified princess (and thus a *dís*), as in *Skáldskaparmál*. But she is so widely attested—in numerous sagas— that many researchers think she was an important Norwegian goddess of Halogaland. Around 960, Thorgerðr is described as a seated wooden statue in Haakon' Jarl's temple, from which a large gold ring is plundered, along with others belonging to the goddess Irpa ("dark one") and Thórr.[180]

Norse sagas preserved fractals of heathen traditions, such as rites and beliefs surrounding the *dísir*. They show that people visited them at mounds and cairns to appeal for advice, blessings and protection. "Dead women come at night," appearing in dreams and on pagan holydays.[181] Sometimes they appear in groups, to warn or perform fateful acts.[182] A common theme has a character dream of a dead person, and awakening, sees a flash of them departing. Thorstein dreamed of his dead mother, who gave him advice, and when he awoke "he thought he caught a glimpse of her as she went away."[183] These apparitions at the edge of sleep could also take animal form. A cow *dís*, the mother of a four-horned ox which Olaf had slaughtered, came to him in a dream. Because he killed her son, she pledged to see to it that his own son, the favorite, would also die. "Olaf woke up and thought he caught a glimpse of her."[184] The world was enchanted then.

The stones raised to the *dísir* were regarded as an opening between the world of the dead and the living: "the Doors," to which people came to call and consult female ancestors. The custom is described in the Eddic poem *Grógaldr*, the "spell-chants of Gróa." A young man is called upon to perform an extremely difficult task. He goes to the cairn of stones over his mother's grave and calls on her to meet him at the "doors of the dead." The spirit of Groa appears to him, and he asks her to chant *galdr* for him:

> Sing for me magic spells / which are beneficial
> mother, help your son.[185]

And the *dís* chants to him of fates that might befall, charms that will protect him in danger. Groa sings spells against enemy ambush, floods, cold, and bondage; for safe sea travel and wisdom. (One line expresses dread of "christian women's ghosts" working misfortune, showing a fear that Christian hostility would be expressed through their *dísir*.) The mother's final blessing has the air of an old proverb:

> May Urd's protection hold you on all sides.[186]

The son goes on to succeed in the task set by his stepmother, which is to become the chosen man of Mengloð, divine lady of the Hill of Healing. The composer of *Grougaldr* believed in the beneficent power of the incantation of the *dís*, and in the survival of spirit beyond death. From the Otherworld, Gróa not only responds to her son's cry at the doors of the dead, but her blessings are seen as affecting events in the world of the living. The poem ends with the mother chanting from the other side of the portal:

ατ τhe doors í stood, on an earth-bound stone, while í sang these songs το thee.[187]

VALKYRIES

Valkyries are well known as fate-spirits of the battlefield. *Valkyrja* means "chooser of the slain." This same word "choose" was used in pagan ritual, "especially in connection with oracles," when the deity indicated which offerings would be accepted through a divinatory rite.[188] The sagas view the valkyries through a military lens, emphasizing their selection of warriors who were to die in battle. But they possessed other qualities that linked them with goddesses, *dísir*, and witches. The valkyries are described as possessing foreknowing wisdom and knowledge of runes. In skáldic poems, they are "all-wise," with shining eyes, and "with the 'thoughtful features' that distinguish those who arrange destinies."[189]

Some sources call valkyries *dísir* (ancestral women); others equate them with norns. The norn Skuld is named in *Völuspá* 30 as first among the valkyries, leading the charge. Another poem calls the valkyries "southern *dísir*."[190] Metal plaques and pendants of women from the Viking era have long been labeled as valkyries, but they may represent *dísir*, other female spirits, or even mortal *völur*.[191]

Recent scholarship challenges the conventional emphasis on valkyries as war-fates, or as maidens who serve Oðinn. According to Alaric Hall, this definition inverts the actual situation, in which "*valkyrja* is most likely a kenning ('chooser of the slain') for *dís* ('supernatural lady')." In the actual written record, "*dís* is extensively attested in Old Icelandic verse and is the basis for many kennings, whereas *valkyrja* occurs rather rarely, and is the basis for none." Hall points out that even the most renowned valkyrie, Brynhildr, is called "*dís* of the Skjoldungs," while the Poetic Edda does not name her as a valkyrie even once.[192]

Valkyries appear as nature spirits, riding their horses in groups of nine or thirteen, or six going north and six to the south.[193] Or they are "three times

nine maidens."[194] As Sváva and her sisters rode in the skies, dew running from the manes of their horses fell in the valleys, and showered hail into the high forests. This fructified the land and gave good crops.[195] Here the valkyries bestow vitality, rather than dealing out death. In this they resemble the *vily*, Balkan forest faeries who go out into the fields, pouring life-giving dew from their hunting horns.[196] Dalmatians spoke of the *vile* bringing storms and hail.[197]

The valkyries chant while weaving magical webs, like the German witch-websters in the *Corrector sive Medicus*. Their weaving is imbued with fateful or oracular power, like the oracular Raven-banner woven by three sisters in the *Vita Alfredi*.[198] In their webs, or in spinning, they lay fate and determine the outcome of battle. Valkyries are shapeshifters, often appearing as a flock of swans.

A rare in-the-round valkyrie from Hårby, Denmark

In *Volundarkviða*, three swan-women flew from the south to the Wolf-lake, "fate to fulfil," and on its shores they spun flax. The linkage of fate and spinning is strongly suggestive, with the line *örlög drýgja*, "determine or carry out fate," repeated twice for emphasis.[199] The swan-women encounter a hunting party of Finnish princes, and take them as lovers, placing them

> *örlög drýgja: "determine or carry out fate"*

under their protection.[200] After nine years, the spirit-women flew away.[201]

Saxo Grammaticus describes similar nature spirits in the story of Hotherius. He was led astray by a mist, in the classic style of faery stories, "and he came on a certain lodge in which were wood-maidens, and when they greeted him by his own name, he asked who they were. They declared that it was their guidance and government that mainly determined the fortunes of war. For they often invisibly took part in battles, and by their secret assistance won for their friends the coveted victories."[202] Then the maidens and their lodge disappeared.

Later on, Hotherius in his wanderings through remote country, "chanced to come upon a cave where dwelt some maidens whom he knew not; but they proved to be the same who had once given him the invulnerable coat."[203] Lithuanian stories also show swan women as those who give the lots in life.[204] Thus the valkyrie tradition comes out of an old cultural substratum; but it had acquired a heavy patriarchal overlay.

The valkyries were fateful goddesses, but the skálds greatly reduced their powers and subordinated them to Óðinn.[205] Though they weave battle destinies, the *Darraðarljóð* calls them "thralls (slaves) of Oðinn."[206] The god punishes them for disobeying his dictates in both the Niflung cycle of the Norse and the German *Nibelunglied*. Sigrdrífa defied Óðinn by granting victory to her own choices: "other heroes she felled than he had willed."[207] Óðinn doomed her to never fight again but be married, pricking her with a sleep-thorn and binding her in a mountain tower until a husband arrived to claim her. In the Norse version, Sleeping Beauty is a woman warrior.

In the prologue to *Sigrdrífumál*, Sigurðr is riding south when he sees light blazing from a mountaintop. He finds a fort with shields inside which a woman warrior lies sleeping in full armor. He removes her helmet and frees her by cutting away the leather byrnie that had grown tight around her body. Sigrdrífa awakens and explains how she came to be there. She gives Sigurðr a drink of mead as a memory drink, reciting an invocation to the day and night, and to the *aesir* and *asynjur*. The drink is not very effective, however, since Sigurðr goes away and forgets all about her. But first, as a love token, he gives her the cursed ring of power that had passed through many hands before he took it from the dwarf Regin. Sigrdrífa then proceeds to impart her rune wisdom to him.[208]

Medieval sagas portray the valkyries as losing themselves in their warrior lovers. *Völsunga saga* says that Brunhildr threw herself on Sigurðr's funeral pyre—and not only herself. As *Nornagests tháttir* tells it:

> **Then Brynhild killed seven of her slaves and five handmaidens, and ran a sword through herself, and bade that she be taken to the pyre along with these people and burned to death. And so it was done, that one pyre was made for her, and another for Sigurd, and he was burned before Bryn-hild. She was driven in a chariot, with a canopy of velvet and costly stuff, and everything gleamed with gold, and so she was burned.**[209]

Brunhildr's funerary suicide is matched by others, like Nanna who is laid on Baldr's pyre alongside him after "dying of grief."[210] Another valkyrie, Svava, dies of sorrow after her brother kills her lover Helgi. In the sagas women mysteriously die after the death of their husband or lover, as Hilda Ellis Davidson documented in depth.[211]

The most chilling reference to wife-sacrifice is the "brides buried in a mound" in *Helgakviða Hundingsbana* II.[212] Historical sources mention wives sacrificed in this way. Saxo Grammaticus related how a wife named Gunnilda immolated herself on her husband's pyre, and how Sygne not only killed herself on her lover's pyre, but all her maids as well.[213]

Brunhilde fares even worse in the medieval German *Nibelunglied*. She resists marriage to Gunther, but Siegfried secretly aids him in three trials of strength, which the valkyrie would have otherwise won easily. (The maiden's combat to determine whether or not she will marry a suitor is retold all the way into Mongolia.) Brunhilde is forced to marry Gunther—but she refuses to have sex with him, tying him up and hanging him from a roof beam. Siegfried intervenes again, breaking her bones and taking away her belt and the ring. She loses her powers and falls into subjugated wifedom.

In this version, too, Brunhilde immolates herself by riding her horse into the flames of Siegfried's pyre. But first she consigns the accursed ring to the Rhine Maidens, on whose shores the pyre was built, instructing them to take it after it was purified by the fire.

The valkyrie Svava helps the warrior Helgi to overcome the giantess Hrimgerth in *Helgakviða Hjövarðzsonar*. The author gives voice to misogynist themes through his valkyrie characters. Sigrdrifa warns Sigurd against taking as lovers "foul witches and harmful hags who haunt the way." Similarly, Brynhild presents Siegfried with her *megin* (personal power): runes of victory, pregnancy, healing plants, and not omitting "the runes of the filtres which will ensure you the fidelity of the captive wife."[214] No female solidarity is to be found here. As Margaret Clunies Ross recognized for most of the epics, "Valkyries are in fact a pretty subservient lot."[215]

Silver woman, Uppakra, Sweden. Some figures may portray dísir rather than valkyries

The valkyries were said to carry those chosen to die in battle to Óðinn's warrior paradise Valhal, rather than to the realm of Hel, the ancient goddess of the dead. (Or rather, they bring half of them, since Óðinn has to split the slain warriors with Freyja, according to *Grímnismál* 14.) Hilda Ellis Davidson suggested that "Odin's expanding role as a warrior god and the concept of Valhalla may have reduced the earlier role of Freyja as the goddess receiving the warrior dead."[216] Valhal copied certain elements of Hel's underworld: its river boundary, its gate of bars and its rooster, symbolizing dawns yet to come.[217]

These mythical revisions date from the militarized society of the Viking age, when Óðinn became "the principal god of the higher ranks of society."[218] Only then did his cult become dominant, popularized by skálds catering to the lordly families, whose rule they legitimized.[219] Even then, the common people remained loyal to the old animistic deities and to Thórr. In fact, "the Óðinn cult aroused a strong national counter current of opposition."[220] It came into conflict with the veneration of Frey /Freyja in Sweden. In Iceland it never surpassed that of Thórr.[221]

The legendary woman warrior Hervör stars in one of the few sagas with a female protagonist, *Hervarar saga*. She is determined to recover her father's magical sword Tyrfing and resists all attempts to dissuade her. As she approaches the grave mound, she calls on her dead relatives to awake. Her father Angantýr appears and rebukes her, refusing to give up the sword. Eventually, however, she "gains Tyrfing for her own." Hervör says of her underworld journey:

i seemed to be lost | between the worlds while around me | burned the fires.[222]

GIANTESSES AND FEMALE POWER

The Norse written record has little to say about goddesses.[223] The *asynjur* are rarely central figures, nor do they do much of anything. As one historian observes, "Of female deities, only Freyja (to a lesser degree, Frigg and Iðunn) receives much attention in the surviving texts."[224] Most of the sixteen *asynjur* listed by Snorri are near-ciphers, mere consorts of the male gods.

Lotte Motz roundly criticized Grimm's definition of "real goddesses" as those paired with a god, and the others only as "half-goddesses." Those literary females are little more than "decorative shadows, prized possessions or abstractions invented by the poets or learned men."[225] The Aesir are mostly spoken of as if they were an all-male group, though gender-neutral words for deity (*goð*, *regin*) did exist. In public temples the wooden idols were male, while the goddesses were in family shrines.[226]

Folk religion was different than the elite skáldic tradition, just as popular Greek religion was not the same as the Olympian pantheon. The giants as an elder generation of deities can be compared to the overthrown Greek Titans. The real female powers are found at the margins of the androcentric poems and sagas—which hardly ever name them as goddesses. Instead they are giantesses, troll-women, *gygjar* (ogres), and *dísir*, *fylgjur*, and *valkyriar*.

A growing body feminist scholarship draws attention to the fact that the most powerful and active—though usually demonized—female figures in Norse lore are the giantesses.[227] They are also the most ancient, befitting their strong association with Earth. They live underground, in caves, mountains, forests, and waters.[228]

The giantesses are primeval powers of Nature: the nine giantesses in the Tree, the nine mothers at the world's edge, the nine waves of the sea. The Three Maidens themselves, the mighty Norns, belong to the giant realm. Giantesses of the great Tree in the *Völuspá* are found again in the late medieval lay, *Hrafnagaldr Óðins*:

> at the north boundary | of the nourishing earth
> under the outmost root | of the noble tree
> went to their couches the giantesses
> titans, spectres, dwarfs and dark elves.[229]

The oldest Eddic poem mentions the primordial cow who licked the ice away from the first giant Ymir, but it does not name her. *Gylfaginning* 6 gives a bit more: "Straightway after the rime dripped, there sprang from it the cow called Auðumla; four streams of milk ran from her udders, and she nourished Ymir." This being became the ancestor of the giants, and from his body came the earth and seas.

The name of the cow comes from the *auð* root, with its meanings of

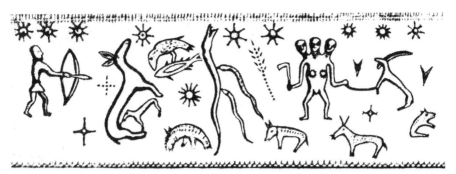

A three-headed giantess, axe in hard, in the company of animals, including a deer and snake (!) suckling their young. Gallehus horn, Denmark.

weaving, fate and wealth (see Chapter 1).[230] Auðumla also feeds Búri, grandfather of the Aesir, whose son Bór fathers Oðinn by an unnamed giantess. Bor's sister, also unnamed and simply called Móðir, "mother," barely gets a mention. In *Rígsthula* she gives birth to Jarl ("nobleman"), underlining the Aesir link to aristocracy. Yet they too are descended from Others—the demonized giants. Clunies Ross marks the "downplaying of the maternal, giant side of their kinship" in this Aesir cosmogony of the *Völuspá*.[231]

Jörd, Earth herself, is also a giantess. Because she and Hloðyn are named as the mother of Thórr, they are assumed to be the same goddess. Hloðyn has some time-depth to her, as demonstrated by five inscriptions to Dea Hludana (Hluthena) in the 2nd century, across a territory extending from the mouth of the Rhine to Friesland.[232] But Snorri demotes Jörd in *Gylfaginning* 10, making her not only a wife of Oðinn, but also his daughter.

It is striking how important giantesses are in Norse cosmology, once the lens is turned toward them. Another key figure is the underworld goddess Hel, a fearsome spirit by most accounts. But this old commentary offers insight: "She, too, is a force of Nature... not a simple agent of destruction; she rather aids Nature's rejuvenation. She originally typifies the idea of life emerging from Death, and of Death being only a transformation of life." Hel's face is half-dark, half-livid: "She thus resembles the Hindoo Bhavani or Maha Kali, the goddess who creates and destroys.... It is noteworthy that the oldest Eddic text should place the first root of the Tree of Existence in the domain of this double-complexioned Mistress of the Underworld."[233]

The bridge to Hel's realm is guarded by the giant maiden Módgud.[234] Angrboða is the mother of Hel, of the world serpent and the Fenris wolf.

She lives with a host of trollwomen in Ironwood.[235] The giantesses are not submissive females, so the sagas mostly depict them as threatening figures. But exceptions do exist in some Eddic poetry. The glorious Menglöð, who sits on the Lyfjaberg (Hill of Healing), has giantess traits. She is called *gýgur* in *Fjölsvinnsmál* 29:6. Nine women are in her company, a recurring giantess theme, and at least one of them, Aurboða, is named elsewhere as a giantess.[236] Her domain is guarded by a giant, and like that of the giantess Gerðr—and the underworld—it is surrounded by flames.[237]

As Judy Quinn observes, giantesses "frequently have some affiliation with the chthonic world, living in rock caves or in the sea and attributed with knowledge about the future or the world in general beyond the hero's ken."[238] She recognizes them as part of a larger Norse pattern of female beings whose wisdom is unbound by time, including giantesses such as Hyndla; the *völur*; and the "taciturn *ásynjur*," who do not reveal their foreknowledge.[239]

Reverence of giantesses as land spirits looks to be a deep cultural substrate in Scandinavia. The name itself comes from the same root as Skaði.[240] Gro Steinsland points to the many sanctuaries (*vé*) that Skaði owns (in *Lokasenna* 51) as a sign that she was venerated in ancient times.[241] That place-names honoring Skaði survived leads toward the same conclusion.[242] So the giantess had not always been a demonized power. Gunnhild Rothe interprets the Oseberg priestess(es) as leading "a cult of giantesses or ancestral mothers who represented the land owned by the ruling family."[243]

Quinn lists various female beings—including *völur*, Norns, valkyries, and *asynjur* like Freyja and Iðunn—who transcend death and decay, and regenerate, or reincarnate.[244] Maria Kvilhaug underlines the connections between these supernatural women: "The female beings transcend the borders between the different worlds. They show up in much the same range of roles in any world, whether it be the world of Aesir, Vanir or giants. They are always the instigators, the teachers, the guides and the consecrators. They are, in fact, the fates, holding the secret purpose of everything."[245] The story of the giantesses Fenja and Menja (below) offers dramatic confirmation of that fateful power.

For Clunies Ross, "the giant world as a whole [is] classified as a female domain."[246] She has good reasons for saying so, but they should be balanced against Lotte Motz's insight that the skálds often placed giantesses in secon-

Swedish church sculpture in Västergötland, 12th century, in sheela-na-gig style

dary relationship as daughters of male giants. In fact, the word *jötun* has no female form—instead we find "trollwoman" and "ogress" (*trollkona, gýgr, flagð*)—and neither does *thurs* (monster, ogre).[247]

The same is true for *tívar*, "gods," which in the singular has only a masculine form (the god Týr).[248] *Tívar* has very old Indo-European roots, shared with Latin *deus*, Greek *zeu*, Sanskrit *dyaus*, but also with Latin *dea*, Indic *devī*, Greek Dione, and goddess words in Gaulish and the Romance languages. So the giantesses are powerful female divinities who seep through the androcentric framework in spite of its linguistic bias.

Clunies Ross describes "the gods and giants and other supernatural figures [as] stalking horses for the interests of human society."[249] (This makes eminent sense if those "human" interests are more explicitly defined as those of men, lords, warriors, and masters; they certainly were not the interests of bondmaids and peasants.) The mythos of female subordination recurs in stories about the giantesses. Skaði comes to the Aesir seeking vengeance for her father's killing (ordinarily a male prerogative) but they treat her "in the manner that was reserved for all women undertaking male roles in Old Norse literature: she was transformed into the object of a marriage."[250]

Gerdr is another example of a giantess who was not demonized and who, like Skaði, became one of the *asynjur*. However, this result is brought about with curses and a "taming wand," fas Skírnir forces her to marry Freyjr. Gerdr resists, repeatedly. She refuses the gold offered her, saying that the

Wolf-mother on a church font in Vester Egede, South Sjaelland, Denmark, 1100s

giants have plenty of their own. In Snorri's version, she says she will never accept the golden apples offered to her "in return for any man's desire."[251] (Her refusal is rare enough in literature; but it is even rarer for a defiant mythic female to survive undefeated.) Gerdr is eminent: her mother is Aurboða, one of the Nine Maidens who sit at Menglóð's knee.[252]

In many stories, men or gods trick the giantesses, or commit violence against them. The Aesir disrespect the giantesses even when they are helping them. The oath-breaker Oðinn deceives and humiliates Gunnloð in order to steal the mead of poetry. The wolf-riding giantess Hyrrokin comes to aid the Aesir and is repaid with violence. Hrimgerth engages in *flyting* (a poetic duel) with Helgi, but is fooled into being caught by the sun and thus turned to stone.[253] Even Freyja sweet-talks the cave-dwelling Hyndla in order to get information out of her for the benefit of her mortal lover.

Several sagas mention a troll-woman riding on a wolf bridled with snakes. One is Helgi's protective deity, who arrives in omen of his death.[254] In *Hemings tháttr*, a troll woman rides a wolf through the air with a trough of blood and limbs as she prophesies the defeat of Harald Harðráði before his invasion of England.[255]

The mighty giantess Hyrrokin came riding on a snake-bridled wolf, in response to the Aesir's call for help when they failed to launch Baldr's funeral ship. She turned her mount over to four berserkers, whose combined strength was unable to restrain it. (Their solution was to kill her wolf.) Meanwhile, Hyrrokin pushed the ship into the water with so much force that the earth shook and flames shot out from the wooden rollers.

Seeing that her strength was greater than his, Thór went into a rage and had to be restrained from trying to split Hyrrokin's head with his hammer.

Instead, he kicked the dwarf Litr into the funeral pyre, incinerating him.[256] According to one 10th century skáld, Thórr did kill Hyrrokin.[257] *Skáldskaparmál* 4 says so too.

Thórr was a famous giant-killer and was always bashing giantesses with his hammer. A 10th century poem describes him as "oppressor of the kinfolk of evening-running women."[258] He breaks the backs of Gjálp and Greip, whose spines are 'the keels of each of the cave-women's age-old laughter-ship."[259] Now there is a concept to meditate on.

The enmity between the ancient hags, and the young male warriors is repeated throughout Germanic, Celtic and Finnic lore; and the storytellers nearly always side with the warriors.

HAGS VERSUS HEROES

Powerful old women's opposition to military men appears throughout the tales and sagas of barbarian Europe. The Russian *skazki* show the Baba Yaga defeating the *bogatyr* heroes, despite their phenomenal strength. As the dragon-hag Baba Latingorka, she fought and killed Dobrynya Nikitich.[260] In Ireland, the Badb (Raven) ordains or foreshadows the deaths of warriors. She appears as the old woman at the ford, washing the clothing of those about to die in battle. Anne Ross comments on the antagonism of old woman to warrior. [261] Tomás Ó Cathasaigh also remarks on an "otherworld goddess vs. hero opposition."[262]

Hags battle Finn and other warriors in Irish and Welsh epics, or place enchantments on them. In one story, a hag gives Fionn MacCumhaill a magic potion and then persuades him to jump over a rock to his death.[263] Both the Irish Fianna and Scottish Fingalians defeat and slay huge supernatural *cailleachan*. In this patriarchal mythos, Finn is the hero, and the hags are the villains. Illustrative is the Irish story of The Enchanted Cave of Keshcorran After Finn MacCumhal angered a family of the Tuatha Dé Danann by hunting a wild boar on their lands, three women set out to work vengeance on him, at the entrance to a megalithic chamber:

The women sought the entrance of the cave that was in the mound, and there sat by each other. Upon three crooked and wry sticks of holly they hung many heathenish bewitched hasps of yarn, which they began to

reel off lefthandwise in front of the cave.[264]

The three crone witches resonate with the wider European theme of spinners of fate, though demonized in this story. By their spinning, the women drained vigor from Finn and Conan, who perceived them as wild-haired hags with fangs and claws and furry legs.[265] Finn went down into an opening in the cave and the hags bound him, as well as all of his men who followed. They were rescued by Goll mac Morna, who fought and beheaded the witches after a terrible battle.

The Caves of Keshcorran, County Sligo, northwestern Ireland

In "The Hunt of Slieve Cuilinn" (= Gullion, the megalithic site discussed earlier) the Cailleach takes the form of a gray fawn to lure the hunter Finn to her lake. Then she appears to him as a beautiful maiden who asks him to fetch her ring from under the water. When he finally emerges from this underworld, he has become aged, whitehaired, and weak. The Fianna who come searching for him do not even recognize him. They go into the cave and force the Cailleach to give him an antidote; but his hair never regains its color.[266] In some versions, the restorative elixir also confers wisdom on Finn.

Various interpretations can be advanced for this story, from the clearly misogynist theme of women's treachery to the motif of faery captivity into a timeless dream-world from which travelers emerge as if centuries had passed. A Scottish version of this story, the "Chase of Ben Gulbin," has the Cailleach Bhéara luring Fingal into a trap. She is angry because he hunts her deer, "the beast of my love." His magic helper kills her.[267]

Sometimes the *cailleachan* will assist a hero, especially when he is being victimized. In the tale of the Great Child, Finn's grandmother saves him when the men who killed his father toss him off a cliff. She takes the form of a crane and flies in to catch him. Or he will help her: in the story of Cailleach an Teampuill (Old Woman of the Temple) Finn saves the four sons of a hag who have been changed into cranes, using three drops of blood from the head of the Cailleach Bhéara's bull.[268]

Much has been made of the dynastic legends in which the sovereignty goddess appears as a loathly hag but transforms into a beauty after the right candidate agrees to lay with her. But far less attention has been paid to themes of powerful old women who oppose men of war, or men with weapons—especially hunters.

In both Irish and Scottish stories, the *cailleachan* have the power of shapeshifting, transforming themselves into wild animals or stunningly beautiful maidens. They can outdo men in feats of strength and outpace them in work and in moving across the landscape. In Ireland, these hags "often oppose the heroes of the early triads."[269]

In Scotland, supernatural *cailleachan* "might be encountered at the wells of which they were considered to be the guardians," or accompanying their deer over the hills where they were once propitiated.[270] As protector of the deer, they were portrayed as having a natural antagonism toward hunters: "The Lochaber Deer-goddess was of bad omen to hunters, but protected outlaws."[271] The idea seems to have been that she sided with underdogs and victims of injustice.

cailleachan vs. hunters

Many legends tell of the Cailleach's fierce struggles with hunters. In a widespread Scottish tale, of which Mackay found at least twenty versions, an old witch attacks a lone hunter out in the mountain wilderness with only his dogs for company. She comes into the bothy, unarmed, sometimes in the form of a cat or a hen that turns into a hag. "She never demands a share of the produce of the chase, but announces her intention of killing the hunter, and *says she knows that he hates her*."[272] (Emphasis added.) A battle ensues. Often the cailleach tries to get the hunter to bind his dogs with one of her hairs. Then she grows large and attacks him: "Long have you been the devoted enemy of my persecuted sisterhood."[273]

The Muilearteach, who raises winds and storms, comes to Scottish hunters in the form of a hag, asking to be allowed near the fire. As she warms herself, she grows large and aggressive.[274] The same story is told of the *glaistig*, a female deer spirit and protector of the deer. (The name is pronounced gláhsh-tek.) She comes to a highland cabin where hunters are gathered, hunkers down by the fire and begins to swell in size. The hag demands snuff from a hunter, and if he is not canny enough to offer it to her on the point of his dirk, she jumps him and begins to choke him. The hunting dogs spring at her, and she tells the hunter to keep them back. She pulls a gray hair from her head to tie them up, but if the hunter is clever, he will use his garter instead.

The *glaistig* goes after him the minute the hounds are tied, saying "Tighten hair." But the hunter says "Loosen garter." With the dogs after her, the *glaistig* backs out the door. They pursue her like a deer until suddenly she turns and fights. The hounds come back mangled and plucked clean of hair. Without these animals and a degree of cunning, the hunters fare ill in combat with the *glaisteag*.[275]

Mala Liatha ("Grey Eyebrows") was also a protector of wild animals, including the wild boar hunted by Diarmaid. She taunted the warrior and interfered with his hunting. He grabbed her by the foot and threw her over a cliff. Then he succeeded in killing the boar, but he had not triumphed after all. A venomous bristle on its slaughtered body pierced his foot and was the death of him.[276] This fateful justice is similar to that meted out by the serpent coming out of the horse's skull in Norse and Russian stories, to deliver a fatal bite to the arrogant lord.

Witch hunt themes intrude on some of the *glaistig* legends. The Tale of the Strath Dearn Hunter treats the supernatural *glaistig* as a human witch. She appears first as a hen, then as a hag, and ends up fighting the dogs. They return to the hunter in very poor shape. He comes home to find his wife has gone off to attend a neighbor woman who seemed to be in terrible pain. Suspicious, the hunter goes to the house and ripping the covers off her, sees that her breasts had been torn off by the teeth of his hounds. The hunter calls the woman a witch and kills her with his sword.[277] Such stories almost always sympathize with the killer, not the slain hag.

A *glaisteag* was captured one night by Big Kennedy of Lochaber. He took his ploughshare and heated it in the fire, then demanded that she swear she would never harm anyone on his land, or ever be seen again in Lochaber.

The hot iron burned her hand to the bone, and shrieking in agony she flew out of the window to a nearby hillside: "and there she put out three bursts of the blood of her heart, which are still visible in the discolored russet vegetation of the hill. With each burst of blood she uttered a curse on Big Kennedy, and on his seed forever: 'Growth like the fern to them, Wasting like the rushes to them, and unlasting as the mist of the hill.'"[278] The story recalls the European ordeal of redhot ploughshares, but here it is forced on a wilderness faery, not a human witch.

A hag is also shown attempting use one of her hairs to magically bind the war-hero Cu Chullain. Or, a *calliagh* pursues Cu Chulainn running toward the sea. He springs to a rock offshore, with the witch in close pursuit, and then he jumps back. The witch falls short and is drowned. The current bears her body north to the Cliffs of Moher, to a place called Cancallee, the Hag's Head.[279] This story is a patriarchalized place-name legend.

The Morrigan

But Cu Chullain's main female opponent is the fateful Morrigan. She confronts him in the form of a red-eyebrowed woman wearing a long crimson mantle, then changes into a crow. Sometimes she appears to him as a hag, or attacks him in animal form. Perched on a branch as a crow, she engages in a word-duel with the warrior. "A dangerous enchanted woman you are," says Cu Chulainn. She promises to come after him as an eel, a gray wolf, and a red-eared cow; he swears he will defeat her, and claims she cannot harm him. But the Crow-Woman replies, "Certainly I can. I am guarding your death-bed, and I shall be guarding it henceforth."[280]

The *Táin Bó Cúailnge* repeatedly presents Cu Chulainn thwarting and disrespecting the Morrigan; but she prevails in the end. The warrior's ultimate doom is set in motion when three old women on the road shame him into breaking his personal *geis* against eating dog flesh. They are painted as villains, but their words to him sum up the conflict between hags and warriors, peasants and aristocrats: "Unseemly are the great who endure not the little and poor."[281] The elders' reproach represents the politically submerged concerns of the grandmothers: the terrible reality of war, and the arrogance of aristocratic heroes in the eyes of the common people.

At last the fateful raven goddess prevails against the celebrated warrior. Appearing in the shape of the maiden Niam, the Morrigan tricked Cu

Chullain into singlehanded combat with an advancing army. Faring to Emain, he saw Babd's daughter washing blood at the ford, a foretold omen of his death. The Morrigan broke his chariot, and the Grey Horse of Macha reproached him. When he fell, the Morrigan swept down from a great height to utter three triumphant cries over him.[282]

The old witch occasionally persists in early Christian stories. An 8th century Breton hagiography tells how St Samson and a deacon were going through a great forest, when they heard a terrifying voice resounding loudly behind them. The deacon ran away, but Samson "saw an unkempt grey-haired sorceress, already an old woman, with her garments ragged and holding in her hand a bloody three-pronged [trident], and in a swift course traversing the vast woods and rushing past, following after [him] in a straight line." She belonged to a family of nine sisters, which the story says are all that remained of a once-large community.[283]

Nine maidens

This fragment recalls a broad tradition of Nine Sisters that existed across northern Europe, from the Nine Maidens of Avalon in the Vita Merlini to the Nine Daughters of Manannan mac Lir, after whom nine Irish lakes were named. Nine Sisters or Nine Maidens also were also names for groups of standing stones in St Columb, Cornwall and Boskednan, Wales. The Old Welsh poem Preiddeu Annwfn spoke of Nine Maidens of the Cauldron:[283a]

> My first utterance,
> it is from the cauldron that it was spoken
> by the breath of nine maidens it was kindled.

A much older classical source refers to the cauldron of transformation of the Nine Gallizenae, shamanic priestesses of the Isle of Sena off the coast of Bretagne. [283b] The Danes invoked the Nine Nouthæ and the English the Nothðæs in their healing charms. Norse sources refer to Nine Giantesses who are the roots of the Tree of Life, or the nine daughters of the Sea.

❖

Louhi of pohjola and The sampo

A powerful crone goddess is counterposed against the brute force of male heroes in the Finnish *Kalevala*.[284] The main action in this "Land of Heroes" epic centers on warriors who attempt to seize the daughters of old Louhi, the Lady of Pohjola. She fights to protect her daughters, whose mates must be chosen by merit, not force. Although she retains divine powers, Louhi is demonized. As a witch and hag, she is automatically the villain, no matter what wrongs the warriors commit.

The old woman declares that whoever is able to forge the magical Sampo will be allowed to marry her daughter. One of the suitors, Väinämöinen, hires the smith Ilmarinen, who performs the feat. The multicolored lid of the Sampo was the vault of heaven, its central post the world Tree. Its pictured cover revolved (as a hand quern does) and ground out chests full of food. When Väinämöinen presents Louhi with the Sampo that he purchased, she passes him over and, true to her word, marries the maiden to the smith who forged the Sampo. But another man kills the daughter, so Ilmarinen returns to obtain another daughter of Louhi. Not surprisingly, she refuses him. He then abducts the maiden, and later turns her into a gull.

Louhi takes the Sampo to the Mount of Copper and guards it with nine locks. It sent out three roots, one into the earth, one to a mountain, and one to the ocean. Väinämöinen believes that the Sampo should belong to him, since he paid the smith to make it. (He does not feel bound to honor the terms of the old woman.) He leads an expedition to Pohjola and captures the Sampo from Louhi. As they flee in a boat, the old woman attacks in the form of a harpy

(shown in painting by Gallen-Kallela). Louhi calls up a terrible storm, wrecking Vainamoinen's magical zither and scattering the Sampo. When the warriors regather parts of its colored cover, Louhi shuts the sun and moon up in a mountain cave. In the end they kill her. The Sampo remains at the bottom of the ocean.

Like Demeter and Amaterasu, Louhi shuts off the pulse of life force when female sovereignty is violated. Though the epic makes her the villain, she retains some divine qualities. She is Lady of Pohjala, the northern land of the dead. There are hints that she is the rightful guardian of the Sampo. Its name relates to the world pillar, which rotates around the North Star, which belongs to her realm, and its speckled lid is named after the heavens. First the Sampo ground out prosperity and happiness, then salt. Now it grinds sand and stone from a whirlpool at the bottom of the ocean.

Elsewhere the whirlpool is described as a signature of Louhi's realm of the North: "Before the gates of Pohjola | Below the threshold of color-covered Pohjola | There the pines roll with their roots | The pines fall crown first into the gullet of the whirlpool."[285]

cosmic quern of the giantesses

The Norse had their own legends about cosmic querns that grind out unimaginable riches, or salt, or sand. For them, it was giantesses who perform the magical feat. A fragment from the poet Snæbjörn refers to nine giantesses as the sea waves turning Grótti, the cosmic mill of the oceans: "Nine skerry-brides fast turn the violent island-mill | beyond the world's edge."[286] Through the ocean's power, the giantesses are grinding out sand along the shorelines: "they who in ages past ground Amlodi's meal."[287] The poet calls them "army-cruel" because the whirlpool emerging from the eye of their sunken mill wrecks ships carrying fighters.[288] It is hags versus warriors again.

These Beings are the deep pulse of the universe, whose totality is symbolized by their number Nine. They are mentioned elsewhere as the Nine Giantesses under the Tree, the Nine Daughters of the Sea and the Nine Mothers of Heimdall. In another verse attributed to Snaebjörn, "The island-mill pours out the blood of the flood-giantesses' sisters, so that bursts from the feller of the land: whirlpool begins strong."[289] (The choppy wording is in the original poem.)

The cosmic mills recur in modern Scandinavian lore. An old blind giantess lived in Gívrinarhol, the "cave of the giantess" in the Faroese island of Sandoy. She ground gold in a massive quern. A man sneaked into her cave to steal some of the gold, and knowing that something was amiss, she raised a cry. A neighboring giantess gave chase, striding across the lake with such force that she left "the Giantess's Footprints" on either side of it. She caught up with the thief, who was able to escape only because at that instant he sighted a church. But people said they could still hear the old giantess grinding gold in the deep cavern of Gívrinarhol.[290]

Like the Irish, Scandinavian people had legends about women who flung great boulders across the land and placed rocks and other geographic features in primeval times. Sometimes they molded the landscape with stones or sand carried in their aprons. In feudal times, these beings are described as falling into bondage.

fenja and menja

In the *Grottasongr* poem, the Danish king Fróði of the Skjoldings bought two maiden captives, Fenja and Menja, who were born of giant kindred. The king set the bondmaids to work at two magical millstones that were so huge that no man was capable of grinding them. The stones had a power of grinding out whatever they were told. Fróði ordered his supernatural thralls to grind out gold for him. So Fenja and Menja labored at the stones, and the greedy king gave them small rest—no longer than the cuckoo remained silent.

As they ground, the giantesses chanted of their mighty strength, and how as children they had tossed boulders in the mountains. One of them was the mill they were grinding on: "as maidens we took on | tasks of great moment: | we ourselves plucked | the mountain-seat from its place. | We sent the stone rolling over the realm of giants | so the ground before it began to quake."[291] The giant maidens go on to tell of their exploits as warriors, toppling and installing princes. The chant foreshadows their overthrow of king Fróði. So does Menja's remark that it had been unwise of him to buy thralls of whose (giant) ancestry he was ignorant.

Ultimately, Fenja and Menja act as fateful beings who intervene in human affairs. The king's attempt to harness natural powers out of greed fails, as "the foreknowing pair" chant down their "master." They prophesy his fall, with enemies burning his hall. In fact, it is they who bring these things about. They enter a giant-rage, their chant mounting as they grind harder and faster, rocking the quern, finally overturning it with their momentum, and splitting the stone: "Ground have we, Frothi, now fain would cease | We have toiled enough at turning the mill."[292]

As Clive Tolley remarks, the legendary "Peace of Fróði" is "a sham which is bought at the price of inhuman cruelty towards the underclasses..."[293] He shows that the *Grottasongr* and *Rígsthula* shared this motif of overworked, despised bondswomen with bare, muddy feet.[294] Another saga, *Helgakvitha Hundingsbana II*, plays the tale of the mighty bondswomen for laughs, with the warrior Helgi in drag. He disguises himself as a woman to avoid capture by his enemies, fooling them into thinking he is a captured valkyrie.[295]

But the 12th century skáld Einarr Skúlason puts the giantesses who overthrow the rule of Fróði into a mythic context: "I have heard that Fróði's maidens ground quite joyfully the serpent's bed."[296] He is explaining that Grotti, the "grinder," is the mill of the ocean, propelled by the power of the giantesses.[297] The same beings figure in Norse kennings for gold: "Fenja's fair meal," and "Menja's good things."[298]

Snorri, and also the prologue to *Grottasongr,* say that after the fall of Fróði, the sea-king Mysingr took the giantesses on his ship. He made them grind salt, which caused his ship to sink. The salt-mill fell into the ocean at the Pentland Firth, where a whirlpool poured out of its eye. The salt-quern of Grotti Minnie and Grotti Finnie survived in Orkney folklore as late as 1895, by which time they were being described as witches.[299] A medieval account by Saxo Grammaticus relates another story in which a Danish witch kills king Frothi III by shapeshifting into a sea-cow and goring him.[300]

Other stories compare the giantesses with ordinary women who had seen their loved ones killed. A Scottish giantess avenged her husband by hurling a battle-ax across Munlochy Bay. "Her aim was as true as her strength was great," and the axe struck the rival giant in his forehead. She called across the water, "That will keep you quiet for one day at any rate."[301] In an episode of *The Flyting of Atli*, the giantess Hrimgerð confronted Atli, a lieutenant of the man who killed her father, in a poetic duel of insults. Atli told her that their fleet was protected with iron "so that no witches may work us ill."[302] (Iron was famous as a protector against faeries, so once again the categories of giantess, witch, hag, faery bleed together.) He bragged that he was hateful "to hags," having often done night-riders to death, and wished Hrimgerð nine leagues under the ground. Then he accused her of holding up Helgi's ships by witchcraft.

Hrimgerth retorted that it was her mother who had done that; she herself was working on drowning part of his fleet. She taunted Atli, calling him a gelding with the whinny of an uncastrated stallion but with his heart in the hind end. She dared her opponent to step on land "in reach of my claws," but he demurred on the excuse of his duty to Helgi. Then the *jötun* witch called out Helgi, her father's killer. Only the help of Helgi's valkyrie lover was able to prevent Hrimgerth from slaying all his men. As the sun rose, the giant woman turned to stone in the legendary manner of trolls and dwarves.[303]

Even where *spákonur* render aid to warriors in the sagas, the heroes insult them. In *Kormaks saga*, the hero and other characters express their disdain for "witch-women." Kormak blames witchcraft for his failure to show up at his own long-sought wedding, and for his failures in battle, no matter how reckless his own actions.[304] Oðinn insults the prophetess he has called up from the grave, after she has answered his questions, calling her the mother of three monsters.[305] In *Hávamál* he expresses his hostility to the wild night hags who ride and sport in the sky.[306]

The question staring us in the face is: why is the mythic female so villain-ized, so predictably made the object of horror, and why do these narratives insist that she must be thrown down? The answer should be obvious, but cultural conditioning has instituted male-hero worship, so that people are habituated to overlook the sexual politics of these myths, without ever questioning them. The demonized archetypes of old women, hags, and witches as "evil" are a means of repudiating their power, of rehearsing their abjection over and over and over, until the message is engrained in the collective unconscious: the female elder cannot win—can never be allowed to prevail. She is a threat to the power of domination.

❖

WITCHES VERSUS WARRIORS

Witches represented a daunting obstacle to conquest in the minds of early medieval warriors. It is written that before the Norman invasion of England, Gyrth had a dream that a great witch stood on the island, opposing the king's fleet with a fork and a trough. Tord dreamed that "before the army of the people of the country was riding a huge witch-wife upon a wolf," and that she tossed the invading soldiers into its mouth.[307]

Similar stories are told of German invasions of Sclavonia.[308] But the myth is even older than that. Such an apparition stopped a Roman general from crossing the Elbe: "the mighty female figure which appeared to Drusus, the first conqueror of Germany, on the bank of the Elbe, and called to him the one word "Back!" which proved so fatal to him."[309]

Conflicts between divine hags and warriors reflect the antagonism between old wisewomen and warlords in real life. Not surprisingly, the soldiers' contempt for witches was accompanied by a strong dose of fear. Anglo-Saxon men believed that witches and elves could make them sick or weak, even kill them. They were afraid of *hagtessen* riding by night, and of spirit warrior-women called *wælcyrean*, the Saxon equivalent of valkyries. Around 1020 Wulfstan of York listed "*wiccan* (witches) and *wælcyrean*" among seven types of sin that anger god.[310]

The 11th century English spell *Wið færstice* interprets a sharp pain in the side as *haegtessen geweorc*, the work of a hag who inflicts magical wounds. The spell draws on ideas of fateful female spirits, whose association with grave-mounds shows them as ancestral women:

> **Loud, oh, loud were the mighty women when they rode over the mound**
> **Fierce were the mighty women when they rode over the land...**
> **I stood under a shield while the mighty women**
> **Prepared their strength and sent screaming spears**
> **If it be the shot of ese, or the shot of *ælfe*,**
> **Or the shot of *hægtessen*, I will help you now.**[311]

The charm attempts to cast out missiles shot by the spirit-women, which cause a pain in the side. It uses the witch-word *hægtessen*: "Be out, spear, not in, spear. If there is here within a bit of iron, the work of *hægtessen*, it must melt."[312] *Hægtessen* (genitive singular) could refer either to a living sorceress or a supernatural woman, but spirits are suggested by the grouping of *hægtessen* with *esa* (Norse Aesir) and *ælfa* (Norse *álfar*, or "elves"). *Hægtesse* is a forerunner of English *hag*, which also carries the meanings of "witch," "old woman," or "terrifying spirit."[313]

In this charm, the "mighty women" are the attackers, but in other healing charms the metaphor for disease is an invading army: "the loathsome foe roving through the land" (in the Nine Herbs Charm, Lacnunga) or the enemy soldiers that the *idisi* thwart (in the Old High German Merseburg Charm I). The *idisi* unravel fetters and set free those who are in bondage.[314] Both of these 10th century charms date from a time of warlord mayhem, when it made eminent sense to use military bands as a metaphor for disease.

Flesh-and-blood witches were believed to be on good terms with the elvish divinities. A 10th-century charm in *Bald's Leechbook* purports to protect against both female sorcery and the elves. (See chapter 5.) Demonized ideas of the witch survive in other charms. In the christianized sowing charm "Æcerbot," the plougher invokes the Lord to guard his field against "witchcrafts sown throughout the land," and beseeches "that no witch be eloquent enough nor any man powerful enough to pervert the words thus pronounced."[315]

The "night-farers," *hægtessen*, and "mighty women" had a Middle Dutch counterpart, the *nacht-ridderen*, in the 13th century poem "De naturrkunde van het geheelal." A passage on stars and sky fires begins, "About the night-riders, and about other devils which make fire in the sky... which seems to us here like torches." After repeatedly being called "devils," the night-riders are identified as "*haghetissen*, and wandering women | 'goodlings' [protective spirits] also | indeed cobolds, water-monsters, *aluen* [elves], *night-maren*, who make themselves known | in the morning, and know well how to get fire."[316] Alaric Hall connects these *haghetissen* to the light-sparking *dísir* in *Helgakviða Hundingsbana* I, and recognizes them as part of "a network of overlapping traditions regarding supernatural, riding women among medieval North Sea cultures."[317]

The Dutch traditions are very close to the English, even using the same name. Both speak of night-riding women—maybe witches, maybe spirits, possibly the ancestral dead. Claude Lecouteux says that the English spell of the "mighty women" and the *hægtessen* may be "the oldest attestation of the Wild Hunt in Great Britain."[318] He shows that this widespread tradition of spectral hosts is about human encounters with the dead—who often appear as an omen of death. It belongs to "the vast complex of ancestor worship, the cult of the dead."[319] The *hœgtessen* have not been considered within this context, due to a greater scholarly preoccupation with witches than ancestor veneration. But the overlap between traditions of witches and the dead is broad, and the elves intersect with both.

witches and waelcyrgean   In 1015, archbishop Wulfstan of York wrote, "Here in England there are witches and *wælcyrgean*."[320] He used this phrase twice, "apparently with the sense of witch or sorceress."[321] Wulfstan repeated this denunciation in king Cnut's Proclamation of 1020, which he co-authored.[322] *Wælcyrge* is an Old English correlate to the Norse *valkyrja*, from *wael* + *ceosan*, "choosers of the slain." The *wælcyrgean* are a kind of Fates that developed in societies given over to war. The raven bore a parallel by-name, *wælcéasiga*, "devourer of the slain."[323] The Irish raven-goddesses Badb and the Morrigan hold a comparable fateful power over the course of battle to that of the Norse valkyries.

Women warriors are presented as demonic forces in a 10th century English manuscript of the Psychomachia *of Prudentius. The wild woman is labeled Ira, "Anger."*

Wulfstan could have been referring to actual women warriors, like Hlaðgerðr, the cross-dressing Danish warrior described by Saxo Grammaticus. However, the English bishop pairs witches with *wælcyrgean* more than once, showing that another meaning is in play.

Wælcyrge carried a strong supernatural charge, possibly with the sense of a *weird* or fate. Several Anglo-Saxon texts connect the *waelcyrge* with the Greek Furies and the Gorgons.[324] Terrifying two-headed monsters are described as having *wælkyrian eagan*, "valkyrie eyes," in the Anglo-Saxon MS Cotton Tiberius B. V.[325]

These flying female beings had a presence in old Anglo-Saxon healing charms, as the "mighty women" in the *Wið Færstice* charm, and the swarming bee "victory women" in the *Wið Ymbe* spell. Philip Purser makes a case that "the language used to name the *wælcyrian* is akin in nature to the epithets and kennings of heroic praise poetry," with honorific terms "that suggest a survival of Valkyrie-veneration surviving late into Saxon England."[326]

In another sermon, Wulfstan added a third term: *wyccan and wælcyrian and unlybwyrhtan*. That last word means "poisoner" or "harmdoer," or translating literally: "unlife-worker."[327] The archbishop used *unlybwyrhtan* in one other place, where he was denouncing sorcerers and enchanters.[328] The positive base of *lybwyrhtan* ("life-workers") has disappeared from view under the clerical onslaught against heathen healers. Only a demonized meaning was allowed to survive.

The formulaic pairing of *wiccan* and *wælcyrian* persisted past Wulfstan's time, as a Middle English stereotype.[329] As late as the 14th century, the anonymous Gawain poet lists *wychez and walkyries* as enemies of the Christian, along with diviners and sorcerers and dream-readers.[330] Another pairing, "witch and whore," was also regularly being hurled at female targets (see chapter 8). Aristocrats and the common man alike reviled the witch, as chapter 8 will show, just as the clergy demonized her.

The female serf was severely disadvantaged physically, economically, and legally, by sex and by class together. Folk religion was the only shield she had against rape from the warlord. The church offered her no protection against feudal violence, seen as a natural outcome of her innate whorishness as a daughter of Eve.[331] Though the oppression of women and peasants was growing, old beliefs in the witch's power endured. A heavily armed man might hesitate to harm an old woman reputed for her *cræft*. Like furies, to whom old sources often compare them, the *hagtessen* were seen as avenging wrongs committed against their kin. The cultural influence of the witch formed the only breakwater to the rising tide of patriarchy that automatically assigned all authority and all privilege to the male, the warlord, and the priest.

7

The witch holda and her retinue

In the year 1000, despite their centuries-long campaigns, churchmen still confronted regional ethnic cultures saturated with heathen belief and custom. Bishops and abbots continued to attack them with missionary zeal. Among their weapons were penitential books designed to ferret out beliefs and customs disapproved by the church. Armed with these manuals, priests questioned villagers about their adherence to the forbidden folkways. They were laboring to stamp out veneration of goddesses and their nature sanctuaries, incantation, divination, herbcraft, contraception, tying-on of herbs and amulets—and beliefs in women who journeyed in the spirit.

Beneficent Mother Earth with serpent and bullock at her breast.
Exultet Roll, 11th century parchment from Monte Cassino, Italy

Around 906, abbot Regino of Prüm wrote a handbook for the use of bishops on visitations to their dioceses. His *Libri duo de synodalibus causis et disciplinis ecclesiasticis* was intended for interrogation and "correction," exhorting people to report those who disregarded church doctrine and who kept pagan ways. Women were especially suspect when it came to magical and pagan matters. Many of Regino's interrogatories began with the words: "Is there any woman who..." Female teachers and birth control practitioners were major targets of this ecclesiastical offensive on folk culture. So were chanters of invocations to non-christian deities.

One passage from this work would resonate for centuries, as the foundation for a medieval mythology of shamanic witches who rode the

Diana dea paganorum

night skies with a goddess. This theme would gradually be transformed into a demonological fantasy that reigned as the defining ideology of the witch hunts; but that process took centuries. It began with Regino of Prüm's condemnation of a popular belief that witches flew by night in the company of an ancient goddess:

> **Certain criminal women, who have turned back to Satan and are seduced by illusions of demons and by phantasms, believe and avow openly that during the night they ride on certain beasts together with Diana, the goddess of the pagans, and an uncounted host of women; that they pass over many lands in the silence of the dead of night; that they obey her orders as those of a mistress; and that on certain nights they are summoned to her service.**[1]

Regino lamented that "a numberless multitude of people... think that there exists some divine power other than the one God."[2] His reference to popular belief in "Diana" was not new. For centuries missionaries fighting to stamp out folk religion had been using this name to denounce goddess veneration, particularly in France and Spain. Back in 585, Gregory of Tours related that a monk had destroyed a statue of "Diana" at Yvois in the Ardennes. He quoted Wulfilaich as saying, "I preached always that Diana was nothing, that her images and the worship which they thought it well to observe were nothing; and that the songs which they sang at their cups and wild debauches were disgraceful..." As a result of his desecrations, the monk broke out in sores all over his body.[3] We are told nothing about how these

The theme of witches riding on animals in the company of a Goddess began to be recorded in the late 800s, and was repeated for centuries. This night rider is clad only in a cape and is blowing a horn. Church fresco, Schleswig, ca 1300.

Gaulish-Frankish people felt about the smashing of their goddess (whatever her real name was) or what her shrine looked like, or what ceremonies took place there. We do know that early medieval sources understood Diana as a forest goddess, a spirit of the wilds, who also sometimes appeared to field workers, and whose followers were known as *dianatici*.

Diana became the great exception to the priestly refusal to name competing pagan deities, as Bernadette Filotas has observed. But she comes to us through the clergy's insistence on the *interpretatio romana*; they used a Latin name which "disguised an indigenous Rhenish goddess of death and fertility..."[4] However, a name of that German goddess managed to leak through the canonical boilerplate (see below).

It is significant that the women themselves said that they rode in the night, even though no one knows what they really believed. This account comes to us third-hand, from a source whose intense bias could not be more clear. Regino contemptuously referred to "little women" who were "deceived by dreams."[5] In his view, in line with church doctrine, the women were possessed and dominated by the devil, who "subjects her to him through her lack of faith and false belief."[6] Vexed by the fact that many people believed that the women's spiritual experiences were real, Regino responded by recommending repression—the punishment of exile. He enjoined bishops "to work with all their might to uproot wholly a dangerous type of sorcery and witchcraft." He urged them to drive anyone who practices it out of their parishes, treating them as heretics.[7] The clergy was not above using fear and intimidation to secure doctrinal conformity in their war on culture—which apparently included running people out of their homes.

The women who go with Diana are first mentioned around 850 in a Frankish text found amongst legal documents of the Frankish king Charles the Bald.[8] This early mention became the first in a long series of priestly anathemata against the belief that witches rode by night with a Goddess.[9] It was eventually incorporated into church doctrine as the Canon Episcopi.

The Witches' Goddess appears next in the late 900s, under a different name, in the *Praeloquia* of bishop Raterius of Verona. He wrote that, "persisting in error to the perdition of their souls," many people paid reverence to Herodias "who they call queen or rather goddess."[10] Raterius added that "one third of the world is given over to her, as if this had been the reward for the prophet's murder." He meant John the Baptist, but failed to explain how a provincial kinglet like Herod got the power to award global dominion. This is priestly mythologizing, of course; but the idea that the goddess controlled a third of the world does appear to be Raterius' estimation of her popularity among the common people in his time and place.

The *Praeloquia* contains the oldest mention of Herodias as a goddess of the witches. Like Regino, Raterius declared that the followers of the goddess were "mostly unfortunate little women" deceived by "tricks of the devil."[11] He explained that Herodias' special appeal to women was caused by deceptions of "the devil," who caused them to sin against the lord of creation. The bishop invoked the anti-god lurking on Christianity's nether side in order to discredit the appeal of a living goddess religion to women.

The biblical legend of Herodias had already been circulating in the Germanic world since around 850, thanks to a retelling of the dance of Salome in the *Heliand*. Louis the Pious had commissioned this vernacular poem with the intention of christianizing the conquered heathen Saxons by rendering biblical stories into Germanic epic style. Later writers picked up the estimate of Raterius that she was venerated by one third of the people. Mentions of Herodias began to percolate into priestly literature on the Witches' Goddess, beginning with the *Decretum* of Burchard of Worms. As her legend spread over the next several centuries, new names were attached to her, some latinate and others from folk culture: Noctiluca, Abundia and Dame Habonde, Bensozia, Richella, Signora Oriente, and Redodesa, among many others.[12]

women who go by night with diana

Around 1015, bishop Burchard of Worms borrowed heavily from Regino's accounts in his influential compendium of canon law, the *Decretum*.[13] Book 10 is titled *De incantationibus et auguribus*: "On Incantation and Divination." It targeted "magicians, soothsayers, prophets, fortune-tellers, various illusions of the devil..." and begins:

> **Bishops and all the men who are their ministers should labor with all their might to eradicate from their parishes the pernicious sorcery and malefic arts, so that if they find any man or woman of this wicked sect, they should eject them in disgrace and dishonor from their parishes.[14]**

The penalty of exile is in line with the more severe punishments ordered in bishops' courts—not the stake as is often imagined, but banishment is still a severe punishment that upends a person's life, (and in some cases shortens it). It would have been especially dangerous for women. There is no way to know how often such a sentence was actually imposed in this period. Fasting was certainly a more common penalty. Banishment continued to be used as a punishment for witchcraft later, by the Inquisition, secular rulers and municipalities.

Still following Regino's text, Burchard moved on to the women who go by night with the Goddess:

> **It is not to be omitted that some wicked women, turned back toward Satan, seduced by illusions and fantasms of the demons, believe and claim to ride on certain beasts in the night hours with Diana goddess of the pagans, or with Herodiade, with an innumerable multitude of**

women, and journey across an expanse of the earth in the silence of deep night, obeying her commands as their mistress, and being called on certain nights to her service. If only they alone perished in their faithlessness, without leading others into their downfall. For an innumerable multitude, deceived by this false opinion, believe that it is true, depart from the true faith, and fall into the error of the pagans.[15]

Burchard's addition of Herodias would ripple through later demonologies, even though he did not mention her when repeating this passage in Book 19.5. §90. The collision of worldviews is in plain view: the bishop admitted that the people believed "that there exists some other divinity or divine power outside of the one god." They believed in a goddess, in fact, though the bishops and canonists all insisted on redefining her as the devil. In a concerted campaign to suppress folk belief in a shamanic goddess, the clergy denied experiences of spirit flight. They insisted that this must be illusory and dismissed it as dreams—nothing like the dreams in the Bible, which were experienced by male prophets, not mere women, and which never involved female deities.

The title of Book 10 connected living witches and diviners with a Witches' Goddess—despite the claim that all this was diabolical illusion. Burchard refers to a "wicked sect," the first glimmering of an accusation that fueled later Inquisitorial witch hunts. He recommends that such women "be beaten with broomsticks and chased out of the diocese."[16] (His choice of weapons is interesting, even if mentions of broomstick-riding would come

Mother Earth in the margins of a Christian scripture. She still has the cornucopia but lies passive, looking up submissively at the Christian god.

Harley Psalter 603 f.50 Placed with Psalm 101

only in future centuries.)

Other than exile, the most severe penance in Book 10 is seven years of selective fasting. It was prescribed for those "devoted to auguries" and women who make divinations.[17] Even those who consulted diviners got five years. But these penalties conflict with those in 10.24, which repeats the ban on women who make divinations, but orders only a year's penance, even though the same phrase is used: *divinationes vel incantationes diabolicas fecerit* ("who makes divinations and diabolical incantations.")[18]

Chant that called in spirit was still very much in contestation. Subsequent canons condemn women who practice magic, who are to be ejected from the parish—a much more severe punishment than fasting— and they denounce people who read auguries, invoke spirits ("demons") —or who consult witches.[19]

wITh ThE wITch hoLdA (STRIGAm hoLdAm)

Burchard's *Decretum* says more about witches and their goddess in chapter 19.5. This section is known as the *Corrector sive Medicus* or, in older sources, as the Corrector Burchardi. It contains detailed accounts of folk beliefs written as an interrogatory for confessors on the hunt for surviving heathen practices. The Latin word *corrector* connoted reprimand, even castigation, as Martin de Braga stated at the beginning of his own *De Correctione Rusticorum* in 6th century Portugal. That manual left no room for ambiguity; its very first line explains its purpose as *pro castigatione rusticorum*, "for punishing the rural people."[20]

In Book 19.5 §70, Burchard got more specific about what the common people believed. Instead of naming Diana as he had in the canonical language of Book 10, he let slip the name of a German folk goddess and identifies her as a witch: "she who common folly calls the witch Holda [*strigam Holdam*], along with a throng of demons transformed into the likeness of women."[21] Here Burchard paired the calumniating Latin witch-word, *striga* with the Germanic name of the beneficent goddess Holda, Holle, Hulla, or Fraw Holt:

Have you believed that a woman can do what some women, deceived by the devil, claim they must do by necessity and by order, that is, with

a demonic throng changed into a woman's form, she who common stupidity calls the witch Holda, must ride animals on certain nights and be counted in their company?"[22]

Once more, whoever believed in the night-flying women was condemned as having been "deceived by the devil." But the women's own explanation for these events was a spiritual one; they said that they made these flights "out of necessity and by order."[23] The idea is that the women are fated to join the Goddess on the night ride, or to become a shapeshifter. Other passages in the *Corrector* illuminate this claim. One speaks of a belief that the Fates ordain certain people with the power to turn into wolves and other animals. In Burchard's opinion, belief in such experiences made one "an unbeliever, and worse than a pagan."[24]

Later copies of the passage naming "the witch Holda" omit the word *striga*, simply naming Holda; or else they include along with *striga Holda* another, inauspicious *striga unholda*[25] (thus pairing a "beneficent witch" and a "maleficent witch"). Understanding that Holda had a positive meaning, the German scribes felt impelled either to correct the text, or to add a negative term to fit the canon's tone.

Burchard kept Regino's reference to Diana, "goddess of the pagans," but in one place he copied Ratherius' mention of Herodias. As Greta Austin explains, the two earliest known versions of the *Decretum* are the Vatican and Frankfurt manuscripts, "which Burchard and his assistants revised and altered extensively."[26] To the account of women who go with Diana in the Vatican manuscript, someone added in the margin, "or with Herodias." That revision was picked up in all later editions of the *Corrector*.[27]

So the influence of Raterius percolated into the canonical literature around the Witches' Goddess, and mentions of Herodias continued to spread. The pronouncement that witches' flights with the Goddess were diabolical delusions came to be called, in its most definitive form, the Canon Episcopii—literally the "bishops' rod." It became the ruling priestly doctrine on witches until viral new diabolist doctrines arose at the end of the Middle Ages. Burchard repeated Regino's claim that the account of the Witches' Goddess came from an early church council at Ankara in 314, and later canonists carried along this false attribution. Quoting from the early church fathers, however distant they were from the situation at hand, always added

Herodias dancing on a boulder, with tree, spring, snake, and cape.
English Harley Psalter, MS 603 f56r, copy of the 9ᵗʰ century Utrecht Psalter.

gravitas. Accuracy was a lesser concern.[28]

Ivo of Chartres included the Women Who Go By Night with the Goddess in his *Decretum* (1092). Gratian followed suit in his *Decretals* (1147), which became the most influential formulation of canon law.[29] The name Canon Episcopii is taken from his version which, once again, calls for a priestly battle against paganism and witchcraft. Its title expands on Regino and Burchard: "Bishops should strive by all means to eliminate divination and the magic arts." Gratian elaborated by specifying *arioli, aruspices, incantatores,* et *sortilegi*[30] ("diviners, omen-readers, enchanters, and sorcerers").

Gratian's canon repeated the demand that episcopal authorities forcibly exile diviners and witches, calling them heretics held captive by the devil. It then launched into the denunciation of "wicked" women who say they ride with Diana on the backs of animals. Gratian added another piece to the edifice: he declared it heretical to believe that these dream experiences really happen in the flesh. This doctrine that shamanic flights with the goddess were nothing but dreams and diabolical illusions would prevail for centuries.

Only at the end of the Middle Ages would it be it countered and displaced by a new doctrine claiming that witches' gatherings and devilish dealings were materially real and happened in the flesh. After 1400 it became dangerous to say anything else.

The Canon Episcopii spread a mythology about witches who go by night with a Goddess over much of Europe. It percolated up to faraway Scandinavia, where the clergy duly translated it into local terms: "It is said in holy books that night-riders or transvecting witches (*kveldriður eða hamleypur*) are believed to travel with the goddess Diana and Herodias for a while over the great sea riding on whales or seals, birds or animals, or over the great land..." The shift to the sea and to whale-riding adapted the canon to the Norse understanding of witchcraft, incorporating a culturally specific word for shapeshifters, *hamleypur*.[31]

NIGHT JOURNEYS, AND THE MIRACLE OF THE BONES

The *Corrector sive Medicus* referred to women who fly by night in several places. It asked if women believe as others do, that at night while their bodies lay in bed with their husbands at their breast, they journey in the spirit, being "raised past locked doors into the air up to the clouds." It says that some women said that they participated in night battles, fighting with other women in the skies, giving and receiving wounds.[32]

This story strongly resembles the shamanic night battles of the Benandanti ("good-walkers") five hundred years later in Friuli, northeast Italy.[33] It also shows similarities to Livonian werewolves who went abroad in the spirit as "defenders of society."[34] These similarities indicate that the women might have understood themselves to be doing something beneficial, and caution against assuming that these flights must have been about harmful sorcery, when in fact there is little to go on.

Another question also asks about women who left their husbands in bed to fly by night, but this time, it says, the aim is to kill christians, cook, and eat them.[35] The description recalls the Old Saxon accusation, recorded in Carolingian capitularies, that witches devoured the hearts of men. Both versions say that the witches replace the hearts with straw or wood stuffing. But the version in the *Corrector* adds, "thus reviving and restoring them to life again."[36]

This line throws a different light on things, spotlighting a pagan resurrection that is an international theme, now known as the Miracle of the Bones. The Witches' Goddess revivifies the cattle that the witches had feasted on at their dances. After the banquet is over, they gather up the bones into the skins, and the Lady regenerates the animals by a touch of her wand, or the witches do it by pronouncing a simple spell like, "Rise, Ronzola."[37] Variations on this story were told all across the Alps. Sometimes it is a goddess who revives the animal, or "three wild women," or the "people of the night"[38] (revenant ancestors).

Stories of a restorative goddess appear in other parts of Europe. As far away as Latvia, trial records say that witches sacrificed a cow to a female "earth demon," who restored it to life.[39] In Belgium, it was saint Pharaildis who revived a goose from skin and bone.[40] John of Salisbury repeated this miracle in his *Polycraticus* (1159), which told of great nightly assemblies in honor of a goddess called Noctiluca or Herodiade. But he mixed in the blood libel, claiming that *children* were being sacrificed to the *lamias*, eaten, and their bones thrown up to be "restored to life" by the Queen of the Night.[41] These allegations of child murder come later, as the priestly literati began to revive Roman accusations of child sacrifice from late antiquity.

Female supernaturals or spirits or ancestors or fates are sometimes confused with living witches, and it can be hard to tell the difference. In the Icelandic *Laxdæla saga*, Án dreams that an old woman slices open his belly, removes his bowels, and stuffs in brushwood instead. This dream is an omen of danger; afterwards his party is ambushed and he is wounded. But later the old woman comes again to remove the brushwood and put his entrails back in place: "and I felt good about this interaction." After this Án recovers completely.[42] So what looks like a dangerous spirit turns out to be a protective one, possibly a *dís*.

A later German tradition warns that the Old Goddess Perchta would punish those who did not observe her holiday by slicing open their bellies and replacing their innards with straw. In these fragmentarily recorded traditions, witches, supernatural women, and goddesses overlap, and sometimes cannot be distinguished from each other.

Another angle to this tangle is a reference in the *Indiculus Superstitionum et pagariarum* to a belief that women "can take the hearts of men, according to the pagans." But the rest of the passage, which involves a relationship of women to the moon, is unclear because of a misspelled Latin word (the mysterious *comendet*). It is not clear if it means that women can "eat" the moon, or "commend" the moon, or commend themselves to the moon.[43] The writer might be referring to love spells.

There is no shortage of evidence for widespread male anxiety about women's witchcraft.[44] Regino was worried that women might kill their husbands with herbs or potions. The *Corrector sive medicus* also lists spells that women supposedly worked on husbands.[45] But these churchmen did not really know what women were doing in their rites. They like other men feared that women were casting spells to cause male impotence or overcome male authority. [46]

One other early source refers to women's night journeys. Burchard's version of the Women Who Go By Night had borrowed the phrase "in the silence of dead of night" from the Arundel Penitential, circa 1000. Its French author asked "If anyone believes that sorceresses rise up in the air in the silence of the dead of night?"[47] This theme of witches flying out by night was in wide circulation.

WOMEN'S RITUAL CUSTOMS

The *Corrector sive Medicus* contains a wealth of fragmentary (and distorted) information about survivals of heathen culture. Like Raterius, its author recognized that it was mainly women who performed and preserved the old ceremonies. Sometimes he addressed his questions to both men and women, but certain kinds of questions—an entire section of them—were addressed only and explicitly to women. His departure from the masculine default emphasizes that it was women who were at the forefront of the proscribed heathen customs. The *Corrector* asked questions like this: "Have you believed, as some [feminine form] have, that..."

Do you believe as some women are accustomed to believe, that...?

Veneration of the Fates appears among the heathen traditions named in the questions addressed to women. Commoners were still performing ceremonial acts to honor the "Three Sisters," as priestly references to the "sisters" and the *parcae* (Latin birth fates) demonstrate. The bishop asked women if they believed that the Fates could assign destiny at birth. Then he revealed more about the offerings that women made to the Fates, asking if they "at certain times of the year spread a table with meat and drink and three knives so that, if those three sisters come, whom past generations and ancient stupidity call the Fates, they can regale themselves?[48] Finally, the prelate rebuked the women for believing in their ancient goddesses, which he equated with the devil:

Do you believe that those called the sisters can help you now or in the future? Foolish woman, don't you know that you are attributing to the devil the power that only divine providence can possess?[49]

But for Rhenish peasant women, the Three Sisters *were* divine providence, to which they appealed for aid in childbirth, healing, and abundant harvests. In the *Corrector sive Medicus*, the women lay tables several times a year, including for their birth ceremonies. However, only a male trinity was acceptable to the jealous priesthood, which refused even to acknowledge these pagan traditions as religion. While the author uses the Latin term *parcae*, his description does not match up with any sources from late Mediterranean antiquity. None of them mention three knives among the offerings—but they are found in French lais of the 1200s and in German woodcuts of the 1400s.

Other customs prohibited in the *Corrector* lead back to the Fates. Women would have directed incantations "in their spinning and weaving" to the divine spinners of webs. The diviners that people invited to soothsay in their homes "according to pagan custom" may have invoked the fates or other folk goddesses when they "cast lots or expect by lots to foreknow the future."[50] Women kept on laying out ritual offering tables for goddesses (*fées*, ancestral women) and appealing to them for abundance and good fortune. Priestly writing on folk religion referred to this custom between 1100-1500 —and even later in certain regions. In Italy, Austria, Germany, France, and Britain, the goddesses so honored were intimately connected with fates and faeries and witches, "the women who go by night."

Tracking the women's night ride with the Goddess is an exercise in medieval detection. It requires piecing together fragmentary information from different sources (which at times conflict) and tracking down the primary sources which are often cited under different names, and are mostly available only in Latin.

The first source is Regino of Prum, *Libri Duo de Synodalibus Causis et Disciplinis Ecclesiasticis*. The title is sometimes translated as *Churchly Disciplines and the Christian Religion*, or cited as *Libri Duo* or *De Synodalibus Causis*. Regino names the Witches' Goddess as "Diana, goddess of the Pagans," the name that bishops and missionaries had been using for centuries when they were forced to refer to native goddesses.

DIANA DEA PAGANORUM

Next comes the *Praeloquia* of bishop Raterius of Verona, who introduces Herodias as the Witches' Goddess. Then the French Arundel Penitential mentions witches who ascend into the skies. It is dated to circa 1000 CE, but the only surviving manuscript is a 13th century English version.[51]

HERODIAS WHOM THEY CALL QUEEN OR RATHER GODDESS

The final source for this formative mythology (850-1015 CE) is bishop Burchard of Worms. Book 19.5 of his *Decretum* of canon law is a penitential guide for priests to question people about their beliefs, customs and behavior. Its title *Corrector sive Medicus* explains it as a doctrinal template which "fully contains medicines for the corrections of bodies and souls."[52] The priests viewed themselves as both discipliners and doctors of the soul. Their model was authoritarian and charged with sexual politics, class politics, and cultural politics. Burchard's questionnaire summarizes and expands on earlier canons of the *Decretum*, but adds a wealth of detail about folk beliefs and customs, making it a key source on heathen culture in western Germany.

DIANA DEA PAGANORUM

DIANA OR HERODIAS

THE WITCH HOLDA

Friedrich Wasserschleben dubbed the interrogatory *Corrector Burchardi*, Most older historians used this name, while modern ones use *Corrector sive Medicus*. Another 19th century scholar, H.J. Schmitz, believed that Burchard had incorporated an entire 10th century Frankish penitential into the *Decreteum*, as Book 19.5. This idea persisted, repeated by such authorities as Henry Charles Lea.[53] Recent studies disprove that theory, demonstrating that Burchard copied from many penitentials and canonists, especially his near-contemporaries Regino of Prum and the Arundel Penitential.[54]

In fact, Burchard's work is a textbook case of intertextuality. He was a compiler who borrowed massively, as he revised, synthesized, altered, and reinterpreted material from earlier penitentials. He copied canons from many older sources, especially Regino of Prüm, from whom Burchard lifted entire paragraphs about the women who go with Diana. He borrowed tell-tale phrases from other sources too, like the "simple priest" for whose use Halitgar of Cambrai (circa 830) intended his penitential.[55]

Source critics disagree on the reliability of the penitential writers as sources on folk belief. Some point to their repetition of older manuals' prohibitions of Roman observances. Burchard's early questions go over themes from 6th century canonists Caesarius of Arles and Martin of Braga that had no relevance to German culture 500 years later.[56]

This habit of copying from older penitentials led Dieter Harmening to view the penitentials as nothing more than priestly ideology, with little authentic cultural content. His most telling example of unreliability is the ever-morphing description of offerings laid on tables for the Calends of January (itself a Roman concept). They are *lapidus* ("stones") in Burchard, but *lampidus* ("lamps") in Atto Vercelli some fifty years earlier, who in turn had borrowed from *dapibus* ("plates") in a Roman synod of 743. Did these changes result from misreadings of the script, or deliberate substitutions? Harmening notes that it was a Roman custom to offer lamps to Fortuna.[57]

But the question remains: was bringing in this ceremony completely irrelevant to local culture, or did the priests make a connection between the Roman fate goddess and native fates (or ancestral mothers) revered by the common people, for example during the Winternights? This gets sticky. West European peoples did borrow

from the Roman culture of their rulers. But neither can we forget that the clergy viewed actual folk customs through a romanizing lens, and that all written sources come from them. For priestly writers, the common people did not count, least of all the women, and the culture they passed on over generations was assumed to be diabolical, something to be eradicated. In priestcraft all that mattered was doctrine, what church authorities said, whether or not it reflected the actual cultures. So they did often play fast and loose with folk belief.

To overcome these difficulties, scholars have devised evidentiary grounds for evaluating the penitentials' testimony about the folk cultures. The criteria set out by Rudi Künzel look for new attestations of observances not recorded before: "a religious phenomenon which does not go back to an earlier prototype."[58] A prime example is the offering table laid for the Fates with "food and drink with three knives."[59] Burchard uses the Latin name Parcae, foreign to rural Germans, but the "three knives" do not appear in any Roman sources, only in vernacular medieval manuscripts.

Another important category of evidence comes from native names and concepts that breach the crust of *interpretatio romana*. They are typically signaled by some version of *quod vulgo vocatur* ("which the common people call ___").[60] Burchard used this phrase to flag German words or names with a strong heathen valence: Holda, *werewulff*, and *belisa* (the witch-herb henbane: see image on next page).[61]

The theme of Women Who Go by Night with a Goddess is the classic example of authentic ethnic culture breaking through the grid of theological jargon. Regino used the priestly lens of *interpretatio romana* in naming "Diana, goddess of the pagans." Next, Raterius supplied a new name, the biblical Herodias, that was widely taken up in later texts. Burchard repeated Regino's *Diana dea paganorum* in his canon law compendium (Book 10.1), and in one place he added Herodias.

But in his manual intended for priests questioning the common people, the bishop introduced a telling description of the witches' goddess: *quam vulgaris stultitia hic strigam Holdam vocant*—"whom in their stupidity the people here call the witch Holda."[62]

For the next four centuries, new names continued to be added to the growing legend of the Witches' Goddess, in both native vernacular and in Church Latin.

Witch spinning in the forest with a distaff loaded with spindles. To her left grows henbane, a witch-herb related to mandrake and nightshade. It turns up in an early medieval Swiss woman's threadbox; in German women's rain rites around 1015; in a 10th century Danish völva's *pouch; and in receipes for witches' flying ointment after 1450. This witch has the power to move the moon and stars in their courses, but the 1532 woodcut by Hans Weidetz—on the eve of the mass hunts—shows her power as blasting, not blessing. He depicts the old woman calling down hail, a common accusation during the witch hunting Terror.*

herodias as witch goddess

Starting with the *Præloquia* of Raterius in the late 900s, the name Herodias appears in some manuscripts along with that of Diana, or even replaces her. How this name got wrapped up into the legend of the Witches' Goddess is an enigma. Herodias was the wife of king Herod in the Christian Bible. According to the books of Mark and Matthew, she got her daughter Salome (also named Herodias) to demand the head of John the Baptist as a reward for her dance.

The story makes Herodias the villain, even though her near-contemporary Josephus clearly states that her husband Herod Antipas treated John as a political threat to his rule. The biblical account was influenced by urban legends then circulating in the Roman world about a prostitute who demands a man's death as her price, and gets it. Thus Christian writers calumniated the unfortunate Herodias, whose father forced her into an arranged dynastic marriage, and who was reviled for taking the unprecedented step of divorcing her husband.[62a]

The name of Herodias first came into play in the Germanic world through the *Heliand*, a vernacular retelling of Bible stories in the style of heathen epics. But its revival of the story of dancing Herodias fails to explain what could have caused such an obscure biblical figure to be connected to women's with shamanic journeys in the night. Dance may well have been a theme that the Herodias story had in common with folk ceremonies. But early medieval accounts of witches do not mention it, though it is central in the later witch mythologies.

In Europe of the 8th to 11th century, and even later, the Bible existed only in rare, Latin volumes monopolized by the clergy and a handful of aristocrats. Very few commoners, none of them women, were literate, and it is unlikely they had ever heard of the Herodian queen, or her daughter. Herodias appears in no church sculpture (the peasantry's primary text on Christian mythology) nor in sermons. There is no reason to assume that Burchard and Raterius were describing a popular belief in the biblical character Herodias as a goddess.

A more likely explanation is that priestly authors, sticklers for scriptural sources that they were, seized on the biblical name because it sounded like that of the folk goddess connected with the witches' shamanic rides. They

The larger context of the dancing goddess in the Harley Psalter 603 f.56. She is approached by naked worshippers. A soldier kicks one of them, while other soldiers rifle through a treasure chest. The pagan goddess is depicted as spatially superseded by the Christian god—but like her he rests on a boulder, with his own flowing cornucopia. One of the male angels surrounding him is dragging away a bare-breasted woman who attempts to approach. She is the only other other woman in the scene, which conveys an abomination of femaleness and of proscribed heathenism. The painting is contemporary with the earliest priestly references to the witches' goddess. Her dance ties in with the developing priestly myth of Herodias, based on biblical accounts of the dance of Salome.[62a]

may have used "Herodias" to approximate the names of the Germanic earth goddess: Erada or Ero or Hero in Old High German, Erda in Norse, Hretha or Hertha in Old Saxon, Eorth in Anglo-Saxon.[63] Ero for Earth appears in the Wessobrunn Prayer, an Old High German text which contains the very archaic expression *ero ni was noh ûfhimil*, "earth was not, nor heaven above." This phrase about what preexisted heaven and earth was omnipresent in old Indo-European, from Vedic, Avestan and Armenian to Greek, Norse, and Old English.[64] One version of the prayer gives Hero instead of Ero, which resembles "Herodias" even more closely.[65]

The likelihood that priestly writers correlated two entities as disparate as the first century Herodian queen and the Germanic Earth Mother is not so farfetched as it might seem. Medieval writers were constantly inventing spurious etymologies in their obsession to explain everything heathen in Biblical or Roman terms. For example, Isidore of Seville tried to derive the name of Britain from Brutus of Troy. Irish and Scandinavian monks went to similar extremes making similar claims of classical or biblical origins for Celtic and Germanic names of deities, heroes, and placenames.

Regino, Burchard and Raterius (a Frank, though bishop of Verona) all hailed from Germanic cultures.[66] In their day, people still openly invoked and venerated Mother Earth. One Anglo-Saxon manuscript reproduces chants directed to her at sowing, for example, with libations of milk, honey, and oil. Even ecclesiastical scribes painted her into their gospel illuminations, with verdure springing up around her, and sprouting up between her toes. In the corners of ivory diptychs and church stonework, Frankish and German artists sculptured Mother Earth under the tree of life, or giving the breast to snakes, humans, cows, deer, and fish. (See figures in this chapter.)

Another piece of the puzzle is a Gaulish tile found in Dauphiné. It shows a woman riding on a goose, with the words: *Fera Comhera*, "with wild Hera."

Carlo Ginzburg suggests that a romanized Celtic goddess known variously as Haera, Era, Hera, or Aerecura may have gotten conflated with Herodias.[67] In late antiquity, Haera was connected to the underworld god Dis, especially in Italy, south Germany and the Balkans, where Roman-era statues of her survive. Other inscriptions to Hera or Haerecura have turned up in Istria, Switzerland and the western Alps. The problem is that the center of gravity for the witch goddess Herodias is further north, among the Franks, Germans, and apparent-

Fera Comhera: "with wild Hera"? the tile from Roussas, Dauphiné, in south France

ly the Dutch, if we go by the Utrecht Psalter. That 9th century manuscript depicts a half-naked woman dancing on a stone beside a tree and snake, complete with worshippers and a cornucopia.

This goddess Hera—or Ero / Hero as Earth—is known to have survived in the Rhineland into the early 1400s, when Gobelinus Persona wrote of a belief among the common people that Lady Hera flew through the air between Christmas and Epiphany, "according to an ancient tradition."[68] Gobelinus attributed this belief to the Old Saxons, saying that Lady Hera was pictured with little bells and other things. He related that the common people called her *Vrowe Here*, and had a saying, *Vro Here de vlughet* ("Lady Hera flies"). And, he continued, "they believed her to confer on them an abundance of material things."[69]

The story of Vrowe Here fits a larger pattern of the Old Goddess. Her fructifying flight across the lands during the Winternights is a familiar theme in folk tradition. This is when Frau Holle was abroad, when Perchta and other forms of the witches' goddess visited homes. A wealth of folklore also ties in the sound of tinkling bells with the approach of the company of the dead, or of the faeries.[70] Holle herself appears in plural form, as beneficent land fairies.[71]

Jeffrey Russell thought that Herodias had probably been chosen because her name resonated with traditions of the wild hunt, whose leader "so often had a name beginning with Ber or Her, like Berhta."[72] Maybe even Madonna Horiens is part of this complex of names, and not a latinate "Milady East." The goddess Horiens taught the witches healing and the virtues of herbs, and resurrected the animals with her wand after they had feasted on them. So Pierina de' Bugatis recounted in a 1390 witch trial at Milano.[73]

Priestly writings forced folk religion through a doctrinal lens, latinizing the names of native goddesses as Diana, Minerva, or assorted "nymphs." They interpolated biblical names like Herodias as substitutes for those goddesses. But the divine status of "Herodias" is beyond doubt, as Raterius calls her "queen or rather goddess."[74] The priesthood further fogged the picture by repeating each other's descriptions of pagan customs and names, and inventing new stories about them. But ultimately, while the authors of canon law could not afford to dismiss the people's veneration of the Old Goddess, they refused to acknowledge her as a goddess, interpreting her as "the devil."

These repetitions show how influential canonical authority was in shaping descriptions of folk religion, and how careless its writers often were of peasant culture's actual contents. One of these new mythologies comes from a sermon of the English cleric Aelfric. He describes Herodias as *moesta hera cui pars tertia hominum servit*, "unhappy mistress who is served by a third part of humanity." ("Hera" appears here again as a Latin word for "mistress.") She perches on oaks and hazels, all night long from midnight to cockcrow, but in the daytime is doomed to float through the empty air, mourning her unrequited love for John the Baptist.[75]

The 12th century Reinardus poem expatiated on this invented love of the princess Herodias for scruffy old John the Baptist. His severed head rejects her caresses and blows her away into the air, where she lives on, wandering in sorrow. But the poem also folds in the folk tradition first glimpsed in Raterius: she has followers, and they constitute one third of humanity.[76] It gives an account of the shamanic flight of the "good women" with three goddesses, identified as Holda, Herodias and "Pharaildis." (Thus the triune goddess was reconstituted under new names). The poet identifies Pharaildis as the daughter of Herodias, and calls her "the best dancer that ever was."[77] He repeats Raterius' remark that "one third of the world serves her."[78]

Like Burchard, the Flemish author introduces a real Germanic name into his account of a Goddess of the Witches.[79] This time it was Pharaildis. The Belgian saint Pharaildis was the patron saint of Ghent, said to have been a devout 7th century princess whose father beat her for refusing to consummate her arranged marriage.[79] Her symbol was the wild goose. Pharaildis is said to have miraculously restored a dead goose to life, tying in with the "miracle of the bones" in legends of the Witches' Goddess.[80] She is not the only goose goddess who survived disguised as a saint, as we will see below.

Pharaildis continued to appear in late medieval Dutch and German sources. Jacob Grimm connected her with Middle Dutch Verelde, seeing her as a Dutch equivalent of frau Hilde or Hulde. He noted a mention of Verhildeburg, much like Holle's mountain, in a 1213 manuscript.[81] Other scholars reject the Verelde derivation of Pharaildis.[82] Ginzburg concurs, but remarks that "the identification of Pharaildis, in the role of a nocturnal guide of souls, remains unexplained." He suggests her association with miraculous revivals as "the key" to her linkage with Herodias.[83] That is part of the puzzle; but Pharaildis had a more direct association with the witches' shamanic flights, in the manner of Holle. By 1456, a Bavarian writer was denouncing witches' flying ointments under the name *unguentum pharelis*.[84]

The theme that "one third" of humanity follow a goddess repeats in the late 13th century poem *Roman de la Rose*. Jean de Meun identified them as the followers of Dame Habonde (Lady Abundia). Her name is recognizable as a medieval descendant of the Gallo-Roman goddess Abundantia. Con-temporary sources confirm that French women were still making offerings to this goddess. In 1282, bishop William of Auvergne described rites for Lady Abundia, Satia, and the "ladies of the night":

Concerning the mistresses of the night, that they are the good women, and great gifts are presented by them to the houses which they visit; especially they persuade the women.[85]

These faery divinities fly into houses through keyholes and feast on the offerings of food and drink laid out for them, without ever diminishing their quantity. They bring prosperity to the households that honor them in this way.[85b] William also reported a belief "that goddesses existed who made such prophecies or predictions at men's birth." He had heard people say that they had overheard goddesses "talking together of the destiny of children being born." The bishop regarded all this as superstition, but warned that it was far more widespread than "the ravings of old women," since it was "repeated almost everywhere," including near his own birthplace.[85c]

The *Roman de la Rose* follows the Canon Episcopii by setting the scene with fantasms that deceive the senses:

By which many people in their folly / believe they are witches [*estries*] by night / Wandering with Dame Habonde / And they say that all over the world / Every third child born / Are in this condition / And that they go three times a week / As if destiny had led them to it... And also that a third of the world / must go thus with Lady Abundia / As if foolish [or crazy: *folles*] old women could prove it / by what they find in visions.[86]

Old women are identified as the source of these traditions—and as dreamers, though in reversed view. "As if destiny led them to it": this phrase returns to the Fates, who conferred the power of shapeshifting to certain people at birth, as in the Corrector sive Medicus. A current of popular culture clearly was running underneath these shifting narratives. Writers injected fragments of local belief into their accounts, even as they adhered to the disdain demanded by church doctrine. They spoke of people, especially women, who were fated to participate in journeys in the spirit, sometimes alluding to shapeshifters or to riding on spirit animals.

Always these witches go in the company of a goddess, whose name was constantly subjected to priestly revisionism. But in one instance, her real identity slipped through, when Burchard named "the witch Holda," making a revelatory connection to a well-known medieval German goddess.

holda / holle, the witches' goddess

Following priestly conventions, the author of the *Corrector sive Medicus* had named Diana and Herodias as the witches' goddess. But in calling her "she whom common stupidity here calls the witch Holda," the canonist provided a tie-in to a vast complex of heathen lore recorded from the Middle Ages into modern times. She is Holda, Hold, Holt, Holde, Holle, Holla, Holl or die Hulla, whose name meant "beneficent, favorable, kind."[87] She was commonly pictured as a long-nosed old spinner.

In Old Saxon, *holdan* means "to care for, to take care of, to cure." The Germans used to invoke good, friendly spirits called *holden*. Two German copyists of the *Corrector* recognized the beneficent meaning of the goddess's name and "replaced it with *unholda*."[88] Demonologists of the late 1400s made the same inversion to *unholda*, but Ulphilas had set the pattern a thousand years before in his Gothic translation of the Bible, rendering *daimónion* as *unholthó*.[89] (Greek *daimon* original meant spirit" rather than "demon.") But other German copyists altered the Latinate *striga* to *friga* (the manuscript characters **s** and **f** being similar) so that it reads Friga-Holda, introducing yet another Germanic goddess into the mix.[90] Apparently Friga made more sense to the scribes than the unfamiliar Latin word *striga*.

Another old reference to Holda comes from the 10th-century poet Walafrid Strabo, who described the goddess as the consummate musician: "Judith strikes the instrument with a sweet-sounding plucker / As if Sappho or Holda had come to us."[91] Six centuries

Earth with snake, tree, and babies.
Bibliothèque Nationale de Paris
Cod. Lat. 9383

later, Martin Luther was still describing Fraw Hulda as a joyous fiddler on holidays—though in far more pejorative terms.[92]

Cultural testaments to the goddess Holda occur across a thousand years, in proverbs and stories, ritual observances and place-names. She appears to humans in various forms and epiphanies, especially in Hesse and Thuringia (central Germany). Women dressed their distaffs full of flax and stood them up overnight for the goddess to inspect on her Winter Nights visit to every house. She presented spindles to hardworking spinners, and tangled or fouled the skeins of lazy ones, or those who failed to respect her holydays. On these divinatory festivals, omens were taken for the coming year.[93]

A 17th century German account shows how the common women would propitiate Frau Holle with offerings: "serving women replenish their spindles or roll large amounts of yarn or fabric around them, and leave them there over night. They say if Dame Holle sees this she will say, 'For every thread there will be a good year.'"[94]

Earth Mother with Snake and Tree in the corner of an ivory bookcover, Tongeren Cathedral, Belgium

Frau Holle, the Good Lady, is the spirit of Earth, who inhabits the ground, its waters, and the air around it. Holy mounts, especially the Horselberg, were known as her sanctuaries and dwelling-places—and they became renowned as places for gatherings of witches.

Holle appears at lakes and springs, especially at noon, when she could be glimpsed bathing in the water. Her yearly circling of the fields fills them with vital power, as Nerthus traveled through the fields in a ritual cart in Tacitus' account of the Germaniae.[95] Transylvanian Germans named certain fields "Frau Holda's ditch" or "trench." Erasmus recorded a story in which Frau Hulda sends out "an army of women" with sickles in their hands.[96]

Addressed as the "Mother of All

Life" and "the Great Healer," Holle is the giver of plenty and of children.[97] People used to tell their children that babies came from Frau Holle's pond, or from her house. Hessian brides who bathed in the Frauhollenteich near Meisner expected to gain health and fertility.[98] In a German folk tale, a girl falls into her well and end up in a faery underworld where Holla lives with her apple tree and her bread-baking oven, bestowing treasure on worthy passers-by, but punishing people who are unkind, lazy and greedy.[99]

Earth nurses a snake at her breast, holding a cornucopia of mugwort. Ivory diptych, Bamberg Cathedral, circa 1000 CE

Holle also receives the dead, who travel in her wake on the great festival eves, especially midwinter. In this she is related to the Norse Hel, lady of the dead, who has power "over nine worlds."[100] She may relate to Dea Hludana, a goddess honored in Roman-era inscriptions of the lower Rhineland, and to the Norse earth goddess Hloðyn.[101] Local orature points out portals to her underworld realm full of treasures, such as the Frau-Holle-Loch wellspring near Fischborn and a deep gorge called the Wildholl-Loch near Seibertenrod.[102]

Holle is a weather-maker in all seasons. When fog hangs over the mountain, said one German proverb, then Frau Hölle has lit her fire in the hill. When snow falls, it is Holle shaking her feather bed. *Die Holle kommt*: she comes in storms, riding the winds at the head of a cavalcade of spirits and witches. These traditions are hinted at in the *Corrector sive Medicus*, and survived in modern Germany, with abundant testimony to them recorded in between. For example, a Hessian witch trial in 1630 convicted a man of going with Frau Holle in the Wild Hunt.[103]

The "witch Holda" and "Diana the goddess of the pagans" had other things in common besides their nocturnal travels with women. Both liked to appear in growing fields of grain during the noon hour. Diana, as the noonday spirit (from the biblical term *demonium meridianum*) appeared to a Gallic woman working in the fields, causing her to fall unconscious to the ground, as Gregory of Tours related in the 6th century.[104] Many European peoples spoke of a goddess who passed through the growing grain at midday. She was the "aunt-in-the-rye," the "corn granny," the *jitnaya baba* ("living crone").[105]

Another spinner-goddess who appeared to field laborers in the noonday was the Wendish *pši-pol'nitsa*. (Her Russian counterpart was the shaggy *poludnitsa*, who watches over the fields.)[106] She especially liked to talk to women tending flax about how to grow it and all the stages of working it.[107] Holle shared this consuming interest in spinning. It was said that this spinner goddess had taught humans to plant flax and to work it into linen. She watched over flax farming and flax-work. Families anticipated her visit to their hearths during her journey across the land in the twelve days following the winter solstice. Spinners made sure to finish the flax on their distaffs before the holyday so as not to offend Mother Hölle, who tangled any flax left unspun on the distaff.[108]

Holle herself was shaggy-haired, like Perchta and the Wendish Pshi-Polnitsa. Holle appears as a long-nosed old woman with large teeth and wild matted hair. A person whose hair sticks out in a tangled mess was said to have "had a jaunt with Holle."[109] The German expression "ride with Holle" referred to both wild-haired people and to those who went on the witches' ride.[110] Much more remains to be told of Holle—but that is for a later volume.

Pši-Pol'nitsa,
Wendish spinner of the fields

Berthe, perchta, and swan-foot spinners

The Spinning Crone appears in Germanic cultures under a multitude of other names: Berhta or Berthe among the Franks and Germans, or Frau Bertha; in south Germany Berche, Bertel, or frau Bert. In Austria and other southern German-speaking regions, the name Berhta metamorphosed into Perchta, Perahta, even Schperchta, or Dame Percht. She was called "Bercht with the long nose," or "with the iron nose." Sometimes she was called die Stempe, "the trampling one," who comes on Twelfth Night.[111] Or she is the Wild Perchta, spirit of the forest.[112]

Always, she remains a spinner, a protector of children and households, who fares forth on the winter festival and whose journey brings fruitfulness to the land. In 1468, the Codex of Augsburg relates this folk tradition: "Diana who is commonly known as Fraw Percht is in the habit of wandering through the night with a host of women."[113] In 1494, *Die Hymelstrass* of Stephen Lanzkrana rebukes the belief in "Frawn Percht, Frawn Hold, Herodyasis or Dyana, the heathen goddess.[114] In the upper Adige, Italians called the night-riding host abroad on the night of Epiphany the Corteo della Berta.[115]

Sometimes the goddess is simply called the "good woman": *diu guote frouwe, la bone dame.*[116] These names mean "good, beneficent lady," just like "frau Hölle," and like the "good women" of French faery culture.[117] Well into the 19th century, Berthe was personified by a young woman in a crown of lights, who distributed gifts to children on the winter holiday. In Schwabia she comes to the house in a crown and holding a wooden spoon on the Thursday before Christmas.[118] A girl crowned with candles also figures in the Winternights tradition of Saint Lucia in Scandinavia.

Perchta, like Holle, traverses the lands during the Winter Nights. In the southern German-speaking regions, the holyday Perchtennacht occurs at the eve of Epiphany, and is celebrated with masks of Perchta and goats, with bells, races, and leaping dances that were supposed to make next year's crops grow high. A 15th century churchman scolded "sinners" who "leave food for Perchta in the 'night of Perchta'

Fraw Percht with a face like a carved wooden mask, late 1400s to obtain prosperity and well-being in the coming year."[119] Such offerings to the goddess are widely attested, and were later consumed as a blessing, like the *prasād* offered to Hindu deities. Austrians of Waidhofen gave the Perchtmilch that they had left out for the goddess to their animals so that they would be healthy and fertile. Tyroleans left fried cakes out on the roof for Perchta, or milk and dumplings. Or the entire household must eat the Bachlkoch, a honeyed porridge, in her honor. Carinthian villagers sought blessings from the goddess by offering dumplings to her on Perchtentag (the feast of Epiphany).[120]

Perchta oversees women's spinning work, which must be finished before the Twelve Nights holyday begins, or she will tangle the fibers. This time is consecrated to her, and must be honored. Tyroleans would say about a shaggy distaff, *Da nistet die Perchta drin*: "Perchta sits within."[121]

Berthe Pédauque

In Frankish tradition, Berthe the Spinner was a wise old woman who spun flax and tales. Like the Cailleach Bhéara, she was proverbially ancient. A widespread saying in Provence and Suisse Romande referred to an event from the remote past as: *Doo temps que Bertha filava* ("from the time when Bertha used to spin"). Italians had the same idea: *nel tempo ove Berta filava*.[122] The Tuscana in Arezzo had it as *al tempo delle fate*, "in the time of the *fatas*."[123] But a 16th century French version closes the door on the pagan past: "The time when Berthe span is no more."[124]

Early medieval legends exalted an exceptional spinster called Swanfoot Berthe, or "Berthe with the big foot." In French, she is called *Berthe Pédauque* or *Berthe au grand pied*; in Latin, *Berhta cum magno pede*, "bigfoot Berhta." Dutch texts render her name as *Baerte met ten breden voeten*, which ties in with later English themes of the broad-footed spinner, and in Low German she was called *Berhte mit dem fuoze*, "Berhte with the foot."[125] The French frequently called her *la Reine Pedauque*, the "swan-footed queen."

In France, the common people called her Berthe *la fileuse*, "the spinner," and held her in such reverence that they used to swear oaths "by the distaff of the Reine Pédauque."[126] (Once more the sacred power attributed to the distaff stands out.) The spinner goddess takes many forms and names. In Franche-Comté, the spinner faery with a goose foot is called Tante Arie.[127]

She also takes the form of a mysterious cave-dwelling serpent woman, the *vouivre*, who is crowned with a precious gem.

Berthe Pédauque was sculptured at the doors of cathedrals and abbeys in Toulouse, Dijon, Nesle, Nevers, and St. Pourcin. Rabelais remarked on the goose-like feet of the statue in Toulouse.[128] Those feet belonged to the old woman tale-spinner later known to the French as *Mère Oye* and to the English as *Mother Goose*. She was credited with a vast repetoire of folk wisdom, tales, proverbs, rhymes, and ditties.[129] Occasionally her name takes variant forms, like Berthe Pédance.

The *reine pédauqe* is named Austris in a legend of Toulouse. It makes her the virtuous daughter of the (pagan) fifth king of Toulouse, in the time of the Visigoths. Struck with leprosy, she turned to the saints, was baptized, and became a healer. Her father built a palace called Peyralade that channeled spring water along an aquaduct into a bath, known as "the queen's baths." Ruins of the aquaduct and bridge continued to be called the "bains de la Régine" or, in Occitanian, *les banhs de la regina Pedauca*.[130]

Rabelais related a legend that Austris or Astie had a marvelous distaff that was never exhausted no matter how much she span. Another of his stories refers to large, goose-like feet "like those that once belonged to the queene Pédaucque at Toulouse." Pedauca also

Berthe Pedauque,
Dijon Cathedral

survived as a faery-name. In a tale of the Ariège, in the northern Pyrenees, a *fée* tries to hide her goose feet.[131]

The French peasantry of Vienne transformed the pagan goddess into Sainte Néomaye or Lumoise, also called Sainte Mi-Oie, "half-goose." She was sculptured with one goose foot, like Berthe Pédauque.[132] Her name varies: Néomadie, Nomadie, Numadie, Nommée, Nomèze, Nosmoise, Nemoise, Nemoie, Néomée, Néoumaye. (The best-known is saint Néomaye at Lésigny in Poitou, whose annual processions were discontinued only in 1950.)

Some versions say that Néomaye was born with the webbed foot, but

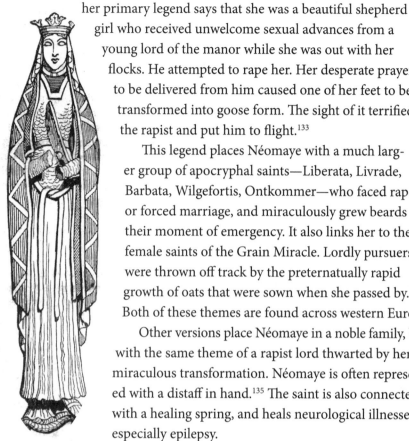

La Reine Pedauque,
(Swanfoot Queen)
at Sainte-Marie de
Nesle church, Troyes.
She may be holding
a weaver's sword.

her primary legend says that she was a beautiful shepherd girl who received unwelcome sexual advances from a young lord of the manor while she was out with her flocks. He attempted to rape her. Her desperate prayer to be delivered from him caused one of her feet to be transformed into goose form. The sight of it terrified the rapist and put him to flight.[133]

This legend places Néomaye with a much larger group of apocryphal saints—Liberata, Livrade, Barbata, Wilgefortis, Ontkommer—who faced rape or forced marriage, and miraculously grew beards in their moment of emergency. It also links her to the female saints of the Grain Miracle. Lordly pursuers were thrown off track by the preternatually rapid growth of oats that were sown when she passed by.[134] Both of these themes are found across western Europe.

Other versions place Néomaye in a noble family, but with the same theme of a rapist lord thwarted by her miraculous transformation. Néomaye is often represented with a distaff in hand.[135] The saint is also connected with a healing spring, and heals neurological illnesses, especially epilepsy.

Several Berthes made their way into the pantheon of saints via the many abbesses who bore this extremely popular name in the 7th and 8th centuries. Some of the saint Berthes became associated with a goose; or they acquired attributes of the spinner goddess and fountain spirits.

Legend said that the 7th-century abbess Berthe of Avenay discovered a spring "and *traced with her distaff* a little furrow from the spring to the convent." The health-giving waters then ran along this path.[136] Once again, the distaff appears as a wand of power. The *Vita* of this Berthe pictures her as spinning while she oversees the construction of her convent.[137]

The spinner goddess was also transformed into Saint Germaine de Pibrac, a shepherd girl whose magical distaff, planted in the earth, watches over her flocks. Another story, about a saint driving away flocks of geese

from the Danube, was hung on the 12th century
Bavarian nun Blessed Bertha, so that an image of
Berthe and her goose could be placed in Christian
chapels.[138]

Where the goose goddess did not undergo
metamorphosis into a saint, a crown was fashioned for her. Medieval chroniclers made Berthe
Pédauque out as the ancestor or mother of the
Frankish conqueror Charlemagne.[139] More recent
historians have attempted to place her elsewhere in
the German dynastic lines, for example as the grandmother of emperor Otto I.

*The swan-footed saint
Néomaye or Néomadie:
a spinner, like Berthe*

But these theories conflict with folk tradition,
which proverbially underlines the great antiquity
of Berthe's spinning. In fact, place names associate
her with stone monuments thousands of years old. Menhirs in several areas
are called Berthe's Distaff or Spindle. Other common placenames refer to the
Fée Berthe, Lady Berthe, or Berthe au grand pied. Reverence was still paid
in the 19th century to a stone in Besne called Berthe's Rock.[140] In this way
the Frankish goddess was assimilated into older megalithic and landscape
traditions of France.

All the fateful spinner goddesses demonstrated remarkable staying power
as their stories were orally transmitted from one generation to the next,
though even though their names were often changed. This transmission was
still going on a century ago in marginalized rural communities. But in the
10th century, it presented an insurmountable obstacle to canonists trying
to eradicate the old beliefs. Priests could scold all they wanted; there was no
question of people giving them up.

Laying tables for the fates

The English clergy also fretted about survivals of goddess veneration
among the common people. The original French version of the Arundel
penitential, circa 1000 CE, condemned people who believed in Herodias
or Diana. But the later English version supplies a cultural context close to
the ritual practices of common women, who revered Three Sisters as fateful

Beings who attended births. It contains a condemnation of offerings by:

> ...she who lays a table with three knives
> for the service of the fates, that they may
> predestinate good things to
> those who are born there.[141]

European women went on preparing votive tables for the Fates and fatas. Here they were called faeries, there the "good women" or *die holden*; in other places the "judges," the "deciders," or the "Three Sisters." Threads scattered throughout early medieval literature lead back to these fate goddesses. Folk tales of the natural world flesh out the shreds so grudgingly surrendered by clerical accounts, as will be discussed in more depth in a later volume. But the scattered and frayed strands now embedded in obscure Latin manuscripts were once woven together in a Holle.

These strands lead back to the Earth goddess who is shown with her cornucopia, suckling serpents and animals and children; whose spinning sacrament is honored during the winter festival; who makes abundant growth spring from the soil; who causes conception and receives the dead; who makes weather and rides in the storm; who journeys in the company of the dead; who appears to fieldworkers in the noonday heat; who lives in the ground and whose faery world lies inside mountains and under the waters of lakes and wells.

Time, like the smoked surface of an old mirror, obscures these reflections of the old religion. Ancient names mixed under pressure with imported and false names, and mutated over centuries of pursuit by priests armed with doctrinal handbooks. By the end of the middle ages, Herodias had trickled into popular culture to became the Italian Irodiade and Aradia, Sardinian Arada, Alpine Redodesa, and Romanian Irodeasa—all syncretic goddesses associated with pagan customs among the peasantry.[142] From Poland to Spain, some peoples adopted the foreign name Diana—contributed, ironically, by the clergy—as a title of their folk goddess, who was understood as a Goddess of the Witches.

The bishops went on preaching sermons against the old customs and prescribing penance for pagan beliefs and observances: bread and water fasts

Earth suckling a serpent. Frankish bronze from Lorraine, circa 800 CE

on church festivals for months or years. The peasants who did attend Mass seem to have decided to ignore the canonical sanctions. Most had faith in their offerings to the Fates, which they loved to do, and which harmed no one.

Even in the 1200s, the 1500s, churchmen were still trying to stamp out peasant belief in the "mistresses of the night," who were also called the "good women who go by night." Often the people seem to understand them as female ancestors, which underlines again the connection of the dead to fates, *fatas*, and the faeries.

People spoke of how hosts of witches rode spirit-animals through the night skies in the company of a pagan goddess and innumerable spirits. The clergy's claim that all this was diabolical illusion failed to displace long-held shamanic traditions. But their interpretations took on a life of their own, which they spread via church canons, penitential manuals and sermons intended to stop out these spiritual beliefs as devil-inspired "delusions."

The priesthood renamed the Goddess with latinate titles and denounced people's ignorance for believing in these traditions. Occasionally they provided local details that betray glimpses of the actual deities. When Albertus Magnus cited the Canon Episcopii, he replaced Holda with the Roman goddess of weaving and wisdom; in his version women go by night with Diana, Herodias and Minerva[143]—who is a weaver.

As people began to pick up elements of these priestly mythologies, the shape of popular culture was altered and overwritten. The names of goddesses changed and the stories began to drift. Church sculpture began the process of transforming the beneficent and nurturing Mother Earth,

with the snake at her breast, into the sexualized image of Luxuria. She still has the snakes but now is now naked and increasingly demonized as the female temptress of misogynist theology. Luxuria (Latin for "sensuality, lust") is one of the Seven Deadly Sins of the church patriarchs. Some of the Luxurias in Romanesque churches draw on nature spirits along the lines of sirenas and sheela-na-gigs. But they become more and more degraded in later sculpture, which shows the snakes biting and devouring, rather than suckling at their breasts.

The old icon of Mother Earth suckling a snake was transformed in Romanesque church sculpture into the figure of Luxuria. *The continuity is obvious in the earliest sculptures, in which she is often surrounded by greenery and animal spirits.*

Church at Mailhat, Puy-de-Dome region

Luxuria means "sensuality," lust being one of the Seven Deadly Sins. Theologically these figures harp on stigmatized female sexuality, Eve and the serpent. The snake rises from her vulva in a church sculpture at Oö, Haut-Garonne, in the northern Pyrenées, circa1000

This Spanish Luxuria is flanked by dragons, from whose mouths the snakes emerge. In folk sensibility she is exuberantly vital, as against the grim woman-hating imagery of theologians. San Pedro el Viejo, Huesca, Aragón, 1100s

A pagan stream of sheela-like Luxurias continues into the 1200s, like this sirena at La Seu d'Urgell, Spain. But this figure who sprang out of heathendom was later increasingly demonized. Instead of her nurturing the snakes, they are depicted as tormenting her. chewing at her now-scrawny breasts. Thus later medieval sculptors transformed her into an object of horror, prey to demons, and a cautionary lesson.[144]

In time the doctrine-makers changed tactics. They still demonized the Witches' Goddess, substituting the christian anti-god for her. But more and more they turned to force to impose their doctrines. In the late Middle Ages, they adopted judicial torture, which enabled them to make women, and some men, "confess" to flying to witches gatherings presided over by "the devil." But that lay centuries in the future. Witch persecutions had not yet absorbed this diabolist theology, which in 700-1100 was still in the process of coalescing. In this period, it was secular lords, and occasionally mobs, who put "witches" to death.

8

EARLY WITCH BURNINGS

T he earliest known witch burnings took place under imperial Roman law, for *maleficia*, "sorcery." Their history is nearly invisible to us, obscured by the attention that literate Roman men gave to the persecution of elite male magicians and astrologers. Patchy evidence survives of witch burnings or drownings in the earliest Middle Ages, in societies ruled by Germanic elites, perhaps because of their adoption of Roman norms. Their laws show the presence of witch persecution from the late 500s through the 700s, in the Lex Visigothorum in Spain, the increasingly repressive Salic law of the Franks, and the Edictum Rothari in north Italy.

These laws are secular, propagated by rulers, but bear the stamp of the priesthood who advised the kings and who wrote the legal texts. It must be remembered that bishops and abbots also ruled as secular lords; the Church was the largest single landholder in Europe. The episcopal councils of Toledo, Narbonne, and Paris, among others, issued their own persecutory codes. Before 800, however, the main punishments for pagans and witches were flogging, enslavement and fines, with 100 and 200 lashes being a common penalty (and the same severe punishment was also decreed for women that performed abortions).[1]

Witch persecution continued in the 800s and 900s. In this period it is still closely interwoven with repression of pagans, even though there are signs that some pagan European societies also persecuted witches. These were patriarchal societies, after all; but the heathen ones had not yet foreclosed female spiritual authority and offices. And, in the old barbarian pattern, they were initially more inclined to prescribe fines in restitution for harm, magical or otherwise, than to burn people at the stake, a practice that appears to come in with Roman influence. They did not penalize healers and diviners.

Around 800, the Frankish emperor Charlemagne issue decrees punishing heathens and diviners with imprisonment, slavery and other penalties. Some of Charlemagne's capitularies ordered death for observing pagan rites:

"those who sacrificed to the devil [Germanic deities] should be killed."[2] His first Saxon edict (circa 781) was especially severe toward the conquered pagan tribes, ordering death for those who refused to convert. If anyone hid from the baptizers "and should have wished to remain a pagan," he decreed,

Repressing heathens: "let him die the death"

"let him die the death." If any "despise" the Lenten fast by eating meat, "let him die the death."[3] This draconian repression followed the genocidal Frankish conquest of pagan Saxony. Further to the east in Sclavonia, out of reach of Frankish armies, Wendish shrines with pagan statues survived on the eastern bank of the Elbe as late as 1069.[4]

Charlemagne issued conflicting laws in different periods. Elsewhere he ordered that people who practiced sorcery or divination must become slaves to the church—already an old strategy of persecuting pagans. His *Admonitio Generalis* (789) ordered punishment for enchanters and sorcerers should be punished. Kieckhefer says that the king enjoined "the strict prohibition of Moses against sorcery." (Though he does not spell it out, Exodus 22:18 and Leviticus 20:27[5] call for the death penalty.) These Carolingian anti-pagan laws are extremely hard to track. There seems to be no translation, much less a study listing them in chronological order. So the information here is given in the scattershot manner that it appears—when it appears.

Around 775 the English king Cathulf wrote to the Frankish emperor urging him to suppress *strigas*, *phitonissas* and other magical practitioners.[6] (This is one of several examples where the Latin witch-word *strix*, *striga*, or *striges* is used in preference to local names; see chapter 3.) The 805 capitulary of Charlemagne is said to be the first to allow torture to be used on sorcerers[7] (although that dubious distinction probably belongs to the Spanish Lex Visigothorum in 589).

Maleficia had acquired a specific magical meaning since the late Roman empire, when it could be punished by burning. The Quierzy laws of Charles the Bald cast sorcery in the mold of poisoning, following the Council of Paris (829). It mixed up witchcraft, incantation, divination and interpretation with "poisoning," and twice called for all of them to be "severely punished."[8] Another translator gives "punish pitilessly."[9]

One piece of evidence shows witch persecution among the Old Saxons. A capitulary of Charlemagne says that the pagan Saxons were burning women who were accused of devouring men, and even eating their flesh: "Whoever, blinded by the devil, and imbued with pagan errors, holds a person to be a witch who eats men, burns her and eats her flesh or makes others eat it, will be punished with death."[10] At least in this instance, the Christian state seems to have acted as a brake on witch persecution. However, it was simultaneously persecuting and even executing Saxons for pagan observances such as divination.[10] It must be kept in mind that this single sentence was written by the mortal enemies of the Old Saxons, who had just carried out a genocidal conquest of their country.

The Franks themselves accused women—under the Latin name *striae*—of eating babies, cattle, and horses. One sermon denounced "certain oafish men who believe that some women must be *striae*" who harm babies and animals.[11] The Franks had also developed the habit of scapegoating witches for catastrophic events. When murrain struck the herds, a rumor spread that the duke of Benevento had sent agents to scatter powders over the land and waters. A mob seized large numbers of accused sorcerers, forced them to "confess" with scourging, torture and threats, and put them to death. Bishop Agobard, who recounted these events, also refers to people being attacked as *tempestarii*, on accusations of causing destructive hailstorms.[12]

Early Spanish law was heavily influenced by the persecutory bent of late Roman law. The Councils of Toledo (eighteen of them!) kept issuing edicts against pagan ceremonies, divination, and sorcery, and exerted strong influence on the Visigothic rulers. In 845, the Spanish king Ramiro I is reported to have burned "a large number of sorcerers, including many astrologers," some of them Jewish.[13] The *Cronicon Emilianense* tells of laws which say "magicians will die by fire."[14]

In 873, the Frankish king Charles the Bald ordered his counts to hunt down *malefici homines et sortiariae* ("evildoing men and sorceresses") and execute them.[15] In these statutes of Quierzy, not only the witches were to be executed, but also those who associate with them.[16] Charles' own mother Judith of Bavaria had been accused of witchcraft, precisely because she fought for his right to inherit a share of his father's imperial lands. His brothers, children of the first wife of Louis the Pious, did not want to share the kingdom with a half-brother. Judith was never tried, but the sorcery charge checked her power. Her enemies had her imprisoned in a convent on charges of sexual depravity and sorcery, and later forced her to undergo a humiliating rite of compurgation (swearing a public oath of innocence).[17]

Judith's friend Gerberga fared much worse. She was a nun, the sister of Judith's political ally, Bernard of Septimania. In order to neutralize the power of the queen, certain courtiers accused Judith and Bernard of being lovers. During the struggle between the sons of Louis the Pious for control of the Frankish domains, prince Lothair looted the town of Châlon-sur-Seine and set it afire. In the mayhem, he seized Gerberga, dragging her out of the convent on the pretext that she was a witch. He then took her to the river Arar and drowned her, "as is customary with sorcerers."[18]

Henry Charles Lea perceptively remarked that this "chance allusion... indicates that much was going on not provided for in the Capitularies."[19] The pretext for Gerberga's summary execution was "on suspicion of tampering with the affections of her friend's husband."[20] In other words, Lothair accused her of helping Judith, his detested stepmother, to magically seduce king Louis into marrying her. His real concern was that her son—his half-brother—was a competitor for their paternal inheritance: the Frankish throne and territories.

Gerberga became the first known medieval European woman to be executed as a witch.[21] Her noble rank is not coincidental to her unusual visibility, as is true for most women named in the sparse accounts of this era. It is also highly unusual, since aristocratic women were rarely executed for witchcraft. Common women were the ones who were at risk of being put to death. Their names are hardly ever recorded in the cases that chroniclers do actually mention.

So it was with the poor woman tried for witchcraft in Freising, Bavaria, in 853. She was a serf belonging to St. Mary's church, which hired out her labor as a maidservant to an aristocrat named Engilpercht. He denounced her to the bishop for having struck down or "poisoned" his daughter "by malevolent efforts and machinations." She was convicted, but her punishment is not recorded; only that her master, the bishop, paid compensation to the man in the form of land.[22] In this case the bishop was acting in his capacity as the secular lord (a very common scenario since the Church was the single biggest landholder in Europe.)

The bishops' courts are often overlooked as an arena of repression.

Henry II forces queen Cunigonde to undergo the ordeal of walking over red-hot plowshares. Germany, early 11th century

Records of trials are in short supply, but occasionally bits of information leak through. Sometime after 800, the Tyrolean bishop Remedius of Chur wrote a set of penalties for sorcerers. The first conviction was punished by shaving the person's head and covering it with tar; the accused would then be led around the countryside on the back of an ass, being beaten all the while. The second time, their tongue and nose would be cut off, and the third time the bishop would turn them over to the secular ruler. In later centuries, this almost always meant execution, though in this period it might refer to judicially-decreed enslavement.[23]

For soothsayers and lot-casters, dream-interpreters, and women who give abortive potions or love charms, bishop Ghärbald of Liège ordered that they "be brought in front of us so that their cases may be heard before us."[24] Going by the penitential books, which generally prescribe fasting for short or long periods of time, the punishments may not have been severe. But enslavement of pagans was still going on in this period, as was flogging. We have just seen how ready the bishop of Chur was to use mutilations for a repeated "offense."

Although burning at the stake is a more familiar penalty for witchcraft, another form of execution in this period was drowning: killing with the power of the elements. That was how Lothair and his men killed Gerberga. Witch-drownings were also committed in Scandinavia[25] and in Britain. An English land deed dated around the year 970 mentions in an aside that an unnamed widow was drowned at London Bridge on accusations of witchcraft. A man named Aelsie and his son disputed her rights to land and property that she held. He accused her of trying to kill him by pushing stakes into a magical poppet. An all-male jury (there was no other kind) convicted and sentenced her to death by drowning at London Bridge. Her son escaped into outlawry, while the king handed the estate over to her accuser. No formal record of a trial exists; the execution is only known because of a random mention in a document on land title transfers.[26]

Pauline Stafford has suggested that Bertilla, the wife of Berengar I, was put to death on charges of witchcraft around the year 911.[27] Her husband was powerful, first as king of Italy and later as the "Holy Roman" emperor. Girolamo Arnaldi points to a couple of verses in the *Gesta Berengari* that "hint in fact of a poisoning which Bertilla would have in some way [supposedly!] brought on herself for having lent her ear to the suggestions of a new Circe. A contemporary gloss to the text of the *Gesta* states that the queen, having listened to the evil counselor, *permutavit statum rationis honeste*." ("She changed/reversed her position regarding the situation due to her honesty/fairness.").[28]

In other words, the author of a panegyric to lord Berengar called the queen's female counselor a witch (by comparing her to Circe). This reference explains why Stafford concluded that Bertilla was targeted for witchcraft. Arnaldi implies that Bertilla had taken a political position that angered her husband, possibly by siding with her family against him.[29] One way or another, as a wife or a witch, Bertilla was killed for being a woman.

Timothy Reuter agrees that Bertilla fell afoul of male power, drawing a parallel between the unspecified charge against her and the accusations of adultery against the queens Uota and Richgardis, and the earlier witchcraft charges against queen Judith and Bernard of Septimania. His discussion reveals another set of executions, which he describes as a "witchcraft scandal," on the charge of "poisoning." (That old Roman term *veneficio* still implied witchcraft.) The *Annales Fuldenses* describe the accusation of adultery laid against the Bavarian queen Uota in 899: "that she had yielded her body to a lustful and wicked union."[30] She was forced to take an oath clearing herself, along with an "extraordinary" number of compurgators (72 of them!) before the leading men of Regensburg.

Uota managed to clear herself, but fresh accusations broke out: "At that same time, and in the same great public meeting ... the king was attacked by paralysis and fell ill." Arnulf's collapse, probably a stroke, was blamed on poisons, which several people were then accused of having given to the king. A man named Graman was convicted of treason and beheaded at Ötting, while another man escaped to Italy. The third suspect was a woman named Ruodpurc, "who was found by strict investigation to have been the instigator of the crime, and perished on the gallows at Aibling."[31] Strict investigation, as Joseph Hansen informs us, meant torturing her until a confession was extracted.[32] Nothing more is known about Ruodpurc, who remains a historical cypher. That a common woman was named at all is unusual.

The cases of Bertilla and Uota relate to a larger pattern of aristocratic women who, while not charged with witchcraft, were persecuted, forced to undergo ordeals, and in some cases, burned at the stake on accusations of adultery. Already in the 6th century Gregory of Tours had written of a Frankish woman who was burned on this charge. So was María of Aragón, the queen of German emperor Otto III, according to Godfrey of Viterbo (and this for a mere attempt, never consummated). St Florent of Saumur wrote that Fulk of Nerra had his wife Elizabeth burned on charges of adultery.[33]

There was also the ordeal of queen Cunigund, accused of adultery by her husband king Henry II. He had the power to literally put her through an ordeal, forcing her to walk over red-hot plowshares to prove her innocence. Adalbert of Bamberg indicates that the royal husband personally sat in judgment over the queen. It comes as no news that such stories are relegated to footnotes and dark corners of history, but suppression of the facts of these cases starts with our earliest written sources. "Both Cunegund's vita, which was produced at the time of her canonization, and [pope] Innocent's bull attempt to conceal Henry's role in the ordeal. The latter gives a circumspect account, attributing Cunegund's trial to diabolical instigation but failing to mention that it was Henry who was chiefly incited..."[34]

Later emendations to Adalbert's biography of the king go to even greater lengths to excuse him. They pretend that the devil disguised as a knight was seen going in and out of the queen's chamber. When Henry was told about it, they then claim, Cunegund herself offered to undergo the ordeal.[35] This is how power, syncophancy, and sexism have distorted the written record we draw on for history.

The Winchester annals (circa 1200) report that the English queen Emma was forced to walk the burning plowshares on charges of having an affair with the bishop of Winchester. Legend says that her own son Edward the Confessor did this to her. Pauline Stafford thinks the story originated with queen Edith of Normandy, whom the king banished from court in 1051. He confiscated her estates, and forced her to swear an oath to clear herself of accusations of adultery.[36]

Queen Richardis of Schwabia was also said to have undergone a fire ordeal on charges of adultery. (Like Cunigund, she was later sainted due to popular sympathy). Her husband Charles the Fat had gone mad, and she ruled in his place, with the assistance of his chancellor Liutward. Courtiers aligned with the king accused the two of adultery. Richardis offered to clear herself through the ordeal, but the king settled for an oath that she had never had sex with anyone (apparently including himself). This allowed him to have the marriage annulled, while Richardis retired to a convent she had founded.[37] She died around 895 and was canonized a century later.

Folk legend said that bears had shown the queen where to build her convent, or that she had revived the cub of a mother bear. Nuns at the convent kept a bear, and images of St Richardis often portray her with a bear. A 15th century painting depicts Richardis being forced to hold a redhot iron in one hand, and the head of her purported lover in the other; in the background she is being burned at the stake, reprising the theme of women burned for adultery.[38] But this back-projected ordeal and execution never took place.

A glimpse of female commoners who underwent this female ordeal appears in a Bavarian council circa 800 CE, in which bishops called for accused witches to be put through the ordeal of red hot iron. It names veneficae, which clergy often used for herbalists generally, and uses a second Latin descriptor, which Filotas does not supply. She translates it as "women necromancers," (a problematic term) but it seems to describe women who acted as oracles for the dead.[39] And what was the punishment if a woman failed the ordeal? Important facts are missing here.

BURNING WOMEN BY IRON AND FIRE: SPAIN

The female ordeal of hot iron was also imposed on women accused of witchcraft in Spain. Spanish law was founded on the harsh Roman codes, which undergird its enforcement of male dominance, slavery and social hierarchy. The reliance on trial by ordeal also reflects influences from the Germanic influx at the end of the empire. The repressive Lex Visigothorum was reworked around 654 as the Forum Iudicum. Its pernicious influence persisted through the middle ages. Translated into Spanish in the 13th century, it carried over the severity of old Roman laws on magic. Article III ordered 100 lashes for invoking deities or spirits (referred to as "the devil"). Article IV gave 200 lashes for sacrificing to "demons" to compel another person's will. And Article V prescribed punishment for all kinds of magic.[40]

a woman who is a witch or sorceress shall either be burnt or saved by iron.

The earliest written evidence for the female ordeal of burning iron appears around 1190 in the Fuero Cuenca: "a woman who is a witch or sorceress shall either be burnt or saved by iron."[41] The Spanish text, written 150 years after the Latin, reads: *Otro si, la muger que fur eruolera o fechizera, quemenla or saluese con fierro*.[42] "And again, the woman who may be an *herbolera* or sorceress, let her be burned or saved by iron." A more explanatory translation reads, "The woman who is an herbalist or witch should be burned alive, or cleared by means of the ordeal of [hot] iron."[43]

Fuero Cuenca Title I. 41 went further, prescribing far more severe penalties for women accused of witchcraft than for the men: "The woman who casts spells on men, animals, or other things, should be burned alive; but if it cannot be proved [by other means], she should be cleared by means of the ordeal of iron. If a man was the spell caster, he should be exiled from the city after being shorn and whipped; if he denies it, he should be cleared by means of judicial combat."[44] The same favoritism toward men is found in the Forum Turolii code (1176) in Aragón, on the other side of the cordillera. It ordered female witches to be burned, but men were only scourged and banished, after shaving a cross on their heads.[45]

Spanish rulers regarded burning at the stake as an appropriate punishment for women, especially for any who refused the prescribed role for wives. Fuero Cuenca ordered death by fire for a woman who deliberately ended a pregnancy (Title §39); for leaving her husband to marry another man (§36); for killing her husband (§43)—a crime that required women of all classes to "take up the iron" to establish their innocence or guilt; for procuring women or johns for prostitution (again, she underwent the ordeal of hot iron if she denied it, §44); or, for having sex with a Muslim or Jewish man (§48)—who were also to be burned.[46] Those female burnings are in addition to laws §41 and §42, which prescribed burning for an herbalist or sorceress. That makes a total of seven reasons for which a woman could be burned alive; and six of them directly enforced the patriarchal sex code on women. The seventh was also sex-marked,

The female ordeal of red-hot iron

since women faced much harsher penalties than men, and were accused more often.

Fuero Cuenca Titles §45 and §46 lay down rules for how these female ordeals should proceed. The trial itself was a punishment, a rite that put extreme pressure on the accused—to say nothing of the pain. First, officials heated up the iron, which was to be four feet long, a palm's width and two finger widths deep. (It was heavy enough, in other words, that its weight would increase the severity of her burns.) They took precautions to ensure that no spells were being cast; the woman was "examined carefully" in case she was wearing any charms to help her pass the test. They set the incandescent iron at a height of four feet. The accused had to wash her hands, dry them, place her hand under the iron, grasp it, and carry it for nine paces. She was expected to "deposit it smoothly on the ground," which meant that dropping the burning iron counted against her. The presiding official immediately covered her hand with wax, wrapped it with flax or linen, and bound that with more cloth. No cooling water or healing salves were allowed. The officer took the accused to his house (!) and examined her hand after three days. "If the hand is burned, she should be burned alive or suffer the penalty to which she is sentenced."[47]

In practice, this meant that the accused woman needed a miraculous recovery to escape being sent to the stake.

if the hand is burned, she should be burned alive or suffer the penalty to which she is sentenced

Though the list of female offences punishable by burnings is long, Fuero Cuenca prescribes burning for men in only a few cases, most of which enforced male rights over women. One penalized men who intruded on a husband's privileges, by raping or abducting a married woman (#25). (If the wife eloped voluntarily, she was burned, too.) The next law extended a man's rights over "his" woman to the entire collectivity of Christian men over Christian women; Muslim or Jewish men were to be burned for sex with a Christian woman, as was she. (No penalty was prescribed for the converse.) Finally, along the same confessionalist lines, both men and women were penalized for selling a Christian into slavery (#47).[48] In no instance was a Christian man subject to burning where women were not; but seven laws prescribed burning exclusively for women—with the addition of a racialized death penalty for Muslim or Jewish men for transgressing the dominance of Christian men.

Women themselves were divided by class, ethnicity, and by whether they complied with the sexual double standard or defied it. In two places, Fuero Cuenca lays restrictions on which women were compelled to undergo the ordeal. The first (#43) follows the law that prescribed burning for witchcraft: "In the other case, no one has to take up the iron other than the prostitute who has fornicated with five men, or the procuress." It must be understood that medieval Spanish law defined any woman who had sex with multiple men as a prostitute, whether she was paid for it or not.) This is repeated in #46: "Only that woman bears the iron who has demonstrated that she is a procuress or one who had fornicated with five men; any other woman who is suspected of larceny, of homicide or of arson should swear or provide a judicial combatant, as is established in the code."[49]

This would seem to cut down the number of ordeals considerably, but both of these passages are appended to other laws, apparently added later. Rafael de Ureña y Smenjaud thinks so: "Women who killed their husbands, committed bigamy, aborted their children, practiced herbal medicine or witchcraft, or cast a spell were liable to this fiery disposition. The same penalty prevailed for a woman caught in flagrant delicto with a Muslim or Jew or convicted of being a procuress. Any woman compelled to endure the ordeal of hot iron and failing to heal properly faced execution by fire."[50]

The clarity of Law #42 could not be more stark: "A woman who is an herbalist or sorceress, burn her, or let her be saved by iron." It contains no extra clauses or special conditions. The emendations must have eased the danger for more privileged women, who were allowed to swear oaths instead of going through the fire ordeal. But no mercy was shown to the most vulnerable of women, the *mala muger* ("bad woman," legally marked for sexual predation) who men could strike, rape, rob, and even kill with impunity.[51]

eaꝛly ḣuṇts iṇ bꝛitaiṇ

The English royal offensive against witches entered history in the royal code of Alfred "the Great." He decreed death or exile for witches and unchaste women. His severity shows the influence of churchly advisors, opening with a number of commands from Exodus, not least: "Do not suffer a witch to live." His law, and that of his successors, associated witches with sexually independent women, and lumped them together with liars and death-dealers:

> **If witches or diviners, perjurers or morth-workers [death sorcerers], or foul, defiled, notorious adulteresses, be found anywhere within the land, let them then be driven from the country and the people cleansed, or let them totally perish within the country, unless they desist and the more deeply make bot [amends].**[52]

The language of this law invited violence against women of sexual independence; but it was utterly unconcerned with male promiscuity. And it was even more severe than Leviticus, extending the death penalty to women who did not themselves practice witchcraft but who consulted charmers and magicians: "Do not let them live."[53]

"*wītcḣ aṇ̃ð wḣoꝛe*"   Alfred's law was not unique in attacking sexually independent women in the same breath as witches. Frankish rulers were the first to introduce the insult "witch and whore," in later recensions of the Salic law—a formula that spread.[54] This stereotypical pairing appears as far away as Hungary, in a pronouncement of the church synod of Szaboles.[55] Witch and harlot both stood outside approved female behavior in a patriarchal society, making them convenient scapegoats. Their power, whether magical or sexual, was easily represented as threatening divine authority (which in practice was indistinguishable from male power). These terms were being used as weapons against women regardless of whether the female individual actually practiced witchcraft (by any definition) or sold sex.

The Anglo-Saxon chronicler Fredegar described queen Marcytrude, wife of Guntram, as *herbaria* and *meretrix* ("witch" and "whore").[56] These epithets were often linked in English laws after 800. The laws of Edward and that same Guthram "class witches and diviners with perjurers, murderers and strumpets," prescribing exile, heavy fines and death for divination and murder alike.[57] Sometimes exile was preferred to execution. In 901 a law of Edward I banished diviners.[58] King Ethelred also ordered witches and prostitutes to be exiled from the kingdom.

"Witch" was often linked with "whore" on the continent as well. In medieval Piemonte, the witch-word *fattuchiera* connoted "prostitute."[59] The Old Swedish Bjärkö Laws show that "whore, harlot, witch, or sorceress" were stock insults leveled against women.[60] The last two examples are later than the early period discussed here, but they reflect an ongoing pattern.

The laws of Ethelstan (928) ordered that witches, homosexuals, people whose bodies were considered monstrous, children born of incest, and bondswomen who stole, all should be burnt at the stake.[61] (This tabulation of likely victims foreshadows some of those at risk in later hunts.) Ethelstan used the "three-fold ordeal" in trials of murder-by-sorcery, with penalties of three months prison, *wergild* (restitution) paid to the family and a 120 shilling fine to the king.[62] (Those who could not pay were sold into bondage; slavery was still around.) By 940 the penalty was again changed to death.[63] A conflict is seen here between old Germanic restitution law and newer penal law that drew on Roman and Biblical precedents. In the early 1100s, the anti-witchcraft laws of Henry I were still indiscriminately mixing "sorcery and image-making" with murder and poisoning.[64]

English kings' pronouncements on witches frequently betray the influence of priestly advisors, who literally wrote the laws. Archbishop

Oujurju. cehming adt accordon quegin quejnun onlujue innobe. jonjuejui.
cilda popd cynie. peohen juehic gopd lujhand. jpobygujbepe juneinu paji
pypunjuiadni juied juejnon. jcu. ep. jue cynip lujulujon. Theceah julhand.
ongun. jpohen comju. Dacjuep daejupe hju ijpeill. waailed folje
jpoiju un luo neinide lujnanuin juhajuep. Syddan comjuoben.

*The 11ᵗʰ century Cotton Claudius manuscript depicts a woman who is
about to be burned on a pyre. Two men are leading her to the fire, directed
by an enthroned king or judge who seems to be pointing to an ordeal iron.
The book is an English Hexateuch, containing biblical texts. It probably
illustrates Exodus 22:18 (Do not allow a witch to live) but reflects the
English cultural context. The witch-pyre (not stake) resembles those
depicted in the German Sachsenspiegel (1220) and the Swiss Wickiana
(late 1500s). Cotton Claudius B I f57r, British Library.*[66]

Wulfstan of York, for example, penned the laws of Aethelred, Edward and
Guthram, and Canute.[65] Like the royal laws, English church canonists of the
late 900s outlawed the worship of trees, stones, wells, and divination "in sun
and in moon and in the courses of stars." The bishops insisted that herbs
must be gathered without incantation (though some allowed exceptions if
Christian deities were named). Sexual politics were also very much at issue.
The canons condemned anyone who "practices witchcraft concerning the
love of any man, or gives him in food or drink or enchantments of any kind
anything so that because of it their love may be the greater..."[67]

    Female sexuality was being demonized in these same clerical sources.
The 10th century Anglo-Saxon *Leechbook* prescribed a salve against elves
and night-goers and women who lie with the devil."[68] This is probably the
earliest reference to a diabolist concept of witches having sex with the devil.

Another occurs in Hungary after the year 1000, when king Stephen I was going after *striges*. (See below.)

An English monastic history of the 1100s projected a sexualized slander on the long-deceased queen Elfrida (Aelfthryth). The *Liber Elensis* calls her a witch, accusing her of the murder of abbot Byrhtnoth, who had died over a century before.[69] The monastic author pictures the abbot riding to court through the New Forest and stopping to relieve himself away from the road. There he saw the old queen Elfrida, all alone in the forest, brewing a potion that allowed her to shapeshift into the form of a mare "so that she might satisfy the unrestrainable excess of her burning lust, running and leaping hither and thither with horses and showing herself shamelessly to them."[70]

Next the monk-author accuses Elfrida of attempting to seduce Bryhtnoth to keep him from reporting her shameless witchery, and when he refused, of having her women murder him by thrusting red-hot metal into his rectum. (The idea was that they could murder him without leaving any visible marks.) To top it off, the monk even claims the queen later confessed to this scurrilous concoction. He invented these accusations long after her death.

"Witchcraft was a serious charge in Anglo-Saxon England," as Elizabeth Norton writes, "and there is no contemporary hint that the queen was suspected of practicing sorcery."[71] (To say nothing of the vicious sexual insults!) It is not to be forgotten that Elfrida was the first English queen to be crowned, and ruled as regent for her son. She had been a major player in monastic reform, exerted authority over convents, and in the legal sphere, acted as an arresting witness in numerous charters. In her time she was arguably the most powerful woman in England. The motivations for the accusations are not far to seek.

The sexualized witchcraft slurs against the eminent Elfrida have parallels with other prominent women. The sorcery charge functioned as a posthumous weapon against the 11th century German abbess Liutgarda. H.C. Lea drew attention to "the opposing accounts" given of her life. One manuscript, "which is doubtless the genuine one, describes her as a cultured and exemplary woman, who ruled her nunnery in the service of God for forty years, leaving a happy memory behind her; another MS. of the same chronicle calls her a blasphemous witch and sorceress, under whose government the convent was almost ruined."[72] In much the same way, Lambert of Ardres accused countess Richilde of Flanders of throwing magical powders to bring victory to her troops in 1071. That she had been defeated and captured on the battlefield presented no problem for the chronicler, who explained that the wind had blown the powders back to her side. But his accusations date to two centuries after the fact.[73]

Witchcraft accusations appear to have been rife among the clergy. In 1030, archbishop Poppo of Trier accused a nun of bewitching him via a pair of shoes he had her make for him from his cloak. He became convinced that wearing these shoes made him lust after her—of course that would be her fault—and other men of the cathedral said the same, after they too tried on the shoes. (Imagine the scene, with accusations flying.) Since the lady was an aristocrat, there was no question of burning her; but Poppo had her expelled from the convent. He then punished her sister nuns with an ultimatum: they could submit to a stricter rule, or leave. They chose to get out of there, after which the archbishop converted the convent into a monastery.[74] These persecutions belong to a larger pattern of destroying female monasteries—and the power of the abbesses—in that period. They show what a large role sexual scapegoating of women played in that process, as it also did in the contemporary Gregorian "Reform."

The calls to witch burning that French and English kings issued in the ninth and tenth centuries were never withdrawn or countermanded. They stood unchallenged for centuries, underpinning local persecutions by feudal lords—who kept no legal records. Witch burning was one tool in the arsenal of oppression that kept women under patriarchal domination and peasants under barons. The Church was unable to interrupt transmission of the older culture in this period. So the clergy took the tack of encouraging feudal rulers to punish witches and openly practiced pagan rites. Militant royal laws against folk religion were enacted at the same time that kings and barons abolished the old tribal rights of free landholders. Consolidating the feudal hierarchy, they gutted the powers of the traditional *folkmōt* councils in favor of hereditary privileges for the aristocracy.

Royal prohibitions of paganism continued into the 11th century, under the Danelaw. King Cnut followed his predecessors (and the influence of bishop Wulfstan) in outlawing all heathenism: "that is, that they worship heathen gods, and the sun and moon, fire or rivers, waterwells or stones, or forest trees of any kind, or love witchcraft or promote morthwork [death-dealing] in any wise."[75] Cnut also forbade the casting of lots, pagan sacrifices, soothsaying "or the striving after suchlike delusions."[76] Like canon law, Cnut's code mixed prohibitions of witchcraft and pagan worship with measures against harmful sorcery.

The great historiographical error of witchcraft literature has been the assumption that more documentation of persecution would exist than the stray mentions that survive for the early middle ages. It is crucial to understand that public records of cases prosecuted under these laws were not kept until after 1200—or much later in some regions. A side mention in a document concerned with other matters is the only surviving evidence of Aelsie's use of witchcraft accusations to expropriate land from an unnamed London widow around 970. No one will ever know how many trials or executions like this took place. We only know about this one through the historical accident of a property record.

However, some "historical" testimony was invented later. Scottish wisewomen would have blended cultural strands from the Celtic-speaking Pictish and Scota cultures, with influences from the Norse and Northumbrian English. For example, lowlanders borrowed the title "spaeing woman" from Norse *spákona*, "prophetic woman." Little is known about them, since they are not mentioned in early written sources.

Holinshed's *History of Scotland* purports to tell of an ancient Scottish king consulting a prophetess about the future around the year 280 CE, but this book was written in 1577, thirteen centuries after the "fact."[77] He claims that when the Scots rebelled against king Natholocus, he sent a trusted follower to consult the renowned Witch of Iona. She was "estéemed verie skilfull in forshewing of things to come, to learne of hir what fortune should hap of this warre." The seeress told the man that the king was going to be murdered, and that he himself would kill him. Fearing that her prediction would come to the king's ears, the messenger panicked at the thought that Natholocus might believe it and eliminate him. So he killed the king.[78]

The same 16th century book alleges that some Scottish women were burned at the stake in 968. It says that king Duff's courtiers blamed treasonous sorcery for his illness. He had fallen into a sweating fever and was slowly failing. Officials initiated a search for a witch to scapegoat. They arrested a young woman who was the concubine of a soldier, who supposedly told his superiors, and so up the chain of command. They forced her to confess, that her mother and other witches were slowly killing the king by roasting a wax image of him over a fire.[79] The scholarly consensus is that this story is "wholly fabulous," an early modern invention.[80] It is suspiciously similar to Livy's account of the coerced role of an officer's concubine in precipitating the Bacchanal persecution in Rome, and may have been inspired by it.

Another spurious claim, repeated in older works on witchcraft, says that the 7th century king Kenneth of Dalriada ordered those who call up spirits and work wonders to be burned.[81] These stories are back-projections, bearing the hallmarks of the later Scottish witch hunts, and attempt to establish precedents for the persecution. In reality, no evidence exists for witch hunts in early medieval Scotland, or for that matter, in Ireland.

ELEVENTH CENTURY PERSECUTIONS

In continental Europe, chroniclers report that mobs of armed men executed women as witches, without trial. Even in the ninth century, the accusation did not have to be true. It made a handy pretext for attacking women. But legal records of witch trials are almost entirely absent, though laws were already on the books in many western European kingdoms. Feudal lords did not need special dispensations to carry out executions by main force. As *haut-justiciers*, they had the power to act as judge, jury and executioner. But in addition to lordly punishments, another kind of persecution shows up: mob lynchings carried out by crowds of men.

"an evildoing sorceress practicing cursed arts with three other women"

Scattered mentions from 800 to the 1100s show instances "in which women were put to death—mostly by burning—for encompassing the death of magnates, though the punishments were mostly irregular and not in pursuance of formal laws..."[82] These attacks were sometimes fueled by the fear of women magically joining up with other women or against men. In 1028 a woman was accused, it is not clear where, of being an "evildoing sorceress practicing cursed arts with three other women."[83] In 1074, after forcing the archbishop to flee Cologne, triumphant rebels threw a woman from the city walls. She was reputed to have "crazed a number of men by magic arts," according to a chronicler.[84]

Accusations of sorcery were also being aimed at Jews, as pogroms spread with the first crusaders in the 11th century. The archbishop of Trier had ordered the Jews to be expelled from the city, and happened to die not long afterward. A rumor spread that Jewish sorcerers had killed him by making a wax image, bribing a priest to baptize it, and burning it on the Sabbath.[85] Both Jews and witches faced repression on accusations of doing harmful magic (as discussed in later volumes).

Charges of harmful sorcery were being used to scapegoat women for natural disasters and crop failures. A northern Russian chronicler described how in 1024 pagan priests known as *volkhvy* ("wolves") denounced wealthy people as grain hoarders. They incited insurrections in which people "rose up and slaughtered the well-to-do."[86] The ruler Yaroslav stopped this first outbreak by executing some *volkhvy* and banishing others. At the time, the conversion of northern Russia had barely begun and was meeting with stiff popular resistance. The conflict had strong class overtones, pitting the wealthy few against the hungry many. Most aristocrats supported the church, while the common people held to their old religion. But in this clash, reactionary sexual politics led to the witch-hunting of women. Rich men, the wealthiest of all, were not targeted in these persecutions.

In 1071 the same chronicler, possibly Nestor, relates that some *volkhvy* had numerous women put to death in the area of Rostov-Suzdal', again during a time of famine and popular revolt.[87] In Novgorod, a volkhv led "all the people" against the prince and bishop.[88] Two *volkhvy* from Yaroslavl' traveled around claiming that they knew who was hoarding grain and were able to find the witches. They began to attack prominent women in the Rostov-Suzdal area, blaming them for failed crops and food shortages by magically devouring the land. With cooperation from aristocrats, the *volkhvy* seized women, young and old, and knifed them in the back while pretending to draw meat and produce from their bodies. They traveled along the Volga and Sheksna rivers, witch-hunting at each settlement, pointing out women: "This one is hoarding grain, this one fish, this one furs." To "prove" this to the credulous, they combined violent physical attacks on the women with sleight of hand: "they cut open their backs at the shoulder blades and by magic extracted from their bodies corn or fish, and they killed many women and expropriated their possessions."[89] These witch-hunters enjoyed great success until they were arrested at Beloozero, questioned, and hanged.

A papal letter of 1080 refers to witch hunts in Denmark. Pope Gregory VII wrote the Danish ruler Haakon to rebuke the belief that priests and women had the power to "make rain and fair weather," or to cause epidemics. He severely chastised the king for allowing women to be put to death. The pope said that women were unable to affect the weather, taking the doctrinal position that such powers were delusional.[90] It was rare enough for the Church to reproach lords for burning witches, but it was unheard of for popes or bishops to take serious action against lords who committed these public immolations.

In 1090, a Bavarian chronicler of Freising recorded that three poor women were accused of being "poisoners" who had destroyed people and crops. A mob took them to the banks of the river Isar and subjected them to the water ordeal, which they passed. The attackers turned to beating them to force confession. The women withstood even this, refusing to yield. But the mob was determined to scapegoat them for the misfortunes of weather and disease, and burned them there on the banks of the river.[91]

The aristocracy found rumors about magical harm-doers useful in their intrigues. They claimed that wax-figure sorcery had killed duke Bernard of

Hardly any visual evidence for witch persecutions exists before 1200. It is difficult to find any images of ordinary women in the early middle ages. The great majority of manuscripts depict men: kings, lords, bishops, prophets, soldiers and, occasionally, laborers. The few women shown are aristocratic, or allegorical figures in the same mold.

Stuttgart Gospels, 9th century Germany. Note the cornucopia: who is she? She may represent Mother Earth giving blessings to the royal couple opposite her.

Gascogne in 1013; bishop Evrard of Treves in 1066; and archbishop Steven of Bourges in 1173.

When king Philip Augustus repudiated Ingeborg of Denmark on their wedding day in 1193, the court murmured that witches had cast a spell over her.[92] Philip himself claimed that she had bewitched him, according to several chroniclers.[93] He subjected Ingeborg to extreme public humiliation, and worse: because she refused to go along with the repudiation, Philip imprisoned her for 20 years in various castles. He made a last attempt to get an annulment on the pretext of witchcraft, but had already antagonized the pope into interdicting the kingdom, so he was not inclined to go along. Lea reminds us that other instances of the sorcery charge were going on, but not being recorded: "bishop Durand, in his *Speculum Juris*, tells us that these cases were of daily occurrence."[94]

Male anxiety about women working impotence magic was widespread, and it fueled "the fiercest condemnations of women's power."[95] Back in the 9th century, bishop Hincmar of Reims was much concerned with impotence caused "by sorcery and by hidden *maleficia*." He even made it the supreme exception to his otherwise rigorous ban on divorce, if the spell could not be undone by exorcism or medicine.[96] In the 11th century, Guibert of Nogent recounted how his father suffered impotence for seven years, while his mother refused the divorce that canon law allowed her under those circumstances. A stepmother was blamed for bewitching him, "but the spell was broken at last, not by priestly ministrations but by an ancient wisewoman."[97]

The Norwegian queen Gunnhild (killed in 980) was rumored to have cast an impotence spell on her young lover Hrut, to prevent him from having sex with his wife Unn.[98] In *Njalssaga*, Unn explains to her father that Gunnhild had cursed Hrut with priapism that enlarged his organ to an extreme size— but only with his wife.[99] The sagas show that Gunnhild was widely reputed to be a powerful sorceress. (Snorri claims in *Heimskringla* that she had learned her arts from two Sámi sorcerers in Finnmark.) But this story grew out of the sexual double standard that threated it as scandalous for a mature woman to take a young lover. Society accepted such liaisons as normal for men, but a woman consorting with a younger partner could only be explained by her having bewitched the man.

Aristocratic women were vulnerable to the sorcery charge in court intrigues. The Benedictine chronicler Orderic Vitalis slandered queen Bertrade de Montfort (1070-1117), claiming that she had attempted to kill her husband Louis—first with witchcraft, then by poisoning.[100] Similarly, the chronicler Adémar de Chabannes attributed the death of Bernard of Gascogne to "womanly plots" and "malefic arts."[101]

In a notorious case in1027, Adémar related that count William of Angoulème fell ill, and rumors spread that he had been bewitched. A woman was accused of using wax and flaxen images to harm the count. She was tried by ordeal of battle, and convicted by the defeat of her male champion. The count's son, Alduin, had the woman tortured, but she refused to confess to sorcery. Next, Alduin tortured three other women until they said that they had helped the first woman to lay the curse. The count himself did not believe the woman had anything to do with his illness and ordered the torture stopped. But he died a few days later. His son Alduin lost no time in having the three accused women burned on the outskirts of town.[102]

Adémar's account of this witch hunt makes many claims of sorcery. He alleged that the man defending the first accused witch "took magic potions" to ensure victory. Nevertheless her champion performed miserably, frozen in place. Adémar claims that after ceding defeat, he vomited out the "potions." His companions (who the monk accused of making incantations to affect the outcome) fled. That the accused woman herself had withstood torture without making a sound did not count in her favor. Adémar explained her steadfastness in the same pitiless terms used by the judges in much later witch trials: "with the devil's assistance in hardening her heart."[103] The three other accused women, probably commoners, were tortured into "confessing" to having made poppets of clay and wax. These were duly "found" buried near springs and in dry places, as well as in the throats of corpses.[104]

Similar charges had begun to proliferate in what R.I. Moore calls "the birth of a persecuting society."[105] Alduin found it expedient to scapegoat women as witches to explain his father's death. Jews and heretics also made convenient targets. In 1010, attacks on Jews followed the news that the caliph al-Hakim had destroyed the Church of the Holy Sepulchre in Jerusalem. Rumors spread that the Jews had sent messages urging him to do it, resulting in massacres and expulsions. A serf was burned as the alleged messenger.[106] In 1022, a group of clerics accused of being "heretics" were burned at Orléans. Richard Landes observes that monastics "played a prominent role in developing the techniques of persecuting defenseless victims."[107]

One of the monks who forged this persecutory climate was Adémar of Chabannes. The second version of his chronicle added seven accusations of poisoning, "mostly against women, some of them adulterous wives, some witches."[108] After 1026, Adémar "had become preoccupied—one might even say, obsessed—with female assassins."[109] He picked up an accusation from the *Miracula sancti Genulfi* that the Frankish king Lothair had been poisoned by his wife, adding the accusation that she was an adulteress ("witch and whore" again). He also claimed that their son Louis had been killed by a magic potion given by his wife Blanca—in spite of the fact that he died in a hunting accident. Adémar's story that Alaiza's uncle Bernard of Gascogne died of a slow poisoning by witches insinuated that Gascon women were given to this sort of thing. One version of Adémar's account of the Angoulême witch burnings offered examples of Greco-Roman witchcraft, followed by the Mosaic law exhortation to put witches to death.[110]

Persecutions also took place in the recently, barely "converted" countries of central Europe. Here, too, noblemen instigated and led the repression. Around 1080, Bratislav II of Bohemia joined with the bishop of Prague, who was his brother, to suppress sorcerers. An early modern account says that they killed over a hundred people:

Bratislaw brought to bear not only steel but fire and water, beheading some, burning others and drowning some Sagae. [111]

The Latin name *Sagae* indicates that the victims were recognized as wisewomen, not harmful sorcerers. Soon after the conversion of the Czechs in the late 900s, religious persecutions were targeting animist sanctuaries. In 1092, the same king Bratislaw ordered the destruction of groves and trees where the Czechs did ceremony and offered pagan sacrifices.[112]

In the early 1000s, the Hungarian king Stephen I turned "sorcerers" over to people they were said to have harmed or to their relatives—in other words, to their accusers. The king named two types of witches, all female: the *striges*, who ride out at night and fornicate, and the *maleficae*, "evildoers." The latter were to be handed over to their accusers. The king made separate provisions for the *striges* (again that Roman *strix*) who were to be placed in the custody of priests for indoctrination and fasting. If they returned to witchcraft (whatever that meant) the indoctrination was to be repeated with the added penalty of branding on the chest with a red-hot iron shape of a cross. A third accusation meant that the clergy turned the woman over to a secular judge, presumably for execution.[113]

The Church's influence loomed large in these Hungarian persecutions, from the Latin name used for witches—in a Magyar country speaking a Uralic tongue—to the branding with crosses. A woman who was accused a second time would literally be branded as a witch, with the possibility of being burned looming over her if someone acccused her a third time. (If later persecutions are any guide, this was not unlikely.) Again, the absence of trial records is general, not just for these laws of witch persecution, so no evidence survives for this period. But consider what impact the awareness of such laws must have had on women, especially after a first formal accusation. Even the proclamation of such laws would have had consequences on the village and family level, as it did in later centuries.

Western European ecclesiastical courts also prosecuted witchcraft cases in the period before 1100. The sparse information available suggests that the bishops did not assign capital penalties, but some of them had dungeons (probably in their capacity as secular lords). The record shows that some, like Remedius of Chur, used severe penalties such as mutilation for witchcraft, as well as public humiliation. But bishops were more likely to prescribe penances such as fasting, pilgrimages or social sanctions on those they convicted of witchcraft. According to Jeffrey Russell, the Church was "lenient because it was not as yet secure or well organized enough to undertake a full campaign against the rebellious."[114]

The priesthood goaded rulers—Alfred of England, Charlemagne of the Franks, Stephen of Hungary, among many others—to repress pagan religion and witchcraft. But rulers needed little urging to extend power over their subjects, striking out with fire and iron. It was feudal lords who provided most of the impetus for early witch hunts. Contrary to popular stereotype, it was secular rulers who burned and drowned and imprisoned witches in the early middle ages. The judicial ordeal, including its use as a witch-finder, developed under feudal lords, and was afterwards absorbed into church procedure, before finally being abandoned.

Witch-burning was entertainment for aristocratic men. The sorcery charge gave them a way to keep women and peasants down while posing as good sons of the Church. Baronial abuses of power, especially violence against women, were a reality in those times. We can only speculate about how aristocratic fear of peasant witches might have acted as a brake on that violence. Scattered reports show that common men were also ganging up on "witches." In later centuries, witchcraft continued to be connected with female defiance and popular rebellion.

There will never be anything approaching a full record of church trials on witchcraft in these "lost centuries" of witch persecution, simply because few written sources survive from this period. An occasional reference suggesting violence against witches slips through, like the Anglo-Saxon prediction that "a girl born on the fifth day of the moon will die worst, for she will be a witch and an enchantress with herbs."[115]

Many myths have grown up around the witch burnings. First came the misconception that they happened mostly in the middle ages, and were committed by churchmen. More recently, a new myth has grown up in reaction against the first. It insists that there were no witch persecutions to speak of in the middle ages; that they began in the Renaissance without any historical run-up, except for the heresy trials, which were the *real* cause of witch hunting. But that is untrue, as will be expanded on in future volumes.

Little history remains from a scantily-documented era, void of judicial clerks and archives, in an era of private law administered by minor dynasts in remote villages. All that remain are the royal laws, scattered accounts strained through the sieve of chroniclers preoccupied with other matters, and preachments showing that sorcery was still very much on the minds of the clergy, aristocrats, and common men.

9

völuspá

The *Völuspá* is the most venerable poem in the Icelandic Edda. Its title means "Prophecy of the Völva" (variously translated as "seeress," "sybil," or "witch"). This is prophecy not only in the sense of prediction, but as a recitation of cosmogony, a sacred history. The poet is riffing on a complex body of myth, but offers only glimpses of it, shards of stories that remain largely unexplained.

The poem begins with an unnamed *völva* who speaks in a majestic ceremonial register to an assemblage waiting to hear her prophecy. She addresses a ritual call to all humanity, in a style reminiscent of the Atharva Veda, which begins, "Hear this, peoples ..."[1]

> **Silence I ask of all holy kindreds**
> **High and low of Heimdall's children:**
> **Thou wilt, Father of Battle, that well I relate**
> **Old tales I remember of men long ago.**[2]

The *völva* announces her kinship with the primeval *jötnar* (giants), who fostered her in primeval times. Some scholars think that she is channeling an ancestral *völva*, or a giantess—or that she is one of those things, if not both.[3] The seeress speaks of nine worlds and nine giantesses who are the essence of the Tree of Life:

> **I remember the kin of giants born long ago**
> **those who once raised me in bygone days**
> **Nine worlds I remember, nine women in wood**
> **With mighty roots beneath the ground**

Nío ívidir, "nine in the tree" is how older sources often read this strophe; but x-rays of the codex show that it actually reads *ívidjur*: "nine (females) in wood. Kvilhaug renders it as "nine witches in wood," literally translating *ívidia* as "within wood."[4] We know from other sources that nine giantesses live under the Tree's nine roots.

These beings are referred to in other poems. The god Heimdallr—who is closely identified with the Tree—says in two surviving lines of a lost poem, "Offspring of nine mothers am I | Of nine sisters am I the son."[5] This verse indirectly shows that the Nine Sisters are the ancestral grandmothers of all peoples, since Heimdall is named as their father in the *Rígsthula*.[6]

Nine worlds i remember, nine women in wood with mighty roots beneath the ground

The nine giantesses are also named in *Hyndluljóð*. "Nine giant women, at the world's edge" bore a hero who is usually identified as Heimdall.[7] Their names, given by the giantess Hyndla, compare with those of giantesses in other Norse texts. Another account gives the nine daughters of the sea god Aegir and goddess Rán as the mothers of Heimdallr. (Like the tree-root giantesses, these water-spirits are sisters.) There are also the nine daughters of Njörd (also a sea god) who *Sólarljóð* describes as carving runes, like the Norns.[8] The Nine Giantesses of the Tree, of the Sea, resonate with other nine-fold sisterhoods.[9]

Now the seeress begins to chant the Norse cosmology. She alludes to mysteries of the Cosmic Tree with its nine shamanic planes. She knows those realms because she has journeyed in them. (Across Eurasia, the World Tree intersects all the worlds, those above and below, which are also numbered as nine in some Siberian and Turkic cosmologies.)

The *völva* recounts the source of her spiritual powers, as is commonly done at the outset of shamanic ceremonies. The giant Vafthrúðnir also says that he has traveled the "nine worlds."[10] And the giantess Hel has "authority over the nine worlds," which Snorri claims that she got from Oðinn when he threw her into Niflheim.[11]

The poem telescopes what would have once been a vast body of Norse myth into a fragmented and often disjuncted account. The *völva* recounts bits of the creation story: how Ymir emerged out of the primordial ice of Ginnungagap, the gaping void that preceded heaven and earth. She tells how the sun and stars and moon did not yet know their courses. Briefly she describes how "all the Powers" gathered for counsel, sitting on their "chairs of destiny" (*rökstóla*) to name the lights in the sky and "order the year."[12] These chairs of destiny have counterparts in "the chairs of the Norns," *a norna stóli,* in which a seer sits for nine days.[13] Stone seats or boulders were probably known by names of this kind, as the Irish speak of stone chairs of the Cailleach or Brígid, or of the druids.

All that the *Völuspá* reveals of the Norse creation story is packed into four stanzas. More has been reconstructed from shards recorded by skálds of the Christian era. They show us a cosmogony that is virtually all male. The only female being involved in creation is a cow who licked the frost away to reveal the first man Búri. (She is unnamed in the *Völuspá*; Snorri calls her Auðumla.) But this story leaves important gaps. The giant kindred are already present from the beginning, uncreated, and it is with an unnamed giantess that the first man mates. Their son Bor fathers Oðinn, Vili and Vé, the three Aesir credited with setting the cosmos in order.

This cosmology belongs to what Margaret Clunies-Ross identifies as "male pseudo-procreation, that is, the pattern by which male creators assume female reproductive capacities to produce offspring on their own without the participation of females."[14] The *asynjur* (goddesses) go unmentioned until far along in the poem. Also missing from the story are the Vanir and Álfar, who appear later as Others whose origins are unaccounted for.

The "powers" are called Aesir for the first time in Stanza 7. They built shrines and temples of timber, and they worked metal into tools, and golden ornaments, which they had in plenty. The Aesir settled in to play at draughts, and to regale themselves in their hall:

> til three thurs maidens came, very
> powerful, from the realm of the giants.[15]

The arrival of the Three Maidens causes consternation among the Aesir for reasons the poem does not explain. Modern interpreters tend to read the Maidens as a threat, without questioning why the first female characters in the narrative would be considered a negative force. Most of them view the Maiden's arrival as portending an end to the golden age of manly play in stanza 7, in line with the poem's progression toward a fated fall of the Aesir.[16]

It is at the crucial moment of the Maidens' appearance that the *völva's* narrative is interrupted by a long section about the creation of the dwarves, with a litany of their names that runs for eight stanzas.[17] The tone of this interpolation is inconsistent with the majestic measure of the verses that precede it. Not only does it break the flow, but the long list of names is completely out of character with the compact, even cryptic, narrative of the rest of the *Völuspá*.

The Dwarves Intrusion breaks the narrative, and it looks as if these stanzas were been added to displace older verses about the Norns. At any rate, they have cost us an explanation of what happened when the Three Maidens came from *jötunheim*. But if we disregard the interpolation, then the *Völuspá* moves from the coming of the Three Maidens directly to the creation of the human pair Askr and Embla, "as yet unfated."[18] The implication is that the Maidens assigned fates to these first humans.

Most scholars see the "Three Maidens" as the Norns.[19] They are also read as giantesses, since they came from the land of giants. However, these interpretations are not mutually exclusive, since the Norns are often understood as giantesses.[20] Like them, they existed before the Aesir came into being. There is no sign of their ever having been born or created. The Three Maidens are the first female powers to be named (since the ice-licking cow is not) in the *Völuspá*. Who could they be, if not the Norns? Norse cosmology knows no other three goddesses who would figure in this sacred history.

THE NORNS

*They laid down fate, they chose lives
for the children of men, destinies of humans.*[21]

The formidable Norns had sway over the entire sweep of existence, and over the gods themselves. Unlike the Aesir, they are ageless beings. They are closely connected with the World Tree, and with the Urðrbrunnr, the most exalted of the three Wells that lie at the foundation of Being. Later sources push the Norns into the background, making Urð's Well the judgment seat of the Aesir[22] and placing Oðinn on the high seat there.[23] What becomes then of the Judgment of the Norns? The king of the gods usurps their place.

After the Dwarf Intrusion, Three Maidens appear by the great Ash Tree that stands over the Well of Urð: "Thence come the Maidens much-knowing." Translators differ about the following line, which varies in the medieval codices themselves: "Three from the hall | beneath the tree standing," says

Hauksbók, using *sal* ("hall"), as Snorri also does. But Codex Regius gives "the waters [*sē* or *sæ*] under the tree."[24] These would be the Three Wells under the Tree described by other texts (and the waters of the underworld).

Now the sibyl names the Three Maidens who come from the Ash that stands green over Urðr's Well.[25] She says that they "score on the wood," marking destinies in runes. These two stanzas are directly followed by the epochal conflict between the Aesir and the Vanir, which is provoked by an attack on a powerful woman.

The quotes above come from the Codex Regius version of *Völuspá*, but the two mentions of Three Maidens are much more clearly connected in the other major medieval manuscript. *Hauksbók* repeats the coming of the Maidens after the Dwarves-Intrusion.[26] It calls the Maidens "mighty and benevolent" (against the readings already discussed which see them as destructive or evil). They come to the man and woman that the Aesir had created from trees (St. 18) to assign their destiny, though this act is not described. Then the poem proceeds directly to the Tree of Life and the Norns. Thus the *Hauksbók* version makes it clear that the two groups of Three Maidens are the same, while repeating their connection to the giants.

The following stanzas (in which the Aesir promise Freyja to a giant in return for his rebuilding Asgarð's ramparts) are much like those in Codex Regius. Then the Hauksbók sequence diverges again, with two added stanzas on the giantess Angrboða: "East lived the crone, in Ironwood, and bore there Fenrir's progeny: of them all, one especially shall be the moon's devourer, in a troll's guise."[27] Angrboða means "sorrow-bringer." She is the mother of Hel, goddess of death, of Iormungand (the world serpent), and of the wolf Fenrir, who tries to swallow the sun. Their father is Loki, who sides with the giants more often than not.

Snorri tells more about Angrboða, saying that she belongs to "the race of wolves": "A witch dwells to the east of Midgarð, in the forest called Ironwood: in that wood dwell the troll-women, who are known as iron wood-women (*iárnvidjur*)."[28] The word translated here as "witch" is *gýgr*, closer to "ogress" or "hag," again reflecting the overlap of these concepts. *Vídjur*, in "iron wood-women," is the same word used earlier in *Völuspá* for the "nine women in wood." This title connects the Ironwood troll-women with the giantesses who are the roots of the great Tree in *Völuspá* 2.

ᴄullveıᴄ - heıᴆr: The prımal völva

After sketching the Norse cosmogony and the Norns, the seeress turns to "the war first in the world."[29] Like so many mythic wars, the conflict begins with violence against a woman. The Aesir attack Gullveig in the royal hall of Oðinn (under his byname Hár, the "High One"). They burn her, repeatedly, but are unable to kill her. Instead she undergoes three rebirths:

> **She remembers the war first in the world**
> **When they riddled Gullveig with spears**
> **And burned her in the hall of Hár**
> **Three times burned, three times born**
> **Often, again and again, but yet she lives.**
>
> **Heiðr they called her when to homes she came**
> **The wise seeress, enchanter of wands**
> **She cast spells in a trance**
> **And was ever the joy of evil women.** [30]

So powerful was Gullveig that when the Aesir burned her in Odin's hall, she regenerated herself three times. The poem sequentially connects the Aesir's spearing and burning of Gullveig—and her survival of it—to her mastery of *seiðr*. She lives on, and goes among the people, bringing the *seiðr* ceremony from house to house, prophesying and calling up spirits. For this, the people call her Heið, "bright, shining," or, as discussed earlier, "heathen." Heið has divine associations in Norse tradition. The goat who eats from the Tree and pours an abundance of ambrosial mead from her udders is called Heiðrún, "bright mystery."[31]

Gullveig means "golden strength, power," or according to some interpretations, "gold drink, intoxication."[32] Most scholars see Gullveig as an aspect of Freya.[33] One of the Norse kennings for gold is "Freyja's tears," and her magical "shining necklace" (Brísingamen) is made from the tears of the sun.[34] But many writers seem determined to interpret Gullveig nega-tively, as a personified "greed for gold." Going with the hostile tone of the last line, about "the joy of an evil woman," they assume that Gullveig some-how deserved the violence—torture, actually—inflicted by the Aesir. These jaundiced readings of Gullveig ignore the fact that, as Maria Kvilhaug points out, "the *Skáldskaparmál* shows that gold is often associated with poetry and

Burning Gullveig in Oðinn's Hall, by the Danish artist Lorenz Frølich, 1895

numinous wisdom."[35] In fact, gold is used as a positive symbol throughout the Edda and sagas.

Britt-Marie Näsström interprets the name as "Gold-thirst," seeing Gullveig-Freyja as a witch who penetrates Asgarðr in order to destroy it—especially by corrupting the women. (From another angle of view, she subverts patriarchy.) Simek makes her "the personified greed for gold."[36] Jenny Blain interprets Gullveig as Love of Gold or Gold Intoxication, and says that most modern heathens, and even academics, view her negatively: 'that she brought to the Aesir the love of gold, and caused problems so that the Aesir attempted to remove the problems by removing Gullveig; or that her magic caused problems for the Aesir, with the same result."[37]

It speaks volumes that one of the most powerful female figures in the Edda (and there aren't many) is still being interpreted in such an adverse way. Blain does acknowledge that some scholars see the passage as reflect-

ing "late heathen mistrust of magic or *seiðr*, misogyny, or indeed both."[38]
Margaret Clunies-Ross puts things in perspective: "The trouble with these
hypotheses is that they do not fit even the slender clues that the text affords
to the Gullveig problem and they project onto Gullveig a negative value....
This is, of course, a typical scapegoating technique and one that is central to
sorcery accusations."[39] Clunies Ross sees the Aesir as trying to destroy Gullveig in order to get rid of the Vanir "trump card"—the power of *seiðr*.[40]

Perhaps wanting to salvage honor for the Aesir, some people interpret
the Gullveig stanza as describing an initiation ceremony, not an attack. This
reading depends on translating the line "they pierced Gullveig with spears"
("pierced" for *studdu*; compare "studded") as "they supported Gullveig with
weapons,"[41] or "hoist on the spears."[42] But an initiation implies that Gullveig
consented, a dubious proposition that fails to explain why the rite would
cause a war, as the stanza clearly states. No allusions to initiations of *völur*
exist—much less ones involving torture with fire and spears.

The prevalent view has long been that Gullveig and Heiðr are the same
figure, as indicated by the seamless transition, and that they are aspects of
Freyja.[43] This idea has been questioned.[44] But the poem proceeds directly
from Gullveig to Heiðr, from "yet she still lives" to "Heið they called her"
(*Völuspá* 21-22).

For Clunies Ross, these stanzas "make it clear that Freyja was thought
to have taught the art of sorcery to human women."[45] Ursula Dronke treats
the story as a transformation of Freyja: "The indestructible Gullveig, thrice
reborn from her triple burning, is transmuted by this alchemy into a witch,
Heiðr (Bright One), who passes into human society, seducing worshippers
away from the Aesir by her sibylline arts.... The legend of Gullveig-Heiðr is
that of the archetypical *seiðkona*—the unburnable witch, the priestess and
prophetess: a hypostasis of the goddess Freyja herself."[46]

Sexual politics loom large in this "first war in the world." A group of men
commit ritualized violence against Gullveig in the royal hall of Óðinn. The
spearing and burning of a woman looks like nothing so much as the torture
of a captive—or like a witch persecution. Gullveig shares the qualities of
Freyja, the *vanadís* who is wise in the ways of *seiðr*. It is her power as a *völva*
that makes her a target, and at the same time it enables her to withstand
the violence. In the view of Margaret Clunies Ross, the Aesir try to destroy

Gullveig because *seidr* "represented a cultural resource that was both desirable and powerful but also threatening to their masculinity."[47] For their part, the Vanir are outraged at the abuse of a woman of their kindred.

This mythic fragment may recall an ancient Indo-European custom of burning women, whether for sorcery or for defying the sexual double standard, in order to assert male lordship. Or it could reflect more recent influences from witch-burning kingdoms to the south. One other Eddic poem, the *Hyndluljóð*, makes a possible allusion to witch-burning: "Loki ate some of the heart, the thought-stone of a woman | Roasted on a linden-wood fire, he found it half-cooked..." It causes him to be impregnated with the ancestors of all ogresses.[48] The witch's heart is called *hugsteinn*, "mind-stone,"[49] or "spirit-stone."

Some readings take this stanza as referring to a cremation, but that hardly warrants the description "cooked" and "half-roasted." Human sacrifice is a possibility,[50] but an execution seems more likely from the description, even more so when we recall the Frankish reference to Saxon men killing and eating witches. Both Gullveig and the unnamed woman are called "evil" (using the same word, *illrar / illri*)[51] and both of them are "burned."

No historical record exists of Norse witch hunts at the time the *Völuspá* was composed, circa 1000 CE. Later sagas speak of burnings and stonings. In late medieval laws, "burning as a means of destroying an individual was chiefly a woman's punishment... and was the favoured method of disposing of sorcerers according to both continental and Scandinavian legal codes."[52] In the same way, burning at the stake functioned as a primarily female punishment in Spain.[53]

But if the makers of later written laws favored burning as a method of executing women, the sagas indicate that in earlier times stoning was more common (though probably less frequent than the later burnings). One source shows men capturing a shapeshifting witch named Dís by putting a skin bag over her head (a method of neutralizing power referred to in other sagas) and then stoning her to death.[54] Also the Dalalagen laws of Sweden say, if a woman convicted of witchcraft was too poor to pay the heavy fine: "let her be meat for stones and strand."[55] Still, no evidence of such executions appears to exist when the *völur* still flourished, up to 1100.

It is worth keeping in mind that the *Völuspá* is recounting events among the gods—not humans. This particular episode is of pivotal importance; it triggers a war between the Aesir and Vanir, an event upon which "the future of the cosmos depends."[56] It is unlikely to feature some obscure goddess. In fact, there are not many major goddesses to choose from, given the low visibility of *asynjur* in the Edda. What other figure than Freyja—the sole named Vanir goddess—could have precipitated a war between the Aesir and Vanir, or have been associated with *seiðr* in her reborn state as Heiðr? That Snorri names Freyja as the goddess who brought *seiðr* to the Aesir is not to be ignored in interpretating these passages.[57] However, although he relies on the *Völuspá* account in *Gylfaginning*, he leaves out the story of Gullveig.[58]

To summarize, the order of events goes like this: the Aesir attack Gullveig in Oðinn's hall, but she survives. Now called Heiðr, she travels about as a *völva*, prophesying. There is a gap in the story after it condemns the seeress for giving joy to an evil woman. It moves to a council of the powers (Aesir and Vanir), who are considering this question: "whether the Aesir should yield the tribute | or whether all gods should partake in the sacrifices."[59] Another translation reads, "whether Aesir should pay a fine / or all the gods should have tribute,"[60] or yet again, "should the Aesir a truce with tribute buy | or should all gods share in the feast."[61]

A common interpretation of the parley views it as wrangling over what restitution should be paid for the injuries inflicted on Heiðr. John McKinnell asks why, if the Aesir injured a Vanir woman, would the Vanir not have attacked first? But that assumes that the Vanir were as warlike as the Aesir, which does not fit their known profile. Their efforts to keep the peace might indicate a different cultural approach to conflict resolution, one well documented in the early Germanic codes: the payment of restitution (*wergild*) for injuries,[62] in large part to avoid destructive blood feuds.

These same lines have also been interpreted as referring to "a religious cult war" over whether the dominant Aesir would permit the Vanir to be venerated and receive offerings in their own right, as deities of a different cultural tradition. Ursula Dronke takes this view,[63] and names several scholars in support of it. More recent writers such as Larrington[64] clearly see this passage as representing a cultural conflict between peoples. The Vanir would be a subordinated or submerged people who had to fight for recognition of their deities. Hermann Pálsson sees a Norse versus Sámi scenario, pointing to the *illrar thjóðar* ("evil nation") version of *Völuspá* in Codex Regius.[65] A more complex picture might be a conflict between an older Germanic populace that had assimilated some Sámi cultural traits, and newcomers who came as conquerors.

The Aesir, prompted by the unrepentant Oðinn, go to war rather than share the tribute or pay damages. He ends the council by hurling a spear. This unilateral move to violence precipitates a disastrous war. The Aesir do not prevail because the potent *vígspá* of their opponents enables them to hold the field: "The Vanir, prophetic in war, tramp the plains."[66] (*Vígspá*, literally "battle prophecy," can be more broadly interpreted as "battle magic.") The infuriated Vanir prevail, and succeed in breaking down the fortress walls of Asgarðr. But about this Aesir defeat, very little is said.

In fact, the *Völuspá* is silent on all but the barest outlines of this conflict, which would have presumably been well known to listeners. The Prose Edda gives a few more details. Snorri tells us that after many battles in which no one prevailed, the Vanir offered a truce, which the Aesir accepted, and that hostages were exchanged as a peace guarantee.[67] They also performed a rite of conmingling, to which we will return. But first it is time to look at the Vanir.

The Vanir

The poet of *Völuspá* never explains who the Vanir are. They are simply there. Eddic literature pairs them in opposition to the Aesir, as a distinct group, in *Gylfaginning, Skírnismál, Sigurdrífumál, and Alvíssmál*. But far more frequently, a different pairing is used: *Aesir ok alfar*, "Aesir and elves."[68]

Amidst the terrors of Ragnarok, as the world devolves into chaos, the *Völuspá* asks, "How fare the Aesir, how fare the Álfar?" Or: "What of the gods, what of the *álfar*?"[69] Not only is *Aesir ok álfar* a common phrase in Old Norse, but it has an exact equivalent in Old English: *esa* and *ylfe*, from a spell in the *Lacnunga*.[70] The shared formula means that this Germanic pairing is probably very old.

The Vanir sometimes seem interchangeable with the Álfar. Frey, the brother of Freyja, was long ago given Alfheim to rule over as a teething-gift.[71] Álfheim could be equivalent to Vanaheim, the Vanir country; both are placed in Sweden, where Freyr is said to have ruled. Another Swedish king who ruled at Uppsala is named Vanlandi ("man from Vanir land") in the *Ynglingasaga*. The connection is matrilineal, from his mother Vana, who married the Swedish king Sveigðir. Freyr himself is called *Svía goð* or *blótgoð* Svía, "chieftain or sacrificial priest of the Swedes."[72] One saga refers to an Alfheim in the far southeast of Norway, near the Swedish border, inhabited by the descendents of king Álfar, who "were all of elfin race."[73]

But these are mythical figures, and the question has been whether they reflect an underlying ethnic history, among other possible layers of meaning. As Snorri put it: "the Aesir had a dispute with the people called Vanir, and they appointed a peace conference and made a truce..."[74] The Aesir :: Vanir opposition may originally have been geographic, since Oðinn was said to have founded the Danish Skjoldung dynasty and the English Scyldings, while Sweden is linked in various ways to the Vanir.[75] The title Yngvi-Freyr links the foremost Vanir god to the Ingvaeones and the Yngling dynasty in Uppsala.[76]

To confuse things further, another formula exists, this one threefold, which contrasts *Aesir / vanir / alfar*, or alternatively *Aesir / alfar / dvergar*— the dwarves. When the giantess Gerðr asks Freyr's emissary if he comes from any of these three groups he answers, "I am not of the *alfa* nor of the *ása* nor of the wise *vana*."[77] *Sigrdrífumál* says of the runes, that were shaved on wood and soaked with holy mead: "They are among the Aesir; they are among the Álfar, some with the wise Vanir; human people have some."[78]

Njördr, with his bag of winds

In *Fáfnismál*, even the Norns are said to come from different kindreds: "some are of the Aesir, some of the Alfar, others of Dvalin's daughters (in other words, the dwarves)."[79]

The wise dwarf Alvís also distinguishes the Aesir, named as gods (ungendered *goðum*), from the Vanir who are called *ginn-reginn* ("powers of enchantment")—and he separates both of them from the giants (*jötnar*, etins) and *álfar* (elves).[80] In *Vafthrúðnismál*, Oðinn asks where the god Njörðr originated, since the Aesir did not rear him, though he has many shrines and altars. The giant replies, "In Vanaheim the wise powers shaped him | and gave him as hostage to gods [*goðum*]; in the age of destiny, he shall yet come home to the wise Vanir."[81] That last phase is often repeated in Eddic poetry: "the wise Vanir." [82] The *Thrymskviða* attributes psychic foreknowing to this spirit kindred: "Even as the Vanir could he see far forward."[83]

The name Aesir (singular Áss) is ancient enough to have cognates in other Germanic languages: *ēse* / *ōs* in Old English; *ensî* / ans in Old High German, *anses* /ans in Gothic, all going back to a Proto-Germanic **ansiwiz* / **ansuz*.[84] The English rune for "A," named *ōs*, compares to the Old Norse form *ōss*. In fact, this Old Germanic deity-name goes back much further—thousands of years—to Proto-Indo-European **h$_a$ensus*, "god, spirit,"[85] or "breath."[86] From the same root came Avestan *ahura* and Sanskrit *ásura* ("deity").

Linguists conjecture that the Proto-Indo-European root **h₂énsus* meant "life force" and "engender." It gave rise to Sanskrit *ásu* "life-force," Hittite *hass* ("to procreate, give birth"), and *ās* ("to produce") in the Central Asian language Tocharian B.[87] Sanskrit *ásu* translates as "powerful spirit."[88]

But Vanir has no correlates in other Indo-European languages—at least, not under that name. Van-names are only recorded for North Germanic, and even there they are greatly outnumbered by references to Álfar, which are abundantly attested in place-names, kennings, and personal names.[89]

However, the Vanir do belong to a widespread Indo-European pattern of a dualist polarity of deities, often referred to as "gods" and "anti-gods," or "not-gods." In India it is *devas* and *asuras*, while in Iran the polarity is reversed, *ahura* designating the divine and *daeva* the demonic. The Norse had a similar polarity, whether it is the Vanir or Álfar who are counterposed to the Aesir.[90]

Some scholars think that the Vanir and Alfar were interchangeable, or at least overlapped. Alaric Hall makes a compelling case for a correspondence, calling attention to the declaration in *Lokasenna* about Aegir's feast: "Many of the *Aesir* and *álfar* were there," a statement later repeated by Loki. Yet the *dramatis personae* include only characters named elsewhere as either Aesir and Vanir.[91] "The obvious explanation for the mysterious *álfar* of *Lokasenna* is to identify them with Snorri's *vanir*."[92] Hall admits that "a variant tradition" does distinguish between the *álfar* and *vanir*—or at least lists them separately—but concludes that "some partial synonymy between *álfr* and *vanr* seems likely."[93] Along the way, he points to a unique "lexical connection between *álfar* and *dísir*"; both have special ceremonies—*álfablót* and *dísablót*—dedicated to them.[94]

Hall compares the Norse association of **vanir :: seiðr** to an Old English pairing of **elves :: siði** (or **siden**, both words being cognate to Norse *seiðr*). Its only surviving Anglo-Saxon form is the word *ælfsiden*, "the magic of *ælfe*."[95] As Hall notes, "the prospect of *ælf* working magic called *siden* or *sidsa* is well-paralleled by Snorri's association of the *vanr* with *seiðr*."[96] A charm in Bald's Leechbook uses jet shavings "against elf and an unknown *sidsa*," another form of the *siden/seið* word.[97]

However, *seið* and *siden* had drifted apart in cultural meanings. Anglo-Saxon sources associate the *ælfsiden* with supernatural causes for illness more than with entranced prophetic ceremonies—though Hall makes a good case for *ylfig* (elvish) inspiration.[98] He notes that *at siða* apparently implied out-of-body travel or shapeshifting.[99] The Anglo-Saxon *wan-seoc*, "made sick by the Wanes" may correspond to "elf-sickness" and to a "more common" usage of *deofulseoc* ("devil-sick"), which meant "possessed," or in modern terms, "mentally ill."[100] If the Wanes in *wan-seoc* correspond to the Vanir, this strengthens the parallel between Wanes/ Vanir and *ælfe* / *álfar*.

Buckets of ink have been spilled on the Vanir question. Older scholarship saw their myth as a historical memory of an indigenous people invaded by the Aesir. They compared Germanic settlers' awe of the Vanir's magical prowess to their distant Arya cousins' perception that the Dasyu that they conquered in India were expert in supernatural arts. In each case light-skinned conquerors fear the magic of a darker people (though some recent scholarship suggests that the Dasyus were enemy Indo-European tribes).[101] That more complex scenario of locally-acculturated Indo-European speakers might have been true for Scandinavia (and for Ireland too).

The Vedas lionize the Aryā as gods (*devas*) and treat the Dasyu as demons (*asuras*). Alain Danielou comments, "It is significant that it was not for their sins that the antigods had to be destroyed but because of their power, their virtues, their knowledge, which threatened that of the gods—that is, the gods of the Aryās." He adds that the Dasyu are called "builders of sinful cities" and—like the Vanir—"expert in magic."[102] The Aryā conquer and enslave them, so that the very name *dāsa* came to signify "slave" (both socially and later in spiritual contexts, as in the name of the poet Kālidāsa).

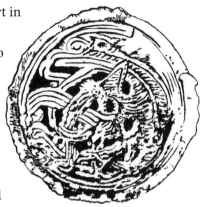

Dragon ornament, Birka, Sweden

But Indic tradition also understands the *asuras* as earthly or materialistic deities, to which certain planets such as Venus are tied, and which are propitiated with mantras and offerings. Sometimes the *asuras* are considered nature spirits, in apparent parallel with the Vanir.

Other similarities between Norse and Vedic themes have been noted. As Freyja, the "goddess of the Vanir," married into the Aesir, so Srī, the Hindu goddess of fortune, abundance and beauty, was from the *asuras* and married the *devas*: "I used formerly to dwell with the virtuous *danavas*."[103] The Danavas are a group of *asuras* who are named as the "children of Danu." This Vedic goddess had a distant European counterpart from whom the Irish named the Tuatha Dé Danann, "Tribe of the Goddess Danand," or of "the gods of Danand." Both the Vanir and the Tuatha Dé Danann were reputed to possess great magical knowledge, and counterposed to invaders: the Sons of Míl in the *Lebor Gabála Érenn*, and the Aesir in the *Ynglingasaga*. Both Indic Danu and Irish Danand are associated with waters, a connection repeated in a litany of river-names from the Rhone (*Rho-danu) to the Don. They are sisters to the Welsh goddess Donwy and to Danaë among the Greeks.

The Aesir are warlike and patriarchal, with the (female) *asynjur* playing only a slim role. The *Völuspá* describes them as metalworkers who "forged precious things, shaped tongs, made tools."[104] Unlike the ancient Sámi, the Indo-European invaders of Scandinavia had bronze weapons and, later, iron. There is archaeological evidence that Indo-European settlers gradually pushed the Sámi further north. This ancient indigenous people also sought refuge from invaders in the inland and upland territory between Norway and Sweden, a region some sagas call Alfheimr, "elf-home."[105]

Norse sources refer to the Sámi as "Finns" (not to be confused with the

Baltic Finns of Suomi, who speak a related language), and often describe
them as "sorcerers." The sagas show the Sámi being sought out for their shamanic knowledge; but Norwegians and Swedes stereotyped and, eventually,
persecuted them. Sorcerers were sometimes cast as darker people; a verse
in *Völuspa hin skamna* declares, "All the sorcerers came from Dark-head."[106]
Other poems project darker people as a subjugated class; the *Rígsthula* views
light, fair-haired people as noble, and dark ones (*svarthar*) as thralls.[107]

Snorri's historical fable claims that the name Aesir means "men of Asia."
He has them coming north from Asia Minor to invade the country of the
Vanir—which he places near Ukraine, not in northern Europe. Snorri first
refers to the Don, ancient Tanais, as Tanakvísl, which he then changes to
Vanakvísl. This attempt to make things "fit" is typical of medieval linguistics,
of a piece with the elite insistence, also shared by Irish monks, on tracing
origins from "Troy" and other Greco-Roman or biblical reference points.[108]
As the "sons of Odin" pressed northward, they set up royal dynasties along
the way. At this point, Snorri converges with other Germanic accounts in
Denmark, England, and Sweden.

Many modern analysts accept Snorri's Odinist claims, in spite of his Asia
Minor fantasy. Yet there is evidence that Oðinn did not become prominent
until the Viking era. He is described as a latecomer who eclipsed the older
veneration of Thórr (and who knows what goddesses).[109] Oðinn's death cult
split away from a pluralist animist cosmology. It introjected a patriarchal
king figure who lords it over all others, along Olympian lines. He is pitiless,
treacherous, and strife-sowing. He demands men be hanged in sacrifice
to him: "Now I give you to Oðinn."[110] The god's "perfidy" extends even to
tricking a man into being sacrificed.[111]

Snorri provides information that helps flesh out stories from the older Poetic Edda, but his retelling of the Norse myths is problematic. As a Christian
skáld, he took pains to recast heathen gods as historical figures (an approach
shared by his Christian counterparts in Denmark and Ireland). He contradicted older sources, and himself. As a skáld who authored a guide to poetic
kennings, his work depended on transmitting cultural traditions that his
audience would recognize—but he did not shrink from distorting them.

Snorri's much-vaunted claim that the Vanir practiced incest could
either be an artifact of Aesir partisanship and Vanir defeat, or of Christian

supercessionism. Dronke exposes its weakness: "There is no reference anywhere to Freyr and Freyja as a divine sister-and-brother wedded pair, nor, outside of *Lokasenna*, to any sister-wife of Njorðr."[112] (A sociological analysis might suggest that partisans of the Aesir projected incest onto a matrilineal society that practiced cross-cousin marriage between patrilines, who were not regarded as related, but there's no evidence for that in Scandinavia.) Yet negative insinuations against the Vanir persist in modern studies. One writer speaks of "the sexual evil represented by the Vanir."[113] Yet at the same time, the sexual violence of the male Aesir is given a free pass.

Another approach to the Norse stories is to understand them as a mythic reflecting pool for societal values and behaviors. The Eddic poems depict the Aesir as a military elite bent on piling up hero-fame and riches, feasting and drinking, gambling looted goods, and fixated on a cult of manhood. But for all their worship of power, these gods are mortal, destructible, and doomed. Odin has one eye, Tyr one hand, Hod is blind, and Heimdallr loses his hearing. The natural order is seen as being under attack: the tree of life is gnawed at from below by the serpent Niðhogg, from above by stags feeding on its leaves; wolves chase the sun and moon to devour them, and the Fenris wolf is chained, awaiting the apocalyptic twilight of Ragnarok. The *Völuspá* projects a sense that the Aesir are in conflict with Nature herself, that they have offended the real Powers—although that is never spelled out.

Dumézil tried to map his "three functions" of priests, warriors, and farmers onto the Norse deities. A long line of scholars followed his identification of the Vanir with the "third function," corresponding to farmers, sexuality, and Nature. By this theory, the Vanir divinities have power over the fruitfulness of the earth, and are associated with plenty, riches, and peace.[114] More recent writers have challenged the Dumézilian model.[115] As Lotte Motz pointed out, Freyr is the prototype for Swedish kingship, so the Vanir are hardly free of lordly associations. Conversely, the *asynja* Iðunn, with her apples of immortality, represents life-force, fruitfulness, and regeneration. The modern stereotype of "fertility" *anything* sheds no light, having become a hopeless cliché. A more meaningful formulation would be to speak of Nature deities in opposition to dynastic-aristocratic gods; but this can't be broken down in strictly Aesir-Vanir terms.

Other cosmological interpretations look at the three (or nine) worlds and the realms of the Aesir, Álfar, Jötnar (giants). They mull over the horizonal planes of Asgarðr, Midgarðr, Utgarðr (which have also been proposed as non-linear concentric realms) and vertical ones that ascend and descend to upper and lower worlds.[116] Is Vanaheimr, "home of the Vanir," supposed to be a physical location, or a plane of existence? It is hard to parse the dual and threefold listings of supernaturals, the larger groupings of Aesir, Vanir, Álfar, and humans as against monstrous giants, thurses and dwarves.[117] As discussed in chapter 6, gendered themes pervade all these oppositions.

Some scholars have argued that Vanir was merely a by-name for the Aesir, whose war in the *Völuspá* was really fought against the giants.[118] Rudolf Simek holds up the scarcity of references to Vanir in skáldic poetry as an argument against their being a separate group. But there is no reason to consider poets hired by the lordly class to sing heroic verse as better cultural witnesses than the oldest Eddic poems. According to John McKinnell, court skálds stayed well away from heathen deities by the 11th century.[119] Simek suggests that "Vanir" was simply an alliterative device (as in *víssa Vana*, the "wise Vanir") for deities who were undifferentiated from the Aesir.[120] But that begs the question of why old sources counterposed the Vanir to the Aesir. The problem is that the existing sources are limited, and all too often withhold crucial information—none more so than the *Völuspá*.

The most extensive references to Vanir come from Snorri, whose worth as a source Simek dismisses—and that skáld undeniably has his flaws. But Snorri did not write the *Völuspá*, or make up all those Vanir titles—Freyja as Vanagoð, Vanadís, Vanabruðr, or those of Freyr and Njördr—that he cited in *Skáldskaparmál*.[121] No skáld would risk looking ridiculous by touting kennings that no one recognized as authentic. In fact, Simek realizes that this was unlikely, and obliquely acknowledges that the kennings come from older poetry. He allows that Snorri was uncertain about their meaning, but he still calls the Vanir "Snorri's creation."[122]

None of this explains the pivotal position of the Vanir in *Völuspá*. The suggestion that the Aesir did not fight a war against the Vanir, but instead against the giants, has no basis in the poem itself. Brief as it is, the war narrative only mentions Vanir. Giants enter into the story only after the war, when the Aesir contract with one of them to rebuild the walls of Asgarð— and that in a different poem. Who would have their fortress rebuilt by an enemy who had just destroyed it?

The theory of Vanir-as-medieval-invention fails to explain several things, such as the special spiritual powers attributed to them in the poetic Edda. *Thrymskviða* says of Heimdallr, "Even as the Vanir could he see far forward."[123] What sense would this make if the Aesir were indistinguishable from the Vanir? It's true that foresight is attributed to Frigg and Gefjon, but the male Aesir are lacking in it. Oðinn in particular boasts of possessing such wisdom, yet goes chasing after women, dead or alive, in order to access it. If Njörðr is really one of the Aesir, then why does *Vafthrúðnismál* prophesy his return to the Vanir after the destruction of the world?[124]

The claim that the Aesir and Vanir are different names for the same gods slams up against the dualistic opposition of gods/not-gods that runs deep in Indo-European tradition. The solution may be that Vanir is only one of several names for these not-gods, another being Alfar. However, other sources contradict this, naming three or four separate groups.[125] Without over-simplifying the multiple collectivities of Norse deities, a striking comparison can be made with another story about gods/not-gods out of India.

The Mead of Poetry, and Vedic Amrita

Snorri says that after the war, the Aesir and Vanir sealed their truce by spitting together into a vat. Out of their combined life-essences, the Aesir fashioned a man, Kvasir, who became a wise teacher to humankind. But the dwarves murdered him, and by mixing his blood with honey, created the Mead of Poetry.[126] This nectar of wisdom made a sage of anyone who drank it. The giants stole it from the dwarves, and Oðinn in turn robbed it from them, as explained in the story of Gunnlöð. (See chapter 4.)

Kvasir is called the wisest of the Vanir in *Gylfaginning* 50. Snorri makes him one of the Vanir hostages in the truce that followed the Aesir's failed war against them.[127] His name is apparently related to Russian *kvas*—an alcoholic drink made from bread, again denoting intoxication. Both originated from a Proto-Indo-European root meaning "to squeeze out essence from some-thing." This meaning also calls to mind the Indian elixir Soma, which the Rg Veda repeatedly describes as an essence pressed out from an herbal preparation.[128]

Ursula Dronke called attention to a striking Indian analogue to the Norse story: the *Sumudra Mathanam*, or Churning of the Milk Ocean.[129] It too tells of a war between two opposing groups of supernaturials who make a truce and cooperate in creating a divine elixir. The *asuras* defeat the *devas*, who then convince them to join together to churn out *amrita* (the nectar of immortality and essence of divine wisdom). The two groups of deities fight again over control of the *amrita*. The eagle-being Garuda bears it aloft, out of reach. The asuras regain control of it, but the gods steal it back by means of a seduction. Vishnu takes female form as Mohinī and deludes the *asuras* so the *devas* can consume the amrita.[130]

Both stories originate in a remote Indo-European past. In one, the divine essence is extracted from milk, in the other from blood. Shared themes include the war, the elixir emerging from a truce, the eagle bearing it away, and its ultimate acquisition via a seduction (both acts carried out by Oðinn in the Norse version). Another similarity is that Lakshmi comes from the *asuras* and marries into the *devas* (Indra), as Freyja comes from the Vanir and marries one of the Aesir (Oðr/Oðinn). Both goddesses are paired with king-figures. Both stories share the cross-dressing disguise. In *Thrymskviða*, the giants steal Thórr's hammer and demand Freyja in exchange for it. Thórr is forced to go *argr*, masquerading as a bride, in order to recover the hammer. Once he has recovered it, he rips off his borrowed women's robes and kills the giants with the hammer. In the Indian story, Vishnu disguises himself as Mohinī and throws off the female robes to slaughter the asuras with his discus weapon.[131]

The *Völuspá* narrative veils in silence key information about the war following the attack on Gullveig, and the ensuing truce. Among the missing details are what happened to Gullveig, how Freyja came to live among the Aesir, and how she came to be paired with Oðinn (under his by-name Oðr). The *Ynglingasaga* fleshes out the picture somewhat, relating that it was Freyja who taught *seiðr* to the Aesir.

One missing episode was brilliantly reconstructed by Ursula Dronke, who called attention to the cryptic passage that immediately follows *Völuspá*'s account of the Aesir war on the Vanir: "Then the deities went all | to the thrones of destiny | sacrosanct gods | and concerned themselves about this | who had tainted all the air with ruin | and given to the giant-race Oðr's girl

[Freyja]?"[132] The poem says that the Aesir committed a violation of oaths and pledges, but doesn't tell that story. To understand what happened in the missing episode, we have to turn to the Prose Edda.

In Snorri's *Gylfaginning*, the war with the Vanir is over, and a truce is in place. But the rampants of Asgarðr are in ruins, and the Aesir feel insecure. So they hire a builder, a giant as it turns out, to quickly construct a new stone fortress. He asks an impossible fee: the sun, moon, and Freyja. In desperation, the Aesir agree, on condition that he finish the walls within a single season, without the help of any man. They feel sure that he will not be able to meet these terms, but the builder brings a stallion of such phenomenal strength that the work proceeds rapidly. In the final three days, it appears that he will meet the deadline. The Aesir are facing disaster. That same sun and moon that they set in their courses, they now stand to lose, and Freyja as well. In a fateful chain of events, the Aesir's attack on Gullveig had caused a war, which destroyed the rampants of their fortress, which they then contracted to have rebuilt—but at the price of an oath that would be unthinkable to fulfill.[133]

The Aesir force Loki—who had convinced them to allow the stallion's help—to stop the giant from winning the reward he was promised for building the wall in one season. Loki turns into a mare and lures the stallion off for a night of sex in the forest, thus preventing the builder from finishing the fortress on time. (In the process, he conceives the eight-legged shamanic horse Sleipnir—one of Loki's two intersex births). Realizing what has happened, the mason goes into a "giant-rage," revealing his real identity as a hill giant. The Aesir bring in Thórr to smash his head, thus breaking their solemn oaths guaranteeing the builder's safety. Like the *Völuspá* itself, Ursula Dronke emphasizes the crucial importance of this oath-breaking, which she sees as leading inevitably to the destruction of Ragnarok at the poem's end.[134]

The *Völuspá* overleaps this entire backstory, jumping from the war with the Vanir straight to the Aesir gathering for council to determine who had made that disastrous deal with the giants.[135] Oðr's wife was Freyja, and it has been asked why, if Gullveig were Freyja, would the Aesir have attacked her if they now feel that they could not possibly do without her? One answer might be that in the interim they had discovered that the Lady of the Vanir embodied the vital force without which life was impossible. Another is that Freyja has several aspects, some of which Eddic poetry treats with ambivalence, if not outright disdain. While she is demonized as Gullveig, and as a *fordaeða* (sorceress), Freyja is no longer described as practicing those arts, nor depicted flying in her "feather-skin." But as Oðinn's consort she is acceptable, and far less threatening than as a *völva* possessed of knowledge and power that frightens the Aesir.

Another way of understanding this myth is to view the Gullveig episode as the Aesir's initial encounter with Freyja, in which they perceive her female power as a threat. Afterward, she is integrated into the dominant order, as other non-Indo-European great goddesses had been—Śrī, Hera, Hebat or Shaushka—under the Aryās, Greeks, and Hittites. She then becomes indispensible to the Aesir, to the point of almost eclipsing the other goddesses. The paucity of (active) goddesses in Norse narratives is comparable to the masculine preponderance in the Vedic texts.[136]

The *Völuspá* leaves a lacuna between the Aesir-Vanir war and the oath-breaking that follows the rebuilding of Asgarð's battlements. The gap corresponds to several missing stories about Freyja, one of the few prominent female actors in the Edda. The Prose Edda describes her father Njörðr and brother Freyr as coming as hostages to the Aesir in the truce. It seems that she accompanied them.[137] How did Freyja come to be Oðinn's consort, and teach him *seiðr*? None of this is told anywhere.

ϝReyja anὄ ϝRiᵹᵹ

Freyja means Lady, sovereign. Her name derives from a Proto-Germanic root that gave rise to Old Saxon *frūa*, Old High German *frouwa*, and modern German *Frau*, "lady."[138] Modern writers like to call her a goddess of love and fertility, and she does embody beauty, music, and lovemaking. But her scope is far greater. She is closely associated with fire and sun and gold, as reflected in her name *logadís*, "flame ancestor." She is Mardoll, "shining ocean," Hörn, "flax," Gefn, "giver," and Syr, "sow" (and so she rides on a boar.)[139] She is the most beneficent of deities, linked to the Earth, plowing and farming, sea-faring and peaceful trade.[140]

Freyja is called Vanadís, ancestral mother of the Vanir, and Vanagóð, their deity.[141] She is protector of the grandmother sanctuaries, *Disarsalr*.[142]

She appears in the form of a mare at the moment of death, "a *dís* claiming her lover," to escort the soul to her rich-seated hall, Sesrumnir, in Folkvangr, "fields of the people."[143]

The land is full of Freyja's sanctuaries. Many places in Norway, and even more in Sweden, are named Freyja-temple, -meadow, -land, -rock, -lake, and -grove. Both countries retain place-names that mean "Freyja's temple" (Norwegian Frøihov, from Freyjuhof) or "Freyja's sanctuary" (Swedish Frövi, from Freyjuvé, literally "Freyja's vé").[144]

There is a noticeable overlap between Freyja :: Oðr and Frigg :: Oðinn. Some linguists see a common origin for Frigg and Freyja, as reflected in placenames and etymology.[145] Both are invoked in birth and the naming of children.[145] Freyja is also paired with Oðinn, as a second wife or concubine.[146] Margaret Clunies-Ross noted that Aesir men take wives from other groups, but never give them—a pattern of conquest. In no case is a Vanir man paired with an Asynja.[147]

Mythically, Frigg seems to fade into the background, except for her ardent efforts to save her son Baldr. Jochens calls attention to the de-emphasis on Frigg: "the Völuspá poet ignores Frigg's imaginative plan to protect Baldr and her forceful attempt to rescue him from Hel... Excluded also are Freyja's vociferous objections to the gods' plan of giving her to the giants in return for the building of a stronghold."[148]

As Loone Ots remarks, the Poetic Edda only mentions Frigg six or seven times: once as crying, another time in a kenning for Oðinn, and twice as an advisor.[149] Yet the skálds' inattention is belied by the importance of this goddess in place-names and day-names—even a constellation—and by the time-depth of her cross-cultural presence. Long after christianization, rural Swedes were invoking Frygge in animal healing charms.[150]

Frigg was revered by the Germans (Old High German Frīja), Saxons (Frike, Freke), Anglo-Saxons (Frīg), and the Lombards of

The Swedish Freyja of Aska, Östergötland. She stands within a dragon ring, wearing multiple necklaces.

northern Italy (Frea). These names all derive from Proto-Germanic Frijjō, which in turn comes from the Proto-Indo-European root *prih-yah. It is related to Indic *priya*, "loved one," and to two branches in Germanic: one that means "love" (also "friend") and the other meaning "free."[151] The strong feminine noun *frīg* appears in poetry as "love" (singular) or "affections, embraces" (plural).[152]

Frigg gave her name to Friday in the Germanic languages: Old English Frīgedæg, Old Norse frijadagr, and modern German Freitag, Dutch vrijdag, and English Friday.[153] Medieval and early modern traditions across Europe associate Friday with witch goddesses.[154] Usually they are also spinning goddesses (like Holle, Perchta, Kostroma, Laima, and many others).

Frigg is a spinner too, especially under her name Hörnflax.[155] This attribute of hers takes on cosmic dimensions in Scandinavian star lore, which names the three stars in Orion's belt as "Frigg's Distaff" (Friggerok or Frejerock).[156] Christianization demanded that the constellation's name be converted to Mariärock. Similar code-switching is visible in the Finnish by-name for the sun, as "God's Spindle." Another constellation is named Freyja's Spindle—or this may be a variant of Friggerok.[157]

Frigg may be depicted on the Frauenbrakteaten (also known as Type

B7, Fürstenberg or Oberwerschen bracteates) medallions made in southern Germany around 500-700 CE. Five of these slim golden amulets show a woman holding a staff, usually interpreted as a distaff. She is in the act of spinning, barebreasted, on a pendant from Oberwerschen (see figure).[158] K. Hauck, the leading scholar on bracteates, saw her as a goddess.

At a couple of sites, spinner bracteates were found in close association with spindles. And there is more: "Grave-goods in the form of distaffs made of precious materials, e.g. jet, ivory or amber, bear

Frauenbracteate, with spinner, from Oberwerschen, Germany

witness to their importance."[159]

Frigg comes off as a matronly wife, yet her name is related to the slang term *frig*, "to caress, rub, pleasure a woman," from Old English *frygian and *frigan*.[160] Her Old Saxon counterpart Freke was still being revered in medieval times as Fru Freke or Vrouw Vreke.[161] Converted into a saint in Belgium, Sint Vreke, she nevertheless kept her sensuality. In her service are mountain-dwelling spirits, the *kabauters* (kobolds), according to a 17th century version of the *Reta de Limburg*. Her witch qualities fade over time: "and Vreke is no longer a great witch (*eene grote heks*) but a goddess with all the alluring charms of Venus."[162]

Freyja has the reputation of a witch, expert in prophecy and enchantment. Her feathered witch-robe (*fjaðrhamr* or *valhamr*) gives her the power of shamanic flight.[163] The shapeshifting Freyja sometimes takes the form of a bird or a sow.[164] Or she rides on a boar, or in a wagon drawn by cats. During her sojourn with the Aesir, she remains the quintessential sorceress. Loki calls her by the witch-word *fordæða*.[165]

It has been suggested that by taking Freyja to wife, the foreigner Oðinn established a claim to sovereignty, as Zeus did in marrying Hera, a pre-Indo-European goddess who was the original mistress of Olympus. But Oðinn was never able to control Freyja, whose far-ranging sexual exploits are alluded to in the *Lokasenna*—and later, by Christian detractors. *Hyndla's Lay* remarks that Freyja gads about at night "like a she-goat straying among bucks."[166] As the *Lokasenna* shows, all the *asynjur*, even wifely Frigg, were vulnerable to accusations of promiscuity, which under the sexual double standard, rendered a female *org* (defiant of gender strictures).

Although Eddic poems and the sagas have relatively little to say about these goddesses, English researchers found evidence that Freyja had been venerated in a Viking settlement in Wiltshire. In the mid-12th century, this community still spoke Norse and used runes, "even for ecclesiastical inscriptions," as discovery of the original tympanum of Oaksey church proved. "[T]heir pagan beliefs died hard," writes Barbara Freitag, demonstrated by "the fact that they inserted the nude figure of the Norse goddess Freya into the wall beside the altar, thus propitiating both new and old gods."[167] This was the famous Oaksey sheela-na-gig, now ensconced in the church's north wall. In the 1920s, an old villager of Pennington told Andy Roberts that "the sculpture had always been called Freya by the local people."[167]

The *Lokasenna* attributes all-knowledge to Frigg and Gefjön. But as Judy

Quinn points out, Loki fools Frigg twice, in the most disastrous instance causing the death of her son Baldr. So what happened to her foreknowing?[169] The inconsistency shows that more than one interpretation of Frigg's foreknowledge was in play. Frigg does not reveal what she knows, as she explains to Loki and Oðinn, "Your fates should never be publicly recounted – what you two Aesir did long ago. Always avoid [revealing] ancient destinies."[170] The silence of Frigg contrasts sharply with the *völur* and the giantesses, who reveal all kinds of things.

Tbe völʌ aꞑꝺ oꝺīꞑꞑ

After the Aesir-Vanir war, the *Völuspá* returns to the seeress who is speaking prophecy. Addressing Oðinn, she declares that she knows the hidden place of Heimdall's horn, "under the radiant, sacred tree." There she sees the foaming flow of a mighty stream "from Fjolnir's pledge | know ye further, or how?" She is alluding to Oðinn's plucking out one eye as the price of a drink from Mimir's well, in order to obtain wisdom. And yet Oðinn comes to the *völva* in search of her foreknowledge.[171]

> alone she sat out, when the lord of gods,
> oðinn the old, her eye did seek.

The *völva* is "sitting out" on the land, in the old heathen way of dreaming. Grounded in primordial consciousness, she is indifferent to Odin's rank, or the rings and necklaces he lays before her to elicit her prophecy. Judy Quinn brings forward a lesser-known version of Völuspá 29, which says, "War-father chose for her necklaces, wealth, wise spells [*spáklig*] and prophecy-wands [*spáganda*].[172] The *spáganda* might well have been envisioned in the form of distaffs, like many of the forged iron staffs of 10th century *völur*. (Indeed, Lorenz Frølich depicted the *völva's* staff in this very form, in the late 19th century before most of them were found: see preceding page.) Carolyne Larrington translates *spáganda* as "a rod of divination."[173] Ursula Dronke renders it as "spirits of prophecy"—but if Oðinn had those to give away, he would have no need of the *völva's* help.

There is nothing the *völva* wants from Oðinn; it is he who is the suppli-cant. She "knows more than Oðinn," comments Ursula Dronke,[174]

Oðinn approaches the völva seeking her prophecy. Lorenz Frølich.

and the *völva* reminds him of that:

> **What seekest to know, why summon me?**
> **Well know I, Ygg, where thy eye is hidden,**
> **In the wondrous well of Mímir**
> **Each morn Mímir his mead doth drink**
> **Out of Fjölnir's pledge: know ye further or how?**[175]

Her mocking tone taunts Odin's pretensions as a wizard; has he not cast one of his eyes into Mimir's well in hopes of gaining second-sight? (Parenthetically, it could be asked: has he not bragged of knowing things that witch-women did not? and did he not boast in *Hávamal* of using his magical prowess to coerce women?) Why, then, does Oðinn bring offerings to the *völva* for her oracular seeing?[176] In the next verse the seeress gives the answer:

> che paces í pachom, yec parcher í see
> see par and wíde che worlds abouc.[177]

Now the *völva* enters into a foretelling of what is to come—but she recounts it in the past tense.[178] Time is irrelevant in this dream-state of seeing. The *völva* sees the valkyries gathering for battle, with the norn Skuld at their head, and she names them. Her tone turns dire: she foresees the doom of Baldr, son of Frigg and Oðinn. The beloved son is to be slain by his own brother, despite his mother's efforts to protect him. The *völva* foresees the binding of Loki who brought about that slaying, and all the woe that follows as things fall apart.

The *völva* repeatedly challenges Oðinn with the refrain: "Know ye further, or how?" *Vituð ér enn, eða hvat?* literally means, "Know you yet, or what?" Lindow translates, "Would you know yet more?"[179] and Dronke: "Do you still seek to know? and what?"[180] Again and again the *völva* repeats this majestic phrase, circling back to it in a rhythmic punctuation that savors of long-established ceremonial verse.

The prophetic giantess Hyndla repeats a similar phrase, "wilt thou know further?" (*viltu ennlengra*) in a poem known as the "Shorter Völuspá."[181] The witch Busla speaks a comparable line (*e a viltu flulu lengri*) in *Bósa saga*.[182] When the old ways remained intact, the *völur* would have pronounced ritualized questions of this kind in their oracular ceremonies. Except for these few fragments, their oracular litanies, their *seiðlati* and *varðlokkur* have been obliterated.

RAGNAROK: DOOM OF THE POWERS

The greater part of the *Völuspá* foretells the end of the Aesir's world. The *völva* names the fell powers who will attack creation—the Serpent gnawing, the Wolf rending—and now another refrain emerges: the chilling image of a terrible hound of destruction:

> **Garm bays loudly before Gnipa cave**
> **Breaks his fetters and freely runs.**[183]

The seeress prophesies the atrocities of war unleashed on humanity, that same war that Oðinn delighted in provoking, and gloried in as a victor. Now he becomes its victim, and falls to a more powerful assailant, undone by his own calculus of "might makes right." The warnings against the rule of violence have gone unheeded, and so the decline into mayhem becomes inevitable:

> Brothers will battle to bloody end
> And sisters' sons their sib betray[184]

The oracle speaks of an "axe-age, sword-age… wind-age, wolf-age," as the world is riven by terrible wars: "Will the spear of no man spare the other."[185] The male Aesir fall in battle. The Tree of Life shudders, as land sinks under the ocean. The sun dims, the stars fall, and the world is on fire.

In this destruction, the fate of the goddesses is left unspoken; the poem alludes only to Frigg's sorrow at the loss of her loved ones. However, at the end of *Heimskringla*—which is notorious for treating the deities as historical characters—Snorri nevertheless comments, "Freyja alone remained of the gods."[186] The life principle survives, in the form of the Vanadís. And so the *Völuspá* concludes by foretelling regeneration after the horrors:

> I see green again with growing things
> the earth arise from out of the sea
> fell torrents flow, overflies them the eagle
> on hoar highlands which hunts for fish.[187]

Another Eddic poem, the *Vafthrúðnismál*, echoes this account. A wise giant predicts that before the wolf Fenrir swallows the sun ("Elf-Beam"), she will bear a daughter orb. "On her mother's path will the maiden fare," after the Aesir fall at Ragnarok.[188] A pair of humans survive too; Life and Life-Speeder, the future ancestors, hide in a grove.[189] Baldr returns, and Njörðr will "come back home to the wise—the future-knowing—Vanir."[190] The surviving Aesir meet on the plain where their ancestors once played draughts, and find the fallen golden pieces in the grass. As Jochens points out, the poem's masculine bias is repeated in St. 63, as the Earth is "repopulated by a pair of males without the mention of women," as it began.[191]

The *Völuspá* concludes by abruptly shifting back to the pagan seeress herself. Having spoken her prophecy, she subsides or falls back: "now she will sink." This passage has always struck me as referring to the *völva* sinking back into her meditative trance after delivering her prophecy, like a shaman at the end of a powerful ceremony.

The seeress of Völuspá has often been interpreted as a giantess who is returning into the earth. But some writers insist on treating her as a dead *völva* who has unwillingly been summoned from the grave, as Oðinn does to the *völva* buried outside the gates of Hel in *Baldrs draumr*. Jenny Jochens remonstrates, "Scholars have often, but without grounds, interpreted the relationship between the two as one in which Oðinn is able to force her to speak."[192] As the *Völuspa* makes clear, the *völva* is *not* dead and buried when Oðinn approaches her, but is engaged in the spiritual practice of "sitting out." Recall, too, how the poem opens with the *völva* addressing an assemblage of hearers in a ceremonial manner. Her prophecies to Oðinn occur within this larger frame story, not the other way around.

Ursula Dronke saw the poem as encompassing two *völur*: one a living prophetess, and the other an ancestral *spákona* who speaks through her. The seeress alternates between "she" and "I." Dronke interpreted that "I" as the voice of a spirit speaking through her: "She knows," and "she sat out," but "well know I, Oðinn," and "the fates I fathom, yet farther I see," and "I saw." So "now she will sink" reads "as if this visionary 'she' must descend like a spirit back into the underworld of the dead—where all the seeds of prophecy lie—now that she has served the purpose for which the human *völva* summoned her."[193]

CHRISTIAN REINTERPRETATIONS

Christian influences are apparent in *Völuspá*, as has often been noted.[194] Toward the poem's end, two lines are inserted proclaiming the Christian last judgement: "Then will come the powerful one to the mighty Judgment."[194] (These lines appear only in *Hauksbók*, not in *Codex Regius*.) The *Völuspá hin skamma* also contains a revisionist foretelling that a great and mighty god will come.[195]

Hauksbók 65 treats Baldr as a sacrificial stand-in for Jesus—he too is resurrected in the end-times—but in a story that is still heathen. Dronke compares a phrase in *Völuspá* 39, 3-4 to a sermon of the English cleric Wulf-stan: "and to designate Baldr as 'sacrifice,' the poet uses a term he could have heard in England used of Christ—*tívorr*: it occurs nowhere else in Norse." But it is used in Old English translations of the Bible.[196]

Themes from Christian Latin texts are evident in the apocalyptic portions of the *Völuspá*. John McKinnell compares them to close parallels in the Vercelli Homily, and in verses in Revelations and Genesis that were used in Easter readings to convert Norse pagans.[197] But he affirms that the poem itself is heathen: "Even if we accept every possible scriptural, liturgical, and homiletic parallel, only about twenty of the poem's sixty-six stanzas show Christian influence, and those that do are not always understood in a Christian way."[198]

Such influences (or tamperings) are unsurprising, considering that the *Völuspá* was written down after the old religion was outlawed. It is striking how much pagan content yet remains in the poetic Edda. The beloved old myths were passed on orally by a population that was nominally Christian. Most importantly, the attributes of the *völva*—her sacred wands, her knowledge of the *seið*, her seership—were rooted in heathendom, a spiritual tradition in which prophecy was a predominantly female sphere.

However colored by christian themes, these prophecies have pagan precedents. Garret Olmsted compared the *Völuspá* to end-time Indo-European prophecies in the Greek *Ergai kai Hemerai* and the Irish *Cath Maige Tuiread*. In the latter, the Morrigan foretells a future collapse of world order. The land loses its fertility, as injustice and war reign: "... many slaves from the mouth of the womb, woods without mast, sea without produce... crimes at every encounter... a slashing of wombs, false judgments from the ancient..."[199]

Ancient mythic and historical traditions survived in the *Völuspá*, notably stories of conquest and patriarchal attackers burning the "prophetic *völva*, enchanter of wands." Pagan society contained its own male supremacist faultlines, as shown by the legendary persecutions of Gothic *haliorunnae*, or the Roman suppression of the "bacchanals," which were really female-led mysteries in a syncretic multi-ethnic spiritual movement.[200]

But repression of the seeresses gained momentum under the Christian regime. The new religion excluded wisewomen from its all-male priesthood, while banning them from practicing their own spiritual ways. The shift is also visible in the omissions and reinterpretations of Christian skálds like Snorri (who drew on Latin Christian texts).[201] Later medieval sagas increasingly villainized and demonized the *völur*.

Christianization interrupted transmission of the old oral traditions, though not entirely. The versions we now possess were edited and revised by the recording clerics, reflecting their own outlook. The skálds could continue performing pagan epics only by salting them with disclaimers to mollify their elite patrons. This may have been when the *völva* Heiðr, and the women who took joy in the *seið* rite, were redefined as "evil." Or maybe that shift dates earlier, to the triumph of Odinism as a ruling ideology, in which male lords treated women's power as a threat.

FEMALE VOICES, FEMALE SPACES

A female author for the *Völuspá* has been proposed,[202] but Jenny Jochens gives compelling reasons for thinking that a man composed the poem— not least its "strikingly male" viewpoint and language. It is told in the voice of a prophetess, but nevertheless the *Völuspá* presents an all-male cosmogony that amounts to an "absence of the goddesses."[203]

Jochens is aware of seven named female skálds, "but they seem almost to be anomalies..."[204] Sandra Straubhaar identifies more, by using much looser criteria that includes the speech of giantesses and other supernaturals. Straubhaar identifies two groups of *skáldkonur* in Norway and Iceland. One group composed in the *drónkvætt* "court meter" that was used by poets in the employ of lordly families. The rest of the female skálds composed in a visionary mode: "Their style is chant-like and simple, using eddic meters, such as *fornyrðislag* ["ancient meter"] and *galdralag* ["meter of "incantation"] rather than *drónkvætt*."[205]

From all female poets, the longest fragment to survive is only eight stanzas long. This paucity says something about how they fared in a male-dominated environment.[206] The failure of culture-keepers to value and preserve women's words, in a constant attrition, has a global context. The words of Korinna, Sosipatra and Hypatía now exist only in fragments. A bit more survives from Sappho—but little in comparison to her male counterparts. The same is true for Gargi in India, or for Wei furen in China, the legendary adept who was credited with founding Shangqing Taoism. Patriarchal literati have a way of disregarding and devaluing women's poetry and women's philosophy.

Among the *galdralag* poems, writes Straubhaar, women skálds refer to incantation, vision, trance and prophecy much more than their male counterparts. She expands on Barði Guðmundsson's association of early Norse female poetry with ceremonial and prophetic culture, veneration of the Vanir, and preservation of the matronymic. Straubhaar agrees with his view that both *seiðr* and poetry were "female-dominated arts in early Nordic society."[207] She speaks of a possible golden age of *skáldkonur,* which was followed by a "dissociation" of poetic composition "from its original, female-dominated cultic or religious environment, in favor of a male-dominated court environment."[208] Straubhaar sees Oðinn's theft of the poetry-mead from Gunnlöð—standing in for the female chthonic deities—as a symbolic summation of this patriarchalizing shift.

The *Völuspá* does not present unmediated female power, nor even a woman's cosmovision. It has been strained through the masculine filter of the skálds. And yet its framework, its defining context, is that of women's prophecy, sought by men and gods alike. Those ceremonies were spaces shaped by women, defined by women, who gave voice to the Divine. They influenced and guided the communities to whom they chanted prophecies. Their oracular power shaped reality, even though they were not immune to the constraints of a patriarchal warrior society. Modern society vaunts the advances made by women, but has no comparable sphere of female power.

The orature of the *völur* gave way to texts written by Christian men. It was subjected to the historical techtonics that shaped what survived, what we can know about. However great their impact once was, in the end the words of those real women were not cherished in memory like those of the skálds, but were allowed to drain away into the sands of time. Only a few shreds of their litanies remain:

know ye further, or how?

swa swa wiccan taecað ::: as the witches teach

So a translator editorialized on an old Frankish condemnation of people who "bring their offerings to earth-fast stone and also to trees and to wellsprings," by adding the Old English phrase "*as the witches teach.*" His comment on a Latin penitential directly contradicts the idea that witches were seen as evildoers. Instead, it intimately associates them with animist ceremonies, earth-based spiritual customs.

The prevailing assumption is that Europe was fully christianized by the early medieval period covered in this book. Many academicians insist on this viewpoint as indubitable fact. But the bishops, canonists, and writers of penitential manuals thought otherwise, and explicitly said so in any number of texts. In the late 700s, the *Homilia de Sacrilegiis* said that anyone who goes to consult diviners "in the hidden place" "is not a Christian, but a pagan." Burchard of Worms was still using the same formula in 1015. In between, the Council of Paris declared that "witches, diviners, and enchanters" practiced "very certainly the remains of the pagan cult."[1] They did not deny the religious dimensions of their competition, but demonized their goddesses.

The subject of these religions has been marginalized at best, and often cast as a threat. Information about the repressed folkways has to be pulled out, and it comes out piecemeal, with yawning gaps. Only by regathering these broken strands together can we envision what the cultural web might have looked like, and bring women back into focus. In revindicating the reviled and forbidden heritages, we begin to grasp what Europe once had in common with other world cultures, whether that was ancestor reverence or sacral sweat-houses, sacred staffs or chanting over herbs.

It is a challenging task to reassemble a mosaic from which most pieces are missing. In mythic history there are both continuities and discontinuities. Even the continuities can be tricky because the literate recorders were hostile witnesses who strained everything through their own doctrinal template. To rule out the later testimony of folk culture, the only form of history from the common people we have access to, is to continue the erasure of authentic narratives, however historically transformed they may be. To foreclose these connections simply perpetuates the politicized eclipse of long-prohibited culture by the supercessionist christian overlay, with its diabolist obsession.

These nine chapters present aspects of a larger story from different vantage points. Here it is historical, there mythic, then archaeological; and all of these must be integrated. The megalithic section in the Cailleach chapter is less neolithic history than an account of culture that has grown up around those sacred places. Culture means tending growth; it is what has grown over time, in place. The word "cult" can no longer be used without the burden of two millennia of pejorative use, but that is what it originally meant: a specific body of ceremony— with all its symbols, icons, stories, songs, dances, litanies, feasts, and sanctuaries—that had grown up over centuries or millennia.

Early medieval cultures changed under constant ecclesiastical pressure. At a certain point in time it was meaningful to say of a popular Germanic folk goddess, "A third part of the world is given over to her." But that meant something different to the clergy than for the people whose beliefs they were describing, especially when it came to who *she* was. Over time, in a rapidly changing cultural landscape, the theme of "one third of the world" following a goddess was unmoored from its original context and transformed with new, sexualizing stories in which Herodias is punished by John the Baptist. As the common culture shifted under pressure, the names of this goddess gave way to priestly redefinition, and mixed and intertwined with it in new ways. Mother Earth nursing snakes became Luxuria the sinful symbol of lust and temptation. Future volumes go into this process in depth.[2]

In spite of everything that we've been taught about the profoundly secondary status of the female, what women did in the spiritual realm mattered. The wisewomen had oracular authority and healing wisdom and ceremonial leadership, even after being stripped of any institutional base. But these female spheres of power faced intense challenges from church, state, and from within the patriarchal family. Sexual politics was closely bound up with witchcraft, with the gendering of *seiðr*, the cries of "witch and whore" in England, and with why the Spanish treated burning at the stake as a female punishment.

At the center of the furnace of cultural transformation was the development of diabolism—a Christian projection of "the devil" onto all ethnic deities. It has had a lasting impact. The namecalling of "devil worship" formed the template for repressing goddess veneration and, later, Indigenous religions on other continents. It still influences scholarly and popular interpretations of witches, witchcraft, and heathen spiritual traditions.

The bottom line is that people who aren't academic specialists have a right to know about this past. I have done my best to uncover it, and more remains to be found out. There's always a better source over the next hill. Future volumes look at priestesses and witches in Greece, Italy, and the Celtic world; the great syncretism of the Magna Mater and the rise of Christianity; sexual politics in the Roman empire and the imperial church. Readers looking for more about Spain, France, and Italy will find it in the forthcoming Vol. VI, *Women in a Time of Overlords*, which goes into the sexual politics of law, and the class and ethnic politics of slavery and serfdom. Vol. VIII, *Priestcraft in the Sword-Age*, looks at Slavic history and culture, the Crusades, theocracy, pagan stones, sheela-na-gigs, and apocryphal saints.

Later volumes follow the explosion of diabolist ideology, the sorcery charge, the Inquisition, torture trials and the witch-hunting Terror: burnings, witches' bridles and "devil's marks." They also survey the Witches' Goddess, faery faith and folk rites, peasant revolts and "heretical" movements, and crusades against pagan Europeans. Further along, the series examines "women possessed" in the crucible of modern "Western" civilization, patterns of persecution, and the export of diabolist ideologies as Europeans colonized the world.

An outline of the Secret History of the Witches can be found at:
www.veleda.net/secrethistory/contents

Excerpts from advance chapters of forthcoming volumes:
See also **https://suppressedhistories.academia.edu/MaxDashu**

Index for this volume: **www.veleda.net/witchesandpagans/index/**

Glossary of terms: **www.veleda.net/witchesandpagans/glossary**

Commentaries: **www.veleda.net/witchesandpagans/commentaries**

Chapter 1: Webs of Wyrd

1. St. 12 and 20. My translation after Bellows, Hollander, Bray. Hauksbók and Snorri have *sal*, "hall," while Codex Regius has *sae*, "lake."
2. Blind, 80
3. *Völuspá* 20; *Gylfaginning* 15, in Lindow, 40. West (383) gives "Happened," "Happening," and "Due."
4. Fick, Falk & Torp, 459
5. Quinn 1998: 31, n. 6
6. Lindow, 39
7. Bauschatz, 13
8. Oxford 2nd Ed, Vol XX, p 102
9. *Fáfnismál* 44. More examples at www.nordic-life.org/nmh/OrlogEddaEng.htm
10. *Gylfaginning* 22; Grimm, 407; 1399
11. Grimm, 857
12. *Fáfnismál* 44
13. Bek-Pedersen, 271
14. Grimm, 406
15. Grimm, 408, cites the Poetic Edda; but *vísa nornir* appears to come from the younger *Hrafnagaldr Oðins* 1.
16. *Grógaldr* 4. See www.nordic-life.org/nmh/OrlogEddaEng.htm
17. Clunies Ross I, 242
18. *Norna-domr*, "judgment of Norns," in *Fáfnismál* 11-15, in Clunies Ross I, 237
19. *Ynglingatal* 24, in *Ynglingasaga* 47
20. Snorri Sturluson, in Branston, 169
21. *Vafthrúðnismál* 48, in Blind, 108
22. *Gylfaginning* 15, in Lindow, 243-4
23. Blind, 109
24. *Gylfaginning* 16
25. Thanks to MaryLena Lynx for making this point, citing Dumont's article.
26. Dumont, online
27. Larrington, 4
28. Bray, 276
29. Lindow, 207
30. *Gylfaginning* 39, *Grímnismál* 25, 26
31. Okladnikov, P. A. *Arkhiv Yakutskogo Filiala: Lenskiye Pesni*. Rest of cite lost.

32. *Vafthrúðnismál* 49, my translation
33. Hall 2004: 38; see also Turville-Petre 1964: 222
34. *Fáfnismál* 13, in Clunies Ross, 244; and www.nordic-life.org/nmh/OrlogEddaEng.htm
35. *Fáfnismál* 12
36. *Reginsmál* 14, in West, 385
37. *Helgakviða Hundingsbana* I, 2-4, in Larrington 1996: 115
38. Larrington 1996: 115
39. DuBois, 112-13
40. Bek-Pedersen, 273; Freitag, 84
41. Karsten, 39
42. Bellows 1923: 242
43. *Fjölsvinnsmál* 22, in Bray, 166; the male default emended to "humanity."
44. Many scholars see this connection of fates and Matronae. See for example Lecouteux (2001: 19); Ginzburg 1993: 105-6 and 117 n. 67; Hodge, online.
45. Grimm, 1400
46. Blind 1879: 191
47. Grimm, 1400. See also West (384) on the Slavic and Baltic fates.
48. Mencej, 73-74
49. Mencej, 72
50. Pócs, 75, n. 119
51. Mencej, 73
52. Mencej, 73
53. Machal 1918: 252
54. Greimas, 112-5
55. West, 384
56. Lecouteux 2003: 164
57. Andersons, 1953
58. Jirasek, 7. Tekla remains a women's name in Hungary and Poland.
59. Borsje, 230; see also West, 384
60. Borsje, 215-17, 222
61. Borsje, 217, n. 14
62. Harf-Lancner, 21
63. *Corrector sive Medicus* 5, 151, in Lea, 184; and McNeill/Gamer, 338
64. *Corrector sive Medicus* 5, 151, in Lea, 184; and McNeill and Gamer, 338

65. Grimm, 415-16
66. Anglia xiii, 31, 104, in Toller, s.v. "Witch"
67. Bauschatz, 14
68. West, 381
69. Mencej 2011: 380
70. West, 380
71. West, 380
72. Pócs 1989: 26
73. West, 381, see also n. 19
74. Ann and Imer, 69
75. Borsje, 218, n. 14
76. Palmer, 91-3, 108-9
77. Originally *fata* was a neuter plural, but came to be understood as a feminine singular word. See Williams, 462.
78. Palmer, 89, 109-14
79. van der Horst, 217-22
80. Harkness, 81
81. Harf-Lancner, 20
82. Harf-Lancner, 22
83. Williams, 457, 462
84. Williams, 463
85. Williams, 465
86. Williams, 463
87. Williams, 464
88. Bauschatz, 8
89. *Etymologiae* 8. 11.93, in Harf-Lancner, 21
90. Bauschatz (10) proposes a derivation of Parcae from *parere*, "to bear," and West (381) from *pario*, "to give birth," by way of *paricae*, "bearers."
91. *Etymologiae*, VIII.11.90, in Cortés, 209
92. *Etymologiae*, X, 103. Cortés, 248; and Grimm, 405
93. Harf-Lancner, 60, 76, 49
94. See etymology of "fairy" in Oxford, Webster's, or any good dictionary.
95. For German studies on the linkage of Matronae, Parcae, and the faery tradition, see Ginzburg, 117 n. 117.
96. Turville-Petre, 227, links the Matronae and Modranecht with the *dísir*, as does Simek 2007: 220, 205-207. See chapter 6.
97. *De Temporum Ratione* 15, in Wallis, 53
98. Rhys 1901: 174
99. Filotas, 76; Beck, 88-89
100. Enright 1996: 247 n. 43
101. West, 383
102. Garman, 47-8
103. Samplonius 1995: 85
104. Described in Enright 1996: 247 n. 43
105. Sebillot 1904: I, 35, my translation.
106. The range of meanings for faery spirits is a vast subject, considered in depth in Dashu, Vol X, forthcoming
107. Picart, online.
108. van Gerrit van Goedesbergh, "Met Witte Wieven in Grafheuvels," online.
109. See Dashu, Vol VI, forthcoming
110. Kauffmann, 16; Grimm, 1399
111. Compact OED, 3731
112. Dorothy Whitelock, *The Beginnings of English Society*, in Branston, 59
113. Whiting and Whiting, 636
114. West, 383
115. Old Frisian law 49.10, in Grimm, 857
116. Halsall, 13, 102
117. *Beowulf* I, 455, in Whiting and Whiting, 636
118. *Heliand* 146, 2, in Grimm, 406
119. *Heliand* 163, 16, in Grimm, 406
120. *Beowulf*, in Grimm, 406
121. Codex Exonius 312, 27, in http://bosworth.ff.cuni.cz/036952; see also Bauschatz, 8
122. R.W.V. Elliott, in Bouman, A.C. "The Franks Casket," *Neophilologus* 3 (1965), 241-9. Proposed readings include Sigurdr's horse weeping over his tomb; the Saxon legend of Hengist and Horsa; the punishment of Rhiannon in horse form (though the figure in question has the head of a deer, not horse); and even the mad Nebuchadnezzar, casting the three hooded women as his wives! Daniel Howlett sees the three

wood-maidens giving Hother a belt of victory in the *Gesta Danorum*; but would an English carver have known this story five centuries earlier?

123. Branston, 60

124. Grimm, 406

125. *Codex Exoniensis* 355, in Grimm, 1399; 406

126. Branston, 59

127. Shetelig and Falk, 435; West, 386

128. Miller 2008: 71-2

129. *Ðonne seó þrág cymeþ wefen wyrdstafum.* Toller translates *wefen* figuratively as "fixed." From "Legend of St Guthlac," Codex Exoniensis, in Toller, 1288; http://bosworth.ff.cuni.cz/036962. On *rūnstæf, see H*alsall, 7.

130. Guthlac 1350f, in West, 383

131. http://bosworth.ff.cuni.cz/036952

132. Whiting and Whiting, 636

133. Branston, 57

134. Branston, 57-8

135. Note in Albert's translation of Boethius, in Branston, 59

136. Barbour, Bruce, I. 87, 148-50, in Whiting and Whiting, 636

137. Gower, 376, written circa ca. 1390. For the pervasiveness of Wyrd in Old English culture, see the wealth of cites at http://bosworth.ff.cuni.cz/036952.

138. Beowulf line 696, in Branston, 58

139. The full line runs, "Ne hert mai think than ioies sere, that iesus christ has dight til his, that weirded er unto the bliss." Curson Ms 23358, in *Compact Oxford*, II, 3731

140. Branston, 57. He discusses the Christian god's competition with Wyrd for the title of all-powerful deity.

141. Romance of Alexander the Great, in Stevenson 1849:10

142. Oxford 2nd Ed, Vol. XX, 102

143. *Legend of Good Women*, in Branston, 60; Grimm, 407, cites Chaucer's *Troilus* 3, 733 as well

144. Vol VIII, 1862, in *Compact Oxford*, 3731

145. Grimm, 407

146. Holinshed, 243-44

147. Branston, 64

148. Heylin, *Microcosmos*, 1625, in Oxford Dictionary 2nd Ed, Vol XX, 102

149. http://shakespeare.mit.edu/macbeth/macbeth.4.1.html

150. Macbeth, Act I, Scene 3

151. www.etymonline.com/index.php?term=eldritch

152. B. Brierley, *Chron. Waverlow*, xv, in Oxford 2nd Ed. Vol XX, 103. *Rice* (pronounced *rikeh*) is cognate with German Reich, Indic Raj, and other Indo-European state-names.

153. Macbeth, Act IV, Scene 1

154. Denham 1895: 81

155. Eckenstein, 39

156. MaryLena Lynx, personal communication, Sept 6, 2014

157. Grimm, 1402

158. Grimm, 1533

159. Whiting and Whiting, 1968; Compact Oxford, 1971, s.v. "weird,"

160. Mather, online

161. See Silverblatt 1987

162. Grimm, 1108-12

163. See http://www.bosworthtoller.com/035323; and http://www.bosworthtoller.com/035322

164. *Loddfáfnir, Hávamal* 111, in Hollander, 35

165. Grimm, 1456

166. Grimm, 585-6

167. Grimm, 584

168. Filotas, 204

169. *Corrector Sive Medicus*, 57, in McNeill and Gamer, 331. See also Caspari, 19. Filotas (205) gives a long list of pagan offerings, including making lights and other devotions at springs, trees, stones and groves, in penitential books.

170. Kauffmann, 38; Grimm, 1454

171. Plutarch, in Kaufmann, 38
172. Brand et al, 379. The poet shows that solitary meditations were dangerous for women; Sir John pushes her head into the stream and rapes her.
173. Grimm, 1166
174. *Canones Edgari* (not really royal laws, but penned by an unknown cleric), in Grimm, 1166
175. *De Auguriis*: Online, 75
176. Book 19.5, 179, in Filotas, 151
177. Filotas, 251
178. Grimm, 1177
179. Grimm, 1166; Filotas, 263
180. Wood-Martin 1895: 308-9
181. Filotas, 197, 262
182. After Tillman's *Folklig Läkekonst* 1962: 56
183. McNeill/Gamer, 198
184. Filotas, 195-6
185. *Compact Oxford* s.v worship; weirding
186. Malinowksi, 220
187. Ibid
188. British Library Cotton manuscript Caligula A, vii. See Earle, online
189. West, 177
190. Grimm, 253
191. West, 177. *Fira* is literally "men," the masculine default.
192. Berger, 66. See also Earle, online.
193. Prologue to the Prose Edda, in West, 177
194. West, 180

Chapter 2: Wyccecræft

1. Leto in Pindar's Nemean Ode 6 and Melia, nymph of the Ismenean Spring in his Fragment 29; Helen in Odyssey 4, and the Graces (Charites) in Fragment 9 of Bacchalides. Thanks to Yonas Theodoros for these citations.
2. Skafte Jensen, 56

3. Pliny, Nat. Hist. 8.74
4. Enna, 44, 78-81
5. http://lolo1955gravoline.blogspot.com/2013/12/ce-que-signifie-vraiment-la-quenelle.html
6. Jeunehomme, online
7. More examples in Beck, 88-89
8. See Ross 1967
9. *Capitula*, in McKenna 101, 98 fn
10. See Ross, 1967; MacCulloch 1918:
11. Levison, online, emphasis added
12. *mulieres in tela sua Minervam nominare...cultura diaboli*, in MacMullen 1997:186 n. 50
13. Flint, 226
14. *Homilia de sacrilegis* III, 9, in Caspari, 7; Filotas, 243
15. Menendez-Pelayo I, 585
16. Filotas, 70-71
17. West, 36-38
18. Gregory 1971, 15
19. Bitel, 130
20. Kinsella, 60-3; Lysaght, 203
21. McCone, 228
22. Enright, 173
23. West 2013: 470-2
24. O'Rahilly, quoted in West 2013: 471
25. *De Devortiis Lotharii*, 656, in Grimm, 1099
26. Grimm, 1119-28
27. Flint, 227; 56-7 n. 60
28. *De Dev. Loth.* 654, in Grimm, 654
29. Clunies Ross II, 38-40. See *Carmina Gadelica* for Scottish chants over cloth.
30. Saxo Grammaticus, *Gesta Danorum* II, online
31. I translated drawing on four sources. Filotas (264-5) provides the key to interpretation: the weavers are ensuring that the warp threads do not get tangled, which destroys the web; but she leaves out the specificity of "incantations," rendered simply as "spells." McNeill and Gamer (330) and (Lea: 1957) make it seem as if the women were attempting

to destroy their own weaving, which as Filotas points out (265) makes no sense. Meaney's translation (185) makes it look like a curse, but this depends on translating *totum*, "all" or "the whole," as "he."
32. *Corrector sive Medicus* 104, in McNeill and Gamer, 335
33. Filotas, 78
34. Sonia Hawkes, in Meaney, 181
35. Meaney 1981: 185
36. Asser's *Vita Alfredi* (the *Anglo-Saxon Chronicle*), in Grimm, 1112; thanks to Eileen Berkun for translation.
37. *Encommium Emmae*, in Grimm, 1112
38. Ellis Davidson 1973: 118
39. Kauffman, 55
40. Tolley, 27
41. The poem is in *Njáls saga*, www. orkneyjar.com/tradition/darra.htm
42. See www.bosworthtoller. com/034302, and Grimm, 997, citing *wælcæsig* in Caedmon 188
43. Ross 1973: 158
44. Wood-Martin, 1902: 278
45. *Cath Maige Tuired: The Second Battle of Mag Tuired*, online
46. Agathias 2,6, in Grimm, 1315
47. Sklute, 208
48. *Bretha Crólige*, in Bitel, 277 n. 64
49. Thorpe, Vol II, 614
50. Johnson, 415. This text purports to be from the laws of king Edgar, but was written by an unknown churchman. See McNeill and Gamer, 409
51. www.bosworthtoller.com/046481
52. www.bosworthtoller.com/012425
53. Flint, 206 n. 7
54. von Cles-Reden, 160
55. Saunders, 89-90; http://bosworth. ff.cuni.cz/017343
56. Flint, 286-87
57. Meaney, 187-88
58. http://irisharchaeology.ie/2013/05/the-moylough-belt-shrine/. The Life of Brigit in the *Book of Lismore* tells how

the saint gave her belt to a poor beggar woman of Huí Maic Uais, "and Brigit said that it would heal whatsoever disease or illness to which it was applied." After that, the woman earned her living from doing healings with this belt. See Duignan (90), thanks to Mary Condren.
59. "Witch," in Murray, et al, Vol X, Part II (V-Z), 206
60. Liberman, 218
61. Oxford English Dictionary s.v. witch
62. Grimm, 1033
63. Grimm, 1033
64. Robbins, 544
65. Grimm, 1033. He (975) translated *wicken* as "to play the witch, tell fortunes," emphasizing the divinatory arts.
66. MaryLena Lynx, personal communication, Oct 1, 2014
67. Summers, 468
68. Dashu, *Woman Shaman: the Ancients*, 2013: www.suppressedhistories. net/wosha_transcript/disc2/staffs.html
69. Law 29, in Bosworth and Toller, www.bosworthtoller.com/026828
70. Dashu, Vol VI, *Overlords*
71. Lionarons, 104
72. Aelfric's *Homilies*, in www.ealdriht. org/witchcraft.html
73. Meaney 1981: 257. Crawford (1963: 111) translates *tham gramlican wiccan* as "these grim witches."
74. Aelfric, "The Passion of St Bartholemew the Apostle," 477, in Thorpe, 184
75. Homilies of Aelfric, online
76. Grimm, 1616; Crawford 1992: 169
76a. De Cauzons, 118
77. Levack 2015: 2. This definition was written by one of the most prominent scholars of witchcraft.
78. Ferraro and Andreatta, 347
79. The classic definition was set down by Evans-Pritchard, 9-10
80. Lecouteux 2001: 86
81. Scot, V, 9. 62, online

82. Cybeleia, 17
83. Storms, 37
84. Weston 1995: 285. She is actually called *ides*; see chapter 4.
85. Matossian, 120
86. T. Gwynn Jones 1979: 126. The original, feminine form in Welsh would have been Ystol Y Gwiddones.
87. Lieberman, 217-18
88. Lieberman, 220. For more see North (97) who shows Anglo-Saxons often used *weoh/wig* to mean "idol."
89. Lieberman, 218. He says that G is commonly exchanged for K or for H in Germanic tongues, but not L, making a change from *wiglera* to *wicce* unlikely.
90. Russell 1980: Appendix
91. Lieberman, 217
92. Lieberman, 218-20. It used to be thought that the Latin word *victim* came from the *wihs root, in the sense of a consecrated sacrifice, but a growing consensus has it deriving from an independent homonym meaning "to fight," along with "victor." Because of phonological complications (Verner's Law shifting H with G), the German verb *wihan*, "consecrate" has been confused with *wigan*, "fight."
93. Lieberman, 218
94. Liberman, 223
95. Hall 2004: 171, n. 218
96. Lieberman, 218
97. Russell 1980: 12. Nor is *warlock* related to Norse *varðlokkr*, contra what is claimed on the internet.
98. Cybeleia, 17
99. Lieberman (221) issues a caution on phonological grounds, since the German "wake" words differ from the Old English, Frisian and Middle Low German forms, as well as the Latin ones.
100. *American Heritage Dictionary*, 2131
101. Cybeleia,18
102. From film script. www.veryabc.cn/

movie/uploads/script/TheSecretGarden. txt Wording in the book differs a bit.
103. *Compact Oxford*, 3798
104. Grimm, 1687
105. Denham (1895: 329) cites old sources that derive rowan from "rune," but the root turns out to mean "red," after the brilliant berries.
106. See Davidson 1949 on beliefs and rites around rowan.
107. Olmsted, 200
108. MacCulloch 1930: 54
109. MacCulloch 1918: 54, 130-31
110. Flint, 228
111. Flint, 247
112. Campbell, 84. Carmichael (284) defines *eolas* (*eoilse, eior*) as "spell, charm, magic, exorcism, knowledge."
113. Wood-Martin 1895: 154
114. Meaney 1981: 10
115. Meaney 1981: 14
116. Both in Grimm, 1174
117. Thorpe, Vol 2, 24
118. West, 337; Grimm, 1233
119. Atharva Veda 4.12. 2-6, in West, 337
120. Turville-Petre, 123
121. http://www.ucc.ie/celt/LGQS.pdf
122. Carmichael, 129-30. Other versions interpolate "Christ" for Bríde.
123. Turville-Petre, 123. For more on this healer, see Dashu, www.source-memory.net/veleda/?p=638
124. Carmichael, 628
125. Day, 48
126. Day, 66
127. Day, 76
128. Trevelyan, 75
129. Trevelyan, 75
130. *Corrector sive Medicus* 92, in McNeill and Gamer, 334
131. Trevelyan, 75
132. Flint, 226
133. Condren, 83; Bitel, 75, calls it a "weaver's hook."
134. See West 2013: 468-73. Thanks to

Mary Condren for this reference.
135. Condren 1989: 83
136. West, 37
137. Mencej, 61

Chapter 3: Names of the Witch

1. Magnusson IV, 452
2. This chapter goes into too many etymologies to provide citations for all the dictionaries I've used. Look them up!
3. *Völuspá* 29, in Hollander, 6 (emended)
4. Lambert, 167
5. Meyer 1906:176; West, 28
6. Lambert, 167. Fedelm is romanized here as Fedelma; also spelled Feidelm.
7. West, 28. On Veleda, see Dashu, www.sourcememory.net/veleda/?p=8
8. Kinsella, 239
9. Kinsella, 239, 356, 124
10. Meyer 1906: 176
11. O Crualaoich, 72
12. Chadwick, online
13. Chadwick / Dillon 1972: 153
14. www.teanglann.ie/en/fgb/banfháidh
15. West, 27
16. Meyer 1906: 176, citing the *Book of Leinster*
17. West, 28
18. Filotas, 219. A *mulier divinator* is also mentioned.
19. *Etymologiae* VIII, 9.14, in Filotas, 228-9
20. Grimm, 1615
21. Filotas, 233, 250
22. Filotas, 96
23. *Homilia de sacrilegiis* III, 5, in Caspari, 6
24. More on the *ariolae* and their rites will be in my forthcoming volume, *Women in a Time of Overlords.*
25. Filotas, 95, 231
26. Filotas, 239
27. *Pseudo-Theodore*, in Filotas, 131

28. Harkness, 70
29. *The Online Etymological Dictionary*, s.v. sorcery.
30. Filotas, 170
31. Filotas, 172
32. Council of Paris to Louis the Pious, in Filotas, 221
33. Wedeck, 257
34. Filotas, 292
35. Filotas, 236
36. Filotas, 243-4
37. Mattias Lexer, *Mittlehochdeutsches Handwörterbuch*, in Brauner, 135, n. 39
38. Anglo-Saxon *swefn reccan*, Old Norse *draum rāda*, in Grimm 1145
39. Flint, 217; Filotas, 227ff
40. Filotas, 220-21. She says that "women tend to vanish behind the inclusive masculine words in all but approximately six percent of the texts studied." But "inclusive" is not the right description for a linguistic convention that obliterates the presence of women.
41. Shetelig and Falk, 423
42. Bosworth-Toller Dictionary: www.bosworthtoller.com/finder/3/fyrht
43. Winchester laws, in Thorpe Vol I, 162
44. Svenson, 18
45. Grimm, 1617
46. Baroja, 150
47. West, 36-8
48. Barandiaran, 79 (using the Spanish *afiletera*); Baroja, 232-3
49. Meaney 1981: 61-63
50. *a pithonibus et aruspicibus uana falsitatis deleramenta garrientibus*, *Prosa de virginitate*, chapter 44, in Hall 2004: 96
51. Antoine Furetière, online
52. Grimm, 1616. Hall 1916: 128 on *galdriggei*; Sweet (72) on *gealdricge* 53; Crawford, 159
54. Theodore XV, 4, in McNeill and Gamer, 198
55. Filotas, 249, n. 195
56. Filotas, 250, n. 207. She says that

this, and a single reference to a *herbaria,* are the only specific references to female practitioners in Caesarius.

57. Filotas, 283
58. Grimm, 1035
59. www.teanglann.ie/en/fgb/piseogach
60. www.etymonline.com/index. php?term=spell
61. Pirmin of Reichnau, in Filotas, 256
62. Chadwick, online. She notes that both stories present *imbas* as originating in Britain, where Fedelm goes to study *filidecht.* But most stories about these arts are about men, especially Finn MacCumhaill. The three arts are named in the *Uraicecht Becc* as *tenm laegda, imus forosnad,* and *dichedul do cennaib.* The Metrical Tractates in the *Book of Ballymote* and *Book of Leinster* also refer to them, again mostly about men in incubation rites with animal sacrifice.
63. Chadwick, online
64. Joyce, 238
65. Chadwick, online
66. Kinsella, 239, 356, 124
67. Chadwick, online
68. Hall 1916: 187. *Leoducræft*: Storms, 37
69. Some of these are given in West, 33.
70. Toller-Bosworth, 631. *Fundian* means "to try, aspire, intend, desire."
71. Fell 1991, 206-8, in Hall 2004: 124
72. Hall 2004: 124.
73. Meaney, 18-19; compare Mitchell, 64
74. *Sigrdrífumál* 17, in Bek-Pedersen, 274
75. Chambers, 539
76. Lambert, 154
77. *Fri brichta ban ocus goband ocus druad,* in Rhys 1901: 295
78. Grimm, 1616, 1068
79. Ralston, 420
80. Flint, 245. Caesarius described some of these acts in Sermo 184
81. Caesarius of Arles, Eligius of Noyon, and a 9th century penitential from Tours,

in Filotas, 254-5; 263
82. *Homilia de Sacrilegiis* V, 17, in Caspari, 10. Audrey Meaney (1981: 12) identifies the "serpents' tongues" as fossilized shark teeth.
83. Grimm, 1236
84. Grimm, 1151
85. Pughe, s.v. *swynaw;* 395; for *dar-swynws* he gives only the male form.
86. Day 49
87. Grimm, 1164
88. Freitag, 74
89. Grimm, 1651
90. Grimm, 1037; Bosworth-Toller online: www.bosworthtoller.com/021917
91. Hall 1916: 192
92. Toller, 647; www.bosworthtoller. com/021917
93. Cockayne, 397
94. Hall 1916: 192 also has "drug, poison, charm: witchcraft."
95. In more reductionist terms, Hall (1916: 192) calls *lybcræft* "skill in the use of drugs, magic, witchcraft."
96. Grimm, 1037, 1616, 1651
97. Meaney, 14; Grimm, 1103; Toller, 647
98. http://bosworth.ff.cuni.cz/021920
99. Cockayne, 397
100. Leechbook III, 41, in Meaney, 228
101. www.bosworthtoller.com/021917
102. L. Ecg. P. i. 8; Th. ii. 174, 34, in www.bosworthtoller.com/021917
103. Moriz, 87
104. Grimm, 1037
105. http://bosworth.ff.cuni.cz/021921
106. *Thurh heora galdor oððe lifesne oððe óðre dígolnesse deófolcræftes,* in Bede's *Historia Ecclesiastica,* 4, 27: http://bosworth.ff.cuni.cz/021920
107. Meaney, 14-15
108. Meaney, 257
109. Filotas, 28
110. Wulfstan. 194, 18, in www.bosworthtoller.com/033509
111. Shetelig and Falk, 415

112. Mitchell, 167. He translates *galldra* as "magic," which is certainly part of its broader meaning, though "incantation" is etymologically foremost.

113. *Svipdagsmál*, 52-54

114. Ellis Davidson, 2002: 163

115. Zurich Pap. MSS B 223-730, in Grimm, 1478-79. Thanks to Christina Schlatter for OHG translation.

116. Grimm, 1652, 1150

117. *mulieribus veneficis et qua diversa fingunt portenta*, in Filotas, 317; Lea 1957: 138 gives Herard's full text.

118. Filotas, 293

119. See Dashu, online: www.academia.edu/9833263/Herbs_Knots_and_Contraception

120. Price 2002: 231

121. Skeat, 375

122. North, 276. I've slightly altered his translation.

123. Filotas, 292

124. Bede IV. 27, in Colgrave and Mynors, 432-33

125. Grimm, 1616

126. Meaney (1981: 65) identifies BL MS Cotton Tiberius Aiii as the source. The term translated as "witch" is Lat. *malefica*; OE *yfeldæd(e)*, literally "evildoer."

127. Leechbook III, BL Royal 12 D, LXI, 62, in Hall 2004: 113. Dated to 850-950 CE (107). See also Meaney, 68

128. Filotas, 276, and passim

129. Filotas, 257

130. *Corrector sive Medicus*, 65, in McNeill and Gamer, 330

131. *Homilia de Sacrilegiis* IV, 15, in Caspari, 9

132. Dömötör, 127

133. Eliade 1972b: 205, or 222

134. Beza, 56-8

135. *Codex Matrensis*, in Delatte, 69, 89, and 117

136. Dömötör, 127

137. Benoit, 81

138. Storms, 187

139. Grimm, 1192

140. Gospel cover of Henry II, Bamberg Cathedral, now in Munich Library. See illustration in chapter 7.

141. Grimm, 1211, gives many examples of these customs.

142. Filotas, 47; 160

143. Rhode, 106-8

144. Pocs 1993: 29

145. Grimm, 1211

146. Shetelig and Falk, 415; *volr*, in Turville-Petre, 317; Kauffmann, 28, renders *völur* as "wand-bearers." An old derivation of *völva* from *velja / valjan*, "to choose," is now rejected.

147. See Dashu, *Woman Shaman: the Ancients*, 2013, on the shamanic staff.

148. Grimm, 1042

149. *Fornaldssaga*, in Grimm, 1399

150. Grimm, 1615

151. *Thorfinns saga Karlsefnis*, in Shetelig and Falk, 415

152. Grimm, 1615

153. Grimm, 1032-33. *Fornald. sög* 3, 205 for *töfranorn*. Hall (147) shows *töfrnorn*, which he translates as "magical norn"; Mitchell (56) gives "sorceress."

154. *Bósa saga ok Herrauðs*, in Hall 2004: 147

155. Dashu, Vol III, forthcoming

156. *Lex Rotharii*, cap. 376, in Centini, 2

157. Grimm, 916; Robbins, 544

158. *pro occultis, et quæ talamascis ac sortilegis solis notæ sunt, et iis quibuscum de earum literarum significatione con ventum est.* (reading *con ventum* as *conventum*) DuCange: http://ducange.enc.sorbonne.fr/talamasca

159. Du Cange: http://ducange.enc.sorbonne.fr/LARVAE

160. Centini, 4

161. Centini, 4

162. Bonomo, 480 fn 48

163. Centini, 3

164. Centini, 3

165. *Physica Curiosa*, in Robbins, 544

166. Grimm, 480; E. Hessus in *Bucol. idyl.* 5, Grimm, 936

167. *Fóstbrœða saga* 14, in Arent, 85

168. Ankarloo 1994: 196

169. *Thrymskviða* 3

170. *Corrector sive Medicus* 5.151, in Hefele, 22-23; McNeill and Gamer, 338

171. Wood-Martin 1895: 118

172. Yeats, 215

173. Gregory, 78

174. Bitel, 219

175. See Schmitz, 1977

176. Bitel, 219

177. d'Este and Rankine, 91

178. Brocard, 44, 58ff

179. Lecouteux 2003: 78

180. McColloch, 81

181. *Helgakvitha* 35, in Bray, 178

182. Ankarloo: 1993: 252-3

183. McColloch, 81

184. Grimm, c 433-5

185. Ankarloo 1993: 252. Lecouteux (2001: 29): "I took a witch's ride to many places this night, and I learned with certainty things I did not know before."

186. Ankarloo 1994: 196; Grimm, 723

187. Blain, 62

188. Grimm, 723

189. Grimm, 1039-41, 1618

190. Hall 1916:144

191. Franck, in Russell, 297, n.15; and www.bosworthtoller.com/finder/3/haga

192. Ruttner-Cova, 152

193. *Hávamál* 154

194. www.etymonline.com/index.php?term=hag

195. Mitchell, 150-51

196. De Vries, 11. The word translated as "skin" here is *hamr*; see chapter 5.

197. www.etymonline.com/index.php?term=hag

198. *Webster's Third New International Dictionary*, 1019

199. *De Civitate Dei* 15:23; *Etymologiae* 18.11.103

200. See https://en.wikipedia.org/wiki/Dusios. I looked for evidence that the second element in *hagedisse* was related to *dísir*, but could find no linguistic grounds for it; and the long í is against it.

201. www.etymonline.com/index.php?term=hag

202. Grimm, 1225

203. www.bosworthtoller.com/finder/3/hægtesse

204. Hall 1916: 143

205. Goldsmith, 110

206. www.bosworthtoller.com/finder/3/hægtesse

207. Goldsmith, 110

208. *Wid fœrstice* charm, in the *Lacnunga*, quoted in www.bosworthtoller.com/finder/3/hægtesse. Grimm, 1244, notes that here *hægtessen* is singular.

209. Crawford, 159-60

210. Grimm, 1244

211. Going by modern stereotypes, Hall (2004: 172) thinks *hœtse* for Jezebel implies "seductress." Given the accusation of "her many sorceries" in II Kings 9:22, it is more likely to have signified "witch."

212. Branston, 43

213. Zurich Pap. MSS B 223-730, in Grimm, 1478-79

214. Daly, 14-15

215. Websters, 1019

216. Grimm, 1041

217. www.bosworthtoller.com/finder/3/hagedisse

218. Grimm, 1039-40, 1478-9

219. Silverblatt, 175

220. See Fogel, 1988

221. Pughe 1832: 179 defines *gwr* as "A being endowed with power, will, or liberty; a man; a person; a husband..."—but the female form is demonized.

222. From Price 2004: 114; these do not appear to be literal translations.

Chapter 4: Völur

1. Simek 2006: 367-68. *Völva* is not etymologically linked to *vulva*, which comes from a different, Latin root meaning "revolve, roll, wrap."
2. Samplonus, 82, 72
3. Enright, 186-7
4. Grimm, 403
5. Dashu, Dec. 2010, online
6. *Ynglingasaga* 7
7. Clunies Ross I, 32
8. Gardeła, 205
9. Quinn 1998: 30-31
10. Quinn 1998: 43
11. Samplonius, 77
12. Ellis Davidson, 1973: 35-38
13. Clunies-Ross II, 34
14. Eliade, 381
15. *Hjealmðérs ok Ölvers*, 20, in Ellis 1968: 123
16. *Thorskfirðinga saga* 17, in Ellis 1968: 124
17. McKinnell 2001: 397
18. Price 2002: 200
19. *Eiriks saga rauða*, in www.gutenberg. org/files/17946/17946-h/17946-h.htm
20. Price, 188; Gardeła 196-197, 203
21. Price 2004: 194
22. Heide, 166-67
23. www.etymonline.com/index. php?term=distaff
24. For a visual comparison of Norse women's staffs with modern wooden distaffs, see www.suppressedhistories. net/articles2/volur.html
25. See chapter 2; Gardeła, 194, n. 4; Mencej, 2011
26. Heide, 165-166
27. Heide, 165
28. Svenson, 2
29. Price 2002: 192ff
30. Price 2004: 116; 198; 203
31. Gardeła, 192-197
32. Clunies Ross I, 250
33. Gardeła, 208
34. Gardeła, 211
35. Klinta burial 59.3, in Price 2002: 183-84. See the staff and a reconstruction at: http://wotanklan.tumblr.com/ post/38551299727/the-klinta-stave
36. Price 2002: 142-149
37. Price 2002: 194-95
38. http://en.natmus.dk/historical-knowledge/denmark/prehistoric-period-until-1050-ad/the-viking-age/ religion-magic-death-and-rituals/the-magic-wands-of-the-seeresses/
39. Davidson 1969: 92
40. www.anundshog.se/artikel.asp?strukturId=404&artikelId=1365
41. Ruffoni, 40-1, 46-7
42. Ruffoni, 44-46
43. Price 2002: 128-130
44. Price 2002: 140
45. Price 2002: 131-139
46. Price 2002: 149-150
47. Price 2002: 154
48. Price 2002: 155-156
49. Gardeła, 202, 208. He remarks that killing with fire or water was a way to break the power of sorcerers and staffs.
50. Blain, 137
51. *Fjölsvinnsmál* 26, in Gardeła, 201, n. 2; 207
52. Ruffoni, 23-25
53. Price, 159-160
54. Ruffoni, 27
55. Ingestad, in Ruffoni, 10, 30-31
56. *Gylfaginning* 24 and 49; *Skáldskaparmál* 28
57. Ruffoni, 24-25
58. Price 2002: 189
59. Stone Cross VIII, B.R. Olsen, 219, in Rickfors, online
60. Price 2002: 161
61. http://archive.archaeology.org/0811/ etc/witches.html
62. Price 2002: 157. He compares her to the Fyrkat *völva*.

63. Price 2002: 75; Dronke 1996: II, 20

64. Price 2002: 127

65. Price 2004: 117. In spite of the strong female context of the material record, Price still places Oðinn's "high seat" before those of the *völur* in his comparisons from saga literature. *Hjallin*: "high seat," in Quinn, 42, n. 21; also as *hjallr*.

66. Price 2002: 164-66

67. Price 2002: 64

68. Price 2002: 162

69. Grimm, 403. Shtelig and Falk render *efla seið* as "fixing *seið*."

70. Kees, 80

71. Svenson, 2; Price 2002: 64

72. Mallory and Adams, 362

73. Heide, 164

74. Hall, 121. Higley, 140, gives the Welsh form as *hut* and the PIE root for all these words as *soito

75. Hall, 117-130

76. Hall, 122, 118; on 37 he cites §6:3.1 for Snorri

77. Hall, 129; www.etymonline.com/index.php?term=uncouth

78. *Varðlokkur* could mean "guardian, protector," "entice," or "bind." Price 2002: 207. The translation of *varðlokkur* as "warlock songs" is spurious.

79. Clunies-Ross, I, 49, translates *froeði* as "knowledge."

80. Shetelig and Falk, 415. *Seiðlæti* are also mentioned in the *Landnámabók*. See Price 2002: 207

81. Quinn, 37-8. Here she translates *seið* as "magic."

82. Magnusson / Morris, 491-92

83. Svenson, 34

84. Quinn, 29

85. Quinn, 46

86. Quinn, 31

87. Quinn, 47

88. Quinn, 41

89. Jónsson 1954: 18, in Quinn 1198: 32

90. Quinn 1998: 40, citing Loth 1965,

48.12; Vigfússon and Unger 1860–68, 1: 580 and 1:259

91. Quinn, 44, cites Sveinsson 1954: 37

92. Lecouteux 2003: 35. He relates this yawning to the deep sigh issued by Sámi *noiadi* as they return to their bodies after a spirit journey. *Heixr* looks like a loan-word from German *Hexe*.

93. Price 2004: 205, 117

94. Gardeła, 205

95. Simek, 370-71. Enright (186) shows that the name was recorded as Balouberg, which linguists reconstruct as Walburg or Waluberg.

96. More on double staffs in Dashú, *Woman Shaman: the Ancients* (2013b)

97. Price 2002: 176; Lea 1901: 305

98. See reconstruction of the burial in Price 2004: 197; and Gardeła, 206

99. Price 2004: 120

100. *Hávamál* 154, in Lecouteux 2003: 94, who adds that this state is called *hamstolinn*, "deprived of one's double."

101. But Price (2002: 178) puts the earliest use of *gandr* for a witch's ride—on a "crooked stick"—in the 1300s.

102. Price 2002: 202

103. Price 2002: 204

104. *Eiðsivathingslov* I: 24, in Price 2002: 175

105. Magnusson, 492

106. Blain, 136

107. Quinn 1998: 29

108. Jochens 1991: 307

109. *Völuspá* 28

110. Samplonius, 77

111. Grimm, 1043

112. Samplonius, 77. Grimm, 1043, cites the *Gulathingen* 137.

113. Samplonius, 79; Dronke 1996: II, 17

114. Grimm, 1037

115. Grimm, 1617

116. *Decretum* XIX, 5.62, in Filotas, 124

117. *Gesta Herwardis*, in Kauffmann, 38; Grimm, 1454

118. Lumley, 218
119. Magnusson, 453; "bewitch," 491-92. He links *galdr* closely to *seiðr*. On "sing," see also www.windsofchange.net/archives/words_of_winds_the_carnival_of_etymologies-print.html.
120. West, 327. Some researchers think *galdr* was delivered in falsetto. Oracular women (*bagirwa*) in the Nyabingi tradition of East Africa spoke in falsetto. See Hopkins 1970: 258-336
121. Ellis 1968: 107-109
122. Craigie, 448, n. 38
123. Jochins 1989: 358, n. 32. Price (2002: 122) notes that *Laxdæla saga* is the only text that uses the –*maðr* ending for a female sorcerer.
124. Snorri, 1889: 289
125. *Sólarljóð* 51, in Price 2002: 208. "Giantesses' sun" is given here for *gýgjur solar*. Contra wikipedia, Price reads the shaman as female. So does Maria Kvilhaug: http://freya.theladyofthelabyrinth.com/?page_id=311
126. Ari Thorgilsson in the 12th century *Islendingabók*, in Blain, 61
127. Ellis Davidson, 1973: 35-38; Price 2002: 176
128. Arnason, *Isl. Thjóðsögur* I, 436, in Magnusson and Morris, 495
129. Magnusson and Morris, 495
130. Price 2002: 73.
131. *Eiriks saga rauða*, 1880, online
132. Price 2002: 73
133. The English word "queen" carries royal connotations absent in the Norse word *kona*, "woman"; both are related to Greek *gyne*, Scottish *quean*, Irish *ban*, Persian *zan*, and many other words from the same Indo-European root.
134. Quotes here and following are from *Eiriks saga rauða*, 1880, online
135. Elizabeth Arwill-Nordbladh, 53
136. Blain, 73. Quinn, 42, n. 21 gives *hjalinn* ("high seat").
137. Price 2002: 228
138. von Schnurbein, 118; Clunies Ross II, 170-72
139. *Flayterjarbók* I, in Gundarsson, online
140. Hardman, online
141. Price 2002: 124
142. Price, 112-114
143. Svenson, 12
144. Hedeager, 128. I disagree with her proposal that these powerful women were "transgender" because they wielded a power beyond that of most women. That removes the most dramatic female sphere of power from the category "women," tightening rather than releasing sexist role definitions.
145. Dronke 1996: VII, 228; see also Kvilhaug 2014: 129-137
146. Dronke, *Poetic Edda* II 1997: 131ff. *Heið* has often been derived from a word for "shining," but see McKinnell 2001: 399
147. Mitchell, 26
148. My translation after Dronke, Bray, Hollander, Quinn, Price, and Bellows
149. Quinn, 34
150. Gundarsson, online
151. Dronke 1996, VII. 225
152. Price 2004: 68-69
153. Quinn, 34
154. Dronke 1996: VII. 224
155. Bray, 284
156. Terene Wilbur 1959, in Jochens, 353
157. Larrington 1996: 8
158. Price 2002: 226
159. Dronke 1996: II, 17
160. Larrington 1996: 7
161. Hollander, 4
162. Bray, 285
163. Bellows, 10
164. Dronke 1996: VII. 228
165. Price 2002: 209
166. In modern Icelandic, according to Google Translate, *hugleikin* translates as

"preoccupied"—and *seið* as "potion"!

167. See Dronke 1996: VII. 225; Price, 228; Svenson, 17; McKinnell 2014: xii, 43

168. Blain, 103

169. View original Codex Regius at www.germanicmythology.com/works/CodRegIMAGES/CR2.jpg

170. Bellows, 10

171. Mitchell, 130; Price, 124

172. Quinn, 35

173. Quinn, 35. This story recalls the English witch-hunt practice of scoring, in which men struck or cut a woman's face in the belief that drawing her blood would release them from her spells.

174. Quinn, 35-36

175. Price 2002: 228

176. Franklin, 263

177. Price 2002: 209

178. Jónsson 1954, 1:8, in Quinn, 39

179. *Friðþjófs saga* 5-8

180. Price 2002: 163

181. https://en.wikipedia.org/wiki/Hereward_the_Wake

182. Davidson, 1969: 131

183. Svenson, 18

184. Price 2002: 117

185. McKinnell 2001: 399

186. *Hrólfs saga kraka* 3, in Price 2002: 162

187. Magnusson, 492

188. *Skáldskaparmál*, quoted in Lecouteux 2001: 47

189. Ellis 1968: 79. The *Sörla Þáttr* blames the situation on a sorceress named Göndul, and ultimately on Freyja, whom Oðinn coerced into the war as the price of returning her necklace.

190. www.etymonline.com/index.php?term=bless

191. *Ynglingasaga* 7

192. *Ynglingasaga* 4

193. Zoega, 176: online

194. Jochens 1989: 350

195. Cleasby and Gudbrand Vigfusson, 208. (Compare Vanadís.)

196. Zoëga, 176, online

197. Cleasby and Gudbrand Vigfusson, 208. The proto-Germanic would be *gudjōn.

198. Shetelig /Falk, 428; Turville-Petre, 221, calls it *Heiðreks saga.*

199. *Hyndluljoð* 10, in Damico, 176; Turville-Petre, 239

200. www.megalithic.co.uk/article.php?sid=12156

201. Shetelig and Falk, 429

202. Ellis 1968: 114

203. Ots, online; Jochens (347-55) calls it the bias of "a culture intensively focused on males and their activities."

204. Völuspá 22:4

205. *Ynglingasaga* 4, in Price 2004: 70; Quinn 30, n. 5

206. *Lokasenna* 24, in Higley, 140; Price 2004: 69

207. *Lokasenna* 24, my translation based on Blain, 123; Price, 69

208. Price 2004: 69

209. See citations at http://thegekkeringfox.blogspot.com/2013/10/did-seidr-use-drum.html. Von Schnurbein (119 n.3) translates *vétt* as "box cover."

210. Price 2002:174

211. Hedeager, 123

212. Quinn, 30

213. *Lokasenna* 21; 29

214. *Thrymr's Lay* 3, in Ots, online

215. Gundarsson, online

216. Price 2004: 119; see 163

217. Quinn 2015, online

218. Eliade, 385

219. Jochens 1991: 307-8. However, in an earlier article (Jochens 1989: 360-61) she goes off the rails, hypothesizing that Norse female prophecy was all based on fakery and a powerless female desire to placate men: "Allowed little choice, women did their best to accommodate the demands. Enough cases turned out well so that the practice caught on, thus

giving rise to the permanent feature of the prophetess."

220. Eliade, 387

221. *Ynglingasaga 7*

222. Eliade, 382

223. von Schnurbein, 121

224. Glosecki, *Shamanism and Old English Poetry* (1989: 14), in Weston, 287, n. 28

225. *Ynglingasaga 7*, in Price 2004: 70

226. *Völuspá* 28, in Jochens 1991: 34, n. 11

227. Lumley, 73. It has been suggested that the *völur* of *Baldrsdraumr* and of *Völuspá* were both of giant kindred. See McKinnell 2001, among others.

228. Even Hedeager (124) says this!

229. Shetelig and Falk, 415

230. See Maria Kvilhaug's discussion of "operative divination" in "Divinatory Seiðr – Saga Texts," online

231. Price 2002: 231

232. Dronke 1996: IX, 263; Bonnetain, online

233. Hall, 146

234. *Skírnismál* 26, online

235. *Lokasenna* 37, in Dronke 1996: IX, 266

236. *Gesta Hammaburgensis* 26

237. Dronke 1996: IX, 253-59

238. H. Lommel, cited by Dronke 1996: IX, 259, n. 1

239. Price 2002: 180

240. Hall 2004: 146

241. *Hávamál* 161-162

242. *Harbarðzljód 20*, in Gardeła, 199, n. 9. Here "witches" translates *myrkriður*, "darkness riders."

243. *Harbarðzljód* 37-39

244. Price 2002: 179

245. Hollander, 27

246. *Hávamál* 113-114, in Hollander, 31

247. Price 2002: 223

248. Dronke 1996: XII, 250, inexplicably refers to these hostile engagements as "Odin's loves."

249. Price 2002: 96

250. Lindow, 211

251. *Gylfaginning* 30; *Gesta Danorum*, III

252. Dronke 1996: 267

253. Lindow, 262–63

254. The name resembles English *witch* but is a latinization of Norse *vitka, according to Hall 2004: 149

255. Lindow, 262

256. See Romeo (289-91) on rapes by a Neapolitan lay exorcist, and de Mello (181-3) on the rapist friar Luis de Nazaré in Brazil.

257. North, 109

258. *Hávamál* 105, in Kvilhaug, 147

259. *Hávamál* 110, in Kvilhaug, 147

260. Kvilhaug, 28-31

261. Price's classification of *seiðr* makes a gendered split into "domestic" and battle magic (2002: 231). But what he calls "domestic" includes the whole world of Nature: working with weather, animals or fish, and the dead, while battle magic is a much narrower category.

262. *Grimnismál* 49, 54 and in *Gylfaginning*, as per Kvilhaug, 117

263. Among them are Swedish archaeologist Martin Rundkvist, and Danish archaeologist Else Roesdahl, quoted in Ellingsgaard, online

264. Price 2002: 163

265. Ellingsgaard, online

266. Clunies-Ross II, 33; Blain, 140

267. Rolf Pipping 1928, in Jochens 1989: 353; Quinn 1998:30; Hedeager, 126. Price 2002: 217 calls the reference in *Bósa saga* a "phallic epithet for the staffs" in this sexual encounter; but there is no *seiðstafr* and no ceremony. Heide (168) points out that *göndull* also means "coarse yarn and other twisted items."

268. *Bósa saga ok Herrauðs* 11, online

269. For a Persian example, see *Rumi and the Hermeneutics of Eroticism*, by Mahdi Tourage (2007: 118)

270. *Thidriks saga of Bern 352*, in Jochens 1996: 259
271. Price 2002: 220-23
272. O' Connor and Kellerman, online
273. Murray, 13. Here he quotes Marc Bloch commenting on the concept of "spindle kin": "...it was as though among the Germans the victory of the agnatic principle had never been sufficiently complete to extinguish all trace of a more ancient system of uterine filiation."
274. Heide, 164
275. See photo essay at www.suppressedhistories.net/articles/emasculating_distaff.html
276. Miller 2010, 83-89
277. See photo essay at www.suppressedhistories.net/articles/emasculating_distaff.html
278. Bodleian MS Douce 215, fol.1r
279. Harley1766_f76v
280. Das Böse Weib, late 1400s. http://landesmuseum.de/sonder/2001/mittelalter/blm/blm_ausst/bilder/boese-weib.jpg
281. www.virginia.edu/artmuseum/supplemental-websites/traces/traces-2007.15.2.html
282. Jones, Malcolm, 72
283. Jones, 75
284. Price 2002: 188, 193; 198
285. Blain, 124, Higley, 139
286. Hedeager, 117
287. Price 2004: 111
288. Higley, 141, provides a striking Welsh comparison from the *Cat Godeu*, which places the seer Taliesin "in a bedcover in the middle between the two knees of kings." North (50) refers to possible Anglo-Saxon "analogues of *seiðmen*," pointing to a Hampshire burial of a male in female dress, with a stone placed on his chest to still his ghost.
289. Dronke 1996: IV, 679
290. Higley, 140
291. http://en.wikipedia.org/wiki/Seiðr
292. Higley, 138
293. *Gulathing* 196, in Hedeager, 115; Blain, 124, 132
294. Higley, 139
295. Hedeager, 119
296. Hedeager, 116
297. Blain, 124
298. http://en.wikipedia.org/wiki/Nið
299. Dronke 1996: 15 defines *nið* as "malice"; Clunies-Ross translates it as "defamation," and Hedeager, 115, as "sexual defamation."
300. Clunies-Ross I, 110
301. Hedeager, 118
302. Hedeager, 115, uses the phrase "perverse sexual acts," but does not supply any examples of what that meant.
303. Blain, 124
304. Clunies Ross I, 70
305. Bandlien 2005, in Hedeager, 115
306. Project Samnordisk Runtextdatabas Svensk - Rundata entry for Vg 67, in http://en.wikipedia.org/wiki/Ergi. (The article also emphasizes the distinction between males who penetrate and those who are penetrated.) See http://en.wikipedia.org/wiki/Saleby_Runestone
307. http://en.wikipedia.org/wiki/Ergi
308. Arent, 85
309. Hedeager, 125
310. Blain, 132, citing Gunnora Hallakarva
311. Solli 1999a: 344, in Blain, 132; Price, 216, 123
312. For example, Clunies-Ross I, 209-10; Jochens 1996: 217

Chapter 5: Runes

1. Filotas, 243
2. Zurich Pap. MSS B 223-730, in Grimm, 1478-79
3. Dr. Hartlieb, *Book of All Forbidden*

Arts, in Grimm, 1773
4. Grimm, 1117
5. See www.pinterest.com/harrasteora/crystal-lenses/ for stunning photos.
6. Meaney 1981: 84, 293-4
7. Grimm, 1108-09
8. Wemple, 213, n. 10, citing E. Salin in *La civilisation mérovigienne*, Paris 1949-59, Vol 4, pp 77-118
9. Wemple, 28
10. Meaney, 1981: 31-33
11. Meaney, 131-3
12. Meaney 1981: 123-4
13. Meaney 1981: 138
14 Fick et al, 64
15. Diut. i 504b, in Grimm, 1277
16. Grimm, 1630
17. Filotas, 15, believes that the Greek word *ethnos* migrated through Armenian *het'anos* and into Gothic.
18. As discussed on the cybalist@yahoogroups.com. See for example George Knyzh "Re: Aryanism and Journal of Indo-European Studies," message 17996
19. H-Africa, Mar 3, 1999, citing *Dictionnaire Littré,* where this is the first definition of "ethnique" given.
20. Filotus, 21 n. 33 cites penitentials from 7th century Spain, 10th century England and 11th century Germany.
21. www.etymonline.com/index.php?term=gentile
22. Pseudo-Boniface sermon, given in Filotas, 23
23. *Homilia de Sacrilegiis*, III.4; .5; .8; .9, in Caspari, 6-7
24. Antenor Nascentes, in the *Diccionario Etimologico da Lingua Portugesa*, links to Latin *brusca* "tree frog." Thanks to Joao S. Lopes, The Indo-European Listserv, Nov 27, 2006
25. Coromines, Vol II, p 283 ff. Thanks to Ton Sales of Universitat Politècnica de Catalunya, on cybalist@ yahoogroups.com, Nov 29, 2006

26. Ton Sales, as above.
27. Aline Macha O'Brien uses the adjective *witchen* to restore the original positive sense of "witch."
28. *Sólarljóð* 79
29. www.etymonline.com/index.php?term=spell; www.windsofchange.net/archives/words_of_winds_the_carnival_of_etymologies-print.html
30. *Sigrdrífumál* 5-19
31. Shetelig and Falk, 411
32. *Grettis saga 78*, in Hight, 199
33. *Grettis saga 78*, online
34. *Grettis saga Ásmundarsonar* 79
35. "Gender and Rune Magic," Feb 1, 2003, in asynjur@yahoogroups.com
36. Halsall, 6. *Reginkunnom* could also be translated "kin to the Powers."
37. Shetelig and Falk, 228
38. Looijenga, 8
39. Grimm, 1225
40. Fletcher, 266
41. Hall 1916: 245
42. Halsall, 7
43. Hall 1916: 245
44. Wilbur 1957: 13
45. Wilbur, 15-16
46. Grimm, 901
47. Shetelig and Falk, 425-6
48. Magnusson and Morris, 377
49. Grimm, 1689. However, the only account of their use is heavily overlaid with Christianity.
50. Bede V, 10, in Bosworth, 971
51. Lea 1957: 402-3
52. Borsje, 217 n. 13. Compare Irish *fid* with Norse *við*, "wood."
53. Halsall, 5
54. Shetelig and and Falk, 415, 219-21
55. *Runa* for *litera*, Grimm 1224
56. Filotas, 243
57. Shetelig and and Falk, 221
58. Halsall, 152
59. Shetelig and Falk, 223
60. *Hávamál*, in Osborn and Longland,

180

61. *Hávamál* 145

62. Gummere, 134

63. Rouche, 520

64. Looijenga 2003: 311-12

65. *mey né manns konu*, in *Hávamál* 163

66. Hollander, 235

67. *Sigrdrifumal* 6-21, in Hollander, 235-38

68. *Sigrdrífumál* 10, in Hollander, 235

69. Hollander, 247

70. Dronke 1969: 120

71. Jordanes, *Getica* 24

72. Wilbur (1957: 16) follows K. Müllenhof (and Grimm, 1225) in deriving *haliorunnas* from the "underworld mysteries". But Lehman (1986:174) likes Scardigli's reading as "hell-runners" (from *rinnan, instead of -rúna), and interprets them "as female shamans." (1973: 70-71)

73. The Gothic legend of witch repression is discussed in greater depth in my forthcoming Vol VI, *Overlords*

74. Michael Scotus, lib. 2. *Mensæ Philosophicæ* 21, in DuCange, http://ducange.enc.sorbonne.fr/ALYRUMNAE

75. McNeill and Gamer, 420

76. *Vaticinantem a sagacitate vocarunt Alyrunam*, in DuCange, http://ducange.enc.sorbonne.fr/ALYRUMNAE

77. Grimm 1225

78. DuCange s.v. *haliorunnae* (Latin plural Jordanes); Grimm 210, 1399

79. Hall 1916: 153

80. Wrenn, *Beowulf*, 262, in Goldsmith, 110

81. Goldsmith, 111

82. O'Brien, 186, on *Beowulf* 163. The full line is *helrunan hwyrftum scriþað*: "those skilled in the mysteries of hell move about." She notes that the compound word is written separately as *hel runan*, a common practice at the time.

83. Wensch 1940: 49, in Wilbur 1957: 17

84. North (104) states that "cognates of hel in all Germanic languages indicate only the abode of the dead."

85. Toller, 1882 s.v. *hægtesse*; Goldsmith, 110

86. Wensch, in Samplonius, 79. See also Wilbur 1957: 16

87. Toller, 631

88. MacMullen 2014, online

89. Grimm, 1226

90. Grimm, 1228

91. Grimm, 1202-3; 1689, 404

92. Grimm, 1402

93. Toller, 630-31

94. Hall 2004: 176 n. 223, says *burg-* "probably means 'protection'..."

95. Toller-Bosworth, 135, refers to "several glossaries among the Cotton MSS." Hall 1916: 53-54 adds "sorceress" also.

96. Weston 1995: 285

97. *Baldrs draumr* 19

98. Hall 2004: 100, 124

99. Meaney 1981: 22

100. Leechbook III, LXI, 61, in Hall 2004: 126-7

101. Hall 2004: 127

102. Leechbook III, 62, in Hall 2004: 113

103. Book I, 64, in Hall 2004: 123

104. Meaney 1981: 239

105. Folio 52v, *Wið ælcre yfelre leodrunan & wið ælfsidenne þis gewrit*, in Hall 2004

106. *Bald's Leechbook* I.64, in Meaney 1981: 22

107. *eft óðer dust and drenc wið leódrúnan*, in Toller-Bosworth, online: http://bosworth.ff.cuni.cz/finder/3/seolcuðe

108. Meaney 1981: 22

109. Hall 2004: 124

110. Hall 2004: 100.

111. Hall 2004: 96

112. Hall 2004: 105

113. Hall 2004: 97

114. Hall 2004: 97-99

115. Lecouteux 2001: 181

116. Davidson 1969: 117. This Olaf should not be confused with the missionary king Olaf, a vicious enemy of heathendom.

117. Hall (2004) proposes that *álfar* referred to male ancestors and *dísir* to female ancestors.

118. Shetelig / Falk, 428; 164

119. Ellis 1968: 111

120. *Homilia de sacrilegiis*, VI, 22, in Caspari, 12; translation of *maiores* as Greater Ones from Filotas, 262

121. *Sepulcrorum violatrix*, in *Lex Burgundionum* XXXIV, 3, in Grimm, 1693

122. Synod of Elvira, Canons 33-34

123. Filotas, 336

124. McNeill and Gamer, 419

125. Filotas, 99

126. Philpott, 488

127. *Vita Dunstani*, in Grimm, 1229

128. Book 10.35, in Filotas, 336

129. Filotas, 338

130. *Corrector sive Medicus*, Burchard's *Decretum* XIX, 79, in Lebbe, 72. Priests were unable to suppress similar customs at Irish wakes until the early 1900s.

131. Filotas, 217; the quote is from the Penitential of Theodore, ca. 700.

132. *Corrector Sive Medicus* 19.82, in Lebbe, 72

133. Filotas, 337

134. Grimm, 333

135. von Cles-Reden, 160

136. Weston, 285

137. *Beowulf* 163

138. Goldsmith, 111

139. *Beowulf* 175-79, in Garnett, 6

140. Shetelig, 411

141. Bosworth Toller online: www.bosworthtoller.com/022054. Thanks to Cefin Beorn and Chase Brown.

142. http://dil.ie/search?search_in=-headword&q=nert

143. Shetelig / Falk, 419

144. Shetelig and Falk, 408

145. Lecouteux 2003: 49. He gave no citation for Snorri's description of *hugr* in *Skáldskaparmál* as the "wind of witches" (on p. 99), so I was unable to determine what word was translated as "witches."

146. Lecouteux 2003: 48. On "caul," 95. On "troll-skin," see De Vries, 11.

147. Lecouteux 2003: 47

148. Ankarloo 1994: 196

149. Lecouteux 2003: 48

150. *Hyndluljóð* 35, in Bray, 221

151. *Edda Snorra Sturlusonar* 9, in Heide, 165

152. Turville-Petre, 228

153. Shetelig and Falk, 408-9, mention *kynfylgja* and *ættirfylgja* as family protectors.

154. Turville-Petre, 228

155. Grimm, 874

156. Shetelig, 408ff

157. Turville-Petre, 230

158. *Vafthrúðnismál* 49, in Shetelig and Falk, 409

159. Ellis 1968: 133

160. Boyer, in Lecouteux 2003: 50

Chapter 6: Cailleachan, Dísir and Hags

1. MacKenzie, 137

2. MacKenzie, 167

3. Mackay, in Rees and Rees, 135

4. Mackenzie 1913: xxxvii

5. Ó Crualaoich, 84

6. Wood-Martin 1902: 216; Ó hÓgain, 67

7. Ó Crualaoich, 90

8. d'Este and Rankine, 69

9. Ó Crualaoich, 100-101

10. West, 379

11. MacKenzie, 162-3

12. O'Donovan and O'Flanagan 1927:96

13. Ó Crualaoich, 113, 115

14. Ó Crualaoich, 116

15. Ó Crualaoich, 144
16. Ó hÓgain, 68
17. MacKillop, 131; Ó hÓgain, 68; 165
18. Ó Cathasaigh, 34
19. Ó hÓgain, 67
20. Gregory 1904: 20-21
21. Wood-Martin 1902: 214
22. Wood-Martin, 305
23. MacKenzie, 140-41
24. http://atlanticreligion.
com/2013/08/26/the-cailleach/
25. http://mountainviews.ie/sum-
mit/226/
26. Βουουίνδα, in Ptolemy 2.2 § 8
27. Ó hÓgain, 209
28. Ó hÓgain, 49
29. Dr. Raimund Karl, online: 1998
30. Ó Cathasaigh, 27.
31. Coffey, 90. He says, "Strange to say, it
has completely escaped notice hitherto."
He mentions (91) an unfinished Dindsenchas that calls the Brugh the "Síd of
Broga," Mound of the House."
32. Senchas na Relec, in Ó Cathasaigh, 31
33. Monaghan 2014: 215
34. Wood-Martin 1895: 166
35. Wood-Martin 1895: 166
36. Ó Crualaioch, 86
37. Ó hÓgain, 67, 119
38. Book of Lecan, in Rees and Rees, 135
39. Meyer 1901: 101-35. A Dindsenchas
explains how Dubad (Dowth, "darkness")
got its name, from the king's rape of his
sister as she was performing a ritual there
to stop the sun in its course, so that a
platform could be constructed there in
a day to stop a cattle-plague: "strongly
she makes her druid spell | the sun was
motionless above her head | she checked
[it] on one spot." The rapist violated the
ceremony, and Dowth was never completed. See Gwynn, 43-47
40. www.maryjones.us/ctexts/dessi2.html
41. Ó Cathasaigh, 34
42. Wood-Martin 1902: 216; Ó hÓgain, 67

43. Wood-Martin 1895: 134
44. For photos of some well-known
Cailleach megaliths, see www.source-
memory.net/veleda/?p=792
45. Ó hÓgain, 68
46. Ross 1973: 156
47. Fossard, 113
48. Tempan, online
49. T.G.F Paterson, Country Cracks –
Old Tales from the County of Armagh,
1939, in Goldbaum, "Slieve Gullion,"
online
50. Wood-Martin 1895: 126
51. Wood-Martin 1895: 135
52. Ó hÓgain, 68
53. Wood-Martin 1895: 130-31
54. Fossard, 133; Goldbaum, Labbacallee
55. Ó Cathasaigh, 29
56. Goldbaum, "Loughcrew," online.
56a. Goldbaum credits Martin Brennan
with discovering the site's equinoctial
aspects, with a link to an excellent video.
57. See photos at www.sourcememory.
net/veleda/?p=792
58. Byrne, online
59. Wood-Martin: 1895: 314
60. Goldbaum, "Loughcrew," online
61. Byrne, online
62. Wood-Martin 1902: 251-3
63. Jones 2007: 209
64. Jones 2007: 249
65. Wood-Martin 1902: 224-5
66. See Freitag 2004; Starr Goode 2016
67. See Andersen 1977
68. Wood-Martin 1902: 247
69. Wood-Martin 1895: 134
70. Ó hÓgain, 68
71. Ó Crualaoich, 148
72. d'Este/Rankine, 35-43
73. Wood-Martin 1895: 129
74. Ó hÓgain, 67-8
75. Ó Crualaoich, 138
76. Ó hÓgain, 67-8
77. Ó Crualaoich, 163-65
78. Ó Crualaoich, 146

79. Ó Crualaoich, 100
80. I'm indebted to Mary Condren for her work on ancient Irish cultural horizons, and for her generosity in sharing sources. See Condren, forthcoming.
81. Ó hÓgain, 68
82. Fossard, 49
83. Ó Crualaoich, 117
84. Carmichael 1900: 283 (see p. 188)
85. Wood-Martin 1902: 216; from Kuno Meyer's 19th century translation
86. Two MSS dating to 1500-1600s are in Trinity College Library, Dublin. Kuno Meyer estimated the poem at circa 1000, according to Wood-Martin (1902: 217). That date was then considered too early, but linguists now think it is too late.
87. Ó hAodha, 315
88. Wood-Martin 1902: 218
89. Wood-Martin, 216
90. Wood-Martin 1902: 219
91. Wood-Martin 1902: 218. In Kuno Meyer's translation, the Cailleach says, "Only women folk I hate," because of their beauty and the pleasures offered them. But this line, which doesn't appear in other versions, is a caution about the vagaries of translation.
92. O hAodha, 318, n. 2. He gives linguistic grounds, since some manuscripts (but not others) show a lenited genitive case, Bhuí instead of Buí.
93. Ó Cathasaigh, 29
94. O hAodha, 309. Mairín Ni Dhonnchadha proposes that the female poet Digdi wrote the *Lament*. See Ó Crualaoich, 48-52. But that name occurs elsewhere as belonging to the Cailleach.
95. Ó Crualaioch, 82-4
96. Mackay 1932: 160
97. Mackay 1932: 153
98. Wood-Martin 1895: 129, 214-6
99. Ó Crualaoich, 148-50
100. Wood-Martin 1902: 283
101. Stokes, 417

102. Ó Crualaoich, 52
103. Ross 1973; 233
104. MacKenzie, 140-41
105. Mackenzie, 143
106. MacKenzie, 140-41
107. MacKenzie, 141-2
108. MacKenzie, 165
109. Ó Cathasaigh, 35
110. MacKenzie, 151
111. Krappe, 295. Thanks to Mary Condren for this source, and to Marylene Lynx for her input on La Vieille. She points to the same theme in Voiteur, six days of the old woman "during which a faery travels through the seasons." Personal communication, Mar. 24 2016
112. "Les Jours De La Vieille En France," online
113. Mackay 1932: 144-74
114. MacKenzie, 164, 144
115. MacDougall, 241
116. "The Cailleach," online
117. MacKenzie, 144
118. Ross 2000: 114
119. MacKenzie, 162-3
120. Wood-Martin 1902: 214-16; O'Crualaoich, 89-90, 146, 114
121. MacKenzie 1935
122. West, 343, on Ben Nevis.
123. MacKenzie, 152
124. Mackay 1932: 152
125. MacKenzie, 152-3
126. MacDougall, 241
127. Carmichael, 494
128. MacKenzie, 151
129. Wood-Martin 1902: 214
130. MacKenzie, 137, 153
131. Monaghan 2009:142
132. Briggs 1976: 106
133. Ross, 233
134. Campbell 1862: 124
135. Briggs 1976: 24, 58
136. MacKenzie, 165
137. Scott 1838: 138
138. MacKillop, 62

139. Briggs 1976: 57-60
140. *Yn Lioar Manninagh*, Volume 1 p. 223, *Manx Natural History and Antiquarian Society*, 1889, in "Caillagh y groamagh," online
141. "Caillagh y groamagh," online
142. George Broderick, in Ó Crualaoich, 89
143. MacKillop, 62
144. W.W. Gill, 'A Manx Scrapbook', London: Arrowsmith, 1929, in "Caillagh y groamagh," online
145. Coda to *Helgakvitha Hundingsbana I*, in Hollander, 237
146. Turville-Petre, 222; Kauffmann, 17-8. Boyer, 622, notes a distant counterpart, *dhisanas*, in Sanskrit.
147. http://bosworth.ff.cuni.cz/finder/3/ides
148. Meaney 1990: 158
149. *Beowulf* 1259, in Wyatt, 184
150. Ellis Davidson 1998: 22
151. *Thæt wæs geomuru ides, Beowulf* 1075, in Hill, 241
152. *Beowulf* 2337 in Grimm, 402. He discovered this correspondence.
153. Chantepie de la Saussaye, 127. West (333) gives "escape the fighters!" Others translate the last word as "warriors."
154. Storms, 187
155. Grimm, 1398. He reads *eydes* as *īdīs* in conformity with the rhyme scheme.
156. Eckenstein, 43
157. *Skáldskaparmál* 68; *Haustlöng*, in Grimm, 1398
158. *Atlamál* 25, in Ellis 1968: 135
159. *Ásmundr Saga Kappabana* 8, in Ellis 1968: 135
160. Ellis 1968: 135
161. *Skáldskaparmál* 28
162. *Guðrúnarkviða* I, 19. Grimm, 402
163. Shetelig and Falk, 428. See *Skáldskaparmál* 42
164. *Hälfs saga* 15; *Atlamál in Groenlenzku*
165. Both in *Grímnismál* 53
166. *Reginsmál* 11; 24
167. *Sigrdrifumal* 9, in Hollander, 235
168. Ellis 1968: 130
169. *Víga-Glúms saga* 9, in Ellis 1968: 131. She gives many examples of these visitations.
170. Ellis 1968: 135
171. Turville-Petre, 225; Boyer 622
172. Turville-Petre, 225
173. Philpott, 486
174. *Egils saga* 205-7, in Grimm, 1398. *Dísablót* are referred to in *Hervors saga* 1 and *Egils saga* 44
175. Kvilhaug 2014: 37-38
176. *Hervarar saga*, in Turville-Petre, 226 and *Egils saga* 43, in Ellis 1968: 136
177. *Ynglinga saga* 29, in Turville-Petre, 226
178. *Vitta véttr*, in *Ylingatal* 21, *Heimskringla* I, online. Some translators say a "witch" is blamed for the king's fall.
179. *Friðthjófs saga* 9, in Ellis 1968: 136
180. In *Njáls saga* 88
181. *Atlamál* is an example, in Lindow, 95
182. Lecouteux (2001: 192) compares groups of *dísir* to widespread continental stories of the Wild Hunt, in which the dead communicate to the living.
183. *Thorsteins Saga Síðu-Hallssonar* 5, in Ellis 1968: 150
184. *Laxdæla saga*, in Arent, 75
185. *Svipdagsmál* 5: 1-3. https://notendur.hi.is/~eybjorn/ugm/svipdag2.html; See also Bray, 159
186. I went with the translation at https://notendur.hi.is/eybjorn/ugm/svipdag2.html but emended "bonds" to "protection." Bray (159) has "May the web of Weird be around thy way," which is beautiful, but not literal.
187. Bray, 161
188. Kauffmann, 55
189. Damico, in Damico and Olsen 1990: 181
190. *Helgakviða Hundingsban*a I, 16
191. Price 2004: 118

192. Hall 2004: 38
193. Kauffman, 55
194. Lecouteux 2003: 212
195. *Helgakvitha Hjovarthsson* 28, in Dronke 1996: VII 230
196. Grimm, 34
197. Pocs 1989: 17
198. Grimm, 1112
199. *Volundarkviða*, stanzas 1 and 3. Lecouteux (2001: 19) has "Young, all wise / For deciding destinies."
200. Hall (2004: 152) compares the fateful swan women to *dísir*.
201. *Volundarkviða*, in Hollander, 160
202. Saxo Grammaticus, *Gesta Danorum* III, online
203. *Gesta Danorum* III
204. Lecouteux 2003: 71
205. Kaufmann, 54
206. West, 385
207. *Fafnismál* 43, in Hollander, 223
208. *Sigrdrífumál* 2-19. This exchange compares with Oðinn's gifts of gold for the *völva's* prophecy in *Völuspá* 29.
209. Hardman, online
210. *Gylfaginning* 49
211. Ellis 1968: 14-15, 46-57.
212. McKinnell 2001: 404
213. *Gesta Danorum* I.8.4 and 7.7.14, in West, 501. He cites Procopius on the Heruli expecting widows to hang themselves beside their husband's graves.
214. Drinker, 45
215. Clunies Ross I, 255, n. 19. In *Grímnismál* 36 valkyries wait on tables, pouring drinks for the warriors.
216. Ellis Davidson 1998: 176, citing Näsström 1995
217. Shetelig and Falk, 431
218. Shetelig and Falk, 416; see also Hedeager, 2011. North (236) speaks of "the aristocratic preoccupation with Oðinn," reflected in court poetry.
219. Bek-Pedersen, 277, n. 3
220. MacCulloch 1930: 29
221. Shetelig and Falk, 416
222. Ellis 1968: 159-60. She shows that the wall of flame around the Otherworld is known from other Norse texts.
223. Shetelig and Falk, 420-21
224. Mitchell, 28
225. Motz, in Lionarons 2005: 272
226. Shetelig and Falk, 421
227. Maria Kvilhaug, Judy Quinn, Lotte Motz, Gro Steinsland, and Gunnhild Rothe come immediately to mind.
228. Clunies Ross I, 55
229. Blind, 104
230. Miller 2008: 71
231. Clunies Ross I, 164
232. Kauffmann, 89
233. Blind, 105
234. Lindow, 142
235. *Gylfaginning* 12-13
236. Menglöð in *Fjölsvinnsmál* 35-42; Aurboða in *Hyndluljóð* 30: 5-8.
237. Clunies Ross I, 113; see also Lindow, 64. Menglö
238. Quinn 1998: 43
239. Quinn, 2005: 9-10
240. North, 23
241. Clunies Ross I, 67. See also North, 98
242. Boyer, 630
243. Rothe 1994, in Ruffoni, 18
244. Quinn 2015, online
245. Kvilhaug, "Burning the Witch!" online
246. Clunies Ross I, 129
247. Judy Quinn (1998: 43) provides a more complete roster of giantess words— *finngálkn, trollkona, gýgr, jotuns dóttir, risadóttir.*
248. Clunies Ross I 49, n. 9
249. Clunies Ross II, 10
250. Clunies Ross I, 119
251. *Gylfaginning* 30-31
252. Clunies Ross I, 142, n. 38
253. *Helgakviða Hjörvarðsson* 26-3
254. *Helgakviða Hördvardssonar* 35. See Lecouteux 2001: 131

255. Tolley, 50
256. *Gylfaginning*, in Lindow, 197
257. Clunies Ross I, 79
258. *kveldrunnina kvinna*, "evening-running women, in Hunt-Anschutz, online
259. *Thórsdrápa* 14, 5-8, in Clunies Ross I 67, n. 26
260. Dixon-Kennedy, 23
261. Ross 1973: 158
262. In Ó Crualaoich, 85; he shows how this antagonism extends to another powerful male category, the priest.
263. Ó hÓgáin, 108-09
264. Ross 1973: 160
265. Anne Ross 1973: 160
266. Augusta Gregory, 1904: 306-309
267. Mackay 1932: 151, 160
268. Matthews, 82
269. Ross, 228
270. Ross, 230
271. Mackay, 159
272. Mackay 1932: 154
273. MacKenzie, 132. In another story (129) a witch helps Finlay defeat the wife of a giant he has wounded, who is now after him. She instructs him how to proceed and aids him in the final battle with "my cunning, black magic wand."
274. Briggs 1976: 304
275. Cite for this story is lost, but Campbell 1862 has several along these lines.
276. MacKenzie, 148-9
277. MacDougall, 231-3
278. Kingshill, 440. Many versions of this story exist, with the curse invariant.
279. Wood-Martin 1895: 133
280. Ernst, 105
281. Ross 1973: 157
282. Markale, 113, 214; McCulloch 1930: 155-6
283. Hall 2004: 176-7
283a. *Preiddeu Annwn* in Darrah, 78; nine daughters in Wood-Martin 1895: 125. Standing stones in https://en.wiki-pedia.org/wiki/Nine_Maidens_stone_row & https://en.wikipedia.org/wiki/Boskednan_stone_circle
283b. Latin Sena, French Sein, means "breast." Nine *dísir* in black and nine in white appear in the Tale of Thiðrandi.
284. The summary of the *Kalevala* that follows draws on Crawford 1894
285. Santillana and von Dechend, 206
286. Quoted by Snorri in *Skáldskaparmál 33*, in www.germanicmythology.com/PoeticEdda/GRM13.html
287. Santillana and Dechend, 363
288. Tolley, 26
289. Santillana and Dechend, 364
290. Craigie, 77-8
291. Tolley, 39. He notes (52) that the same words were used for their dislodging of the stones from the mountains as for their turning as a mill.
292. *Grottasongr*, Hollander 158
293. Tolley, 17
294. Tolley, 54
295. Preface to *Helgi Hundingsbana* II, at www.sacred-texts.com/neu/poe/poe20.htm
296. Tolley, 25
297. Santillana and Dechend, 362
298. Tolley, 24-25
299. Tolley, 33, 36
300. See Tolley 14-15.
301. MacKenzie, 100-1
302. Hollander, 173
303. Hollander, 173, *Helgakvitha*. In *Alvísmál*, Thor questions the "allwise" dwarf, detaining him until dawn, so that he turns to stone.
304. www.sagadb.org/kormaks_saga.en
305. *Baldrsdraumr* 13, in Lindow, 70
306. *Hávamál* 154, in Bray, 107
307. Branston, 101
308. Grimm, 403-4
309. Kauffmann, 55
310. Saunders, 89
311. *mihtigan wif*, in Hall 2004: 10-12; Storms, 50; Grimm, 1244

312. Hall, 11
313. Hall: 2004: 171. See also Weston (285) on the overlap of the meanings *human witch* and *spirit-women*.
314. Jeep, 112-13
315. Berger, 65
316. Hall 2004: 177-8
317. Hall 2004: 177-8
318. Lecouteux 2001: 202
319. Lecouteux 2001: 199
320. MacCulloch 1930: 253. The quote is from *Sermo ad Anglos: her syndan wiccan & wælcyrian.* Wulfst. 298, 18. *Wiccan* and *wælcerian*; and 165, 34. See http://lexicon.ff.cuni.cz/ s.v. *wæl-cyrge.* Both forms, with and without g, appear.
321. www.bosworthtoller.com/034306
322. Purser, 3
323. Shetelig / Falk, 431. They compare *wælcéasiga* to Old High German *kiosan*, "eat, partake of."
324. www.bosworthtoller.com/034306
325. Purser, 62
326. Purser, 92. He says that the charms treat the "mighty women" as powers to be exorcised—but also to be placated.
327. Wulfst. 298, 19, in www.bosworth-toller.com/033509
328. Wulfst. 194, 18, Ibid. All these words are in the masculine default.
329. Hall 2004: 173
330. Purser, 67-68
331. See Vol. VIII, *Priestcraft*, forthcoming.

Chapter 7: The Witch Holda and Her Retinue

1. *De synodalibus causis*, in Filotas, 75. Burchard took this description word for word into his *Decretum*
2. Cohn, 211
3. Gregory of Tours, VIII, 15. Behringer, 52, identifies the shrine-destroying monk as St. Wulfilaich.

4. Filotas, 357. Regino is the first to wrongly ascribe these lines to an ancient council at Ancyra, followed by Burchard of Worms.
5. MacMullen 1997: 201 n.1
6. Filotas, 314
7. Filotas, 313: *sortilega et malefica ars*
8. Filotas (312) says the text came from a Frankish council or capitulary; Baroja (61) dates the text to 872. Neither one of them quotes from this obscure source. Neither does Behringer, 49. What does this important missing piece say?
9. Lea, 178-81; Grimm, 476; Bonomo, 18
10. *Praeloquia* 1.10, in Bonomo, 19. For quasi *reginam imo deam*, Filotas (75) gives "a queen, in very truth, a goddess."
11. Grimm, 283-84: *talibus praestigiis infelices mulierculas*
12. These goddesses are discussed in volumes IX and X of the *Secret History of the Witches* series, forthcoming.
13. Austin (39) says that "over one third" of the canons come from Regino's book
14. *Decretum* 10.1, in Grimm, 1741, my translation. Ginzburg (1991: 90) gives: "So that the bishops shall expel witches and enchanters from their parishes." Russell (79) interprets the passage as "drive out... those who believe and practice the wild ride," which is substantially correct, if not literal.
15. *Decretum* Book 10, in Grimm 1741-42, my translation
16. *Decretum* X, in Filotas, 315
17. 10.8, in Austin, 177
18. Austin, 178
19. Canons 10.29 and 10.30, in Austin, 270-72
20. Martin de Braga, at www.thelatinlibrary.com/martinbraga/rusticus.shtml
21. *Decretum* 19. 5, 70, in Lea 1957: 185
22. Gagnon, 122-23; 196; my translation
23. Book 19.5 §70
24. Book 10.1, in Austin, 176

25. Behringer, 50
26. Austin, 10
27. Gagnon 59, citing Regino 2.371
28. Austin (199-201) describes how "forgery and textual tampering" was widespread, with canons being invented and council names falsified.
29. Bonomo, 21
30. *Decretum* 26. 5. 12
31. Mitchell, 134
32. *Decretum* XIX 5 §171
33. See Carlo Ginzberg, 1985
34. Lecouteux 168 and passim
35. *Decretum* XIX, 5, 170, in Filotas, 315
36. *iterum vivos facere et inducias vivendi dare*, in Behringer 1998: 43. Gagnon (145) translates "give them time to live."
37. Behringer, 41. He gives "Rosina"; one of my Italian sources has it as "Ronzola."
38. Behringer, 39-42. In *Gylfaginning*, it is Thórr who kills his goat to feed his hosts, and instructs them to put the bones back in the skins, reviving them. See Lecouteux 2003: 53
39. Pócs 1993: 27
40. Behringer, 42-43
41. Kloss, 101
42. *Laxdæla saga* 49, in Arent, 127; quote from Lecouteux 2003: 46
43. Filotas, 129-30
44. Flint, 231-37
45. Filotas, 280. Dashu, Vol VIII, gives more detail about the sexual politics of witchcraft in the *Corrector sive Medicus*.
46. Flint, 233
47. Arundel 1.460, in Gagnon, 145, n. 74. *Si quis in aerem in quiete nocti silentio se a maleficis feminis sublevari crediderit?*
48. Lea 1957: 184
49. Bonomo, 25
50. Burchard #60, McNeill/ Gamer, 330
51. Gagnon, 46-47
52. Wasserschleben, 407
53. Lea 1957: 182

54. Gagnon, 102, 45-48, 85
55. Gagnon, 49
56. Gagnon, 51-3. I am indebted to his summary of the source criticism.
57. Gagnon, 55-56
58. Gagnon, 58
59. *Corrector Sive Medicus,* XIX.5 §153
60. Gagnon, 57-8
61. §151, *quod teutonica werewulff vocantur,* and §194 *quod Teutonice belisa vocantur,* in Gagnon, 65
62. 19 .5. 70, in Gagnon, 58
62a. On the life of Herodias, and for analysis of the Harley scene, see www.sourcememory.net/veleda/?p=595
63. Grimm, 250
64. West, 340-41
65. Grimm, 250
66. Grimm, 283, on Raterius.
67. Ginsburg 1991: 104. He translates Fera Comhera as "with cruel Hera," which I read as "wild Hera," as in "feral." See Pascal, 102; Green 1992: 82
68. Lea, 177. Ginsburg (1991: 104) locates this myth in the Palatinate region.
69. Gobelinus Persona, after Schilter, voc. Cherioburge, in Duncan, 73, and Grimm, 254
70. Lecouteux (2011) documents traditions of the company of the dead.
71. Gardenstone, 99
72. Russell 1972: 49. He also refers to male figures such as Herne and Herlechin.
73. Ginzberg 1991: 92-93
74. Grimm, 283-84
75. *Homilies of Aelfric,* I, 486, in Grimm, 284-85. Mann (93) identifies Aelfric as the oldest source for the Herodias myth.
76. Mann, 92
77. Ysengrimus II 73-94, in Mann, 93
78. *Ysengrimas,* Grimm, 285; Bonomo, 28
79. Mann, 93
80. Behringer 1994: 42-43
81. Grimm, 285
82. See Mann, 94

83. Ginzburg 1991: 148
84. Johannes Hartlieb, *Book of All For-bidden Arts*, in Schaff, Vol. 5, Part 2, 527
85. *De Universo*, in Grimm, 1059, trans-lated by Eileen Berkun
85b. *De Universo*, 12, in Russell 1972: 146
85c. *De Universo*, in Harf-Lancner, 53
86. Lea 1957: 175, my translation. "Witches" translates Old French *estries*.
87. Grimm, 456, points to the expres-sion *die guten holden*, comparing them to the Irish *daoine shi* and Welsh *dynion mad*, faery names that mean the "good people."
88. Filotas, 76. Focusing on the Latin word, she thinks that people thought of Holda as a "baby-eating, man-eating *striga*," rather than the beneficent god-dess that her Germanic name indicates.
89. Grimm, 1007
90. Filotas, 76, suggests "generous Friga."
91. Grimm, 1367
92. Grimm, 269
93. Waschnitius, 105, 36, 48, 62, in Reaves, online
94. Johannes Prætorius, in Lecouteux 2001: 219
95. Waschnitius 1913: 89, in Ellis Davidson, 66
96. Reaves, 7
97. Rüttner-Cova 1986: 78
98. Waschnitius, 89, in Reaves, online
99. For more on Holle, see Motz 1984, and Dashu, Vol X, forthcoming.
100. Boyer, 631
101. Simek, 154-55
102. Gardenstone, 80-81
103. Waschnitius, 87, in Reaves, online
104. Grimm, 1162
105. Ralston 1970
106. Oinas, 103
107. Grimm, 1162
108. Grimm, 269, 1368
109. Grimm, 269
110. *mött de Holle fahren*, in Motz 1984:

154, 156
111. Grimm, 1370; 277-79
112. Motz 1984: 155
113. *Thesaurus pauperum*, Tegernsee MS 434, in Kraus, 169
114. Waschnitius, 47, in Reaves, online
115. Lecouteux 2001: 150
116. Grimm, 430 (medieval spellings)
117. Some scholars equated Berthe with the Germanic earth goddess: "Nerthus or Hertha (Frau Bertha), the earth." See for example Tillinghast, 164.
118. Motz 1984: 153
119. Motz 1984: 151
120. Motz 1984: 152-54
121. Waschnitius, 33, in Reaves, online
122. Lumley, 279
123. Bonomo, 454
124. Sebillot, 332; Grimm, 280
125. Grimm, 280
126. Grimm, 1371
127. Johns, 75
128. Grimm, 1371
129. Baring-Goulds, 17
130. Nicolas Bertrand relates the story of Austris in *De Tolosanum Gestis*, 1515. http://fr.wikipedia.org/wiki/Reine_Pédauque#cite_note-7
131. Harf-Lancner, 99
132. Mineau & Racinoux, 356-7
133. http://tinyurl.com/h8ddhzd
134. See Berger, 1985; and Dashu Vol VI, forthcoming
135. http://tinyurl.com/h8ddhzd
136. Dunbar, 117
137. Sebillot 1894: 4
138. Dunbar, 120
139. MacCullogh, 47
140. Sebillot 1907: 332. See www.suppressedhistories.net/secrethisto-ry/oldgoddess.html for more on the Stone-Raising Spinner Goddess.
141. McNeill and Gamer (349) read *Per-sonarum*, "persons," as *Parcarum*, "fates." See also MacColloch, 38

142. Behringer 1994: 52; Magliocco 2009:43; Leland 1998: 127-33
143. Grimm, 1057. A later volume will look at these transformations of the Old Goddess in more depth.
144. On the pagan and demonized forms of Luxuria, see: http://tinyurl.com/h873zjr Also: http://tinyurl.com/gorsn3a

Chapter 8: Early Witch Burnings

1. I document witch laws from 550-800—since no trial records exist—in Vol VI, *Women in a Time of Overlords*
2. Kieckhefer 1976: 179
3. Davis, 122
4. *Annales Weissenburgenses,* in Flint, 210 n. 31
5. Kieckhefer, 1976: 179
6. Flint, 62
7. Russell 1972: 73
8. Baroja, 56
9. Cauzons, 118
10. Hefele III, 993; Filotas, 311
11. Filotas, 311-12
12. Lea 1901: 415
13. Lea, 429. I discuss Spanish repression in the 7th-8th centuries in Vol VII.
14. Ureña y Smenjaud, 79, citing Menenez y Pelayo 1880: 570
15. Russell 1972: 73. For more details on these early medieval persecutions, see Dashu, *Women in a Time of Overlords.*
16. Quierzy-sur-Oise statutes, in Russell 1972: 73.
17. McNamara, 170
18. Lea 1901: 414. Fournier, 63; McNamara, 171. The Latin phase used is *more maleficorum,* in *Historiarum Libri IIII,* I, v, and *Vita Hludovici Imperatoris,* in Flint, 82.
19. Lea 1901: 414
20. Flint, 156

21. Wemple, 95. The source is Reinhold Rau, ed. *Anonymi vita Hludowici imperatoris* 44, 53 (in Enright, 67, n. 63)
22. Hansen 1900: 115
23. Filotas, 288. Russell 1972: 73; Wemple, 81, 95; Nelson, 239, 254 n. 104; Stafford, 29
24. Filotas, 292
25. Mitchell, 164
26. *Borough Customs of London,* 1904, in Cohn, 153-4; Crawford, 167; Flint, 230
27. Stafford, 188. She must have thought a reference to Bertilla's female counselor as Circe referred to the queen herself.
28. Arnaldi, online. Thanks to Demetra George for translation of the Latin.
29. Arnaldi, online. Thanks to Roberta Cimino, for supplying this information on <medfem-l@list.uiowa.edu>: "Bertilla of Spoleto: witchcraft or adultery charges?" Mar 27, 2015
30. Reuter, 138-39
31. Reuter, 138-39; Kieckhefer 2000: 187
32. Hansen 1900: 116
33. *Annales de Saint-Aubin,* in McCracken, 191, n. 19
34. Elliott, 129
35. Elliott, 129
36. Stafford, in Elliott, 129 n. 146
37. Lea 1973: 233-4; Schulenberg, 344-5
38. http://en.wikipedia.org/wiki/Richardis
39. Filotas, 234-5. She does not supply the Latin term, and notes that the only copy is seven centuries later than the Conciliam Rispacense. See chapter 5 for my critique of using "necromancy" for Germanic ancestor oracles.
40. Corry, 79-80
41. Book II, Section 1, Article 35, in Baroja, 82. His citation differs from Ureña y Smenjaud, 84, who gives it as Article 42.
42. Corry, 82
43. Ureña y Smenjaud, 84

44. Ureña y Smenjaud, 84

45. Wedeck, 257; Lea 1957: 139

46. Ureña y Smenjaud, 83-85

47. Ureña y Smenjaud, 85

48. Ureña y Smenjaud, 85

49. Ureña y Smenjaud, 85

50. Ureña y Smenjaud, 10

51. See Dillard, 1990, on the *mala muger* and the legal definition of prostitute

52. Benjamin Thorpe, *Ancient Laws & Institutes* (1840) in Ewen, 1929: 3

53. Ewen, 3

54. *Stria et meretrix*, in Franck, 627; Wemple, 223, n. 77

55. Lea 1957: 1253

56. Flint, 382. Weston (287) shows that the *hægtessen* were linked with *ganea*, "whore," in glosses.

57. Lea 1901: Vol III, 420

58. Wedeck, 257

59. Centini, 3

60. Mitchell, 152

61. Lederer, 196-7

62. Ewen, 3-4; Lea, 420

63. Wedeck, 257

64. Ewen, 5

65. Flint, 41

66. www.bl.uk/manuscripts/Viewer. aspx?ref=cotton_ms_claudius_b_iv_ fs001r

67. Crawford, 165

68. Crawford, 164

69. *Historia Ecclesiae* II.56, also known as the *Liber Eliensis*. See Norton, 5.

70. Norton, 6

71. Norton, 6

72. Lea 1901 Vol 3: 419-20

73. *Historia comitum Ghisnensium*, in Ingstrand 2009, online

74. Lea 1901 Vol III: 419

75. Thorpe, 379

76. Cnut II, 5, Storms, 115

77. Holinshed, online

78. Holinshed, online

79. Holinshed, online

80. Russell 1972: 308

81. Cauzons, 133

82. The words are Lea's summary (1957: 139) of documentation in Hansen's *Zauberwahn*.

83. Grimm, 1068, n. 2: *malefica mulier artes maleficas cum tribus aliis mulieribus exercens*

84. Lea 1901: 419; Grimm 1068, n 2: *mulier homines plerumque magicis artibus dementare infamata*

85. Tractenberg (1939: 7) gives a date of 1066; Kieckhefer (2000: 83) gives it as 1130; and Brann, 58, as 1059.

86. Fennell, 80

87. Hubbs, 21-2

88. Franklin, 263

89. Fennell, 82

90. Baroja, 57, has "innocent women"; Lea 1901: 143, 417; Flint, 114

91. *Annales S. Stephani Frisingensis*, in Cohn, 155; Russell 1972: 321, n. 20

92. Summers, 360-1; Cauzons, 166-7

93. Mitchell, 169

94. Lea 1901: 418

95. Flint, 233

96. Flint, 293-94. See forthcoming Vol VI, *Overlords*, for more details.

97. Lea 1901: 418

98. Flint, 233

99. *Njalssaga* 5-8

100. Fish, online

101. *At Bernardo, insidiis muliebribus, maleficis artibus corpore fatescente, vitae privato. Corpus Christianorum Continuatio Medievalis*, vol. 129, III. 38, p 160, in https://en.wikipedia.org/wiki/Bernard_I_William_of_Gascony

102. Fournier, 63-65; Cauzons, 168-9; Kieckhefer 2000: 187

103. Landes, 180

104. Landes, 180

105. Moore, 140-44, in Landes, 188

106. Landes, 46

107. Landes, 188

108. Landes, 189. But Landes projects a "poisoning" of William of Angoulême onto his daughter-in-law, Alaiza. No evidence exists that the count had been poisoned, but Landes paints Alaiza as a power-hungry schemer, and even speaks (185) of "the crimes of Alaiza"!

109. Landes, 190

110. Landes, 190

111. Dubravius, *Historia Bohemicae*, 1687, in Lea 1280. I've regularized names.

112. Russell 1972: 96. For more on the military "conversions" of the Czechs, Wends, and Poles, see Vol VIII, *Priestcraft*, forthcoming.

113. Fournier, 53. *Striges* is the plural of the Latin *strix*.

114. Russell 1972: 71

115. BL MS Cotton Tiberius Aiii, in Meaney 1981: 65

Chapter 9: Völuspá

1. West, 92

2. The translations that follow are my synthesis of Clunies-Ross, Vol I; Dronke 1996: VII, 225-232; Hollander, 1962; Larrington 1996; Lindow 2003; Kvilhaug 2014; and other editions linked at www.germanicmythology.com/index.html#Resources

3. Clunies Ross (I. 153) remarks "if not a giantess herself." McKinnell (2001: 397; 413) proposes that she is a giantess with the *völva*-name Heið.

4. Kvihaug 2014: 10. Price (2002: 109) gives "nine wood-giantesses"; Larrington (6) has "nine women."

5. These lines come from from *Heimdalargaldar*, which Snorri quotes in *Gylfaginning* 25, here translated by Faulkes, 25-26.

6. See *Rígsthula*, and *Völuspá* 1:1-4

7. *Hyndluljóð* 37-38, www.sacred-texts.

com/neu/poe/poe15.htm

8. *Sólarljóð* 79. Kvilhaug's translation, online

9. See chapter 6

10. *Vafthrúðnismál* 43

11. *Gylfaginning* 34

12. Stanzas 6, 9. Such councils are also described in *Thrymskviða* 14 and *Baldrs draumr* I. Jochens 1989: 350

13. Kvilhaug, *Sólarljóð* 51, online

14. Clunies-Ross I, 59

15. Clunies Ross (I, 67, n. 26) translates *ámátcar mioc* as "very powerful; Hollander (3) as "awful in might." Jochens (1989: 353) notes that *ámátkar,* the Maiden's "mightiness," is "a term normally used for witches." *Thurs* means "giant, ogre."

16. Clunies Ross, I, 201

17. *Völuspá* stanzas 9-16

18. *Völuspá* 17; Cod. Reg. *orloglasa* and Hauksbok *orluglausa*

19. *Völuspá* 20. See Larrington, 264; Ellis Davidson (1998: 120) thought that this passage might give "two pictures of the norns, ominous or benign according as they bring evil or favorable fortune."

20. Kauffmann, 16

21. *Völuspá* 20, in Clunies-Ross I, 203

22. *Gylfaginning* 17, 30-21

23. *Hávamál* 111

24. See Dronke 1997; Price 2002: 110

25. *Völuspá* 25

26. *Völuspá* 24, Hauksbók, online. "Mighty and benevolent": stanza 17.

27. The text and translation below are taken from www.germanicmythology.com/works/hauksbokvoluspa.html, which explains that translators take *thussa* as *thursa*—"ogresses, giants"

28. *Gylfaginning* 12, online

29. St. 21 in Codex Regius; st. 26 in Hauksbók

30. My translation, drawing on Turville-Petre, 157; Hollander, 4; Bray, 283-85;

Bellows, 10; McKinnell 2001: 394

31. *Grímnismál* 25; *Gylfaginning* 38-43

32. Kvilhaug, 137

33. McKinnell, 394

34. Turville Petre, 158-9

35. Kvilhaug, 137

36. Näsström 1998: 68, 91, 128; and
Simek 1996: 122. I'm indebted to Maria
Kvilhaug (2004; 135-37) for these cites.

37. Blain, 102

38. Blain, 102

39. Clunies Ross I, 205. The scapegoating seems as effective now as it was then.

40. Clunies Ross I, 199; 206

41. Turner 1823, online

42. An online search shows that many
contemporary heathens favor this translation. Kvilhaug (2004: 138) suggests
that the burning was an initiatory passage in which Gullveig overcame death
itself, possibly becoming a goddess in
the process. Blain (102) speculates that
it could have been an initiation by fire
that gave Gullveig knowledge of *seiðr*.

43. Exponents include Gabriel Turville-Petre, Ursula Dronke, Rudolf Simek,
Carolyne Larrington, and John Lindow,
among many others.

44. McKinnell (2001: 396-9, 412-3)
thinks that Gullveig is an idol, and views
Heiðr as the prophetess of *Völuspá*, and
a giantess to boot.

45. Clunies Ross, II, 33

46. Dronke 1996 VI, 58

47. Clunies Ross I, 210

48. *Hyndluljóð* 41, in Larrington, 258

49. Clunies Ross I, 184

50. Dronke 1996: III, 660

51. Jochens 1989: 353, n. 22

52. Ström 1942: 189, quoted in Clunies
Ross I, 208, n. 16

53. See chapter 8. The reason for the
qualifier "primarily women" is that Jewish and Muslim men were also subject to
burning if convicted of having sex with

Christian women.

54. *Thorsteins saga Víkingssonar*, Mitchell, 87-88

55. Mitchell, 165

56. Dronke 1996: VII, 223

57. Heimskringla I: Freyja "was the
first to teach *seiðr*, common among the
Vanir, to the Aesir." in North, 85

58. Clunies-Ross I, 200

59. *Völuspá* 23, in Larrington, 7

60. Lindow, 51

61. Hollander, 4

62. McKinnell 2001: 395

63. Dronke 1996: VII, 226-7

64. Larrington 1996: 7

65. See McKinnell 2001: 402; & chapter 4

66. *Hauksbók*, online

67. *Ynglingasaga* 4

68. *Völuspá* (Codex Regius 50; Hauksbók 41); *Hávamál* 142 and 159, *Grímnismál* 4; *Skírnismál* 7, 17, 18; *Lokasenna*
2, 13, 30; and *Þrymskviða* 6

69. Codex Regius 50, Hauksbok 40

70. The *wið færstice* spell, in Hall, 43;
MacCullough 1930: 120 on the phrase
"*aesir* and *alfar*". See chapter 5.

71. *Grímnismál* 5

72. Shetelig / Falk, 420

73. *Thorsteins saga vikingssonar*, in Ellis
1968: 113

74. *Snorra Edda* 57, in Samplonius, 261

75. Hedeager, 17

76. Shetelig / Falk, 420

77. *Skírnismál*, 18: 1-3

78. *Sigrdrífumál* 18

79. *Fáfnismál*, 13, my translation

80. *Alvíssmál* 20. Kauffmann (13) wrote,
"It is significant that the word *goð* was
originally of neuter gender, to include
masculine and feminine."

81. *Vafthrúðnismál* 39 (*víssum Vönum*)
in Bray, 52. I've emended "Wanes" to
Vanir, and *aldar rök* to a more literal
translation than "in the story of time."

82. Simek 2010: 12 lists the attestations

for *víssa vana*

83. *Þrymskviða* 14, in Bellows

84. West, 121; Hall and Grimm; Joao Lópes on proto-Germanic, in cybalist@ yahoogroups.com, July 21, 2006

85. Mallory and Adams, 410

86. Lindow, 49

87. D.Q. Adams, "King", in *Encyclopedia of Indo-European Culture*. London: Fitzroy Dearborn, 1997: 330

88. Mallory and Adams, 410

89. Hall, 35-37

90. West (160) highlights a concept of "the former gods" found in Hesiod (Greek), the Rg Veda, and Hittite texts.

91. Hall 2004: 34, 43-45

92. Hall 2004: 44

93. Hall, 45, 50

94. Hall 2004: 40. His thesis is that *álfar* are male and *dísir* female ancestral spirits, which he compares with a masculine gendering of the elves in Anglo-Saxon. According to Shetelig and Falk (428) the *álfablót* were "less frequent" than those to the *dísir*.

95. Hall, 118-122

96. Hall 2004: 130

97. Meaney 1981: 72-3

98. Hall 2004: 96-7

99. Hall 2004: 120

100. North, 52

101. This was the consensus, at least, on the IE linguistics listserv *cybalist*. See George Knyzh "Re: Aryanism and Journal of Indo-European Studies," Message 17996, cybalist yahoogroup.

102. Danielou, 141

103. Danielou, 141

104. *Völuspá* 7

105. Kauffmann, 13

106. "Sorcerers" for *seiðberendr*, in Bray, 220. That term denotes gender-nonconforming males.

107. *Rígsthula* 7

108. However, Bernhard Salin, an expert on the Norse animal style, proposed that Scandanavia had been colonized by an invasion from the Black Sea region. More recently Lotte Hedeager (2011: 95-105, 154-55) has hypothesized Hunnic influence, via steppe art of the animal style, on Nordic metalwork and carving.

109. Clunies Ross I, 183

110. Clunies Ross I, 194

111. Clunies Ross I, 71; 274

112. Dronke 1996: V, 102

113. McKinnell, 2001: 413

114. Boyer, 623

115. Motz, 1996; Simek 2010: 13

116. Hastrup 1985, in Hall, 50

117. Hall, 41-42

118. Eugen Mogk may have been the first, in "Zur Gigantomachie der Völuspá," 1924

119. Simek 2010; McKinnell 6, online

120. Simek 2010: 10-13

121. *Skáldskaparmál* 20; 28; 37; in http://heimskringla.no/wiki/Skáldskaparmál

122. Simek 2010: 18

123. *Þrymskviða* 14

124. Larrington, xiv, 7, goes with the classic interpretation of the Vanir.

125. West (164) proposed that the Vanir were a separate, possibly subaltern group, who were absorbed.

126. *Skáldskaparmál* 57

127. *Ynglingasaga* 4

128. *Rg Veda* IX, i; xvi; passim

129. Dronke 1996, IV: 679ff

130. *Mahabharata*, Adi Parva, Astika Parva, Section 18. The story is also told in the Bhagavata and Vishnu Puranas.

131. Dronke 1996: IV, 679-80, citing *Mahābhārata* and *Bhagavata-Purana*

132. Dronke 1996, VI: 58ff

133. *Gylfaginning* 42

134. Dronke 1996: VI, 59, 83

135. *Völuspá* St. 25

136. Lionarons (2005) notes that most of the goddesses Snorri names are empty

abstract categories who mainly function as consorts for the male gods, but aren't mentioned in the Edda or sagas.

137. Clunies Ross I, 207
138. Orel, 112
139. *Gylfaginning* 35; *Hyndluljóð* 5
140. Boyer, 627
141. *Gylfaginning* 35
142. Hall (2002: 45, n. 46) says, "... Freyja, seen as the pre-eminent, divine *dís*, is usually assumed to be the *dís* of the Dísarsalr ('hall of the *dís*') mentioned in *Heiðreks saga* and *Ynglinga saga*."
143. Dumezil, 73
144. Turville-Petre, 178
145. Lindow, 129
146. Ellis Davidson 1969: 90
147. Clunies-Ross, I, 97-100
148. Jochens 1989: 352-53
149. Ots, online
150. Grimm, 1232
151. Grimm, 301-03; North, 255-57; https://en.wikipedia.org/wiki/Frijjō
152. OED s.v. "Friday"
153. www.etymonline.com/index.php?term=Friday
154. See Dashu, "The Old Goddess," online
155. Boyer, 627
156. Grimm, 302, 722. He compares (727) Friggerok to the Balkan star-name *babini sčtapi*, "old women's staff (or distaff)."
157. Grimm 1500, citing *Kalevala* 32, 20
158. Enright 1990: 54-70
159. Pesch, 386
160. https://en.wiktionary.org/wiki/frig
161. Grimm, 304
162. Eckenstein, 32
163. *Thrymskviða* 3; and in Snorri
164. Price 2002: 108
165. *Lokasenna* 32; Grimm, 1033. "Doing" or "making" is a common root of "sorceress" words; see chapter 3.
166. Bray, 235-7

167. Freitag, 25
168. Freitag, 27
169. Quinn 2015, online
170. *Lokasenna* 25, in Quinn 2015, online
171. *Völuspá* CR 27; H 23
172. Quinn 2015, online, quoting MS Gl. kg. sml. 2365, 4o
173. Larrington, 8
174. Dronke 1996 II, 18; 19
175. *Völuspá* 28, in Hollander, 6. Another translation has, "What do you ask of me? Why test me? I know everything, Óðinn, where you hid your eye." Neckel and Kuhn 1983, 7, in Quinn 1998: 34
176. *Völuspá* 29. 1–2
177. *Völuspá* 29. 3–4, in Hollander, 6
178. Clunies Ross, I: 237
179. Lindow, 143
180. Dronke 1997: 16
181. *Völuspá hin skamma*, in *Hyndluljóð* 50. Lindow has, "Do you wish yet more?"
182. Yngona Desmond, "Re: Freyja," asynjur yahoogroup, May 11, 2008
183. Völuspá 43, in Hollander, 9
184. Völuspá 44, in Hollander, 9
185. Hollander, 9
186. *Heimskringla* 133, in Laing and Anderson, 289
187. Hollander, 12
188. *Vafthrúðnismál* 47, in Hollander, 50
189. *Vafthrúðnismál* 45
190. *Vafthrúðnismál* 39, in Dronke 1996 II, 13. She sees the Vanir as unaffected by Ragnarok, since they "are always alive in the world of the dead."
191. Jochens: 1989: 356
192. Jochens 1989: 358
193. Dronke 1996: II, 19
194. Dronke 1996. II, 3-21; McKinnell 2008, online. Lindow, 313, has "the powerful one will come from on high, he who rules all."
195. Dronke 1996 II: 15
196. Dronke 1996: II, 20, n. 30; and 21,

n. 31
197. McKinnell 2008: 9-11, 12-20
198. McKinnell 2008: 22
199. Olmsted, 29. Other lines in
these prophecies have a more
patriarchal slant.
200. See Dashu, Vol III,
forthcoming
201. Hall 32-33
202. See Jochens 1998: 344 n. 1
203. Jochens 1989: 347-50, 354
204. Jochens 1989: 346, n. 8
205. Straubhaar 1993: 594-596
206. Straubhaar 1993
207. Straubhaar, citing Barði
Guðmundsson (1967)
208. Straubhaar, 595

Conclusion

1. De Cauzons, 118
2. See titles of *Secret History of
the Witches* series at the end of
this book.

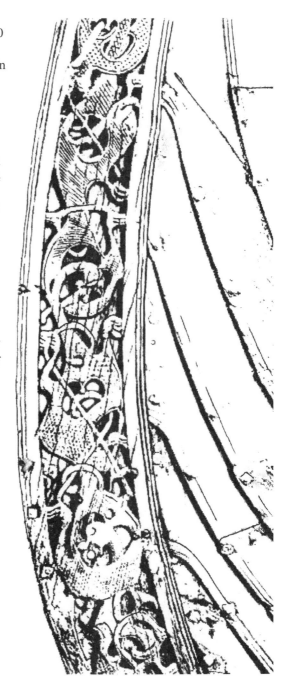

*Prow of the Oseberg ship: a ceremonial
burial of two Norwegian priestesses in 834 CE*

Aelfric, "The Passion of St Bartholemew the Apostle," in Benjamin Thorpe, *The Homilies Of The Anglo-Saxon Church*, London: The Aelfric Society, 1844

American Heritage Dictionary, 3rd Edition. Boston: Houghton Mifflin, 1992

Andersen, Jørgen, *The Witch on the Wall: Medieval Erotic Sculpture in the British Isles*, George Allen & Unwin, London, 1977

Andersons, Edgar, et al. *Cross road country: Latvia*. Waverly, Iowa: Latvju Grāmata, 1953

Ankarloo, Bengt, "Blakulla, ou le sabbat des sorciers scandinaves," in Jacques-Chaquin, Nicole, and Préaud, Maxime, eds, *Le Sabbat des Sorciers en Europe: XVe-XVIIIe siecles*, Paris: Jerome Millon, 1993

_____. "Magies scandinaves et sorciers du nord," in *Magie et Sorcellerie en Europe du Moyen Age à Nos Jours*, ed. Robert Muchembled, Paris: A. Colin, 1994

Ann, Martha, and Imer, Dorothy Myers. *Goddesses in World Mythology: A Biographical Dictionary*. New York: Oxford University Press, 1993

Anonymous. "The women and gold treasure of Tuna." Online: www.anundshog.se/artikel.asp?strukturId=404&artikelId=1365

Anonymous. "Caillagh y groamagh: The woman who sat by the sea..." The Atlantic Religion blog. Sept. 19, 2014 Online: http://atlanticreligion.com/tag/caillagh-y-groamagh/

Anonymous. "The Cailleach." The Atlantic Religion blog. Aug 26, 2013. Online: http://atlanticreligion.com/2013/08/26/the-cailleach/

Anonymous. "Les Jours De La Vieille En France." http://la.vieille.free.fr/jjbase-joursfrancea.htm

Aranzadi, Juan, *Milenarismo vasco: Edad de oro, etnia y nativismo, La Otra Historia de España*, Vol 7, Taurus, 1981

Arent, Margaret A. *The Laxdæla Saga, translated from the Old Icelandic*. Seattle: University of Washington. 1964

Arnaldi, Girolamo, *Dizionario Biografico degli Italiani* - Vol. 9 (1967), s.v. "Bertilla." Online: www.treccani.it/enciclopedia/bertilla_(Dizionario-Biografico)/

Arwill-Nordbladh, Elisabeth, "Ability and Disability. On Bodily Variations and Bodily Possibilities in Viking Age Myth and Image." in *To Tender Gender: the Pasts and Futures of Gender Research in Archaeology*. eds. Ing-Marie Back Danielsson and Susanne Thedéen, Stockholm Studies in Archaeology 58, 2012

Austin, Greta. *Shaping church law around the year 1000: The Decretum of Burchard of Worms*. Burlington VT : Ashgate, 2009.

icine, George Allen and Unwin Ltd, London, 1952

Banks, M. M. "Scoring a Witch above the Breath." *Folk-lore* XXIII. London: The Folklore Society, 1912

Barandiarán, Jose M. de, *Mitología Vasca*, Editorial Txertoa, San Sebastian, 1979

Baring-Gould, William and Ceil, *The Annotated Mother Goose*, Bramhall House, New York, 1962

Julio Caro, *The World of the Witches*, translated by Nigel Glendinning. London: Weidenfeld and Nicolson, 1961

Bauschatz, Paul, *The Well and the Tree: World and Time in Early Germanic Culture*, University of Massachusetts Press, Amherst, 1982

Beck, Noémie. "Goddesses in Celtic Religion. Cult and Mythology: A Comparative Study of Ancient Ireland, Britain and Gaul." Disssertation, Dec. 2009, online: http://theses.univ-lyon2.fr/documents/lyon2/2009/beck_n/info

Behringer, Wolfgang, *Shaman of Oberstdorf: Chonrad Stoeckhlin and the Phantoms of the Night.* Translated by H.C. Eric Midelfort. Charlottesville: University Press of Virginia, 1994

Bede, *A History of the English Church and People,* tr by Leo Sherley-Price, Baltimore: Penguin, 1968

Bek-Pedersen, Karen. "The Norns: Representatives of Fate in Old Norse Tradition." In *Goddesses in World Culture, Vol II: Eastern Mediterranean and Europe.* ed. Patricia Monaghan, Praeger: Santa Barbara CA, 2011

Bellows, Henry Adams, *The Poetic Edda,* Scandanavian Classics, Vols XXI and XXII, New York: The American-Scandanavian Foundation, 1957

Benoit, Felix and Bruno, *Hérésies et Diableries à Lyon et Alentours,* Editions Horvath, 1987

Berger, Pamela, *The Goddess Obscured: Transformation of the Grain Protectress from Goddess to Saint,* Beacon Press, Boston, 1985

Beyer, Harald, *A history of Norwegian literature,* translated by Einer Haugen, New York: New York University Press for the American-Scandinavian Foundation, 1956

Beza, Marcu, *Paganism in Roumanian Folklore,* EP Dutton, NY, 1928

Bitel, Lisa M., *Land of Women: Tales of Sex and Gender from Early Ireland,* Ithaca: Cornell University Press, 1996

Bjarnadóttir, Valgerður Hjördís, "The Saga of Vanadís, Völva and Valkyrja: Images of the Divine from the Memory of an Islandic Woman," Masters Thesis, CIIS, San Francisco, 2002

Blain, Jenny, *Nine Worlds of Seid-Magic: Ecstasy an Neo-Shamanism in North European Paganism.* Online: http://coreyemmah.weebly.com/uploads/2/2/1/8/22181700/blain_-_nine_worlds_of_seid.pdf

Blind, Karl, "The Teutonic Tree of Existence," in *Fraser's Magazine,* Vol 15, No. 85, Jan 1877 (pp 108-117)

_____. "Shakspere's Weird Sisters." *The Academy* Vol. 15, 1879, pp. 190-191.

Bonnetain, Yvonne S. "Riding the Tree." Online: www.dur.ac.uk/medieval/www/sagaconf/bonnetain.htm Acc: May 21, 2009

Bonomo, Giuseppe, *Caccia alle Streghe: La Credenza nelle Streghe dall secolo XIII al XIX con particolare referimento all'Italia,* Palermo: Palumbo, 1959

Borsje, Jacqueline, "Fate in Early Irish Texts." Utrecht University Repository. Online: http://dspace.library.uu.nl/bitstream/handle/1874/37337/Fate_Borsje.pdf?sequence=1.2002

Bosworth, Joseph & T. Northcote Toller. *An Anglo-Saxon dictionary, based on the manuscript collections of the late Joseph Bosworth*; edited and enlarged by T. Northcote Toller. Oxford: Clarendon. (1998 reprint of 1898 edition). Online: https://books.google.com/books?id=oXlii1KgDngC&source=gbs_navlinks_s

Bouman, A.C. "The Franks Casket." *Neophilogus* 3 (1965), 241-49.

Boyer, Regis, "Some Reflections on the Terra-Mater Motive in Old Scandinavian Sources," in *Germanische Religionsgeschichte: Quellen und Quellen-Probleme,* ed.

Beck, Heinrich; Ellmers, Detler; and Scheir, Kurt. Berlin: DeGruyter, 1922

John Brand, John, Sir Henry Ellis, and James Orchard Halliwell-Phillipps, *Observations on the Popular antiquities of Great Britain: Chiefly Illustrating the Origin of Our Vulgar and Provincial Customs, Ceremonies, and Superstitions.* Vol. 2. London: G. Bell, 1901

Branston, Brian, *The Lost Gods of England*, Thames and Hudson, London, 1957

Brauner, Sigrid, *Fearless Wives and Frightened Shrews: The Construction of the Witch in Early Modern Germany*, Amherst: University of Massachusetts Press, 1995

Bray, Olive, (Ed. & trans.) *The elder or poetic Edda, commonly known as Saemund's Edda*, London, The Viking club, 1908

Briggs, Katharine, *An Encyclopedia of Fairies: Hobgoblins, Brownies, Bogies and Other Supernatural Creatures*, Pantheon, 1976

Briggs, Katharine, *A Dictionary of British Folk-Tales in the English Language:* London: Routledge & K. Paul, 1970

British Library Manuscripts, Online: www.bl.uk/

Brocard-Plaut, Michele, *Diableries et Sorcelleries en Savoie*, Editions Horvath, 1986

Brundage, James A., *Law, Sex and Christian Society in Medieval Europe*, Chicago: University of Chicago, 1987

Buchan, David, ed., *Folk Tradition and Folk Medicine in Scotland: The* Lyons, #276 Edinburgh, 1994

Byrne, Martin. "Megalithic art at Cairn T." Online: www.carrowkeel.com/sites/loughcrew/cairnt2.html

Campbell, John Francis. Popular Tales of the West Highlands, Volume 3. Scotland: Edmonston and Douglas, 1862

Campbell, John Gregorson, *Witchcraft and Second Sight in the Highlands and Islands of Scotland: Tales and Traditions Collected Entirely from Oral Sources*, Detroit: Singing Tree Press, 1970

Canellada, Maria Josefa, *Folklore de Asturias: Leyendas, cuentos y tradiciones*, Ayalga Ediciones, Spain, 1983

Carmichael, Alexander, *Carmina Gadelica*, Edinburgh: Oliver and Boyd, 1984

Caspari, C.P. *Homilia de sacrilegiis: Eine Augustin fälschlich beilegte.* Christiana, 1886. Online: https://archive.org/details/MN41409ucmf_4

Cath Maige Tuired: The Second Battle of Mag Tuired. CELT: Corpus of Electronic Texts, Online: www.ucc.ie/celt/online/T300010/text168.html

Cauzons, Thomas de, *La Magie et la Sorcellerie en France*, Librarie Dorbon-Ainé, Paris, 1910/11

Centini, Massimo. "La Stregoneria In Piemonte: Fonti Storiche E Tante Leggende." Torino 1955. Online: www.incontritramontani.it/Files/Atti/ITM2008 - Centini.pdf

Chadwick, Nora. "Imbas Forosnai." *Scottish Gaelic Studies*, Vol. 4, part 2, Oxford University Press, 1935. Online: http://searchingforimbas.blogspot.com/p/imbas-forosnai-by-nora-k-chadwick.html

Charon, Veronique, "The Knowledge of Herbs," in *The Pagan Middle Ages*, ed. Ludo Miles, translated by Tanis Guest, Woodbridge UK: Boydell Press, 1998

Cheetham, Samuel, and Smith, William, *A Dictionary of Christian Antiquities.* London: J. Murray, 1908

Cleasby, Richard, and Gudbrand Vigfusson. *An Icelandic-English dictionary.* 1874. Online: http://lexicon.ff.cuni.cz/png/oi_cleasbyvigfusson/b0208.png

Clément, Catherine, *Opera: The Undoing of Women.* University of Minnesota Press, 1999.

von Cles-Reden, Sibylle, *The Realm of the Great Goddess: The Story of the Megalith Builders,* Englewood Cliffs NJ: Prentice-Hall, 1962

Clunies Ross, Margaret, *Prolonged Echoes: Old Norse Myths in Medieval Northern Society.* Odense, Denmark, Odense University Press. 1994

Cockayne, Thomas Oswald. *Leechdoms, wortcunning, and starcraft of early England.* London: Longman, Green, et al. 1864. Online: https://archive.org/details/leechdomswortcun02cock

Coffey, George, "On the Tumuli and Inscribed Stones at New Grange, Dowth, and Knowth." in *Transactions of the Royal Irish Academy,* Volume 30. Dublin: The Academy, 1896, online

Cohn, Norman, *Europe's Inner Demons: An Enquiry Inspired by the Great Witch-Hunt,* New York: Basic Books, 1975

Colgrave, B. and R.A.B. Minors, eds. and tr., *Bede's Ecclesiastical History of the English People,* Oxford: Clarendon Press, 1969

Colm, "The Moylough Belt Shrine." May 14, 2013. http://irisharchaeology.ie/2013/05/the-moylough-belt-shrine/

The Compact Edition of the Oxford English Dictionary. New York: Oxford University Press, 1971

Condren, Mary, *The Serpent and the Goddess: Women, Religion and Power in Celtic Ireland,* San Francisco: Harper and Row, 1989

_____. *Brigit (full title to be announced).* Dublin: New Island. 2016

Coromines, Joan, *Diccionari etimològic i complimentari de la llengua catalana,* Vol II. Barcelona: Curial. 1980-1992

Corry, Jennifer M. *Perceptions of Magic in Medieval Spanish Literature.* Bethlehem PA: Lehigh University Press, 2005

Coulton, G. G., *Life in the Middle Ages,* Cambridge, 1928

Craigie, William A., *Scandinavian folk-lore: illustrations of the traditional beliefs of the northern peoples,* Paisley, Scotland: A. Gardner, 1896.

Crawford, Jane, "Witchcraft in Anglo-Saxon England," (1963) in Levack Vol II: Witchcraft in the Ancient World and Middle Ages, 1992

_____ "Evidences for Witchcraft in Anglo-Saxon England." *Medium Ævum* 32.2 (1963): 99-116.

Crawford, John Martin, *Kalevala, The Epic Poem of Finland,* Cincinnati, 1898

Crist, Sean. *Germanic Lexicon Project.* Online: http://lexicon.ff.cuni.cz/

Cybeleia, Joanna Hypatia. "Why Are Witches Called Witches?" *Reclaiming Quarterly,* No. 9, 2009, pp. 17-19 Online: www.reclaimingquarterly.org/web/history/RQ99-17-History-WhyWitches.pdf

Daly, Mary. *Gyn/Ecology: The Metaethics of Radical Feminism,* Boston: Beacon Press, 1978

Damico, Helen, and Olsen, Alexandra Hennesy, eds, *New Readings on Women in Old English Literature,* Indiana U Press, Bloomington, 1990

Damico, Helen, "The Valkyrie Reflex in Old English Literature," in Damico and Oslen, 1990

Danielou, Alain, *The Gods of India: Hindu Polytheism*, New York: Inner Traditions International, 1985

Dashu, Max. "Kings Vs. Witches." (2000) Excerpt from *Secret History of the Witches, Women in a Time of Overlords*, Vol. VI, forthcoming. Online: www.suppressedhistories.net/secrethistory/kings_witches.html

_____. "The Old Goddess." (2000) Excerpt from *Secret History of the Witches*, Vol. X, forthcoming. Online: www.suppressedhistories.net/secrethistory/oldgoddess.html

_____. "The Grand Inquisitor of Toulouse." (2000) Excerpt from *Secret History of the Witches*, Vol. XI, forthcoming. Online: www.academia.edu/9734999/The_Grand_Inquisitor_of_Toulouse

_____. "Herbs, Knots and Contraception." (2004) Excerpt from *Secret History of the Witches*, Vol. VI, forthcoming. Online: www.academia.edu/9833263/Herbs_Knots_and_Contraception

_____. "Veleda, the prophetic female voice." (Dec. 2010) Online: www.sourcememory.net/veleda/?m=201012

_____. "Xi Wangmu, Great Goddess of China." In *Goddesses in World Culture*, ed. Patricia Monaghan. Santa Barbara CA: Praeger, 2011

_____. "Notre Dame de la Vie: Our Lady of Life." (April 2012) Part 1. Online: www.sourcememory.net/veleda/?p=539

_____. "Notre Dame de la Vie: Archaic Celtic Goddess." (April 2012). Part 3. Online. Part 2: www.sourcememory.net/veleda/?p=522

_____. "A Goddess in the Harley Psalter." (June 2012) Online: www.sourcememory.net/veleda/?m=201012

_____. "Raising the Dead: Medicine Women Who Revive and Retrieve Souls." (March 2013) Online: www.sourcememory.net/veleda/?p=638

_____. *Woman Shaman: the Ancients*. (Video) Oakland CA: Suppressed Histories Archives, 2013.

_____. "Seiðstaffs of the Völur." (2015) www.suppressedhistories.net/articles2/volur.html

_____. "The Emasculating Distaff." (2016) Online: www.suppressedhistories.net/articles/emasculating_distaff.html

_____. *Women in a Time of Overlords*, Vol VI of *Secret History of the Witches*, Veleda Press, forthcoming

Davidson, Hilda Ellis, *Roles of the Northern Goddess*, London/New York: Routledge, 1998

_____ *Scandinavian Mythology*. London: Hamlyn, 1969

_____ "Hostile Magic in the Icelandic Sagas," in *The Witch Figure*, ed. Venetia Newall, London, 1973

Davidson, Thomas, *Rowan Tree and Red Thread*, Edinburgh: Oliver & Boyd, 1949

Day, Cyrus Lawrence, *Quipus and Magic Knots: The Role of the Magic Knot in Primitive and Ancient Cultures*, Lawrence: University of Kansas Press, 1967

Delatte, Armand, *Herbarius: Recherches sur le Ceremonial usité chez les Anciens pour le Cueillette des simples et des plantes magiques*, Paris, 1936

Denham, Michael Aislabie, *The Denham Tracts : a collection of folklore reprinted from the original tracts and pamphlets printed by Mr. Denham between 1846 and 1859* (1892), London: Published for the Folklore Society, by D. Nutt, 1895

Dexter, Miriam Robbins. *Whence the Goddesses: A Source Book*. Oxford: Pergamon Press, 1990

Dillard, Heath, "Women in Reconquest Castile," *Women in Medieval Society*, ed. Susan Mosher Stuard, University of Pennsylvani Press, 1976

Dillard, Heath, *Daughters of the Reconquest: Women in Castilian Town Society*, 1100-1300, Library of Iberian Resources, http://libro.uca.edu/dillard.htm

Dillon, Myles, and Chadwick, Nora K., *The Celtic Realms*, Weidenfeld and Nicolson, London, 1972

Dinneen, Patrick S. *Foclóir Gaedhilge Agus Béarla An Irish-English Dictionary*, Dublin: Irish Texts Society / M. H. Gill & Son, 1904

Dixon-Kennedy, Mike. *Encyclopedia of Russian and Slavic Myth and Legend*. Santa Barbara CA: ABC-CLIO, 1998

Dömötör, Tekla, *Hungarian Folk Beliefs*, Bloomington: University of Indiana Press, 1981

Douglas and Greenaway, eds, *English Historical Documents*, London: Eyre and Spottiswoode, 1961

Drinker, Sophie, *Music and Women: the story of women in their relation to music*. New York: Coward-McCann, 1948

Dronke, Ursula, ed/trans., *The Poetic Edda*, Vol I: Heroic Poems. Oxford: Clarendon Press, 1969

_____. "Völuspá and Sibilline Traditions," in *Myth and Fiction in Early Norse Lands*. Aldershot UK: Variorum, 1996. II: 3-21.

_____. "Voluspa and Satiric Tradition," 1996, VI: 57-86.

_____. "Eddic Poetry as a source for the history of Germanic religion," 1996, IV: 656-684

_____. "The War of the Aesir and Vanir in Völuspá." 1996, VII: 223-237

_____. *The Poetic Edda: Vol II, Mythological Poems*. Ed. & tr. Dronke, 1997.

DuBois, Thomas. *Nordic Religions in the Viking Age*. University of Pennsylvania Press, 1999

DuCange, *Glossarium Mediae et Infimae Latinitatis*, Niort, 1883-87

DuCange, Charles du Fresne, et al., *Glossarium mediæ et infimæ latinitatis*. Niort: L. Favre, 1883-1887. Online: http://ducange.enc.sorbonne.fr/

Duignan, Michael, "The Moylough (Co. Sligo) and Other Irish Belt-Reliquaries."- *Journal of the Galway Archaeological and Historical Society*, Vol. 24, No. 3/4 (1951), pp. 83-94

Dumézil, Georges, *Gods of the Ancient Northmen*, ed. Einar Haugen, Berkeley: University of California Press, 1973

Dumont, Darl J., "The Ash Tree in Indo-European Culture." *Mankind Quarterly*, Volume XXXII, Number 4, Summer 1992, pp. 323-336. Online: www.musaios.com/ash.htm

Dzērvītis, Aleksandra. *Latvju raksti*. Toronto: Amber, Latvian Federation in

Canada, 1973.

Earle, John "Anglo-Saxon Literature." www.archive.org/stream/anglosaxonliter-a17101gut/17101-0.txt

Eckenstein, Lina, *Woman Under Monasticism: Chapters on Saint-Lore and Convent Life*, Cambridge UK: University Press, 1896

Eirik the Red's Saga. Translated by John Sephton, 1880. [EBook #17946, Mar 8, 2006] www.gutenberg.org/files/17946/17946-h/17946-h.htm

Ellis, Hilda Roderick, *The Road to Hel: A Study of the Conception of the Dead in Old Norse Literature*. New York: Greenwood, 1968

Eliade, Mircea. *Shamanism: Archaic Techniques of Ecstasy*, Princeton: Bollingen, 1972

————. *Zalmoxis: The Vanishing God, Comparative Studies in the Religion and Folklore of Dacia and Eastern Europe*. Chicago: University of Chicago Press, 1972b

Óluva Ellingsgaard, "Var Odin en kvinde?" *Videnskab DK*, January 2010. Online: http://videnskab.dk/kultur-samfund/var-odin-en-kvinde

Elliott, Dyan, Spiritual Marriage: Sexual Abstinence in Medieval Wedlock. Princeton NJ: Princeton University Press, 1995

Enna, Francesco, *Fiabe sarde*. Milano: A. Mondadori, 1991

Enright, Michael, "Goddess Who Weaves: Some Iconographic Aspects of Bracteates of the Fürstenberg Type." *Frühmittelalterliche Studien* 24 (1990), pp 54-70

————. *Lady with the Mead Cup: Ritual, prophecy and lordship in the European warband from La Tène to the Viking Age*. Dublin: Four Courts Press, 1996

Ersnt, Windisch. "The Appearance of the Morrígu to Cuchullin before the Táin bóCuailnge." In *The Cuchullin Saga in Irish Literature*, Issue 8. Ed. Eleanor Hull. London: D. Nutt, 1898

d'Este, Sorita, and David Rankine, *Visions of the Cailleach: Exploring the Myths, Folklore, and Legends of the Pre-eminent Celtic Hag Goddess*. London: Avalonia, 2009

Evans, Ivor H., *Brewer's Dictionary of Phrase and Fable*. New York: Harper and Row, 1981

Evans-Pritchard, E. E. *Witchcraft, oracles and magic among the Azande*. Oxford: Clarendon, 1937

Evans-Wentz, *The Fairy-Faith in Celtic Countries*, Humanities Press, NJ, 1978

Ewen, C. L'Estrange, *Witch Hunting and Witch Trials*, Kegan Paul, Trench, Trubner & Co, London, 1929

"The Expulsion of the Déssi [Déisi]." ed. Mary Jones. Celtic Literature Collective. Online: www.maryjones.us/ctexts/dessi2.html

Faulkes, Anthony, tr. *Edda*. London: Everyman, 1995

Fennel, John L. *A History of the Russian Church to 1488*. New York: Routledge, 2014

Ferraro, Gary, and Susan Andreatta. *Cultural Anthropology: An Applied Perspective*. Tenth edition. Boston: Cengage Learning, 2014

Fick, August, with Hjalmar Falk and Alf Torp, *Wörterbuch der Indogermanischen Sprachen: Dritter Teil: Wortschatz der Germanischen Spracheinheit*, 1909.

Filotas, Bernadette. *Pagan Survivals, Superstitions and Popular Cultures in Early Medieval Pastoral Literature*. Toronto: PIMS, Jan 1, 2005

Fischer, Katherine, ed. and tr., *The Burgundian Code*, Philadelphia: University of Pennsylvania Press, 1949

Fish, Karen. ""Descendants of Charlemagne," Online: www.ffish.com/family_tree/descendants_charlemagne/d1.htm

Fletcher, Richard, *The Barbarian Conversion: From Paganism to Christianity*, New York: Henry Holt and Co, 1997

Flint, Valerie, *The Rise of Magic in Early Medieval Europe*, Princeton: Princeton University Press, 1991

Fogel, Daniel, *Junipero Serra, the Vatican and Enslavement Theology*, San Francisco: Ism Press, 1988

Fossard, Lee. "La Vieille dans la toponymie du Royaume-Uni et de l'Irlande : trace d'un ancien culte voué à la Nature ?" *Linguistics*. 2014. Online: http://dumas.ccsd.cnrs.fr/dumas-01080422

Fournier, Pierre-François, *Magie et Sorcellerie*, Moulins: Editions Ipomée, 1977

Franck, Johannes, "Geschichte des Wortes Hexe," in Hansen, *Quellen und Untersuchungen zur Geschichte des Hexenwahns und der Hexenverfolgung im Mittelalter*, Hildesheim: G. Olms, 1963 (1901)

Franklin, Simon, *Writing, Society and Culture in Early Rus, c. 950-1300.* Cambridge University Press, 2002

Freitag, Barbara. *Sheela-na-gigs: unravelling an enigma.* London and New York: Routledge, 2004

Friðþjófs saga, Online: www.vikinganswerlady.com/seidhr.shtml

Furetière, Antoine. *Dictionnaire universel*, 1690, online: http://hypo.geneve.ch/www/cliotexte/sites/Histoire/Sorcellerie/corpus.html Acc 3/29/08

Gagnon François, "Le Corrector sive Medicus de Burchard de Worms (1000-1025): présentation, traduction et commentaire ethno-historique." MA Thesis, Université de Montréal, August 2010

Gardenstone, *Goddess Holle: In Search of a Germanic Goddess.* Hamburg: Books on Demand, 2011

Alex G. Garman, *The Cult of the Matronae in the Roman Rhineland: A Historical Evaluation of the Archaeological Evidence.* Lewiston: Edwin Mellen Press, 2008

Gardela, Leszek. "A biography of the seiðr-staffs: Towards an archeology of emotions." *Between Paganism and Christianity in the North.* ed. Leszek P Slupecki and Jakub Morawiec. University of Rzeszow, 2009

Garinet, Jules, *Histoire de la magie en France, depuis le commencement de la Monarchie jusqu'à nos jours.* Paris: Foulon, 1818 https://archive.org/details/histoiredelamagi00gari

Garnett, James M. *Beowulf: An Anglo-Saxon Poem, and the Fight at Finnsburg.* Boston: Ginn, 1893

Gazi, Stephen, *A History of Croatia*, New York: Philosophical Library, 1973

Gesta Herwardi. Online: https://en.wikipedia.org/wiki/Hereward_the_Wake

Gimbutas, Marija, *Ancient Symbolism in Lithuanian Folk Art*, Philadelphia: Memoirs of the American Folklore Society, Vol. 49, 1958

_____. *The Balts*, New York: Frederick Praeger, 1963

Ginzberg, Carlo, *Night Battles: Witchcraft and Agrarian Cults in the 16th and 17th Centuries*, translated by John and Anne Tedeschi, New York: Penguin, 1985

_____. *Ecstasies: Deciphering the Witches' Sabbath*, New York: Pantheon, 1991

van Goedesbergh, Gerrit, "Met Witte Wieven in Grafheuvels," (etching) in Picardt, Johan. *Korte Beschryvinge van eenige Vergetene en Verborgene Antiquiteten,* 1660. Online: https://nl.wikipedia.org/wiki/Witte_wieven

Goitein, Hugh, *Primitive Ordeal and Modern Law,* London: George Allen and Unwin, 1923

Goldbaum, Howard. "Labbacallee Wedge Tomb." *In Voices from the Dawn: the Folklore of Ireland's Ancient Monuments.* Online: www.voicesfromthedawn.com/labbacallee/

_____. "Slieve Gullion." www.voicesfromthedawn.com/slieve-gullion/

_____. "Loughcrew Passage Tomb Complex (Sliabh na Caillíghe)." www.voicesfromthedawn.com/loughcrew/

Margaret E. Goldsmith. *The Mode and Meaning of 'Beowulf'.* London and New York: A&C Black (Bloomsbury), 2014

Goode, Starr. *Sheela na gig: The Dark Goddess of Sacred Power.* Simon and Schuster, forthcoming

Gostling, Frances M., *Auvergne and Its People,* Macmillan, NY 1911

Gower, John. *The English Works of John Gower: (Confessio amantis).* Early English Text Society, 1900

Gray, Elizabeth, translator, *Cath Maige Tuired: The Second Battle of Mag Tuired.* Online: www.sacred-texts.com/neu/cmt/cmteng.htm

Greimas, Algirdas J. *Of Gods and Men: Studies in Lithuanian Mythology.* Bloomington: Indiana University Press. 1992

Gregory of Tours, *History of the Franks.* Online: http://legacy.fordham.edu/halsall/basis/gregory-hist.asp

Gregory, Isabella Augusta, *A Book of Saints and Wonders of Ireland,* Gerrards Cross, Bucks: Colin Smythe, 1971

Grettis saga. Online: www.snerpa.is/net/isl/grettir.htm

_____. Gods and Fighting Men. London: J. Murray, 1904

Grimm, Jacob, *Teutonic Mythology,* Vols I-IV, translated from 4th edition by James S. Stallybrass, London: George Bell & Sons, 1883

Gummere, F. B. *Germanic Origins: A Study in Primitive Culture.* New York: C. Scribner, 1892

Gundarsson, Kveldúlfr. "Spae-Craft, Seiðr, and Shamanism." Online: www.hrafnar.org/articles/ kveldulf/spaecraft/ Acc: 4/5/15

Gwynn, Edward, trans. *The Metrical Dindshenchas:* "Cnogba." CELT: Corpus of Electronic Texts, 2004. University College, Cork. Web. 29 June 2011. www.ucc.ie/celt/published/T106500C.html, pp 43-47.

Hall, Alaric Timothy Peter, "The Meanings of Elf and Elves in Medieval England." Dissertation at the University of Glasgow, 2004. www.alarichall.org.uk/ahphdful.pdf

Hall, John R. Clark. *A Concise Anglo-Saxon Dictionary,* 2nd ed. Cambridge University Press / New York: Macmillan, 1916, online: http://lexicon.ff.cuni.cz/texts/oe_clarkhall_about.html

Halsall, Maureen, *The Old English Rune Poem: A Critical Edition,* U of Toronto Press, 1981

Hansen, Joseph, *Quellen und Untersuchungen zur Geschichte des Hexenwahns und der Hexenverfolgung im Mittelalter,* Hildesheim: G. Olms, 1963 (1901)

Hansen, Joseph. Zauberwahn, *Inquisition und Hexenprozess im mittelalter und die entstehung der grossen Hexenverfolgung,* München, 1900

Hansen, Joseph, Zauberwahn, *Inquisition und Hexenprozess im Mittelalter und die Entstehung der grossen Hexenverfolgung,* Aalen: Scientia Verlag, 1964

Hardman, George, L. (translation) *The Story of Nornagest.* (2011) Online: www. germanicmythology.com/FORNALDARSAGAS/NornaGestrSagaHardman.html

Harf-Lancner, Laurence. *Les Fées au Moyen Age: Morgane et Mélusine.* Genève: Slatkine, 1984

Harkness, Albert Granger, "The Scepticism and Fatalism of the Common People of Rome as Illustrated by the Sepulchral Inscriptions," *Transactions and Proceedings of the American Philological Association,* Vol. 30, Johns Hopkins Press, 1899

Harva, Uno, *Mythology of All Races, Vol 11: Finno-Ugric & Siberian,* Archaeological Institute of America, Boston: Marshall Jones Co., 1927

Hauglid, Roar, *Norske Stavkirkir: Bygningshistorisk Bakgrunn og Utvitkling,* Oslo: Dreyers Forlag, 1976

Hauksbók. Online: www.germanicmythology.com/works/hauksbokvoluspa.html

Hefele, Carl Joseph. *Histoire des conciles d'après les documents originaux.* Hildesheim / New York: Georg Olms Verlag, 1973

Heide, Eldar, "Spinning seiðr," in *Old Norse religion in long-term perspectives: Origins, changes, and interactions. An international conference in Lund, Sweden, June 3–7, 2004.* Ed. Anders Andrén, Kristina Jennbert & Catharina Raudvere http://eldar-heide.net/Publikasjonar til heimesida/Spinning seidr, Lund conf Heide.pdf

Hedeager, Lotte. *Iron Age Myth and Materiality: An Archaeology of Scandinavia, 400-1000.* Abingdon: Routledge, 2011.

Hefele, Karl J. von. *Histoire des conciles d'apres les documents originaux.* Vols I and II. Translated by H. Leclercq. Paris: Letouzey, 1907

eds. Henningsen, G, and Ankarloo, B, *Early Modern European Witchcraft: Centres and Peripheries,* Oxford, 1988

Herbert, Kathleen, *Looking for the Lost Gods of England.* Anglo-Saxon Books, 2007

Herlihy, David, *Women in Medieval Society,* Houston: University of St Thomas, 1971

Hight, George Ainslie, translator, *The Saga of Grettir the Strong: A Story of the Eleventh Century.* London: J.M. Dent, 1913

Higley, Sarah Lynn. "Dirty Magic: Seiðr, Science, and the Parturating Man in Medieval Norse and Welsh Literature." *Essays in Medieval Studies* 11, pp 137-149 Online: www.illinoismedieval.org/ems/VOL11/higley.html

Hill, Joyce, "Thæt Wæs Geomoru Ides: A Female Stereotype Examined," in Damico and Olsen, 1990

Hodge, Winifred, "Matrons and Disir: The Heathen Tribal Mothers." Online: http://haligwaerstow.ealdriht.org/Matrons.htm

Hole, Christina, *Witchcraft in England,* Charles Scribner's Sons, NY 1947

Holinshed, Raphael. *The Historie of Scotland,* Vol. I, 1577, online: www.cems. ox.ac.uk/holinshed/extracts2.shtml

Hollander, Lee M., *The Poetic Edda*, Austin TX: University of Texas Press, 1962

Elizabeth Hopkins, "The Nyabingi Cult of Southwestern Uganda," in *Protest and Power in Black Africa*, ed. Robert Rotberg and Ali Mazrui, New York: Oxford, 1970, pp 258-336

vab der Horst, P.C., "Fatum, Tria Fata; Parca, Tres Parcae." *Mnemosyne*, Third Series, Vol. 11, Leiden: Brill, 1943

Hubbs, Joanna, *Mother Russia: The Feminine Myth in Russian Culture*, Bloomington: University of Indiana Press, 1988

Hunt-Anschutz, Arlea. "Gender and Rune Magic," Online: asynjur@yahoogroups.com, Feb 1, 2003

Hurd-Mead, Kate Campbell, *A History of Women in Medicine, from the earliest times to the beginning of the 19th century*, Haddam CT: The Haddam Press, 1938

Ingstrand, Stefan, "Éowyn under Siege: Female Warriors During the Middle Ages." April 6, 2009. Online: www.strangehorizons.com/2009/20090406/ingstrand-a.shtml

Insoll, Timothy, ed. *The Oxford Handbook of the Archaeology of Ritual and Religion*. New York: Oxford University Press, 2011

Isidore of Seville. *Etymologías*. Translated by Luis Cortés y Góngora and Santiago Montero Diaz. Madrid: Biblioteca de Autores Cristianos, 1951

Jacques-Chaquin, Nicole, and Préaud, Maxime, eds, *Le Sabbat des Sorciers en Europe: XVe-XVIIIe siecles*, Jerome Millon, Paris, 1993

Jamieson, John, *An Etymological Dictionary of the Scottish Language*, Supplement, Vol. 2. University Press for W. & C. Tait, 1825

Jeay, Madeleine and Kathleen Garay, *The Distaff Gospels: a First Modern English Edition of Les Evangiles des Quenouilles*. Peterborough ON: Broadview, 2006

Jeep, John. *Medieval Germany: An Encyclopedia*. Routledge; 2001

Jochens, Jenny, *Women in Old Norse Society*, Ithaca: Cornell U Press, 1995

_____, "Völuspá: Matrix of Norse Womanhood." *Journal of English and Germanic Philology*, University of Illinois Press. Vol. 88, No. 3 (Jul. 1989), pp 344-362

_____, "Old Norse Magic and Gender: þáttr þorvalds ens Vídforla." *Scandinavian Studies*, University of Illinois Press, Vol. 63, No. 3 (Summer 1991), pp 305-317.

_____. *Old Norse Images of Women*. Philadelphia: University of Pennsylvania Press, 1996

Johns, Andreas. *Baba Yaga: The Ambiguous Mother and Witch of the Russian Folktale*. Frankfurt and New York: Peter Lang, 2004

Johnson, John. *A collection of the laws and canons of the Church of England: from its first foundation to the conquest, and from the conquest to the reign of King Henry VIII*. Oxford: Parker, 1850

Jones, Carleton, *Temples of Stone: Explaining the Megalithic Tombs of Ireland*. Cork: Collins, 2007

Jones, Francis, *The Holy Wells of Wales*, Cardiff: University of Wales Press, 1954

Jones, Malcolm. "Folklore Motifs in Late Medieval Art II: Sexist Satire and Popular Punishments." *Folklore*, Vol. 101, No. 1 (1990), pp. 69-87 Taylor & Francis.

Jones, Prudence, *A History of Pagan Europe*, London & New York: Routledge, 1995

Jones, T. Gwynn, *Welsh Folklore and Folk-custom*. Cambridge, England, 1979

Guðni Jónsson and Bjarni Vilhjálmsson, eds. *Bósa saga ok Herauðs*. Online: http://tinyurl.com/huaf55y

Jordanes, *The Origin and Deeds of the Goths*, translated by Charles C. Mierow, www.ucalgary.ca/~vandersp/Courses/texts/jordgeti.html

Jordanes, *GETICA Sive De Origine Actibusque Gothorum*, translated by Freedrich Yeat. Online: www.harbornet.com/folks/theedrich/Goths/Goths1.htm

Joyce, Patrick Weston. *A social history of ancient Ireland: treating of the government, military system, and law; religion, learning, and art; trades, industries, and commerce; manners, customs, and domestic life, of the ancient Irish people*. Volume 1. Ireland: Longmans, Green, and Co, 1903

de Jubainville, H. d'Arbois, *The Irish Mythological Cycle and Celtic Mythology*, translated by Richard Irvine Best, New York: Lemma, 1970

Karl, Raimund, "Celtic Religion: what information do we really have," Part 4, Celtic Well listserv, Dec 13, 1998

Karsten, Sigfrid Rafael. *The Religion of the Samek*. Brill Archive, 1955

Kauffmann, Friedrich, *Northern Mythology*, Alden House, London, 1903

Kieckhefer, Richard, *European Witch Trials: Their Foundation in Popular and Learned Culture, 1300-1500*, Berkeley and Los Angeles: University of California Press, 1976

_____. *Magic in the Middle Ages*. Cambridge University Press, 2000

Kingshill, Sophia, The Lore of Scotland: A guide to Scottish legends. Random House, 2012

Kinsella, Thomas, ed. *The Táin: From the Irish Epic Táin Bó Cualinge*. Oxford University Press, 2002

Kloss, Waldemar. "Herodias the Wild Huntress in the Legend of the Middle Ages. II." *Modern Language Notes*, Vol 23, No. 4 (April 1908), pp 100-102

Krappe, A. Haggerty. "La Cailleach Bheara: notes de mythologie gaélique." *Etudes Celtiques*, Vol I, 1936, pp 292-302.

Kraus, Jörg. *Metamorphosen des Chaos: Hexen, Masken und verkehrte Welten*. Königshausen & nmNeumann, 1998

Kvilhaug, Maria, *The Maiden with the Mead: A goddess of initiation in Norse mythology*. Dissertation, University of Oslo, Spring 2004. Online (Dec 16, 2014): www.duo.uio.no/bitstream/handle/10852/23958/18497.pdf?sequence=1

_____. "Sólarljóð – the Song of the Sun," translated by Maria Kvilhaug, Online: http://freya.theladyofthelabyrinth.com/?page_id=311

_____. "Burning the Witch! The Initiation of the Goddess and the War of the Aesir and the Vanir." Online: http://freya.theladyofthelabyrinth.com/?page_id=206

_____. "Divinatory Seiðr – Saga Texts." http://freya.theladyofthelabyrinth.com/?page_id=255

Laboulaye, Edouard, *Recherches sur la Condition Civile et Politique des Femmes*, Paris, 1843

Lacarra, José María, *Investigaciones de la historia navarra*, Col. Diario de Navarra 25, 1983

Lambert, Pierre-Yves, *La Langue Gauloise: Description linguistique, commentaire d'inscriptions choisies*, Paris: Editions Errance, 1994

Landes, Richard Allen. *Relics, apocalypse, and the deceits of history : Ademar of Chabannes, 989-1034.* Cambridge MA: Harvard University Press, 1995.

Larner, Christina; Lee, Christopher Hyde; and McLachlan, Hugh, *A Source-Book of Scottish Witchcraft*, University of Glasgow, 1977

Larrington, Carolyne, trans. and ed. *The Poetic Edda.* Oxford World's Classics, 1996

Latourette, Kenneth Scott, *A History of the Expansion of Christianity: 1000 Years of Uncertainty*, New York: Harper & Brothers, 1937-45.

Lea, Henry Charles, *A History of the Inquisition of the Middle Ages*, New York: Harper and Bros, 1901

_____. and Howland, Arthur C., *Materials Toward a History of Witchcraft.* New York: T. Yoseloff, 1957

_____. The Ordeal. Philadelphia: University of Pennsylvania Press, 1973 (1866)

Lebbe, Christophe, "The Shadow Realm Between Life and Death."in *The Pagan Middle Ages*," translated by Tanis Guest, ed. Milis, Ludo, Woodbridge UK: Boydell, 1998.

Lecouteux, Claude, *Phantom Armies of the Night: The Wild Hunt and the Ghostly Processions of the Undead.* Translated by Jon E. Graham. Rochester VT: Inner Traditions, 2001

_____. *Witches, Werewolves and Fairies: Shapeshifters and Astral Doubles in the Middle Ages.* Translated by Clare Frock. Rochester VT: Inner Traditions, 2003

Lederer, Wolfgang, *The Fear of Women.* New York: Grune and Stratton, 1968

Lehmann, Winfred P; Helen-Jo J Hewitt; Sigmund Feist. *A Gothic Etymological Dictionary: Based on the Third Edition of Vergleichendes Worterbuch der Gotischen Sprache.* Leiden: E.J. Brill, 1986

Leland, Charles. *Aradia, or the Gospel of the Witches: a new translatin by Mario Pazzaglini and Dina Pazzaglini.* Blaine WA: Phoenix, 1998

Levack Brian P, *The Witch-hunt in Early Modern Europe*, Longman, NY 1987

_____. *Witchcraft in the Ancient World and the Middle Ages.* Vol. II of series: *Articles on Witchcraft, Magic, and Demonology: Anthology.* New York: Garland, 1992

_____. Ed. *The Witchcraft Sourcebook*: Second Edition. Abingdon UK: Routledge, 2015

Levison, *Vita S. Eligius*, MGH SS Mer. 4, 669-742, Online: www.fordham.edu/halsall/basis/eligius.html

Liberman, Anatoly. *An Analytic Dictionary of the English Etymology: An Introduction.* Minneapolis: University of Minnesota Press, 2008

John Lindow, *Norse Mythology: A Guide to the Gods, Heroes, Rituals, and Beliefs.* Oxford / New York: Oxford University. 2002

Lionarons, Joyce Tally, *The Homiletic Writings of Archbishop Wulfstan*, Boydell & Brewer, 2010

_____. "Dísir, Valkyries, Völur, and Norns: The Wiese Frauen of the Deutsche Mythologie." in *The shadow-walkers: Jacob Grimm's mythology of the monstrous.* ed. T. A. Shippey. Turnhout: Brepols, 2005

Looijenga, Tineke, *Texts and Contexts of the Oldest Runic Inscriptions.* Leiden: Brill, 2003

Lumley, E. *Northern Mythology: Comprising the Principal Popular Traditions and Superstitions of Scandinavia, North Germany, and the Netherlands*, Volume 1 (Google eBook) 1851.

Lysaght, Patricia, *The Banshee: The Irish Death Messenger*, Boulder: Roberts Rinehart, 1986

Macalister, R. A. Stewart. *Lebor Gabála Érenn: The Book of the Taking of Ireland*. http://www.ucc.ie/celt/LGQS.pdf

MacCulloch, John Arnott. *Mythology of All Races*, Vol III, Celtic, Boston: Marshall Jones, 1918

_____. *Eddic Mythology* (Vol. II of *Mythology of All Races*), Archaeological Institute of America, Boston: Marshall Jones, 1930

_____. *Medieval faith and fable*, London: George Harrap, 1932

MacDougall, James, *Folk Tales and Fairy Lore in Gaelic and English*, Edinburgh: J. Grant, 1910

Machal, Jan. *Mythology of All Races, Vol III: Slavic*, Boston: Marshall Jones, 1918

MacKay, J.G. "The Deer-Cult and the Deer-Goddess Cult of the Ancient Caledonians." *Folklore*, Vol. 43, No. 2 (Jun. 30, 1932), Taylor & Francis, pp. 144-174

MacKenzie, Donald, *Scottish Folk Lore and Folk Life*, London: Blackie, 1935

MacKillop, James, *A Dictionary of Celtic Mythology*, Oxford/New York: Oxford University Press, 1998

MacMullen, Ramsay, *Christianity and Paganism in the Fourth to Eighth Centuries*, Yale: New Haven, 1997

_____. "The end of ancestor worship," in *Historia* 63 (2014) pp. 487-513

MacPherson, J.M., *Primitive Beliefs in the Northeast of Scotland*, London: Longmans Green & Co, 1929

Magliocco, Sabina, "Aradia in Sardinia: the Archaeology of a Legend." in *Ten Years of Triumph of the Moon*, ed. Dave Green and Dave Evans. Harpenden UK: Hidden Publishing, 2009

Magnússon, Eiríkr, and William Morris. *The Heimskringla: Or, The Sagas of the Norse Kings from the Icelandic of Snorre Sturlason*, Volume 4. London: B. Quaritch, 1905

Malinowski, Bronislaw. "The Meaning of Meaningless Words and the Coefficient of Weirdness." In *Coral Gardens and Their Magic*, 1935, vol. 2, "The Language of Magic and Gardening," 213-222.

Mallory, J.P. and Adams, Douglas Q. Adams. *Encyclopedia of Indo-European Culture*. London: Fitzroy Dearborn, 1997

Mann, Jill. *Ysengrimus: Text with translation, commentary and introduction*, Brill: Leiden and New York, 1987.

Markale, Jean, *Women of the Celts*, London: Cremonesi, 1975

Mather, Cotton, *The Wonders of the Invisible World*, 1693, Online: www.hawthorneinsalem.org/paper/10341/

Matossian, Mary Kilbourne, "Vestiges of the Cult of the Mother Goddess in Baltic Folklore," in Ziedonis, Arvids; Puhvel, Jaan; Silbajoris, Rimvydas; and Valgemae, Mardi, eds, *Baltic Literature and Linguistics*, Columbus OH: Association for the Advancement of Baltic Studies, 1973

Matthews, John, *Taliesin: The Last Celtic Shaman*, Inner Traditions / Bear & Co, 2002

McCone, Kim. *Pagan Past and Christian Present in Early Irish Literature*. Ireland: An Sagart, 1990

McCracken, Peggy. *The Romance of Adultery: Queenship and Sexual Transgression in Old French Literature*. Philadelphia: University of Pennsylvania Press, 2013

McNamara, Jo Ann Kay, *Sisters in Arms: Catholic Nuns Through Two Millennia*. Cambridge: Harvard University Press, 1996

McKenna, Stephen, *Paganism and Pagan Survivals in Spain up to the Fall of the Visigothic Kingdom*, Washington DC: Catholic University of America, 1938

McKinnell, John. *Essays on Eddic Poetry*. eds. Donata Kick, John D. Shafer University of Toronto Press, 2014

_____. "Völuspá and the Feast of Easter." 2008. Online: http://userpage.fu-berlin.de/alvismal/12vsp.pdf

_____. "On Heiðr," *Saga-Book* 25/4, 2001: 394-417. Online: www.heathengods.com/library/viking_society/2001_XXV_4.pdf

McNeill, John T. and Gamer, Helena M., *Medieval Handbooks of Penance*, New York: Columbia University Press, 1938

McQueen, Malcolm, "Stones for All Seasons", *Circles Magazine*, Spring 88, Scotland

Meaney, Audrey, *Anglo-Saxon Amulets and Curing-Stones*, Oxford, England: British Archaeological Reports, British Series 96, 1981.

_____, "The Ides of the Cotton Gnomic Poem," in Damico and Olsen, eds., *New Readings on Women in Old English Literature*, Bloomington: Indiana University Press, 1990

de Mello e Souza, Laura, *O Diablo e a Terra de Santa Cruz: Feitiçaria e Religiosidade Popular no Brasil Colonial*, São Paolo: Companhia das Letras, 1987

Mencej, Mirjam, "Connecting Threads," *Electronic Journal of Folklore*. Vol. 48 Estonian Institute of Folklore, 2011. www.folklore.ee/folklore/vol48/mencej.p5d5f

Menendez y Pelayo, Marcelino. *Historia de los Heterodoxos Españoles*, Volume I. (1880-82) Madrid: Biblioteca de Autores Cristianos, 1998

Meyer, Kuno. "The Expulsion of the Deissi." *Y Cymmrodor. 14, 101-135, 1901 Expulsion of the Deisi*, A Version: Laud 610 & Rawlinson B 502, Celtic Literature Collective, Online: www.maryjones.us/ctexts/dessi2.html (1/03/15)

_____. *Contributions to Irish Lexicography*, Volume 1. Tübingen: M. Niemeyer, 1906

Miles, Ludo, ed, *The Pagan Middle Ages*, tr Tanis Guest, Woodbridge UK: Boydell Press, 1998

Milanich, Jerald T, "Laboring in the Fields of the Lord," *Archaeology Magazine*, Jan/Feb 1996

Miller, J. L. "Paškuwatti's Ritual: Remedy for Impotence or Antidote to Homosexuality?" *Journal of Ancient Near Eastern Religions* 10:1, 2010, pp 83–89.

Miller, William Ian. *Audun and the Polar Bear: Luck, Law, and Largesse in a Medieval Tale of Risky Business*. Leiden: Brill, 2008

Mitchell, Stephen A. *Witchcraft and Magic in the Nordic Middle Ages*. Philadelphia: Penn, 2011

Mogk, Eugen Mogk. "Zur Gigantomachie der Völuspá." *Folklore Fellows Commu-*

nications, 58 Helsinki: Academia scientiarum Fennica, 1924

Monaghan, Patricia. *Encyclopedia of Celtic Mythology and Folklore*. New York: Facts on File, 2009

Monaghan, Patricia. *Encyclopedia of Celtic Mythology and Folklore*. New York: Infobase Publ, 2014

Monroe, D.C. and Sontag, R.J., *The Middle Ages: 395-1500*, New York: The Century Company, 1928

Heyne, Moriz, *Fünf Bucher Deutscher Hausaltertümer, von den ältesten geschichtlichen Zeiten bis zum 16. Jahrhundert*, Volume 2, Leipzig: Hirzel, 1901

Moss, Leonard W., and Cappanari, Stephen C., "In Quest of the Black Virgin: She is Black Because She is Black," in *Mother Worship: Theme and Variations*, ed. James L. Preston, Chapel Hill: University of North Carolina Press, 1982

Motz, Lotte, "The Winter Goddess: Perchta, Holda, and Related Figures." *Folklore*, Vol 95, No. 2, Taylor and Francis, 1984, 151-166.

Motz, Lotte, "Kingship and the Giants." (1996) Online: journals.lub.lu.se/index.php/anf/article/download/11555/10242

Mowatt, D.G., tr, *The Nibelunglied*, New York: Everyman's Library, 1962

Murray, Alexander C. *Germanic Kinship Structure: Studies in Law and Society in Antiquity and in the Early Middle Ages*. Toronto: PIMS, 1983

Murray, Bradley, Cragie, and Onions, eds., *A New English Dictionary*, Oxford: Clarendon Press, 1928

Muthmann, Friedrich, *Mutter und Quelle: Studien zur Quellenverehrung im Altertum undim Mittelalter*, Mainz: Archaeologischer Verlag, 1975

Nelson, Janet L. "Queens as Jezebels: The Careers of Brunhild and Bathhild in Merovingian History," in *Medieval Women*. Edited by Derek Baker. Basil Blackwell, 1978. http://biography.yourdictionary.com/fredegund#6U50MPsVjCuEVdLr.99

National Museum of Denmark. "The magic wands of Viking seeresses?" (2014) Online: http://natmus.dk/en/historisk-viden/danmark/prehistoric-period-until-1050-ad/the-viking-age/religion-magic-death-and-rituals/the-magic-wands-of-the-seeresses/

_____. "A seeress from Fyrkat?" (2014) Online: http://natmus.dk/en/historical-knowledge/denmark/prehistoric-period-until-1050-ad/the-viking-age/religion-magic-death-and-rituals/a-seeress-from-fyrkat/

Newall, Venetia, *The Witch Figure*, Boston: Routledge & Kegan Paul, 1973

Neumann, Eric, *The Great Mother: An Analysis of the Archetype*, Princeton NJ: Princeton University Press, 2015.

Jose Manuel Nieto Soria, "La mujer en el Libro de los Fueros de Castiella," in *Las Mujeres en las ciudades medievales*, Seminario de Estudios de la Mujer, Universidad Autonoma de Madrid, 1983

Noonan, John T. Jr., *Contraception: A History of Its Treatment by the Catholic Theologians and Canonists,* Cambridge: Belnap Press, 1965

North, Richard, *Heathen Gods in Old English Literature*, Cambridge: Cambridge University Press, 1997

Norton, Elizabeth, *Elfrida: The First Crowned Queen of England*. Stroud, UK: Amberley 2013

Nutt, Alfred. *Studies on the Legend of the Holy Grail, with especial reference to the hypothesis of its Celtic origin.* The Folk-Lore Society, Vol. 23. London: Glaisher, 1888

O'Brien, Katherine O'Keefe, *Reading Old English Texts*, Cambridge: Cambridge University Press, 1997

Ó Cathasaigh, Tomás. "The eponym of Cnogba." *Éigse* 23: 27-38. 1989

O' Connor, Patricia, and Kellerman, Stuart. "The flip side of distaff." The Grammarphobia Blog, April 21st, 2008. Online www.grammarphobia.com/blog/2008/04/the-flip-side-of-distaff.html

Ó Crualaoich, Gearóid, *The Book of the Cailleach: Stories of the Wise-Woman Healer.* Cork, Eire: Cork University Press, 2003

O'Donaill, Níall. *Foclóir Gaeilge-Béarla.* Ireland, 1977. www.teanglann.ie/en/fgb/

O'Donovan, John, and Michael O'Flanagan. *Letters Containing Information Relative to the Antiquities of the County of Meath, Collected during the Progress of the Ordnance Survey in 1836.* Bray, 1927, online: www.voicesfromthedawn.com/loughcrew/

Ó hAodha, Donncha. "The Lament of the Old Woman of Beare." In *Sages, Saints, and Storytellers: Celtic Studies in Honor of Professor James Carney.* Ed. Donnchadh O Corráin, Liam Breatnach, Kim McCone. Maynooth: An Sagart. 1989

Ó hOgain, Daithi, *Myth, Legend, and Romance: An Encyclopedia of the Irish Tradition*, New York: Prentice Hall, 1991

Oinas, Felix. *Essays on Russian Folklore and Mythology.* Columbus OH: Slavica, 1984

Olmsted, Garret, *The Gods of the Celts and the Indo-Europeans*, Innsbruck: Archaeolingua, 1994

Okladnikov, P. A. *Arkhiv Yakutskogo Filiala: Lenskiye Pesni.* Lost publisher, date.

Orchard, Andy, *Dictionary of Norse Myth and Legend.* London: Cassell, 1997

Orel, Vladimir. *A Handbook of Germanic Etymology.* Leiden: Brill, 2003

Osborn, Marijane, and Longland, Stella, *Rune Games*, Routledge, Kegan & Paul, Boston, 1982

Ots, Loone, "The Position of the Woman in the Poetic Edda." *Folklore*, Vol 7, Online: http://haldjas.folklore.ee/folklore/vol7/llone1.htm

The Oxford English Dictionary, Second Edition, eds J. A. Simpson and E.S.C. Weiner. Clarendon: Oxford, 1989

Palmer, Robert E.A., *Roman Religion and the Roman Empire*, Philadelphia: University of Pennsylvania Press, 1974

Parsons, Ben. "'Verray goddes apes': Troilus, Seynt Idiot, and Festive Culture." *The Chaucer Review*, Vol. 45, No. 3 Penn State University Press (2011), pp. 275-298

Pattetta, Federico, *Le Ordalie*, Turin: Fratelli Bocca, 1890

Pertz, Georg Heinrich. *Monumenta Germaniae historica: Capitularia regum Francorum*, Vol. 1. Germany: Hahn, 1835

Pesch, Alexandra. "Gold Bracteates and Female Burials: Material Culture as a Medium of Elite Communication in the Migration Period." In *Weibliche Eliten in Der Frühgeschichte / Female Elites in Protohistoric Europe*, Ed. Dieter Quast. Internationale Tagung, Vols. 13-14. (June 2008) im Rahmen des Forschungsschwerpunktes »Eliten«. Mainz: Verlag des Römisch-Germanischen Zentralmuseums, 2011. Online: www.academia.edu/11230220/GOLD_BRACTEATES_AND_FEMALE_BURI-

ALS._Material_Culture_as_a_Medium_of_Elite_Communication

Peters, Edward. *The Magician, The Witch, and The Law*, University of Pennsylvania Press, 1978

_____. *Europe: The World of the Middle Ages*, Englewood NJ: Prentice-Hall, 1977

Philpott, Miss B. "Germanic Heathenism," in *The Cambridge Medieval History*, Volume 2, eds. Henry Gwatkin and James Whitney. New York: Macmillan, 1913

Pócs, Eva, *Fairies and Witches at the Boundary of Southeastern and Central Europe*, Helsinki: FF Communications, Vol CV, #243, 1989

_____, "Le Sabbat et les mythologies Indo-Europeennes" in *Le Sabbat des Sorciers en Europe: XVe-XVIIIe siecles*. ed. Jacques-Chaquin, Nicole, and Préaud, Maxime, Paris: Jerome Millon, 1993

Price, Neil, "The Archaeology of Seiðr: Circumpolar Traditions in Viking Pre-Christian Tradition." *Brathair* 4 (2), 2004: 109-126. Online: www.brathair.cjb.net

Neil S. Price, T*he Viking Way: Religion and War in Late Iron Age Scandinavia*. Uppsala: Department of Archaeology and Ancient History, 2002 www.pdf-archive.com/2013/08/27/the-viking-way-neil-s-price/the-viking-way-neil-s-price.pdf

Pughe, William Owen. *A Dictionary of the Welsh language, 2: explained in English; with numerous illustrations, from the literary remains and from the living speech of the Cymmry*. Volume 1. T. Gee, 1832

Puhvel, Jaan, "The Baltic Pantheon," in Ziedonis, Arvids; Puhvel, Jaan; Silbajoris, Rimvydas; and Valgemae, Mardi, eds, *Baltic Literature and Linguistics*, Columbus OH: Association for the Advancement of Baltic Studies, 1973

Purser, Philip A. "Her Syndan Wælcyrian: Illuminating the Form and Function of the Valkyrie-Figure in the Literature, Mythology, and Social Consciousness of Anglo- Saxon England." Dissertation at Georgia State University. May 10 2013.

Quinn, Judy. " 'Ok verðr henni ljóð á munni'—Eddic Prophecy in the fornaldarsögur." *Alvíssmál* 8, 1998, pp. 29-50. Online: userpage.fu-berlin.de/~alvismal/8ljodh.pdf

_____. 'What Frigg Knew: The Goddess as Prophetess in Old Norse Mythology', in *Dee, profetesse, regine e altre figure femminili nel Medioevo germanico*, Atti del XL Convegno dell'Associazione Italiana di Filologia Germanica, ed. Maria Elena Ruggerini e Veronka Szőke (Cagliari: CUEC, 2015), pp. 67-88. Online: www.academia.edu/8992612/_What_Frigg_Knew_The_Goddess_as_Prophetess_in_Old_Norse_Mythology_

_____. "Women in Old Norse poetry and sagas," in *A Companion to Old Norse-Icelandic Literature and Culture*, ed. Rory McTurk, Blackwell Companions to Literature and Culture 31 (Oxford: Blackwell, 2005), pp. 518-35

Ralston, W.R.S., *The Songs of the Russian People, as illustrative of Slavonic Mythology and Russian Folk Life*, New York: Hashell House, 1970

Rampton, Martha, "Burchard of Worms and Female Magical Ritual." In *Medieval and Early Modern Ritual: Formalized Behavior in Europe, China and Japan*. Ed. Joelle Rollo-Koster. Leiden: Brill, 2002, pp. 7-34

Reaves, William P. "Odin's Wife: Mother Earth in Germanic Mythology," 2010. Online: *www.germanicmythology.com/original/earthmother.html*

_____. "Resources For Researchers: The Nine Worlds Of Norse Mythology." Online: www.germanicmythology.com/index.html#Resources

Rees, Alwyn and Brinley, *Celtic Heritage: Ancient Tradition in Ireland and Wales*, London: Thames and Hudson, 1961

de Reu, Martine, "The missionaries," in Miles, 1998

Reuter, Timothy, ed. *The Annals of Fulda: Ninth-century Histories*. Manchester, UK: Manchester University Press, 1992

Rg Veda, online: www.sacred-texts.com/hin/rigveda/rv09001.htm

Rhode, Eleanor, *A Garden of Herbs*. London and Boston: P. L. Warner, 1921

Rhys, John, *Celtic Folklore: Welsh and Manx*, Oxford: Clarendon Press, 1971

_____. Celtic Folklore: Welsh and Manx, Vol. I. Clarendon Press, 1901

Richards, Mary, and Stanfield, B. Jane, "Concepts of Anglo-Saxon Women in the Laws," in Damico and Olsen, 1990.

Rickfors, Flemming. "Völuspá - Vølvens Spådom." Online: www.verasir.dk/show.php?file=chap35-20-0.html

Riddle, John M, Estes, J. Worth, and Russell, Josiah C, "Ever Since Eve: Birth Control in the Ancient World," *Archaeology magazine*, March/April, 1994

Riesman, David, *The Story of Medicine in the Middle Ages*, New York: Holber, 1935

Rivers, Theodore John, tr., *Laws of the Alemans and Bavarians*, Philadelphia: University of Pennsylvania Press, 1977

Rohde, Eleanor Sinclair, *A Garden of Herbs*, New York: Dover, 1969

de Rojas, Fernando, *La Celestina* (Burgos, 1499) Madrid: Clásicos Castellanos, 1945

Romeo, Giovanni, *Inquisitori, esorcisti e streghe nell'Italia della Controriforma*, Florence: Sansoni Editore, 1990

Ross, Anne, *Pagan Celtic Britain*, London: Routledge and Kegan Paul, 1967

_____. "The Divine Hag of the Pagan Celts", in Venetia Newell, ed., *The Witch Figure: Essays in Honor of Katharine M. Briggs*, London: Routledge Kegan Paul, 1973

_____. *Folklore of the Scottish Highlands*. Stroud: Tempus, 2000

Rouche, Michel, "The Early Middle Ages in the West," in *A History of Private Life, Vol I: From Pagan Rome to Byzantium*, ed. Paul Veyne, Cambridge: Belknap Press, 1987

Ruffoni, Kirsten, "Viking Age Queens: the example of Oseberg." Master's thesis MPhil Nordic Viking and Medieval Culture, University of Oslo, 2009-2011 Online: www.duo.uio.no/bitstream/handle/10852/26632/Ruffoni_Master.pdf?sequence=2

Russell, Jeffrey Burton, *Witchcraft in the Middle Ages*, Ithaca: Cornell University Press, 1972

_____, *A history of witchcraft: sorcerers, heretics and pagans*, New York: Thames and Hudson, c 1980

Ruttner-Cova, Sonja, *Frau Holle, die gesturzte Gottin: Marchen, Mythen, Matri-archat*, Basel: Sphinx Verlag, 1986

Salin, Edouard. La Civilisation Merovingienne, Vol. 4. Paris

Samplonius, Kees. "From Veleda to the Völva: Aspects of female divination in Germanic Europe." in *Sanctity and Motherhood: Essays on Holy Mothers in the Middle Ages*. Ed. Annekke Mulder-Bakker, New York: Routledge, 1995

Santillana, Georges, and Hertha von Dechend. *Hamlet's Mill: An Essay on Myth and the Frame of Time*. Boston: Gambit, 1969 de la Saussaye, P.D. Chantepie, *The Religion of the Teutons*, Boston: Atheneum, 1902

Saxo Grammaticus, *Gesta Danorum*, online: www.archive.org/stream/thedanish-history01150gut/1150.txt

Saunders, Corinne J. *Magic and the Supernatural in Medieval English Romance.* Martlesham UK: Boydell & Brewer, 2010

Sayers, William. "Old Irish Fert 'Tie-Pole,' Fertas 'Swingletree,' and the Seeress Fedelm," in *Etudes Celtiques* 21 (1984), pp. 171-183.

Schmitz, Hermann Joseph. *Die Bussbücher und die Bussdisciplin der Kirche*, Graz: Akademische Druck-U. Verlagsanstalt, 1958 [1883], Vol II, 407-452

Schmitz, Nancy, "An Irish Wise Woman: Fact and Legend." *Journal of the Folklore Institute*, Indiana University Press Vol. 14, No. 3 (1977), pp. 169-179

Schmidt's *Jahrbuecher*, Volumes 25-26, 1840, p 293 Online: Google Books

von Schnurbein, Stefanie, "Shamanism in the Old Norse Tradition: A Theory between Ideological Camps." *History of Religions*, Vol. 43, No. 2 (November 2003), pp. 116-138, Online: www.jstor.org/stable/10.1086/423007

Scot, Reginald. *The Discoverie of Witchcraft*. 1584. Ann Arbor, MI; Oxford (UK) Text Creation Partnership, Online: http://name.umdl.umich.edu/A62397.0001.001

Scott, Sir Walter, *Letters on Demonology and Witchcraft* (1884 ed), East Ardsley, Wakefield: S. R. Publishers LTD, 1968

_____. The poetical works of Sir Walter Scott: first series, containing Minstrelsy of the Scottish Border, Baudry's European Library, 1838 Online: Google eBooks

Sebillot, Paul, *La Folklore de la France*, Vols I-IV, Paris: Librairie Orientale et Americaine, 1904

_____, *Legendes et curiosites des metiers*, Paris: Godefroy, 1894

Simek, Rudolf, *Dictionary of Northern Mythology*. Cambridge: Brewer, 1993

_____. "The Vanir: An Obituary." *Retrospective Methods Network Newsletter*, University of Helsinki, Dec 2010. Online: www.helsinki.fi/folkloristiikka/English/RMN/RMN Newsletter DECEMBER 2010.pdf

Shakespeare, William, *Complete Works*, Chicago: Scott, Foreman & Co, 1961

Shetelig, Haakon, and Falk, H. S., *Scandinavian Archaeology*. translated by E. V. Gordon. New York: Hacker Art Books, 1978. (Reprint of 1937 ed. Clarendon Press)

Silverblatt, Irene, *Moon, Sun, and Witches: Gender Ideologies and Class in Inca and Colonial Peru*, Princeton: Princeton University Press, 1987

Skafte Jensen, Minna. "Artemis in Homer," in *From Artemis to Diana: The Goddess of Man and Beast*, ed. Tobias Fischer-Hansen and Birte Poulsen. Danish Studies in Classical Archaeology: Acta Hyperborea, Vol 12. Copenhagen: Museum Tusculanum Press, 2009.

Skeat, Walter W., *A Concise Etymological Dictionary of the English Language*, New York: Clarendon Press, 1901

_____. ed. and tr. *Aelfric's Lives of saints: being a set of sermons on saints' days formerly observed by the English church, edited from Manuscript Julius E. VII in the Cottonian Collection*. London: Early English Text Society, 1881. Issue 76; Issue 82 (Google eBook)

Sklute, L. John, "Freoðuwebbe in Old English Poetry," in Damico and Olsen 1990

Skírnismál. Online: www.sacred-texts.com/neu/poe/poe07.htm

Sturluson, Snorri, *The Stories of the Kings of Norway Called the Round World (Heimskringla)*. Vol IV. eds. Eiríkr Magnússon, William Morris. London: B. Quaritch, 1905

_____. *The Heimskringla: Or, The Sagas of the Norse Kings from the Icelandic of Snorre Sturlason*, Volume 4. Samuel Laing and Rasmus Björn Anderson, London: J.C. Nimmo, 1889 (Google eBook)

_____. *Heimskringla I*, online: http://vsnrweb-publications.org.uk/Heimskringla I.pdf

_____. *Gylfaginning*, online: www.germanicmythology.com/works/hauksbokvoluspa.html

Spangenberg, Lisa, "Were There Women Druids?" Online: http://members.aol.com/lisala/, 1997

Stafford, Pauline, *Queens, Concubines and Dowagers: the King's Wife in the Middle Ages*. Athens: University of Georgia Press, 1983

Steinhauser, Walter. "'Eidechse' und die Schreibung des Sekundärumlautes. *Zeitschrift für Mandartforschung*, 30 Jahrg., H. 4 (Apr 1964), Franz Steiner Verlag, pp 331-334

Stevenson, Charles H., *Law in the Light of History*, London: Williams and Norgate, 1939-1940

Stokes, Whitley, ed. "The Death of Muirchertach mac Erca." *Revue celtique*, Volume 23, Vieweg, 1902, pp. 395-437

Storms, Godfried, *Anglo-Saxon Magic*, The Hague: M. Nijhoff, 1948

Straubhaar, Sandra Ballif. "Skáldkonur." In *Medieval Scandinavia: An Encyclopedia*. Philip Pulsiano et all, eds. New York: Garland, 1993, pp. 594-596

Stuard, Susan Mosher, ed., *Women in Medieval Society*, University of Pennsylvania Press, 1976

Summers, Montague, *The Geography of Witchcraft*, London: Routledge & Kegan Paul, 1927

Svenson, Rig, "The Chicanery of Seiðr." Online: www.academia.edu/10553742/The_Chicanery_of_Seiðr 2015

Svipdagsmál, online: https://notendur.hi.is//~eybjorn/ugm/svipdag2.html

Sweet, Henry. *The Student's Dictionary of Anglo-Saxon*. New York and London: Macmillan, 1897

Tacitus, *The Complete Works of Tacitus*, tr Alfred John Church and William Jackson Brodribb, New York: Modern Library, 1942

Tempan, Paul, "Irish Hill and Mountain Names." Online: www.mountaineering.ie/_files/Paul Tempan Irish Mountain Placenames – Feb 2012.pdf

Thatcher, Oliver, *The Library of Original Sources*, Vol. IV, Milwaukee: E. F. Henderson, 1915

Thorpe, Benjamin, and R. Price, eds. & trans. *Ancient Laws and Institutes of England*. Vols. 1 and 2. London: Commissioners of the Public Records, 1840

Tillinghast, William, *Ploetz' Manual of Universal History*, Houghton Mifflin, Cambridge, 1915

Tillman, Carl-Herman. *Folklig Läkekonst*. Sweden: LTs Förlag, 1962

Toller, T. Northcote, ed., *An Anglo-Saxon Dictionary based on the MS collection of*

Joseph Bosworth, Oxford: Clarendon Press, 1882

_____ *An Anglo-Saxon Dictionary : Based on the Manuscript Collections of the Late Joseph Bosworth, D.D., F.R.S. : Explanation of References* Online: http://ebeowulf.uky.edu/cgi-bin/Bosworth-Toller/ebind2html3.cgi/bosworth?seq=11

Tolley, Clive, ed. *Grottasöngr: the Song of Grotti*. London: Viking Society for Northern Research. 2008

Tourage, Mahdi. *Rumi and the Hermeneutics of Eroticism*, Leiden: Brill, 2007

Trachtenberg, Joshua. *Jewish Magic and Superstition: A Study in Folk Religion*. New York: Behrman's Jewish Book House, 1939

Elaine M. Treharne. *Old and Middle English: c.-890-c.1400: An Anthology*. Malden MA: Blackwell, 2004

Trevelyan, Marie, *Folk-lore and Folk-stories of Wales*, London: E. Stock, 1909

Turner, Sharon, translation of *Völuspá* (1823) Online: www.germanicmythology.com/works/elderedda/voluspaTurner1823.html

Turville-Petre, E.O.G., *Myth and Religion of the North: The Religion of Ancient Scandinavia*, London: Weidenfeld and Nicolson, 1964

Rafael de Ureña y Smenjaud, ed. *The Code of Cuenca: Municipal Law on the Twelfth-Century Castilian Frontier*. James F. Powers, translator and introduction. University of Pennsylvania Press, 2000

Vanina y Neyra, Andrea. "El Corrector sive Medicus de Burchard de Worms: una visión acerca de las supersticiones en la Europa medieval." Online: www.academia.edu/1404207/Conferencia_El_Corrector_sive_medicus_de_Burchard_de_Worms_una_visión_acerca_de_las_supersticiones_en_la_Europa_medieval

Vigfússon, Guðbrandur, *An Icelandic-English Dictionary: Based on the Ms. Collections of the Late Richard Cleasby*. Oxford: Clarendon Press, 1874

Völuspá, in Codex Regius. Online: www.germanicmythology.com/works/codex-regiusvoluspa.html

de Vries, Eric, *Hedge-Rider*. City not given: Pendraig, 2008

Ward, Christie. "Women and Magic in the Sagas: Seiðr and Spá". Viking Answer Lady Web Page. Online: www.vikinganswerlady.com/seidhr.shtml

Wall, Margarethe, "The Gold Figure Foils ('Guldgubbar') from Uppakra" in *Continuity for Centuries* (167-221) Online: www.uppakra.se/backup/docs/uppakra10/U10_06.pdf

Wallis, Faith (Translation). *Bede, the Reckoning of Time*. Liverpool University Press, 1999.

Watkins, Calvert, "Indo-European and the Indo-Europeans," *American Heritage Dictionary*, 3rd Ed, Appendix. Boston: Houghton Mifflin, 1992

Wedeck, Harry E., *A Treasury of Witchcraft: A Sourcebook of the Magic Arts*, New York: Citadel, 1970

Wemple, Suzanne Fonay, *Women in Frankish Society: Marriage and the Cloister 500-900*, Philadelphia: University of Pennsylvania Press, 1981

West, Maire. "Weavers beams, weaving rods and the Prophetess Fedelm." In *Saltair Saíochta, Sanasaíochta agus Seanchais: A Festscrift for Gearóid ma Eoin*. Eds, Dónall Ó Baoill, Donncha Ó hAodha, Nollaig Ó Muraile. Dublin: Four Courts, 2013

West. M. L. *Indo-European Poetry and Myth*, Oxford: Oxford University Press, 2007

Weston, L. M. C. "Women's Medicine, Women's Magic: The Old English Metrical Childbirth Charms." *Modern Philology*, Vol. 92, No. 3 (Feb., 1995), pp. 279-293

Whiting, Bartlett Jere and Whiting, Helen Wescott, *Proverbs, Sentences and Proverbial Phrases from English Writings Mainly Before 1500*, Cambridge UK: Belknap Press, 1968

Wilbur, Terence H. "The Word 'Rune.'" *Scandinavian Studies*, Vol. 29, No. 1 (Feb, 1957), University of Illinois Press, pp. 12-18

Williams, Noel. "The Semantics of the Word *Fairy*: Making Meaning out of Thin Air." *The Good People: New Fairylore Essays*. Ed. Peter Narváez, Lexington KY: University Press of Kentucky, 1997

Wood-Martin, W.G., *Pagan Ireland: An Archaeological Sketch*, London: Longmans, Green & Co, 1895

_____. *Traces of the Elder Faiths of Ireland: A Handbook of Irish Pre-Christian Traditions*, Vol II, London: Longmans, Green & Co, 1902

Work-Makinne, Dawn. "The Rhineland Deae Matronae: Collective Female Deity in Germanic Europe." in *Goddesses in World Culture*, ed. Patricia Monaghan, Vol 2. Santa Barbara: Praeger, 2011

Wyatt, David R. *Slaves and Warriors in Medieval Britain and Ireland: 800 - 1200*. Leiden and New York: Brill, 2009

Young, Serinity, *An Anthology of Sacred Texts By and About Women*, New York : Crossroad, 1993

Zoëga, Geir T. *A Concise Dictionary of Old Icelandic*. (1910) Online: http://norse. ulver.com/dct/zoega/

IMAGE CREDITS

In 1970 Max Dashu founded the Suppressed Histories Archives, to research and document women's history on a global scale. She built up a collection of 15,000 slides and 30,000 digital images. From these archaeological and historic images she has created 150 visual presentations on female cultural heritages.

Dashu began to present slideshows in 1974, mostly at feminist bookstores and coffeehouses, to make women's history accessible. She has since presented hundreds of visual talks to all kinds of audiences: at universities, conferences, museums, bookstores, community centers, libraries and schools, in North America, Europe, and Australia. She has keynoted at numerous conferences, and published in numerous journals and anthologies such as *Feminist Theology* (2005) and *Goddesses in World Mythology* (Praeger 2010).

This book is the first volume to be published in the series *Secret History of the Witches*. Dashu teaches online courses (see below) based on forthcoming volumes in the *Secret History* series. In lieu of grants—independent scholars have to work very hard—the courses are funding those books' completion.

Max Dashu has also produced two videos: *Women's Power in Global Perspective* (2008) and *Woman Shaman: the Ancients* (2013), as well as a series of posters on female iconography. Page views of her articles (and advance book excerpts) consistently remain in the top 0.5% on Academia.edu. Daily posts on the Suppressed Histories Archives page on Facebook are followed by 148,000 people from around the world.

Dashu offers live webcasts of her visual talks, including *Rebel Shamans: Women Confront Empire*; *Deasophy*; *Witch Hunts*; *Female Rebels and Mavericks*; and *Female Icons*. A full listing of presentations (or rather of those digitized so far) as well as articles can be found at the Archives site:

www.suppressedhistories.net

See current courses and webcasts at: **www.sourcememory.net**

You can sign up for notifications about events and publications at:
http://madmimi.com/signups/79799/join

secret history of the witches
by max dashu

The current volume (VII) is the first publication
in the series *Secret History of the Witches*
See www.veleda.net for forthcoming volumes and excerpts

Advance excerpts from unpublished volumes are also found at
www.suppressedhistories.net and at
https://suppressedhistories.academia.edu/MaxDashu